Harris Gaylord Warren is chairman of the history department at Miami University in Oxford, Ohio. He was educated at Purdue and Stanford Universities and received his Ph.D. from Northwestern. He has taught Latin American history at Louisiana State University, and was professor of history at the University of Mississippi from 1946 to 1957. His books include *The Sword Was Their Passport: A History of American Filibustering in the Mexican Revolution* and *Paraguay: An Informal History*. Upon completion of current research projects, he plans to do a book on "Herbert Hoover and the Great Prosperity."

For GORDON *and* GWENDOLYN

Harris Gaylord Warren

Herbert Hoover

AND THE

Great Depression

The Norton Library   NEW YORK

W · W · NORTON & COMPANY · INC ·

BOOKS THAT LIVE

The Norton imprint on a book means that in the publisher's
estimation it is a book not for a single season but for the years.

W. W. NORTON & COMPANY, INC.

Printed in the United States of America
2 3 4 5 6 7 8 9 0

CONTENTS

INTRODUCTION

Nearly every author who has written about the years before the New Deal has been impressed by their uniqueness. The combination of people, events, and circumstances produced during the 1920's resulted in something that may be described more easily than it can be understood. These were the years when Herbert Clark Hoover was Secretary of Commerce and President of the United States, and these were the years when Hoover proved that he was the greatest Republican of his generation.

In writing a political and economic history of Hoover's struggle with the Great Depression, the author is severely handicapped by not having access to the Hoover papers at Stanford University. There is, however, a tremendous mass of published sources which can be exploited, a mass so large that several generations of historians will not exhaust it. Fortunately, Mr. Hoover and several other people prominent during his presidency have published their memoirs.

Emotional storms generated by depression misfortunes still cloud the vision, color the judgment, and mislead the memory of millions who lived through the Great Depression. It is extremely difficult, almost impossible, to persuade such people to substitute reasoned judgment and historical fact for passion and prejudice.

Herbert Hoover is one of those men whose lives become so much a part of the fabric of their times that history cannot ignore them. History wants to know everything about such men, not just what they themselves choose to tell; but the career of Herbert Hoover before 1914 still is primarily an unwritten story. Some day someone is going to have to burrow into what records may remain in an effort to eliminate uncertainties. This has to be done because no one can explain the Hoover of the Harding Administration, the Hoover who made the Department of Commerce such an efficient advance agent for American business, the Hoover who confounded professional politicians by winning the nomination and election of 1928, and the Hoover who tried so manfully to save the nation from inevitable consequences of long accumulating follies, unless we know more about what the young Hoover was doing after he graduated from Stanford University.

Herbert Hoover is the main actor in this book, but the spotlight was not on him alone during the first four years of the Great Depression. There were many developments, many events, in which the President was little more than an interested spectator, as helpless as the rest of us; but there were few events national in scope or effect that had no connection with the worried man in the White House.

The problem of how to treat major events or developments is especially difficult when dealing with a short period. One may, as did John Kenneth Galbraith in *The Great Crash,* 1929 (Boston: Houghton Mifflin Company, 1955), concentrate on one major development; or, as did Joe Alex Morris in *What A Year!* (New York: Harper & Brothers, 1956), range over the length and breadth of an entire year. In either case, the author must look back and ahead in order not to lose perspective and to provide the necessary setting.

No one, it seems to me, has done justice to the Hoover Administration. His friends have joined in uncritical praise and his enemies have magnified his failures while ignoring his great achievements. The result is a distorted picture of what some historians are calling 'the age of Roosevelt.' Projected against the customary biased, prejudiced, and grossly unfair accounts of Hoover's presidency, the New Deal assumes an unnatural and unreal luster. Forgotten is the fact that what Hoover did was in a very real sense preparation for the next steps known collectively as the New Deal. Herbert Hoover was too progressive for the conservatives and too conservative for the radicals. While Mr. Hoover's rivals should be thankful that he and not one of them was President from 1929 to 1933, the country, too, should be grateful.

HARRIS GAYLORD WARREN

Oxford, Ohio
January, 1959

PREFACE TO THE NORTON LIBRARY EDITION

When Herbert Hoover died on October 20, 1964, the nation's press, from country weekly to metropolitan daily, united in paying tribute. He was "a great citizen, a great statesman, above all a great American." Some three decades earlier, journalists generally were not using the adjective "great" to describe the frustrated man who bore unfairly so much blame for not restoring economic prosperity to a stricken world.

The popular image of Hoover as President became a caricature even before he left office. This distortion needed to be corrected, and that was the task attempted in the first edition of this book in 1959. Considering his historical significance, relatively little scholarly work about Hoover has been produced since then, and I feel that my interpretations, while always subject to correction, are basically sound.

Hoover became President in one of the most critical periods in modern history. The world, still staggering under the burden of four years of carnage, was a world in turmoil. These were revolutionary times, the fruit of vast technological changes and ideological conflicts, in which a comfortable status quo could not exist. No one then could grasp the complex picture in its entirety, no one had a ready solution to problems still unsolved. Hoover was uncompromising in his opposition to socialism, but he probably understood his times far better than most men; in an impatient era, he understood the need for patience. But although he was not afraid of innovation, he was cautious in politics and lacked the boldness and daring that had made him successful in business.

Many presidents have suffered from vicious, unrestrained attacks by irresponsible writers and speakers. These Hoover endured in unprecedented volume. His name was prefixed to the Great Depression, to slums, to squatter's hovels. Many an economic villain escaped exposure as unwarranted blame focused on President Hoover. But although he left office scorned or ignored by the millions who once praised him, he never lost faith in his country. Always ready to serve, he devoted much energy and wealth to philanthropy while time slowly restored him to public favor.

During the long years of Democratic supremacy, Hoover was a restrained, intelligent critic of policies that violated basic tenets of his economic philosophy. His was a loyal opposition; he attacked ideas, not personalities. He made the most of his limited influence as the former leader of a party in disfavor. He found in President Truman a spirit very close to his own; and the friendship of these two men, who differed so widely in temperament, gave Hoover further opportunities to serve the nation he loved so well.

Always an admirer of Woodrow Wilson, in whose sub-cabinet he served brilliantly, Hoover resented the unfair criticisms of his former chief. One of his last books, *The Ordeal of Woodrow Wilson*, is a penetrating analysis of Wilson's problems and a fine critique of his actions. Hoover's relations with such men as Wilson and Truman demonstrated a breadth of interest, of compatibility, that transcended political partisanship.

Herbert Hoover's meteoric rise from poverty to wealth, from complete obscurity to international renown, is a fascinating example of the American dream come true. This book presents a small part of that story. What had started to be a "life-and-times" project had to be narrowed, for Herbert Hoover was notoriously uncooperative with historians. He allowed extremely limited access to his papers; collections in the recently opened Hoover Library at West Branch, which Hoover dedicated in 1962, are still incomplete. No adequate biography of Hoover can be written until his papers are opened freely to scholars. Then the biographer will confront a formidable task in reconstructing a life that lacked but a decade in spanning a century. But this must be done, for Herbert Hoover was a giant on the American scene and he, too, has left "a lonesome place against the sky."

HARRIS GAYLORD WARREN

Oxford, Ohio
August 1966

Herbert Hoover and the Great Depression   **TEXT**

CHAPTER I

HERITAGE OF NORMALCY

1. *Diagnosis*

March 4, 1929, and Herbert Clark Hoover became the President of the United States. His reputation as engineer, humanitarian, and statesman calmed the fears of doubters and reinforced the hopes of believers. Very much a part of the exuberant 'twenties, he was the symbol of prosperity created by enlightened economic statesmanship.

This was the symbol that made him a national hero. His carefully directed public relations built upon a splendid war record and brought to him a popular esteem magnificent in proportions. He was a new kind of businessman, an ideal public servant who could harmonize selfish objectives of the market place with ideals long in the public domain. So completely did the public accept him as one pure at heart and noble in spirit that he escaped from the Harding muck and mire with scarcely a splatter. But he could not escape the Great Depression; he did not foresee it. And when he brought to bear upon that catastrophe the remedies dictated by the philosophy in which he put complete faith, he was bewildered by the apparent failure of principles that could not fail. His was the heritage of Normalcy.

The United States in the 'twenties was approaching the end of a crowded, dynamic shakedown cruise. Techniques of the industrial revolution had triumphed. Business combinations resulting in great holding companies, banker control, mechanization of agriculture, mass production and mass marketing, mass advertising and impersonal journalism, mass education and massed population, had transformed America. Major basic inventions that were to revolutionize the American way of life had gone to drawing boards for refinement. Automobiles and tractors and airplanes and mysterious devices were at different stages in their development. Before 1925, comparatively few farms were fully mechanized or served with electricity; people still ran out of their houses to see an airplane in the sky. By 1930, horses were disappearing from the fields and airplanes passed unheeded. Radios and electric refrigerators became household necessities in the same decade when women began to smoke in public, bob their hair, shorten their dresses, encase their heads in helmets, and drop their waistlines midway between knee and hip.

Every year of the 1920's brought a full measure of excitement. There were great achievements in science, fantastic fortunes in finance, gigantic combinations in business, and billion-dollar corporations. Religious controversy swirled around the poles of fundamentalism and modernism. The Ku Klux Klan rode through the country and left a touch of its blight nearly everywhere. Underworld violence kept pace with the furious brawling over Prohibition. New sounds came to dominate the city streets: honking horns, deafening clatter of pneumatic riveters, concrete mixers, and, finally, blaring radios.

One could isolate various strands of this potpourri of life and study them as movements, trends, and isms. But that is not the way it happened. The great names and the new names in all phases of life jostled one another in newspapers, magazines, and movies. Great events and latest moves in social, political, and economic continuities tangled in a mass that could challenge and bewilder historians for a millennium.

The 1920's were a time for optimism, for seeking out new horizons. The greatness of Albert Einstein was more than dimly sensed. Wave after wave of unrestrained and delirious enthusiasm swept over the country when Charles A. Lindbergh, young and vigorous and modest, flew the *Spirit of St. Louis* from New York to Paris. This was a new age! America knew it and welcomed its prolonged birth with screeching sirens and ticker tape, with colossal ornate movie palaces and soaring skyscrapers, with new housing developments and golf courses, with high tension transmission lines and concrete highways, with a new model Ford and tri-motor giants of the airways.

Even while the worst flood in the nation's history was pouring down upon the lower Mississippi, engineers successfully demonstrated television. At the end of April 1927, the image of Herbert Hoover was sent from Washington to New York. Hoover and television, Hoover and prosperity, Hoover and efficiency, Hoover and the flood. Nobody, nothing, kept Herbert Hoover out of the news because Herbert Hoover was a genuine American hero. In the same week that television was born, Chicago accepted William Hale Thompson as its champion to keep King George out of America; in the same week Billy Sunday and Dr. John Roach Straton summoned God to smite Sinclair Lewis, author of *Elmer Gantry;* and a judge sentenced two innocent Italians to death for a crime committed by someone else years before.[1]

Any other week would bring much the same fare. Disaster in nature, new strikes in the coal fields, somebody roaring for or against some scheme to relieve agriculture, new mergers in business, Babe Ruth in a batting slump, another innocent citizen killed by a Prohibition agent, a new high in the stock market. These were the things that people heard and read about. They were corings from a drill cutting the newly deposited stratum of life in America. Some there were who surveyed the scene from a crow's nest where they could see the wake stretching to the horizon, where they could guess what lay ahead in the shrouding mists. But a prophet of doom is never heeded until the disaster he foretold is upon the people.

Faith in a better future, in a more prosperous and glorious future, is part of the American tradition and ingrained in the American character. Success, worldly success, was good; the gospel of wealth preached it; the democratic faith made it possible. We were young at heart after World War I; we had not been hurt badly in any material way. The blood we shed and the goods we spent in France were not really missed. For the dead we raised a monument in Armistice Day and the Tomb of the Unknown Soldier; for the goods we raised a monument called the War Debts. We paid obeisance to both; however much we pretended, we knew that the dead do not return.

There was more, much more to the 'twenties than the superficial and the spectacular. No o   read the great newspapers and maga-zines and novels of the   noting the space given to problems of agriculture   manufacturing. Her-bert Hoover, presiding   nt of Com-merce, went about hi   solve these problems and to rec   he best things of the 'twenties, he   eas while con-vincing a large pr   s expert in the knowledge of the

For the benefi   recorded promi-nently that liter   what their prob-lems were in t   proposed were not tried, because   roups did not want them to be t   e did not know how terribly seri   sed our position in a shrinking   nterdependence of nations. We had allowed unanswered questions to accumulate until, suddenly, they all demanded answers at once. The America that elected Herbert Hoover to the presidency in 1928 was an optimistic America. There was faith that this widely heralded engineer, humanitarian, administrator, and efficiency expert, this citizen of the world, could provide the guidance and the answers. There was faith, too, in the mission of America to spread democracy and prosperity all over the world.

The dream was shattered and the faith obscured by a combination of economic conditions that caused the Great Depression. There had been plenty of signs for the wise to heed, but the solemn warnings of Walter Lippmann and Norman Thomas, the pessimistic admonishings of Roger Babson, could not be heard above the clanking of cash registers. Too large a segment of the nation's population lived in a fool's paradise brilliant with dreams of great wealth. The Republicans, unrepentant after the Harding scandals, ignored the indictment of outraged citizens, ignored the millions of bankrupt farmers, denied labor's reasonable demands for justice. The New Day had arrived. Poverty was to be banished from the United States, prosperity was here to stay.

This conclusion could be reached only by ignoring the heritage of Normalcy. Prohibition was a farce, a failure, a nightmare. Banking practices had undermined basic foundations, and stock and commodity exchanges had become gigantic gambling casinos. European collapse was being prevented only by American loans. Monopolies through consolidations had proliferated with reckless disregard for federal laws, and the oligarchy of concentrated wealth had expanded. The textile and coal mining industries were in desperate straits; foreign developments of intense significance for the future were taking place; and new sets of social values were emerging from the wreckage of Calvinistic America. To borrow a phrase from Frederick Lewis Allen, the United States was walking backward into the future. Yet Herbert Hoover could say these were the years when Republicans showed 'rare courage in leadership and constructive action.'[2]

2. *Concentration of Wealth*

A notable characteristic of the 1920's was the further concentration of wealth. This process is inevitable in a free enterprise system but it need not be without controls. The Federal Trade Commission in 1926 reported on the basis of an incomplete survey that 60 per cent of the wealth was owned by 1 per cent of the people. Prosperity of a sort seemed general in 1926, yet the average income of 44 million people did not exceed $1,000 in that year. It was even less in 1927. Two years later came the Great Crash, and in that year of crisis 3 per cent of the income receivers got 18.5 per cent of the total national income.[3]

Big incomes became larger in the decade and more people received large incomes. Only 33 people confessed to having received more than a million dollars each in income in 1920. There were 511 in that class in 1928. The number of people with incomes over $10,000 more than doubled during the decade. One could, with justification, conclude that it was a wonderful economy that permitted so many people to have so much income, that opportunities for economic advancement abounded in America. Comfort could be found in the thought: 'We have a great many rich people in this country today, but none of them seems to be doing any harm. . . .'[4]

Fortunate people with incomes over $10,000 in 1928 were favorite targets for soak-the-rich schemes. About 10 per cent of those who filed income tax returns were in that category,[5] and they replied to all criticisms with a mighty wail that government, through heavy taxation, was killing individual initiative. So long as Andrew Mellon remained in the cabinet, the rich had no need to worry on that score.

Fears that produced the Sherman Anti-Trust Act in 1890 were more than justified by events in the 'twenties. Business combinations in oil, railways, and steel dominated the trust movement after the Civil War. These young giants became single-eyed monsters and after World War I their tribe increased until concentration of wealth in gigantic corporations all but destroyed old concepts of competition. The 200 largest non-financial corporations controlled more than 44 per cent of corporate assets of that category in 1927; their assets in the 1920's increased more than three and a half times as fast as national wealth. The conclusion is inescapable that corporate wealth was increasing with great speed, that more and more of the national wealth was coming under control of giant corporations.[6] Less apparent was the fact that a considerable amount of corporate and national wealth would not have been in existence at all had it not been created by the giant corporations.

Concentration of control accompanied the concentration of wealth.

In 1927, less than 2,000 individuals were directors of the 200 giant non-financial corporations.[7] Demonstrating a singular lack of economic statesmanship, these managers failed to return to labor a reasonable proportion of the wealth labor created. In the 'twenties, real wages increased 13 per cent, returns to industry as a whole increased 72 per cent, dividends in rails and industrials went up 285 per cent. Instead of going into wages and salaries, into higher prices for agriculture, accumulated capital went into stocks and bonds to create a bloated market.[8] This was the result of control by irresponsible industrial imperialists.

The man who was called upon to rescue the country from the inevitable consequences of industrial imperialism had faith in a free enterprise system. The rules of the free enterprise game were written by the recipients of its greatest benefits. People, acting collectively through government, were not permitted to combine for protection against giant monopolies which were engaged in the process of concentrating more and more wealth in the hands of an ever smaller proportion of the population. The theory, supposedly, was that business would provide its own competition, thereby serving the public interest. Government might regulate but big business in the 1920's became so big that effective regulation in the public interest was impossible. Hoover's promotion of 'associated activities' unwittingly made the federal government a benevolent accomplice in the process of consolidating competing units, a process blessed because it supposedly lessened waste.[9]

Concentration of wealth and productive capacity in a comparatively small number of corporations made the economic structure stiff and unresponsive to needed changes in policy. A gigantic bureaucracy ruled the economic order and determined prices to meet the demands of business politics.[10] In an economy dedicated not to free enterprise but to monopoly, to the elimination of competition, the monopolies well nigh succeeded in destroying one another and the country too. Vast regimented industries and financial institutions had no real concern with that American individualism which was at the heart of President Hoover's philosophy.[11] Tremendous changes in American society had occurred, making necessary still more changes to restore the lost balance. The old formulas were valid no longer. But the high priests of the Grand Old Party who mumbled the hoary credo and shook the sacred gourds could not believe that their medicine had lost its magic. They still believed that masters of money had created our modern industrial society, that government could best serve the country by serving its financial lords.

3. *Credits and Debits*

Bankers, the policy forming officials of financial institutions, cannot escape considerable blame for the orgy of speculation that misled so many people into believing that the beast of poverty, at least in America, had been slain. There were 25,330 banks in the United States on 30 June 1929, and it is no exaggeration to assert that thousands of them were grossly mismanaged. A bank failure is a social catastrophe and an economic crime. There were 1,827 suspensions in the years 1927 to 1929, and 5,102 more were to go under during the next three years. During the six years before the market crash, banks failed at the rate of two every day; for the six years ending in 1932, banks failed at the rate of more than three every day! Depositors, however, lost only one-fourth of their deposits. The loss of confidence in banks was far more serious than the loss of deposits, for banks had become the cathedrals of the 'twenties and bankers were the priests of prosperity.[12]

Carelessness, ignorance, and greed were leading causes of bank failures. A great many banks went under because they loaned too much credit on too little security. Interest earned on call money was high enough to attract large supplies of funds and low enough to encourage speculation on an ever-rising market; attractive discount rates encouraged over-buying; excessive loans on real estate helped operators to bid up prices. New stocks and bonds issued in the United States from 1919 to 1929 reached the astronomical total of $43,767 million. There were plenty of 'securities' to absorb the apparently endless supply of money and credit in the hands of eager buyers. The Federal Reserve Board refused to apply deflationary pressures. Easy credit, lack of effective regulation of corporate financing, huge corporate credit balances, and an insatiable appetite for goods contributed to inflation.[13]

There was a huge domestic and foreign market in spite of depressed sectors in the economy. Installment buying and foreign loans made it possible to keep goods moving to people who lacked the purchasing power to buy them outright. By 1929, many billions of dollars were outstanding in consumer credit, real estate mortgages, and foreign loans. The good times, the Harding-Coolidge prosperity, came in no small measure because of selling on credit. In goods alone, domestic and foreign credit absorbed $11,500 million during the eight years ending in 1929.[14]

With almost no warning at all, World War I completely reversed the traditional economic relationship of the United States to other nations. Before World War I, long-term foreign investments in the United States amounted to about $6,700 million, while our investments abroad were about one-half as large. Then European nations began to borrow heavily from banks and individuals, and finally from the United States Treasury, to finance their war effort.[15] Our associates (we would never call them allies) spent $10,470 million for the purchase of American goods and for repayment and servicing of loans floated in the United States before the first Liberty Loan Act was passed in 1917; in the next five years they borrowed another $9,379 million and spent most of it in the United States. In casting up accounts after the war, the World War Foreign Debt Commission by 1926 had settled on $11,704 million as the principal to be paid, plus interest payments almost as large.[16]

These war debts could be paid primarily by selling goods and services to the United States. An alternative, of course, would have been for us to accept direct payment in goods and services. But, engaged as we were in economic warfare by means of the protective tariff, that alternative was politically impossible. We loaned goods and would not take goods in payment. England, for example, could have built battleships to our specifications and we could have taken those battleships on account. But that would have denied orders for battleships to our own industry, that would have employed Britishers instead of Americans. There are economists who insist that our course was wise. To have accepted payment in goods would have increased unemployment, since our own industrial capacity was more than enough to produce all the goods we could or would consume. Be that as it may, the unpaid war debts were part of the heritage of that normalcy which Herbert Hoover had helped to make and whose complex problems he inherited in 1929.

The United States enjoyed a 'favorable' balance of trade during the 'twenties. The annual average value of merchandise exports from 1921 to 1929 was $4,578 million and the average value of merchandise imports was $3,906 million. The difference between the totals was made up by tourist expenditures, service remittances, loans, and investments. From these sources foreign countries obtained dollars to buy American goods, to make war debt payments, and to service investments.[17]

America's private capital market in the 'twenties was a happy hunting ground for foreign borrowers. Private portfolios held some $4,600 million in long-term securities by 1925, a figure which, added to the intergovernmental debts, made the United States a creditor second only to Great Britain. During the next four years American bankers competed recklessly for the privilege of selling foreign bonds to their investors. Loans, floated honestly and dishonestly, reached a total of more than $5,000 million from 1925 to 1929. Foreign loans floated in the United States provided $7,500 million in new capital for other countries from 1919 to 1929. The market boom of 1928 diverted funds to domestic speculation and caused a drastic curtailment in foreign issues without which some economies were certain to suffer severe strains.[18]

The collapse of our over-extended domestic and foreign credit structure began even as President Hoover was looking forward to four years more of prosperity under Republican blessing. Increasingly numerous reports of business depression abroad caused little alarm, and Republican tariff masons were reaching again for their trowels to raise a wall that would practically guarantee the cessation of imports that might compete with American industry.

4. *Agricultural Migraine*

'Farmer' is a word well loved by politicians of some faiths, feared by a few, and ignored by none. There is a mystic tie between the word and 'the roots of democracy,' a strong connection with the born-in-a-log-cabin complex. Farmers en masse were widely regarded as a solid, conservative, All-American balance wheel that would prevent wild gyrations of the democratic machine. The distress of those who held this conviction increased as the economic plight of farmers grew steadily worse in the roaring and prosperous 'twenties.

There was no one farm problem and hence no single panacea. Farmers were all agricultural producers, but there was wide variation in their problems of production and marketing. Something like a common denominator can be found in the price structure. Except for the corporate farms and the limited activities of successful co-operatives, farmers bought at retail and sold at auction. They paid what was asked and took what was offered. Another common denominator was the inability of farmers as a group to combine for control of production, and without production controls there could be no satisfactory price control.

The farmer entered the 1920's with surplus facilities, the result of many factors. While European countries were concentrating on building up their industrial plants in the nineteenth century, there was an ever-increasing demand for American agricultural products. Millions of acres of new land came into production, swelling the volume of agricultural produce seeking markets abroad where they were needed to pay for our imports. This market contracted before World War I as western European nations adopted policies to increase their own agricultural production. Domestic demand had not increased with sufficient speed to absorb the surplus which still sought markets abroad and helped to depress world prices. World War I brought a great reduction in European production, and expanded acreage in the United States made up the difference. As prices rose, more and more land was brought into cultivation; land increased spectacularly in value, and many farmers borrowed large sums at high interest rates to finance the purchase of over-priced land. At the end of the war, European countries again took measures to restore their own agricultural production; they also increased purchases in areas where they sought expanded markets for their industrial production. All of these factors served to curtail markets for surplus crops. Prices of farm products plunged from about 250 per cent of the 1913 level in July 1919 to 63 per cent of the 1913 level early in 1921. Seven years later, after a slow recovery, farm products had a purchasing power 10 per cent under the 1913 figure.[19]

The 'twenties brought tremendous changes in American agriculture. The triumphs of agricultural sciences resulted in huge increases in production per man hour. Mechanization not only displaced farm workers but also released great areas from the production of crops needed to feed draft animals. Changes in styles of clothing reduced per capita demand for cotton and wool. Dietary changes reduced per capita consumption of several products, and such substitutes as oleomargarine cut heavily into the consumption of others. Still there was no decline in efforts of science to increase and to improve production, in promotion of reclamation and irrigation to bring more land into cultivation.[20]

Masses of statistics gathered and explained by numerous public and private agencies agreed that agriculture was not receiving a just share of the national income. Farmers all over the nation were not netting enough from their work in the 'twenties to maintain a decent standard of living. They were steadily falling farther and farther behind the non-farm population, being unable to acquire 'many of the services and conveniences taken for granted by city people.'[21] Whatever yardstick was taken—medical facilities, school opportunities, labor-saving devices, and frequency of ownership or use of many modern inventions—revealed that the farm population lagged far behind the rest of the nation. No matter how one measured farm values, farm income, or farm ownership, the figures were always disheartening.

The farmer was stretched on a Procrustean bed, with head and foot moving in opposite directions. Taxes went up, interest rates remained high, wages increased; the tariff on manufactured goods greatly raised the prices of things farmers had to buy; transportation costs increased. The Esch-Cummins Act of 1920 provided needed raises in freight rates, but it came when farm prices were on the way down. Higher rates hit the farmer twice—on what he sold and on what he bought. He could find small solace in talk about the Great Lakes—St. Lawrence Waterway and the Mississippi system to permit cheaper transportation.[22] Credit facilities, it is true, improved remarkably in the 'twenties; but what the farmer needed was higher prices for his products or a drastic reduction in prices fixed by others. He was unable to obtain either, and the result was that political and economic migraine known as the Farm Problem.

Herbert Hoover, busy with building his Department of Commerce empire while he kept his eye on the White House, made himself something of an expert on the farm problem. He could not know that his plan, devised to conform to his political and economic philosophy, would be such a weak and puny thing in the path of economic catastrophe.

5. *Labor and Laissez Faire*

Labor was struggling in the 'twenties to win recognition and public support of unions. Its objectives were primarily economic and social, directed toward gaining a position of strength in an industrial society whose rulers tortured the original meaning of laissez faire to mask their own arbitrary interference with publicly revered economic laws. The American Federation of Labor, strongest national labor organization, had played down political activities and preferred to work through established parties to achieve its ends. This decision opened the way for Communist infiltration and for radical labor leaders to capture the spotlight during the great strikes of 1919–22, during which organized labor lost so many of its World War I gains.[23]

Conservative leadership of the American Federation of Labor remained unchanged when William Green succeeded Gompers in 1924. Gompers had been opposed to the industrial unionism advocated by John L. Lewis. Green, who had been an industrial unionist while in the United Mine Workers, reversed his stand to support craft unionism. Thus the A.F. of L., when most in need of dynamic leadership, failed the cause of unionism.[24]

A major objective of industrial management was to destroy organized labor. This was, indeed, what many employers meant when they talked of 'normalcy.' It was normal for employers to refuse collective bargaining; it was abnormal to bargain with a labor leader. In pursuing their objective, industrialists used every weapon in a well-stocked arsenal: control of the press to provide publicity uniformly unfavorable to labor, political pressure to secure legislation favorable to industry and to prevent pro-labor legislation, employment of strike breakers on a large scale, injunctions to hamper labor activities, spies to report on union members and plans, the blacklist to deny employment to labor 'agitators,' and the yellow dog contract to prevent laborers from joining unions. Such men as Elbert H. Gary, John D. Rockefeller, Jr., and John J. Raskob preferred wage increases to the recognition of unions.[25]

Industrialists advocated the American Plan, which was merely the Star Spangled Banner wrapped around the open shop. Hundreds of open shop associations spread anti-union propaganda which few unions were able to counter successfully.[26] Using the guilt by association and guilt transfer techniques, industrial propagandists equated unionism with un-Americanism. The National Association of Manufacturers, the League for Industrial Rights, and other groups enthusiastically supported the open shop drive. The president of the N.A.M., John E. Edgerton, in 1925 pictured the labor leaders as holding union members in a 'slavery such as this country never knew before.'[27]

Added to industry's unbending anti-unionism was the hostility of federal courts whose judges, not infrequently, had achieved prominence as corporation lawyers. Yellow dog contracts, the hated agreements not to join unions, were declared valid in outrageous violation of a basic civil right. Courts emasculated the Clayton Act, once mistakenly hailed as labor's Magna Charta, and the Supreme Court invaded state rights by denying Arizona's right to enforce a sweeping anti-injunction law. The reactionary decision in Adkins v. Children's Hospital (1923) invalidated minimum wage laws. Only one bright spot appeared: approval of the Railway Labor Act of 1926 which guaranteed freedom of union organization among railway workers, a privilege extended to no other large body of laborers engaged in interstate commerce.

Company unions and welfare capitalism were deceptive bones thrown to labor in the 'twenties. More than 400 company unions enrolled about 1,370,000 workers in 1926. Profit sharing, sale of stock to employees, bonuses, group insurance, old age pensions, free clinics, recreational programs, company magazines, and company lunch rooms were characteristic features of welfare capitalism in the Age of Normalcy. Labor, of course, had no guarantee that these altruistic driblets would continue during economic distress.

By disregarding unfavorable statistics, labor and industrial leaders could congratulate themselves on the dawn of a new day. Strikes declined rapidly after 1925, a record marred primarily by sporadic flareups in the coal mines and by disastrous strikes in southern textile mills. Labor's real wages increased by an average of 20 per cent; however, the increase was very uneven and does not reveal the whole story. While some hourly rates went up substantially, others already too low declined still more. While average annual wages rose from $1,171 in 1921 to $1,408 in 1928, there were millions of families whose income fell under $1,000 per year at a time when a decent standard of living required twice that amount.[28]

The vaunted industrial system that drew so much praise from its chief beneficiaries increasingly failed to provide opportunities for employment. In fact, there was so little concern, in government and business, that statistics on employment notoriously failed to reveal how many were unemployed. Estimates for 1928 ranged as high as 8 million. The Secretary of Labor reported that factory employment in March 1928 had declined by 1,874,000; but he did not know how many were unemployed. John B. Andrews, secretary of the American

Association for Labor Legislation, complained that 'All estimates were actually based on little or no factual material. . . . And we have no comprehensive means for measuring unemployment.'[29]

Political and industrial leaders need not worry about such a temporary phenomenon as rumored unemployment. Immigration restriction had all but closed our ports to the European hordes, and the wonder-working providence of an endlessly expanding economy would provide work for every honest and upright citizen. Fortified by this comforting philosophy, they could look beyond the coal fields and the blighted mill towns and await the parade of new automobiles which would drop off, two by two, at every garage in the country.

6. *Social Confusion*

People in or past middle age in the 'twenties still thought in terms of the 'nineties or, at best, in turn of the century patterns. In their lives the Big Change, as Frederick Lewis Allen so aptly called it, had taken place. Small dwellings replaced the larger unit for the middle classes; professional people were steadily slipping in the unequal race to make dollar income keep up with prices and taxes; the handicapped were increasingly becoming burdens of the community as homes became too small to house indigent relatives. The hired girl ceased to be a social institution. Her passing was made easier by cheaper ready-to-wear clothes, labor-saving kitchen gadgets, smaller families, and smaller homes—all of which enabled many a housewife to devote more and more time to playing bridge, reading frothy magazines, or making use of a newly found leisure in pursuit of culture and community service.

There was much concern over tremendous trivia as young people wriggled out of inherited whalebone. Puritanism was outmoded anyway in a world of radios, saxophones, tractors, and talking pictures. People middle-aged found it hard to accept changes forced on them by rebellious sons and daughters, especially by the daughters. But in spite of all predictions that disaster impended, the Lost Generation of the 'twenties carried on to fight World War II, legacy of the good old days, and to be world leaders in the age of sputniks.

In these years of change, fruition, and seed time, the farce of Prohibition played on and on before a scornful domestic and jeering foreign audience. Mobs of native and alien gangsters, co-operating with public officials, grew fat in the sympathetic environments of large cities. The spectacular careers, objectives, and methods of these men were compared with those of earlier tycoons in business, finance, and industry, and the parallels were so apparent that they made people uncomfortable.[30]

A combination of circumstances caused this new hierarchy of crime to fasten its tentacles on the life of every large city, but Prohibition gave big gangs a chance to grow bigger and to become so powerful that their influence was to extend even to the national capital. Organized crime flourished primarily because a majority of citizens were too lazy, ignorant, indifferent, or cowardly to insist upon honesty in government. In the years of Normalcy, in the years of depression that followed, there was no relentless, organized drive for reform until efforts to repeal the Eighteenth Amendment took on the thin aspect of a crusade. Repeal proved at least one thing: Prohibition was not and never had been a major cause of racketeering.

Passion for uniformity and for standardization became a virulent social disease. Large-scale industry, the fantastic mobility created by millions of automobiles, nationalized radio programs, advertising, publishing, and motion pictures, all served to create uniform patterns. There were national organizations without number working for uniformity among persons of similar occupations. There were national organizations which sought to defend democracy by attempting to enforce conformity with their institutionalized prejudices. The Ku Klux Klan, the American Legion, and the Daughters of the American Revolution defined Americanism. The Anti-Saloon League and the Woman's Christian Temperance Union attempted to assert a moral dictatorship over the entire country.

There was a morbid fear of free thought. So many people were afraid because they were lost in the rubble of smashed ikons. In their panic, in their surrender to hysteria, in their blind groping, they sought refuge in laws to scotch the teaching of Darwin's theory of evolution, to compel teachers to swear eternal abhorrence of free inquiry, to make it illegal for American citizens to exercise their constitutional liberties. Calculating and cynical enterprisers capitalized on this hysteria by directing it against freedom of association, freedom of speech, and freedom of teaching, the factors which alone could unmask their hypocrisy and rapaciousness.

Confusion in values created a cult of business worship that fostered unbounded faith in a businessman for President. Business had created the great abundance, business would abolish poverty, business would bring the New Day safely through its chaotic dawning. Referring to the common man, Gerald W. Johnson wrote: 'Of all the layers of illusion in which time and circumstance had wrapped him, the thickest and most opaque was the illusion of the sapience and puissance of the American businessman in general and the American financier in particular.'[31] So a businessman became President and presided for four years over the shambles businessmen had done so much to create.

CHAPTER II

THE RISE OF HERBERT CLARK HOOVER

1. *Iowa to Washington via the World*

Seriously and apparently with solemn intent a small group of men walked along the edge of an Iowa stream on a summer day in 1928. Their leader was a serious, square-set man in a double-breasted suit, a rich and famous man who had come home for a day. His face was full, his eyes blue, and sandy brown hair was showing gray. He was looking for the swimming hole under the willows down by the railroad bridge, while upwards of 15,000 people were crowding into the nearby hamlet of West Branch.

More than four decades before, Herbert Clark Hoover had taken his last swim in the old swimming hole and set out upon journeys that were to take him into fabulous adventures and, at last, back to West Branch. Here he would begin his active campaign to persuade his countrymen that their fabulous prosperity would be secure under continued Republican guidance.

Familiar scenes and a few familiar people remained in the little village. There was the small neat house where Jesse Clark Hoover and his bride, Huldah Minthorn, had lived among their Quaker friends. There was his first teacher, Mrs. Molly Brown Curran, long retired from the classroom, to sit prominently in a front row under the huge tent and hear the ponderous periods of a presidential candidate, and, later, to be questioned by reporters seeking to clothe stereotyped symbols with stereotyped words.[1]

For this was the staged homecoming of the only prodigy son of West Branch, a rural community of 745. Quakers from Ohio had started the settlement in the 1840's. Eli Hoover and his wife Mary joined the migration. Mary died at West Branch in 1852, leaving five children among whom was Jesse Clark Hoover, not yet six years of age. Eighteen years later, Jesse married Huldah Randall Minthorn in the Methodist Episcopal Church at nearby Graham. Their second son, Herbert Clark Hoover, was born on 10 August 1874 in the small, neat house near Jesse's blacksmith shop. The mother was a woman of fine intellect, much in demand as a speaker at meetings of the Friends;

the father was a sober, industrious, and self-reliant Christian gentleman.²

The future President knew little of parental care. His father died of typhoid fever in December 1880 and the widowed mother was a victim of pneumonia on 22 February 1883. In the little time remaining to her after her husband's death, Huldah Hoover flung herself into religious work. Her three children lived with relatives during the summers. After his mother's death, Herbert entered the home of his uncle Allan Hoover on a farm near West Branch and lived there until August 1885, when a family council decided to send him to Newberg, Oregon. There another uncle, Dr. Henry John Minthorn, had resigned an Indian Bureau job to become principal of the Pacific Academy. Herbert earned his board and tuition at the Academy, as did his brother Theodore, who soon joined him at Newberg. The doctor gave up his academic career in 1888 to open a real estate office, the Oregon Land Company, in Salem. A year later the three Hoover children—Theodore, Herbert, and May—were at last together in the same town. Herbert worked in the land company's office and took a course at the Capital Business College. At the age of seventeen, 'on a shoestring of money and a thimbleful of preparatory education,' Herbert Hoover entered the newly established Leland Stanford Junior University as a member of the Pioneer Class.³

Hoover was by no means a slave to books while he was at Stanford. Much of his time was spent in working, and some went to student politics, in which he played a minor role. After one year in mechanical engineering, Hoover changed to geology, which he studied under the famous John Casper Branner. His summer vacations were devoted to geological field work. Following graduation in May 1895, Hoover worked for the United States Geological Survey, then found a laborer's job at $2.00 per day in mines at Nevada City. A few months later he obtained a clerical position with Louis Janin, a wealthy mine operator and consultant who had extensive western interests. Within a short time Janin gave him important assignments that took the young geologist to many parts of the West. Janin then recommended him to the London firm of Bewick, Moreing and Company, which sent him to Australia as a mine scout in 1897. Herbert Hoover was then only twenty-three years of age, earning nearly $7,200 a year, and well started on a spectacular career.⁴

Hoover's work in Australia satisfied his employers. At the very time the youngster was managing the Sons of Gwalia, a mine whose purchase he had recommended and in which he had an interest, Charles Algernon Moreing was in China conferring with one Chang Yen Mao, a 'big operator' type who had become director of the Chinese Engineering and Mining Company.[5]

Chang Yen Mao, head of the Bureau of Mines of Chihli and Jehol provinces, wanted a technical adviser, a chief engineer. He also wanted Moreing to float a large bond issue to provide capital for the Chinese Engineering and Mining Company. Moreing advised employment of an American who would be free of European pressures, and who could look after the bondholders' interest and serve as technical adviser at the same time. Upon Chang's authorization, Moreing offered Hoover the job at $20,000 a year plus expenses. Hoover left the Sons of Gwalia late in 1898, arrived in London in January to learn more about the Chinese deal, then sailed for Peking via California. At Monterey he married his college sweetheart, Miss Lou Henry (1875–1944) on 10 February 1899 and sailed with her for China the next day. From Peking, Hoover directed harbor improvements and port and railway construction, operated mines, prospected for gold, and investigated the extensive anthracite deposits west of the city. Caught at Tientsin by the Boxer Rebellion in June 1900, Hoover aided in provisioning the beleaguered foreign colony and Chinese refugees.[6]

One of the most controversial parts of Hoover's early career proved to be the few months he spent in China. During the Boxer Rebellion, troops of five nations seized property of the Chinese Engineering and Mining Company. The bondholders had invested some $5 million in the company, an investment endangered by Russian seizure of the Kaiping mines. Gustav Detring, Chang's mentor, advised transferring the property to Moreing, who would organize a British company to preserve its assets. Detring got a deed from Chang; Hoover signed the agreement for Moreing and then, in the fall of 1900, sailed for London with the deed. Moreing and others organized the Oriental Syndicate; Hoover became General Manager at a higher salary and a 'small interest in the reorganization.'[7] How much was this small interest? Corey, telling the truth about Hoover, neglects to say; but his enemies guess as high as $250,000.[8] Whatever it was, the small interest must have been substantial. Hoover managed the company until the fall of 1901, when Belgians gained control. He resigned and returned to London as a junior partner in Bewick, Moreing.[9]

The affair of the Chinese mines might well have ended then had not Chang Yen Mao attempted to recover full control of the Kaiping property. The ensuing litigation in 1905 developed an intricate account of domestic graft and international piracy. Hoover's detractors used the affair in smear campaigns in 1928 and 1932, and his defenders found it hard to cancel the damage done by such mud slingers as Hamill, Wood, and Liggett.[10]

During the years from 1902 to 1915, Hoover's activities took him to many parts of the world. A detailed account of these years has never been written, and so far as the public is concerned, long periods of his life 'were utterly blank.'[11] Mr. Hoover himself devoted less than fifty pages in three volumes of memoirs to these thirteen important years, during which he made a fortune that has been estimated as high as $4 million. Although his salary alone was $100,000 a year, Hoover left Bewick, Moreing in 1908 to become an independent mining engineer.[12]

When World War I began, Hoover was in London, and soon he plunged into the task of repatriating stranded nationalists. He did not at once give up all of his business activities but remained for a year or more as a director in many companies. His residence, Red House in Kensington, was a mecca for many citizens of the world. Although he preferred to return to the United States, Hoover stayed in Europe to direct relief for Belgium. Walter Hines Page, Will Irwin, and Belgian officials joined in urging him to accept the task, for which his many contacts in France, Germany, Belgium, and Russia made him an ideal choice when the relief program required expansion. From that time forward, all income Hoover derived directly or indirectly from public office went for charitable enterprises. This was still true in March 1957 when Hoover, in his eighty-third year, decided to retire completely from public service. The Belgian relief task was tremendous and Hoover accomplished it magnificently over a four-year period. So great was his fame that an Austrian astronomer gave the name Hooveria to an asteroid between Mars and Jupiter.[13]

President Wilson called Hoover home in May 1917 to become head of the United States Food Administration, although it was August before Congress passed the Lever Act creating the organization. According to Hoover and his friends, the entire Food Administration, with such agencies as the United States Grain Corporation and the Sugar Equalization Board, came through the trial with a fine record.

But farmers particularly were critical and complained that processors and distributors were allowed to make high profits at the expense of consumers and producers.[14]

Hoover's role in the peace negotiations kept him in the background but his relief work as head of various organizations was especially significant. This emergency work on the continent was little appreciated in the United States, although taxpayers paid more than $100 million of the cost. Hoover and his American Relief Administration were important in preventing chaos in post-Armistice Europe, for the vast American agricultural surpluses which he distributed not only averted an economic collapse at home but saved lives and governments abroad. Hoover and his men were a preview of the later UNRRA, without the support of a United Nations. They restored communications, conquered epidemics, moved millions of tons of food and other supplies, and overcame tremendous obstacles created by the British and French.[15]

There is no doubt that President Wilson and Herbert Hoover agreed in the use of food as a weapon to stem the Bolshevist tide. Food overthrew the Soviet regime of Bela Kun in Hungary and installed Admiral Nicholas Horthy's reactionary regime. Baron Mannerheim received aid in overthrowing Finland's socialist government. But when the enemies of Wilson and Hoover charge them with having kept the continent in turmoil, they enter the world of fantasy. Equally unreal is the conclusion that Hoover's relief service was an example of unalloyed humanitarianism based on the Quaker philosophy of service.[16]

Herbert Hoover had become a name familiar in every household in the country because of his work as Food Administrator. Few there were who did not know that 'to Hooverize' meant to economize, to save and to share. The public had still more occasion to hear from this remarkable man whose stature grew from day to day. There was talk about the 1920 presidential election, and Hoover's name was mentioned with increasing frequency; there were news stories and articles in which Hoover was the central figure.

The American Relief Administration was a post-Armistice organization created to keep the Congressional appropriation of $100 million separate from other relief funds. Officially, the A.R.A. died on 30 June 1919; but the need continued, so Hoover and his principal aides re-created a private A.R.A. to solicit funds primarily to feed European children. Extensive publicity accompanied this drive for funds. Prominent was the 'food draft,' a means by which Americans could pay for food at their bank by buying a draft that called for delivery to specified persons in Europe. This brilliant scheme enlisted thousands of helpers, bypassed foreign exchange, and moved the food from European warehouses to needy families. Expecting to end children's relief activities late in 1920, Hoover discovered that more effort was required.

The European Relief Council, formed in June 1920, brought various relief agencies together in an attempt to raise money. President Wilson aided the drive, but even more spectacular were the Invisible Guest dinners. Invited to dine on simple relief rations at rough tables, guests who paid from $100 to $1,000 a plate would find that their host was an 'empty high chair with a lighted candle before it symbolizing the Invisible Guest.'[17] At one such dinner, Hoover and General Pershing sat on either side of the Invisible Guest and spoke for him. More than $1 million was collected at that dinner.

Again there was extensive publicity. Hoover spoke in many cities and published appeals for contributions. A fund of more than $29 million was collected for distribution to participating agencies. Hoover also obtained congressional approval for what amounted to giving nearly $76 million worth of grain to five countries.

These postwar relief activities were climaxed by an appeal from Maxim Gorky in July 1921 to relieve the Russian famine. This task Hoover directed by long distance through William N. Haskell, experienced in Armenian relief. Another drive for funds, which produced over $30 million, again dramatized Hoover's role as a great organizer. When the work ended in the spring of 1923, Maxim Gorky was lavish in his praise.[18]

Publicity derived from these postwar relief efforts added more laurels to a brow already heavily crowned. Hoover, deep in his campaign to reconstruct America, became even more prominent and popular.

2. *The Great Secretary*

Whenever people canvassed presidential possibilities for 1920, Hoover's name inevitably came up. There was considerable public doubt whether he was a Democrat or a Republican, a burgeon from old roots or an air plant seeking a host. Ray Stannard Baker, Frank Cobb, Franklin K. Lane, and Colonel E. M. House considered him a Democrat and took the lead in sparking a mild boom in 1919. Even after Hoover told Cobb, editor of the *New York World*, that he was a Republican, Democrats refused to be silenced. Louis B. Wehle, who served in various posts under Wilson, thought that a Democratic ticket of Hoover and Franklin D. Roosevelt would be a winner.[19]

Republicans, too, were interested. George Horace Lorimer, influential editor of *The Saturday Evening Post*, sought him out as a Republican. Hoover was flattered but he had no illusions about his candidacy. He did want a cabinet post and his friends advised him to let the boom run to increase his prestige. The Old Guard, personified by Boies Penrose, James E. Watson, Simeon D. Fess, and Philander C. Knox, made no secret of their dislike. They regarded Hoover at best as a late convert and could not forgive him for having strongly supported President Wilson's plea for a Democratic Congress in 1918. Although friends entered his name in several primaries, and for both major parties, only in California did Hoover approve their efforts. His reason for challenging Hiram Johnson was to bring out pro-League sentiment. Hoover made no campaign but polled 210,000 votes to Johnson's 370,000. Johnson joined the 'orgy of personal abuse and slander' directed by the isolationist press against Hoover.[20] Neither man forgot and Johnson was still in the Senate when Hoover was in the White House.

Hoover and his friends were not through with the Old Guard. Judge Nathan Miller of New York placed his name in nomination at the Republican convention and it was probably not chance that placed so many enthusiastic backers in the gallery.

Hoover's support for a cabinet position was so strong that the Old Guard was forced to agree to his appointment as Secretary of Commerce. Harding, so runs the story, forced Penrose and Knox to accept Hoover in order to continue Mellon as Secretary of the Treasury.[21] This explanation gives too much credit to Harding, long a machine politician. There was a liberal faction in the Republican party, aside from the western insurgents, which included William Allen White and Judge Miller. In order to preserve harmony, the Old Guard surrendered to their demand that Hoover be included in the cabinet. To take this administrative post, which he filled until 1928, Hoover refused an offer from Daniel Guggenheim of a full partnership in the

Guggenheim empire and a 'guaranteed *minimum* income of $500,000 a year.'[22]

Before accepting Harding's offer, Hoover insisted on having a voice in 'all important economic policies of the administration,' and he wanted other cabinet members to know it.[23] His objective was neither personal glory nor power. His passionate conviction was that society as a whole could benefit most through efficient use of natural resources for maximum production. Everything that touched on this goal was Hoover's business. He set out to reconstruct America, to create a society in which the postwar confusion so evident in Europe could be avoided. In undertaking this task, no man in American public life gave a greater demonstration of unselfish devotion to his country and to its people.

After so much activity since 1914, Mrs. Hoover was happy to settle in Washington. She purchased the colonial house at 2300 S Street overlooking the city and transformed it into a home. Here Allan, the younger son, kept the neighbors amused and his parents properly apprehensive. Tame ducks on the front porch were harmless but pet alligators in the bathtub met with mild objections. Here, too, the Hoovers received a never-ending stream of guests. Prominent among them were Justice and Mrs. Harlan F. Stone and the Mark Sullivans. Members of Congress, whose support was needed for many Hoover projects, came to dinner. On one occasion Senator Peter Norbeck, entranced with his own conversation, ate a small Belgian lace doily with his ice cream.[24]

Hoover began his cabinet career by summoning an advisory conference of 300 business, agricultural, and labor leaders. While subcommittees were at work evolving policies, Hoover reorganized the Department of Commerce. No longer would its major purpose be to turn on coastal lights at night and put the fish to bed. He cut out dead wood, reorganized bureaus, raised salaries, and added new agencies. A Housing Division was created in 1922; three years later Hoover captured the Bureau of Mines and the Patent Office from Interior; in 1926 Congress authorized the Aeronautics Branch and in 1927 a Radio Division.[25] Despite tremendously broadened activity, the Department's increase in employees and appropriations was moderate.

A major task assumed by the Economic Conference in September 1921 was relief of unemployment caused by the short postwar depression and precipitate demobilization. Under Hoover's energetic direction, state and local committees sprouted over the land to solicit funds, encourage public works, and persuade employers to spread work and hasten maintenance activities. Co-operation between local and state governments with industry and labor, Hoover believed, was the proper way to undertake unemployment relief. In this way only could we escape 'that ultimate paternalism which would undermine our whole political system.'[26] As President he resorted to the same measures less than a decade later, and he never admitted any better way of doing things.

Hoover's program of reconstruction became a crusade to eliminate waste by promoting co-operation without lessening sensible competition. There were ten areas for specific attack, including labor relations, research, water power, electrification, business cycles, business practices, and rail transportation. Three thousand conferences or committees attacked various aspects of economic problems and some of them recorded impressive accomplishments.[27]

Hoover's activities in the Department of Commerce were amazing in scope. He suggested a practical remedy for the coal industry's troubles, urged reorganization and simplification of federal agencies, started safety conferences to reduce traffic accidents and to promote uniform traffic codes. He encouraged official and private scientific research. Opposition to his program, Hoover complained petulantly, came not from business and labor but 'from the conglomeration of professors and intellectuals tainted with mixed socialist, fascist, and antique ideas.'[28]

To rejuvenate foreign trade, Hoover appointed 'a perfect public servant,' Dr. Julius Klein, to head the Bureau of Foreign and Domestic Commerce. Its agents ferreted out opportunities for American business, and the commercial attaché became a fixture of diplomatic missions. Hoover fought foreign monopolies intended to victimize the American consumer and shared with State and Treasury advisory supervision over private foreign loans. This supervision aroused banker hostility and caused Harding, Coolidge, and Mellon to retreat. Even bad loans, Hoover commented, helped to promote American exports and so were a cheap form of relief by preventing wider unemployment.[29]

Two activities especially carried Hoover's name to the people, but in neither case was his purpose to publicize Herbert Hoover. He had formed, in 1920, the American Child Health Association, which carried on an extensive program until 1935. Hoover's interest in housing led to intensive work by the Department to promote better homes. This campaign embraced a study of all major housing problems, from building codes to finance.

Persuaded that industry and labor must co-operate for efficiency in production, Hoover sought industrial peace. He favored collective bargaining but opposed the closed shop, unsuccessfully encouraged private unemployment insurance, favored a child labor amendment, and sparked such a skillful publicity campaign against 'barbaric' hours in the steel industry that Judge Elbert H. Gary abolished the twelve-hour day. Hoover clashed with banker-managers when he tried to settle the railway shopmen's strike in 1922, but later he helped in the development of the Railway Labor Mediation Board, created by Congress in 1926.[30]

Dismayed by haphazard conditions in commercial aviation, Hoover in 1922 urged measures to control and to develop a potentially powerful agency of commerce. Constant work bore fruit in 1926 when Congress passed the necessary legislation, and Hoover at once organized the Aviation Division, later called the Aeronautics Branch. Great progress in commercial aviation was a direct result and Hoover as President continued his active interest.

Radio broadcasting literally burst upon the country and threatened to create complete chaos. Regulatory powers, already vested in the Department of Commerce, were strengthened in 1927. Aimee Semple McPherson, white-robed evangelist of Los Angeles, objected to bureaucratic interference with her use of God's wave lengths. Tactfully the Radio Division brought the noted revivalist into line.[31]

The proper relation of government to business was a perpetual worry to Hoover, who recognized that the problem 'involved the destiny of the American scheme of life.' Abuses there were, but they were marginal; nevertheless, they must be cured to right wrongs and to deprive left-wingers of 'propelling texts.' Where necessary, government regulation must apply the cures; but Hoover wanted business to police itself. To the achievement of this goal he applied himself most diligently.

The much maligned trade association was to be the agency for avoiding wasteful competition and for eliminating marginal faults. Overzealous enforcement of the antitrust acts Hoover considered a 'perversion of justice.' After studying Dr. Klein's exhaustive report on associations, Hoover recommended ways for co-operation within the law and assigned to a staff within Commerce the task of preparing 'codes of business practice and ethics.' Before promulgation, each code was passed on by the Department of Justice and the Federal Trade Commission. These codes were not to be confused with Open Price Associations, which were brazen price-fixing devices that aroused Hoover's opposition.

William E. Humphrey, appointed to the Federal Trade Commission in 1925, agreed fully with Hoover's objectives in promoting these associated activities. He did not believe in elimination of competition, but he refused to publicize wrongdoing and slapped wrists very gently. If the trade associations actually were, as some critics charge, used to evade the antitrust acts, the blame lay with the Federal Trade Commission and not with the Department of Commerce.[32]

In reporting upon his last year as Secretary of Commerce, Hoover was complacent: 'The volume of production and consumption for the year . . . and the physical quantity of exports and imports were very large, unemployment was relatively unimportant . . . and the standard of living . . . remained higher than anywhere else in the world.'[33] Nearly all indexes showed new highs and the Department continued its efforts to smooth out the business cycle. Four years earlier even the *New Republic* had admitted editorially that Hoover was a great Secretary of Commerce, but that 'is like saying that he is a big five-footer.' Forced to subordinate ideas to loyalties in a feeble administration, Hoover was judged to be 'but a shadow of his old figure.'[34] The shadow was so substantial that it dominated Republican politics in 1928.

Hoover was very much in the news in 1927. His was the image first sent by television; and while people were still pondering the meaning of that latest technological marvel, a great disaster struck the Mississippi Valley. Heavy rains drenched the tributary valleys in April and soon the Mississippi River poured over its banks and crashed through levees in one of the greatest floods in history. By the first of May, the loss of life was heavy and many thousands of people fled their homes as the water drowned more than 2 million acres of crops.

Governors of afflicted states called for Hoover. From headquarters at Memphis the world's greatest relief expert mobilized federal, state, local, and private agencies. Hoover was everywhere, in person or by proxy. Whether they saw him at the broken Melville levee on the Atchafalaya watching water pour through a crevasse, in the Evangeline country warning scoffing citizens of the danger rushing from the north, or descending from his special train in one of many inspection tours, people felt better because Mr. Hoover was there.[35]

The publicity value of Hoover's flood relief was incalculable. Charles A. Lindbergh crowded Hoover out of the headlines but not out of the news at the end of May. For three months Hoover and the flood was a top news story; then President Coolidge wrote a few words that made Hoover a leading contender for the presidency.

Early in his career as cabinet member, Secretary Hoover had impressed observers with his encyclopedic knowledge, apparently limitless energy, great administrative skill, and an alleged lack of political intelligence. It was said that he found it difficult to make political decisions and that politics baffled him. Perhaps the criticism is just; but this baffled amateur, admittedly with great aid from professionals, beat the career politicians at their own game. In sharp contrast with his presidential experience, Hoover displayed an extraordinary talent for publicity through extensive newspaper, magazine, and film contacts. When Will Irwin in 1928 pieced together the campaign film 'The Master of Emergencies,' he had 'some ten miles of miscellaneous cinema films showing Hoover activities since 1914' from which to select. There is considerable truth in the comment: 'All his advertising has made him appeal to the American imagination, but not to the American heart.'[36]

President Coolidge threw politicians into a frenzy with his cryptic 'I do not choose to run' statement of 2 August 1927, which he handed to reporters at his Black Hills retreat. Most of the party lodge brothers who were tired of Coolidge took it for granted that taciturn Calvin meant what he said. People close to Coolidge were convinced that he wanted to be renominated; but William Allen White, the great liberal from Kansas, believed that Coolidge refused to clarify his statement because he wanted Hoover to follow him, not Charles G. Dawes or Frank O. Lowden. The eastern industrialists wanted Dawes and distrusted Hoover, who was not 'of the Wall Street kind.' Hoover would perpetuate Coolidge's policies.[37]

Many reporters and politicians professed to be mystified by Coolidge's simple expression of preference but Hoover accepted the statement at face value.[38] The Senate attempted to nail down the lid on

Coolidge's political career with an anti-third term resolution introduced by Robert M. La Follette, Jr. George Rothwell Brown versified in the *Washington Post:*

> That famous phrase, 'I do not choose,'
> Is once more headlined in the news;
> La Follette thinks it's much more fun
> To make it read 'You shall not run.'

When the resolution came to a vote on 10 February 1928 it passed by 56 to 26. The Senate, in effect, told Coolidge that it, too, did not choose to have him run for the presidency in 1928.[39]

Hoover's many friends, seeing in him an engineer who might drain the paludal reaches of Republican politics, urged him to announce his candidacy while others were still wondering what Coolidge meant. The Secretary of Commerce may have been wondering, too, but he was not worrying. In 1926 he had hired George Akerson, a very capable and conservative reporter wise in the ways of politicians, as his private secretary. At once this indefatigable worker began to build a Hoover machine and to keep his employer in the public eye. Hoover and Akerson were a good combination; soon there was a marked increase in the flood of publicity emanating from the Department of Commerce. Walter Folger Brown, the former Toledo political boss who had shed his Bull Moose antlers, came in as Assistant Secretary of Commerce.[40]

There were many Hoover boosters who felt that he would be good for the country. None were more convinced than George Horace Lorimer and his prominent trio of *Post* contributors, Isaac Marcosson, Samuel G. Blythe, and Garet Garrett. A Hoover drive definitely was under way by October, almost indecently close on the heels of the Coolidge announcement, and by January 1928 there were enough Hoover clubs to be united in a Hoover-for-President Association.[41]

Prominent people jostled one another on the Hoover wagon. Senator Walter E. Edge of New Jersey, the revered Thomas Alva Edison, and several Scripps-Howard editors pronounced for Hoover in January. John Taylor Adams, former chairman of the Republican National Committee, came from Dubuque to open Hoover headquarters in Washington. James W. Good, formerly member of the House from Iowa, organized the Midwest for Hoover before the Kansas City convention. Colonel Horace A. Mann, one of Harding's cronies, brought southern Republicans and anti-Smith Democrats together.[42]

All of this cost money, and the campaign for delegates required many a deal at the level of 'practical' politics. Hoover played this game with a skill worthy of Indiana's James E. Watson.

While Good, Mann, and many others were at work, Will Irwin was seeing his *Herbert Hoover, A Reminiscent Biography* through the press. Altogether more than 700 Hoover supporters carried on a preliminary campaign that made the Old Guard frantic. The first public indication that the very energetic Secretary of Commerce was available came on 12 February, two days after the Senate vote on the La Follette resolution, when Brown entered him in the Ohio primary. [43]

Hoover's avowed candidacy for the nomination automatically turned more spotlights in his direction. More reporters covered his activities, Irwin's biography went through five printings, and Samuel Crowther pictured him as the one man 'who can now lead to a fuller life—who can lead to the previously impossible state in which poverty in this country can be put on a purely voluntary basis.'[44] Such encomiums may not have swayed many voters but they helped to perpetuate the myth of a superman. When the Republican convention met at Kansas City, there was an overwhelming popular demand for Hoover. Elder statesmen Elihu Root and William Howard Taft were among his supporters, although Taft hoped until the end that a miracle would put Coolidge in for another term.[45]

3. *Hoover's Individualism*

The popular favorite was, to most people, simply a great reputation. His picture, familiar to millions, failed to reveal the inner fires that fed his spirit. His face was too heavy, too full to permit a dramatic play of expression; but his eyes were clear and his features retained the buoyancy of youth. Very properly, hiking or fishing photographs were almost as numerous as more serious poses. Hoover loved the open spaces, particularly if cut by a good trout stream. Unlike Coolidge, he would never dream of fishing with worms, nor did he ask Secret Service men to bait his hooks and take off the catch. He exercised regularly, enjoyed a massage, and by sessions with his 'medicine-ball cabinet,' which was much in the news after the inauguration, he reduced his weight from 210 to 183 by January 1932. For pets he preferred large dogs, like Tut, his favorite German shepherd.

An innate shyness caused Hoover to be ill at ease with strangers and casual acquaintances. He was described as shy, awkward, diffident, and even embarrassed in formal social intercourse; in a small circle of intimates he was a lively conversationalist and a fascinating raconteur. Such a man would never be a slapper of backs, a generator of anecdotes, an arms-around-the-shoulders good fellow. He lacked the qualities generally ascribed to successful politicians. Yet time and again reporters remarked on his ability to 'instil in those surrounding him a spirit of intense loyalty.'[46]

A great ambition, for himself and for his country, was the force that carried Hoover into the White House. He believed firmly in the great doctrines of democracy—the fundamental law, the free but responsible individual, and the mission of America to carry democracy to the world. These beliefs were fortified by David Starr Jordan's 'gospel of liberal democracy' which he heard at Stanford.[47]

Herbert Hoover entered Stanford when many strong currents of thought were stirring up the rising tide of nationalism. Henry George, champion of social justice, was nearing the end of his long crusade to reform the economic order. Lester Frank Ward, first of American sociologists, was preaching democratic socialism. Edward Bellamy's *Looking Backward* had been a best seller for three years, and scores of Nationalist clubs were seeking to promote the brotherhood of man. William Graham Sumner, that prodigious intellect and champion of laissez faire, taught self-reliance and warned against the welfare state. Sumner's teachings at Yale had a national audience and were to be echoed, consciously or unconsciously, in Hoover's writings and in his many speeches.

Hoover's political and social philosophy was not complicated. He held fast to a few major premises; and when he deviated from those principles, his explanations often were diffuse and confusing. However often circumstances forced emergency departures, Hoover always returned to reiterate his faith in those principles. His experience in the 1920 presidential steeplechase probably caused him to pause and to examine his mind. A lover of system and order, he could not permit either the public or himself to go on wondering about his basic philosophy. His *American Individualism*, written in 1922, was the result. There are many contradictions in this little book, and statements that the most charitable critic would have to ignore; but even Morris R. Cohen, who acknowledged that Hoover 'is still the most significant character in our public life,' was not unkind in his *New Republic* review.[48]

The central doctrine of Hoover's philosophy was individualism, and it was his view that individualism, together with certain corollaries, was the American system. It was this system, the virile growth of individualism, that made America great, and it was within this system that the remedies for all inequities existing in the social order must be sought.

Individualism meant for Hoover equality of opportunity for every person to play the role 'to which his intelligence, character, ability, and ambition entitle him . . .' The corollary to equality of opportunity was freedom from political, social, or economic domination by any group. Government would protect this equality, treating all men as equal before the law, preventing a class struggle, and promoting co-operation for maximum production.[49]

Social responsibility must go with equality of opportunity. While society made possible the full expression of self-interest and rewarded individual enterprise with special premiums, the individual must co-operate for the common good. He must have a sense of responsibility and of service. Industrial leaders must promote co-operation and work for maximum distribution of wealth. The community must work as a unit to preserve the democratic ideal of equality and self-reliance, and to provide subsistence and improvement for the unfortunate.[50]

Individualism, in the Hoover system, is the creator of democracy, and democracy, in turn, is the mechanism through which individualism functions in politics.[51] The proper functions of government, therefore, are to umpire and regulate, to encourage co-operation, and to coerce where necessary to maintain equality of opportunity. Government must stay out of business, and must not compete with its own citizens. 'Government can and must cure abuses. What the government can do best is to encourage and assist in the creation and development of institutions controlled by our citizens and evolved by themselves from their own experience and directed in a sense of trusteeship of public interest.'[52] Individualism with stewardship—this is what Justice Stephen J. Field had preached in 1895.

This general philosophy did not prevent active government participation in economic affairs. Hoover definitely favored government regulation to preserve competition, conserve natural resources, prevent abuses, and to protect individual liberties. Government should regulate only when necessary to achieve these objectives, and federal regulation should be resorted to only when state and local governments were unable to protect equality of opportunity and the public interest.[53]

Hoover defined co-operation with business in broad terms. He supported the tariff as a protector of labor, industry, agriculture, and the family budget. Farmers' co-operatives should be organized with federal aid, then sent on their way to promote the welfare of their members. Government must help industry to achieve full employment, 'to provide a job for all who have the will to work.' Government must not deprive labor of equal opportunity by unfair use of the injunction; and unions must not deprive the worker of the right to a job by insisting on the closed shop.[54]

Hoover's system did not preclude all government business enterprise. There were, he admitted, some areas in which local governments could operate successfully; but this was an exception to the general rule that a government, dominated by politics, cannot operate a business. There were, also, some areas in which business enterprise by state and federal government was admissible. Public funds could be used in scientific research, and building highways and other public improvements which were the by-products 'of some great major purpose.' But such enterprises as the sale of electrical energy to the consumer, or the operation of transportation systems, were inadmissible. He would approve the use of federal funds to subsidize private enterprise; he would oppose as socialistic direct government performance of the subsidized service.[55]

These standards for government intervention followed logically from Hoover's philosophy of individualism. Extension of government would undermine rugged individualism, the development of the individual according to his ability, and equality of opportunity. 'You cannot extend the mastery of government over the daily working life of a people without at the same time making it the master of the people's souls and thoughts.'[56]

For many decades Hoover called for faith in the future, for daring and imagination in exploring new frontiers, for seeking democratic solutions to economic and political problems. His dream for America was one of the purest idealism, a dream he believed could be made into reality. Regardless of success or failure, no President worked harder to make of America a land where men and women may walk in ordered freedom in the independent conduct of their occupations; where they may enjoy the advantages of wealth, not concentrated in the hands of the few but spread through the lives of all; where they build and safeguard their homes, and give to their children the fullest advantages and opportunities of American life; where every man shall be respected in the faith that his conscience and his heart direct him to follow; where a contented and happy people, secure in their liberties, free from poverty and fear, shall have the leisure and impulse to seek a fuller life.[57]

There was nothing new in Hoover's philosophy except, perhaps, the boldness with which he attempted to reconcile rugged individualism and social responsibility. Even in this he had noted predecessors, including Andrew Carnegie. Critics of Hoover's individualism doubted, scorned, or jeered at his attempts to bring right and left together in a common middle effort. John Dewey could see no human insight in Hoover's humanitarianism, no hope in his materialism. Robert Morss Lovett, professor of English at the University of Chicago and a *New Republic* editor, found in Hoover the 'chief spokesman for a philosophy which is hostile to everything in democracy except its catch words.' Walter Millis, journalist and historian, saw Hoover as a chameleon taking on the coloring of his surroundings, a bureaucrat who coddled rugged individualists. Oswald Garrison Villard, editor of *The Nation,* could not forgive Hoover for his silence during the Harding scandals, for accepting reactionary attitudes toward domestic and foreign problems, for having 'forgotten all that stuff he was talking, when he came back from Europe, about a new deal and a better political life in America . . .'[58]

One of the best pre-convention analyses of Hoover described him as a 'beaver-man' in six columns illustrated with a picture of gracious Lou Henry Hoover. Calling him a people's choice, *Time's* political analyst wrote with rare foresight:

The central fact militating against Candidate Hoover is that many people cannot understand what he stands for. He is no forthright protagonist of an ideal or program. He puts forth no clearcut political or social theory except a quiet 'individualism,' which leaves most individuals groping. Material well-being, comfort, order, efficiency in government and economy—these he stands for, but they are conditions, not ends. A technologist, he does not discuss ultimate purposes. In a society of temperate, industrious, unspeculative beavers, such a beaver-man would make an ideal King-beaver. But humans are different. People want Herbert Hoover to tell where, with his extraordinary abilities, he would lead them. He needs, it would seem, to undergo a spiritual crisis before he will satisfy as a popular leader.[59]

But the delegates who converged upon Kansas City were not worried. Their man may not have been an ideal leader but he was indeed popular, except with the parading farmers who carried signs inscribed 'Anyone BUT Hoover!'

4. *Hoover and Curtis*

There was small chance of stopping Hoover as more than 2,000 Republican delegates and alternates met at Kansas City, Missouri, on 12 June to hear Senator Simeon D. Fess deliver from memory a dull recital of party virtues. New Hampshire's Senator George H. Moses, the permanent chairman, did a much better job of tub-thumping, challenging the Democrats to come out of their corner and fight.

The platform was a long-winded document, full of pious nothings, little of which need be taken more seriously than the normal quadrennial foolishness. Analyzing platforms is a fruitless task, since what the candidates say is more important, and what they say is often a barrage of obfuscation. The plank on agriculture promised the Federal Farm Board, and that promise was fulfilled. As an illustration of blundering all around the subject and saying nothing in particular, let us read the plank on public utilities:

Republican Congresses and administrations have steadily strengthened the Interstate Commerce Commission. The protection of the public from exactions or burdens in rates for services by reason of monopoly control, and the protection of the smaller organizations from suppression in their own field, has been a fundamental idea of regulatory enactments. While recognizing that at times Federal regulations might be more effective than State regulations in controlling intrastate utilities, the party favors and has sustained State regulations, believing that such responsibility in the end will create a force of State public opinion which will be more effective in preventing discriminations and injustice.[60]

Bravely the Republicans tooted: 'No better guaranty of prosperity and contentment among all our people at home . . . can be given than the pledge to maintain and continue the Coolidge policies.'[61]

'Fighting Bob's' son and namesake, Robert M. La Follette, Jr., presented a meaningful minority platform that received nothing more than respectful attention. Farm relief advocates failed to obtain endorsement of McNary-Haugenism; anti-prohibitionists failed to obtain approval for returning the liquor problem to the states for solution.[62] It was the last major victory of the dry forces and Bishop James Cannon, Jr. gloated.

A California lawyer, John L. McNab, set off a well-planned ovation when he nominated Hoover. Other candidates, including Lowden, James E. Watson, Guy Goff, and Charles Curtis, vainly formed an alliance to stop the favorite. Whether Coolidge really wanted the nomination is very doubtful, although his hearty protests that he did everything possible to stop a draft are a bit suspicious.[63] Failure of anti-Hoover forces was measured by the first roll call when Hoover won the nomination with 837 of the 1,084 votes.

Senator Curtis swallowed his pride and agreed to be the vice-presidential nominee, although less than a week earlier he had spoken of Hoover as a man 'for whom the party will be on the defensive from the day he is named until the close of the polls on election day.'[64] The prophecy would have been better had the date been extended to 1933. Curtis had turned a complete cartwheel. The caustic pen of H. L. Mencken dubbed him

the Kansas comic character, who is half Indian and half windmill. Charlie ran against Hoover with great energy, and let fly some very embarrassing truths about him. But when the Hoover managers . . . threw Charlie the Vice-Presidency as a solatium, he shut up instantly, and a few days later he was hymning his late bugaboo as the greatest statesman since Pericles.[65]

Grateful for the nomination, Hoover made the customary genuflection: 'It is vital to the welfare of the United States that the Republican Party should continue to administer the government. If elected by my fellow countrymen, I shall give the best within me to advance the moral and material welfare of all our people and uphold the traditions of the Republican Party so effectively exemplified by Calvin Coolidge.'[66]

CHAPTER III

CRUSADE FOR PROSPERITY—1928

1. *Happy Warrior*

The life of Alfred Emanuel Smith is a political success story in good Horatio Alger style. That it was not to reach a White House climax may be attributed to whims of fate, not to any insuperable faults in the man who was born in a New York tenement on 30 December 1873. Al Smith grew up in the South Street neighborhood where he was born, opposite the wharfs of the East River, in the shadow of the Brooklyn Bridge. Leaving school at the age of fifteen, two years after his father's death, he became a truck chaser, handy man for an oil company, and bookkeeper for a commission house in the Fulton Fish Market, where he spent seven years. Life and not books, he liked to boast, was his teacher.[1]

If a poor young man wanted to enter politics in New York, it had to be by way of Tammany. Smith began his political career at the very bottom, working at the polls and doing odd jobs for the precinct leader while trying to sell real estate for a living. Eventually his faithful service and personal charm brought work with the Commissioner of Jurors. Smith celebrated this small promotion by marrying Katherine Dunn on 6 May 1900. Three years later he entered the New York Assembly and soon became the champion of such reform measures as workmen's compensation, equal pay for women teachers, and better care for the handicapped. As majority leader of the Assembly in 1911, he supported William F. Sheehan for United States Senator and encountered the successful opposition of Franklin D. Roosevelt.[2]

Smith's services in the Assembly and in a state constitutional convention consolidated his Democratic position and won high praise from such Republicans as Elihu Root and George W. Wickersham. After a term as sheriff of New York, he moved on to become president of the Board of Aldermen. Elected governor in 1918, he occupied the executive mansion at Albany until 1928, with the exception of the 1921–2 term.

Throughout his four terms as governor, Smith revealed a genuine humanitarian instinct. During the postwar Bolshevik scare, he kept his head, championed minority rights, and fought against the expulsion of Socialists by the Republican Assembly. He vetoed bills to degrade education by requiring teachers to prove their undiluted Americanism to the satisfaction of professional flag wavers, to permit the state's attorney general to prosecute 'radical' candidates, and to license private schools. His veto messages in defense of freedom of speech, thought, education, and political action reveal a champion of liberty in the highest American tradition.[3] Tammany Hall no longer dominated him by 1923, and his prominence made him a leading candidate for the Democratic presidential nomination in 1924.

Al Smith would have been the first to deny that he was the perfect public servant; but his record as governor of New York for four terms fully justifies his being called one of the best state governors in American history. He reorganized and consolidated New York state government, constantly championed reform and welfare legislation, aided materially in getting the Workmen's Compensation Law, won adequate appropriations for public education, pushed a unified park system plan through the hostile legislature, reduced agricultural taxes, carried out large-scale public improvements, defended democratic principles, and reduced the spoils system of appointments —all of this and more against a legislature which was under Republican control except for two years when the Senate was Democratic.[4]

In all of Smith's career, there is no evidence whatever that the Roman Catholic Church ever dictated a political decision. He was a good Catholic but no one believed more firmly in separation of church and state. An Episcopalian layman, Charles C. Marshall, addressed an open letter to Smith in March 1927 asking how he could reconcile Catholic dogma, papal encyclicals, and other pronouncements with the Constitution and American principles of government. Marshall, in short, charged that one could not be at the same time a good Catholic and a good American. Smith's reply was a masterful defense of religious liberty.[5]

Interest in Smith's religion was inevitable when political forecasters were agreeing that he would be the favorite in the 1928 Democratic convention. Admirers hastily took to their typewriters to praise the man, the executive, the great liberal-conservative. Some defended him because he was a Catholic, some because he was a wet, some because he was a great governor and an excellent politician. Republicans attacked him because he was a Democrat; religious bigots screamed their hysterical fears of Rome; the Ku Klux Klan unleashed the full force of its venom. Bishop James Cannon, Jr. and his dry crusaders served warning that they would never fight under the banner of one thrice damned with Rum, Romanism, and Tammany Hall. The campaign of vilification, begun in 1924, slowly gathered fury in 1927 and reached its climax in November 1928.[6]

The Democrats who gathered at Houston, Texas, could choose from an unusually large number of well-qualified candidates. Thomas J. Walsh, James A. Reed, Walter F. George, Albert C. Ritchie, Joseph T. Robinson, Harry Byrd, Cordell Hull, and Atlee Pomerene were among the capable and willing. But even before Claude G. Bowers delivered his rousing, invective-studded keynote address, there was little doubt that Smith would win. Joseph T. Robinson, one of the ablest members of the Senate, presided as permanent chairman and became the vice-presidential nominee. Another Democratic pillar, Senator Key Pittman of Nevada, presided over drafting the platform.

This document called the Democracy to battle stations. After very proper excoriation of the 'sordid corruption and unabashed rascality ... [of] eight blighting years of Republican rule,' the platform made obeisance to lower taxes, efficiency, a just tariff, a farm board, prosperous mining, a constructive foreign policy to retrieve American prestige, promotion of waterways, conservation of natural resources, efficient transportation, protection for labor, a study of unemployment, aid to veterans, restricted immigration, free speech, an honest effort to enforce the Eighteenth Amendment and the anti-trust laws, and several other matters to prove that Democrats were nice people.[7]

On hand to nominate Smith again was the convalescent Franklin Delano Roosevelt, well on the way to recovery from an attack of poliomyelitis that had threatened in 1921 to end his political career. After adopting the platform, the convention nominated Smith on a revised first ballot on 28 June. In accepting the nomination, Smith let it be known that he would try to put an end to Prohibition.[8]

2. *Campaign Patterns*

Alfred E. Smith's reputation for political finesse and liberal statesmanship could not escape comparison with Herbert Hoover's fame as engineer and administrator. He was better liked than Hoover, who often was described as cold, aloof, dignified, unapproachable, and petulant. Smith looked and acted as a normal man should. He was quick to smile, had a spontaneous sense of humor that broke into laughter easily and naturally. His emotions were connected with his muscles. He knew the value of a good press and knew how to get it. His liberalism attracted such pundits as Walter Lippmann; his urbanism attracted the fire of such agrarian Republicans as William Allen White.

Al Smith entered the campaign handicapped by the belief that New York was America, that its values and its various ways of life were American values and American ways of life. Hoover knew the country far better, at least in a statistical way, and he had seen far more of it than Smith.[9] Whether either candidate really understood America is a moot point.

As the campaign of 1928 got under way, both parties prepared to spend unprecedented sums. The national committees alone ran through more than $16 million; the Republicans managed to spend about $9.5 million. Many solid Protestant Republicans and Democrats counted it a small price to keep the Pope out of the United States.

Any lingering idea that Hoover was a political neophyte should have been dispelled by the care with which he organized his campaign. Dr. Hubert Work of Colorado, Coolidge's completely undistinguished Secretary of the Interior, was chairman of the Republican National Committee, but Hoover gave the orders. The key headquarters was the luxurious, elephant-garnished office in Chicago where James W. Good presided. Democrats put great faith in John J. Raskob's enlistment of other millionaires to help Smith. Raskob, normally a Republican, was not a good political organizer, regardless of how skillful he had been as a high official of General Motors.[10] Hoover would hear more, much more, from Raskob.

Very significant for the future was how the campaign helped to stabilize, or to congeal, some of the Republican opposition to Hoover. Popular demand made Hoover the nominee and carried him into the White House. The Old Guard accepted with ill grace this 'amateur' who threatened their control of the party. None of the major Republican machines favored Hoover, and none of them campaigned vigorously for him. Progressives were hopeful rather than happy. William E. Borah vouched for the candidate because of his stand on Prohibition; Smith W. Brookhart, Iowa's rabidly dry senator, persuaded himself that Hoover could be trusted on farm relief; and Gifford Pinchot was at least dubious. George W. Norris, who scathingly denounced both Hoover and the party, campaigned for Progressives regardless of party label.[11] The Norris-Hoover feud, begun as early as 1921, ended only with the death of Nebraska's greatest statesman.

Both candidates were in favor of peace, equality of opportunity, protection of the American home, the welfare of American children. Both pronounced in favor of developing inland waterways and conserving natural resources. Both favored better relations with Latin America, although Smith could be more forthright in denouncing current policies. An analysis of his major speeches shows that Hoover dealt too much in generalities, banalities, and exhortations. Smith attacked vigorously in twenty major speeches; Hoover evaded masterfully in seven homilies.

Al Smith was far too colorful a figure not to attract considerable attention wherever he went. Large crowds would gather to see him, to hear him, and to wish that he were a Methodist or a Baptist. At Oklahoma City Smith delivered the one sermon of his campaign—a plea for religious toleration.[12] A biographer's prophecy, written in 1927, had come to pass:

There will be many, if this man runs for the presidency, who will bristle at the thought of his Catholicism. Spellbinders of the Republican Party will view with alarm for hours on end the perils of Rum and Romanism. It may be that the ludicrous hobgoblins of the Ku Klux Klan will dust off their robes and hold solemn rallies under the banner of intolerance. But vast throngs will crowd into the halls where he speaks, to laugh at his jokes and be won by the first real personality in politics since Roosevelt. And the melody of a city song will sweep the prairies.[13]

Most of the excitement was synthetic so far as the candidates were concerned. Democrats did not fail to ring the changes on corruption until they frayed the ropes and cracked the bells. There was no need to manufacture or to hunt. The record was there: Elk Hills, Teapot Dome, Salt Creek, the Veterans' Bureau, Prohibition, and so on and on. Claude G. Bowers set the pattern when he called the Republicans a party of 'pillage and privilege.'[14] Judging from his *Memoirs,* Hoover knew little about the Harding scandals, spent little time in condemning them, and mentioned them only when absolutely necessary.

As a candidate, Hoover sidestepped the muck with a general announcement that he was against sin. But where was his sense of humor when he said: 'The record of these seven and one-half years constitutes a period of rare courage in leadership and constructive action. Never has a political party been able to look back upon a similar period with more satisfaction. Never could it look forward with more confidence that its record would be approved by the electorate.'[15]

Republicans could ignore their malodorous record, supremely confident that their golden wand of prosperity would wave away all sins. They counterattacked with the cry of 'Tammany!' and pointed to rotten Democratic machines which, allied with racketeers and lords of vice, ruled many a great city.

3. *Prosperity, Prohibition, Prejudice*

No political party and its leadership have suffered more cruelly from the climax of events than did the Republicans after 1928. The market crash was but a spectacular explosion in the economic storm that was sweeping over the country even as votors went to the polls. The Great Depression came so soon after the election that the rash political oratory of Republican campaigners was remembered and hurled back with devastating effects.

Republicans, with Hoover setting the pace, continued to identify their party with prosperity. Largely ignoring the rising volume of unemployment, bank failures, and farm distress, politicians whooped it up for prosperity. So did the publicists, complacent and overconfident: 'We have put poverty on so nearly a voluntary basis that we have been forced to find a new definition for poverty . . . We have set about making prosperity and not poverty universal.'[16] Democrats, of course, were labeled as midwives for a depression certain to be born if Smith were elected.

Hoover recited the great economic gains that had been centuries in the making, and gave Republican policies much of the credit. He endorsed full employment, admitted that full employment rested not only on 'a strong and progressive economic system but upon the sound policies of and the vigorous co-operation by the government to promote economic welfare.' Mr. Hoover did not define what he meant by sound policies or specify what the federal government could do to maintain full employment. Republicans had ended the unemployment of 1921 by 'a nation-wide employment conference' and 'a program for the systematic organization of the whole business community to restore employment.' Labor's prosperity depended on 'sound governmental policies and wise leadership,' which Republicans had provided.[17] Hoover could say such things without cracking a smile, fully believing them, as he believed that 'Never in our history was the leadership in our economic life more distinguished in its abilities than today, and it has grown greatly in its consciousness of public responsibility.'[18] One wonders if he was thinking of his own leadership in the Department of Commerce.

Nothing that Smith could say about farm distress, the 4 million unemployed, and the 669 bank suspensions in 1927, seemed to make much impression.[19] There was not enough concentrated suffering to show sharply through the prosperity fog. A majority of the voters probably believed that the country was prosperous, and no one could persuade them that it was not.

Prohibition was a far better issue, one that could cause genuine excitement and evoke intensely emotional responses. Mr. Hoover was a reluctant champion of the dry cause, since he did not believe in trying to promote temperance by legislative fiat; but he did not say so during the campaign. At Stanford he repeated: 'I do not favor the repeal of the Eighteenth Amendment. I stand for the efficient enforcement of the laws enacted thereunder. . . . Our country has deliberately undertaken a great social and economic experiment, noble in motive and far-reaching in purpose.'[20] On another occasion he announced that 'The purpose of the Eighteenth Amendment is to protect the American home. A sacred obligation is imposed on the President to secure its honest enforcement and to eliminate the abuses which have grown up around it; I wish it to succeed.'[21]

Smith was by all odds correct in asserting that enforcement efforts were a farce, crime and corruption had invaded the liquor field, and racketeers flourished in every large city in the land. He wanted the allowable alcoholic content of beverages to be increased pending an amendment that would return liquor control to the states where it belonged, urged the need for realistic thinking, and called for a national referendum.[22] Church groups, particularly Methodists and Baptists, hated Smith for these views. Mabel Walker Willebrandt, long identified with enforcement, helped to spread the conviction that Prohibition was a Protestant achievement under attack by a Catholic minority.[23] Attitudes on Prohibition crossed party lines so thoroughly that it is impossible to label either party as wet or dry.

Both candidates toe-danced around the touchy water power question. In his acceptance speech, Hoover endorsed general development of water resources. Anything resembling government ownership he would oppose as socialistic. Smith condemned waste of natural resources, dishonest propaganda of utility corporations, campaigns of falsification, lobbying in state and national government, sinister efforts of the National Electric Light Association to censor textbooks, and all attempts to defeat public ownership. While not proposing government distribution of power, Smith urged public ownership of of power sites and generating facilities in order to guarantee fair rates and equitable distribution.[24]

Hoover recognized the existence of a farm problem, promised a farm board, aid to co-operatives, adequate tariffs, stabilization corporations, reorganization of the marketing system, and vaguely suggested lower transportation costs by developing inland waterways. Apparently Republicans were about ready to stop talking and do something, since Hoover promised that 'The working out of agricultural relief constitutes the most important obligation of the next administration.'[25]

Republicans were especially vulnerable on the farm problem and Smith made the most of his opportunity. His jibes on numerous occasions would have been body blows had they been delivered by a dry Protestant. Hoover in 1924 had prescribed a remedy for surplus crops: make the price so low that surplus production would be unprofitable. Smith could not believe that his opponent really expected tariff tinkering to be of any great benefit to agriculture. He warned that stabilization corporations 'made up of voluntary associations of producers' could not possibly stabilize agriculture without government intervention. While not pledging himself categorically to McNary-Haugenism, which had so many enemies in the East, Smith stood squarely behind 'an effective control of the sale of exportable surplus with the cost imposed upon the commodity benefited.'[26]

The Republican *Campaign Text-Book* of 1928 set the tariff pitch for party choristers. After the Democrats won in 1892, this novel interpretation of history asserted, the country experienced one of the worst panics in its history. 'Industry throughout the country was completely paralyzed. . . . Before the close of this panic, brought on by the Democratic tariff policy, practically all of our industrial plants were closed, 50 per cent of our railroads and 30 per cent of our national banks were in the hands of receivers.'[27] Hoover stood squarely behind the high protective tariff and the time-honored deception perpetrated by the Republican party to make the country as a whole pay tribute to a powerful few. The tariff protected high wages, the tariff would help solve the farm problem, the tariff caused American prosperity, the tariff would continue to keep the United States prosperous. Mr. Hoover had figures, plenty of figures, which proved to his satisfaction that the Republican tariff did not prevent Europeans from earning money to buy from us. Altogether, from trade and other items, foreign countries had a purchasing power of over $6 billion and only $320 million was due annually on debt settlements, so the tariff could not be attacked on that score, either![28]

Smith, as could be expected, defended the modernized Democratic tariff stand for reasonable protection. He excoriated tariffs made by log-rolling, praised the Tariff Commission created in 1916, and condemned the Republicans for having emasculated the commission. He advocated taking the tariff out of politics and urged such rates 'as will to the very limit protect legitimate business enterprise, as well as American labor from ruinous competition of foreign-made goods produced under conditions far below the American standard.' He also reassured business that there was nothing to fear from Democrats on the tariff.[29] Smith, like many other Democrats, weaseled and squirmed on the tariff issue.

Smith could plead in vain, almost in desperation, for sober judgment on the record and not on insinuations and innuendo. At Oklahoma City on 20 September he spoke in the Coliseum packed to its 10,000 capacity. He reviewed his record as governor of New York, challenged the Republicans to find any breath of scandal connected with his administrations, and cited endorsements from such distinguished people as Charles Evans Hughes, Nicholas Murray Butler, and John Dewey to show that he was not the Tammany Tiger in disguise. Smith refused to be silent for political expediency while Republicans high in the party zealously promoted the campaign of slander. Nearly all of the Oklahoma City speech was a defense of his record and an attack upon the effort, directed by ex-Senator Robert L. Owen of Oklahoma, to inject religion into the campaign.[30]

Bishop James Cannon, Jr. was far more effective than any other public figure in playing religious prejudice for all it was worth in the dry, Protestant South. It was Cannon who transformed the campaign in the South 'into what was almost tantamount to a religious war.'[31] Still, Cannon and the Reverend Bob Jones accused Raskob and Smith of introducing the religious issue! The accusation merely served as an excuse to pour out torrents of abuse against Romanism. Cannon organized the Anti-Smith Democrats for Hoover and made speech after speech attacking Smith for his nullification of Prohibition. The fighting bishop was also very effective in the Middle West, where wavering farmers who still preferred Lowden had to be persuaded that Hoover was better than Smith. Bishop Cannon astutely shunned any but the most casual relations with Republican leaders.[32] More sober in campaigning against Smith was Senator Borah, who sincerely decried religious prejudice. His speeches in the South, where Hoover's popularity already was high in many quarters, must be credited with having done much to turn both bigots and more sensible people toward the Republican candidate.[33]

4. *And Hoover Won*

The final count of votes cast on 6 November 1928 gave Hoover some 21,392,000 and Smith only 15,016,000, making the popular vote much closer than the electoral count of 444 to 87. Smith carried only Mississippi, Alabama, Georgia, South Carolina, Arkansas, Louisiana, Massachusetts, and Rhode Island. Hoover and the Republican party had broken into, not smashed, the Solid South and they did it on the issues of Prohibition and religion, however much the victor might discount the religious factor. Still, Democrats in six Southern states, to whom a Republican was more hateful than a Catholic, remained loyal to ancestral memories of ghostly gray battalions. 'A legend went against a personality, and the legend won.'[34]

Leaders of business could contemplate both the campaign and election with equanimity. Neither party carried a genuine threat to vested interests. Happily, a leading business journal reported: 'Business stood the campaign well. . . . And the time may come when business will not shiver at *any* proposal of politics, knowing and realizing that trade makes its own laws no matter which party is in power and that natural laws *must* in the end prevail over artificial and political.' After all, bureaucracy was the only real issue—not tariff, water power, farm relief, Prohibition, or any other artificial political issue.[35] This attitude, born of monolithic prejudice, typified people who confused a parade of slogans and banalities with thought processes.

Republicans won the election of 1928 because they had the inertia of prosperity mythology on their side. Hoover did nothing and said nothing to shatter faith in the myth of eternal boom, and 'Adult Americans elected him for the same reason that would have led Americans under the age of ten to elect Santa Claus.'[36] Democrats should have been fighting for years to get rid of the rascals but they had not done so, and John J. Raskob's campaign for his friend and fellow Catholic fell far short of success. Hoover believed that 'general prosperity, Prohibition, the farm tariffs, Tammany, and the "snuggling" up of Socialists' defeated Smith.[37] In the midst of their rejoicing, Republicans need not worry about persuading voters that 'the sun rises because the rooster crows.' Prosperity is here because the Republicans are in office.[38]

Perhaps Smith was unduly sensitive about bigotry and the whispering campaign, but there is no doubt that these factors contributed largely to Hoover's plurality. Hoover's sincere rebuke of fanatics could not reverse a traditional animosity toward Catholicism that had existed, often in virulent form, since colonial days. 'I don't believe in mixing politics and religion; but, by gum, I ain't gonna vote for no Catholic!' is the way one farm hand wrapped up the whole issue. The Ku Klux Klan was by no means dead in 1928; fear and hatred of Romanism, deeply imbedded in rural areas throughout the country, was very powerful in the Solid South. Nevertheless, much of the Bible Belt would come far closer to voting for a wet Catholic than for a Republican; some states simply would not accept a candidate both Catholic and wet.

Senator James Thomas Heflin, the rabble-rousing stumper from Alabama, may not have been speaking for all who voted against Al Smith, but his tirade of 12 June 1930 sheds some light on why so many Democrats bolted to Hoover in 1928. North Carolina voters had just rejected their 'Little Giant,' aging Senator Furnifold McLendel

Simmons, at a primary election. Heflin delivered himself of a eulogy which included this attack on Smith:

My God, just think of it, the great Democratic Party of Jefferson and of Jackson and of Wilson going to Tammany for leadership, with its alien program and interests and its social equality plan and practice, and its foreign secret understanding and practice of slipping in hundreds of thousands of foreigners in violation of the laws of our country to swell the vote of Tammany and help make America Catholic. Take that and thrust it in the face of the great Democratic Party of the South and tell us that we must bow down and worship this new hideous and hateful image which is set up in front of us by the John J. Raskob régime. He is a Republican and an officer in a foreign government. He holds an official position in the kingdom of the Roman Catholic Pope . . . Shades of Jefferson! [39]

Herbert Hoover meant what he said in the campaign. He would seek legislation to enact his promises into law, and he would fight steadfastly against every proposal that did not harmonize with his political and economic principles. He truly believed that Republican policies had been responsible for prosperity, that those policies were sound, and under his leadership they could be applied effectively to solve any problem that might arise. Few if any Presidents have taken office with a program of action constructed so carefully and followed so faithfully.

CHAPTER IV

CHANGING THE GUARD

1. *Ideas and Men*

An overcast sky greeted Herbert Hoover as he looked out the window of his S Street home on March 4. Washington was like that, and the very practical President-elect thought nothing of omens as he dressed casually for an hour of work before breakfast. There was time to play for a few minutes with his grandchildren, Peggy Ann and Herbert 3d, before returning to unanswered mail. Boris, his Serbian valet, helped the Chief into formal morning clothes at 10 A.M. and smoothed the shiny high hat that would get so wet before the day ended. Senator Moses then arrived to lead the presidential party to the White House.

Calvin Coolidge was even more gloomy and taciturn than usual. After completing last official duties, the President wandered through the White House, taking a final, silent farewell of the rooms he had known and of the greatness they implied. Mrs. Coolidge tried especially hard to be gracious to the servants who were being treated so brusquely by her husband. Some reporters observed that Coolidge greeted the Hoovers at the door as they arrived; but 'Ike' Hoover, chief usher, remembered that the President dressed tardily and descended to the Blue Room where the Hoovers, Curtis, and other dignitaries waited. There was no small talk as Coolidge greeted his guests with a curt nod and announced sharply: 'Time to go!'

President Coolidge and the man who did choose to run led the procession behind a cavalry escort. Coolidge enjoyed the crowd's applause and thawed as he neared the Capitol. Frequently he raised his hat in acknowledgment; modestly, Hoover bared his own head infrequently. Smiling dutifully beneath their snug helmet-like hats, Grace Goodhue Coolidge and Lou Henry Hoover in a second car followed their distinguished husbands down Pennsylvania Avenue.

Obeying tradition, the President signed the last bills that were to bear his name while the President-elect waited to get along with the day's business. In the Senate chamber they stood by while Charles

Curtis was sworn in and Charles Dawes returned to private status. Then dignitaries and functionaries stepped out into the drizzle for the main event. The ladies were lost in the crowd and Hoover was plainly annoyed until George Akerson escorted them to their prominent seats on the platform.

Herbert Clark Hoover placed his hand on a new Bible opened to the Sermon on the Mount and repeated the oath of office after Chief Justice William Howard Taft. The Bible was then turned back to Proverbs 29:18: 'Where there is no vision, the people perish; but he that keepeth the law, happy is he.' The Chief Justice offered his congratulations and Calvin Coolidge remained seated as he reached up to shake hands. Rain fell steadily. Indians in full war paint sought shelter under the Capitol portico as President Hoover, wiping the rain from his face, moved under an umbrella to read his sober inaugural.[1] After acknowledging congratulations, the Hoovers drove to their new home for a quick lunch and then to the reviewing stand, where they enjoyed the two-hour inaugural parade despite the heavy downpour.

There is little reason to suspect that the President's address aroused enthusiasm among those who heard it or those who read it. Prohibitionists would find comfort in the promise to investigate 'the whole structure of our Federal system of jurisprudence,' and rugged individualists approved the promise to keep government out of business. Internationalists might hope for membership in the World Court as the President delivered his eloquent plea for peace, understanding, and world co-operation. Hoover would seek economy in public expenditure, reorganize executive departments, expand public works, and promote welfare activities.[2] In the four years of his presidency, Hoover stood firmly for this program.

The President also presented his interpretation of American ideals. While he found it difficult to put into words the 'embedded ideals and aspirations' of the American people, those intangibles would be expressed by attaining

The preservation of self-government and its full foundations in local government; the perfection of justice whether in economic or in social fields; the maintenance of ordered liberty; the denial of domination by any group or class; the building up and preservation of equality of opportunity; the stimulation of initiative and individuality; absolute integrity in public affairs; the choice of officials for fitness to office; the direction of economic progress toward prosperity and the further lessening of poverty; the freedom of public opinion; the sustaining of education and of the advancement of knowledge; the growth of religious spirit and the tolerance of all faiths; the strengthening of the home; the advancement of peace.[3]

A quarter of a century later, after a terrible depression and the most destructive war in history, Herbert Hoover might have re-read with pardonable satisfaction:

Ours is a land rich in resources; stimulating in its glorious beauty; filled with millions of happy homes; blessed with comfort and opportunity. In no nation are the fruits of accomplishment more secure. In no nation is the government more worthy of respect. No country is more loved by its people. I have an abiding faith in their capacity, integrity and high purpose. I have no fears for the future of our country. It is bright with hope.[4]

One year after these words were spoken, he might have wondered.

Hoover's concept of the presidency was sufficiently broad and understanding to permit plenty of room for action. The President, he believed, is the chief administrator, responsible for national defense, law enforcement, and maintenance of peace. He is a party leader. 'As adviser to Congress . . . he must demonstrate constant leadership by proposing social and economic reforms . . . He must be the conserver of natural resources, and he must carry forward the great public works in pace with public need. He must encourage all good causes.'[5] Hoover, following these precepts, tried to provide far more leadership than came from Calvin Coolidge; like his predecessor, he wanted to respect Congress, avoid battles with legislators, and obtain reforms without blasting them out.

Hoover's cabinet was made up of conservatives, with no genuine liberal or progressive included. Perhaps one or two might be called Manchester liberals, or people whose ideas were a century or more behind events. Six members of the cabinet were millionaires. Mellon, generally regarded as the most powerful man in Washington, was also one of the richest men in the country. No President could ignore him. On the whole, the new cabinet members were competent; except for Henry L. Stimson, all were mediocre.

The new President wanted Frank B. Kellogg to remain as Secretary of State, but 'Nervous Nellie' was tired of the heavy load he had carried. Senator William E. Borah's earnest campaigning had laid the President under an inescapable obligation; but Borah preferred to remain in the Senate.[6] The third choice was Henry L. Stimson, who returned from the Philippines to head the cabinet. Stimson we may accept as a great public servant without quibbling. The new secretary was a Teddy Roosevelt Progressive who had refused to bolt when the Bull Moose tossed his itching antlers in 1912; he did not belong in the company of such men as La Follette and Norris. Stimson was not an isolationist and so contributed balance to a party that included those confirmed western ostriches, Borah and Hiram Johnson; indeed, he at least imitated a sword-rattler who would have welcomed a Far Eastern war in 1931–2.[7] This was no political appointment. Stimson brought additional prestige to the cabinet and *Time,* with singular discourtesy, put Stimson's picture instead of Hoover's on its March 9 cover.

Andrew Mellon, who continued to preside over the Treasury, was a banker-industrialist whose very wealth made him suspect. His major objective in taxation was to lower income taxes on the rich and to transfer the cost of government more and more to people less and less able to bear it. Some ecstatic writers pictured Mellon as the personification of post-war America, the champion of giving everyone a chance to get rich. He was the champion of organized business, the champion of tax refunds and lower income taxes in the high brackets; but he was also the champion of balanced budgets and reduced national debt, of keep-the-government-out-of-business, of the dribble-from-the-top theory of prosperity. The great organs of publicity, the metropolitan newspapers and conservative monthly magazines, expressed their editorial approval. With Mellon in the cabinet, surely the golden wand would remain untarnished.[8] Hoover was pleased to name him as ambassador to Great Britain in 1932; it was, of course, pure coincidence that a move was on in Congress to impeach Mellon, probably on charges impossible to sustain. Ogden L. Mills, who stepped into Mellon's place, loomed in Hoover's estimation as an intellectual giant. Mills and Hoover had been mutual fans since 1920 and it was Mills more than any other man who guided the financial policies of the Hoover Administration.

A nasty rumor circulated about the appointment of William D. Mitchell as Attorney General. Hoover had promised the position to his old friend and ardent supporter, William J. Donovan, but reneged under pressure from anti-Catholic and Prohibition forces.[9] Mitchell had been a very competent Solicitor General.

Other cabinet members were acceptable but far from brilliant.

Neither James W. Good, who died on 18 November 1929, nor Patrick J. Hurley was outstanding as Secretary of War. Charles Francis Adams, who made a comfortable Secretary of the Navy at a time when the big emphasis was on naval disarmament, could not forget his illustrious ancestors. Hoover was very proud of Arthur M. Hyde, a Ford dealer who came out of Missouri's politics to be Secretary of Agriculture. Being from Missouri, however, is no guaranty of ability either to diagnose agricultural ills or to prescribe proper medicines. Hyde entered office knowing little about agriculture, in spite of his ownership of three farms, and left unchanged. Ray Lyman Wilbur, president of Stanford University and one of the President's few intimate friends, may have understood the West 'above most men,'[10] but as Secretary of the Interior he would deal with more than Western problems. Robert Paterson Lamont, Hoover's first Secretary of Commerce, was competent but unimaginative. Hoover retained James J. Davis as Secretary of Labor; when Davis entered the Senate in December 1930 William N. Doak, a labor politician of mean stature, replaced him.[11] Walter Folger Brown, a master politician from Ohio, functioned smoothly as Postmaster General.

In every department and many independent agencies were capable Hoover men, 'new patriots' who sacrificed the chance to increase their wealth in order to serve their country. Among them should be noted F. Trubee Davison in the War Department, Ernest Lee Jahncke and David S. Ingalls in Navy, Julius Klein in Commerce, Earl D. Church as Commissioner of Pensions, Charles J. Rhoads as Commissioner of Indian Affairs, and Charles Evans Hughes, Jr. in Justice.[12]

The presidency often blurs the President's personality. Every incumbent will react differently to the manifold duties that must be discharged, to the pitiless and constant publicity. The real Herbert Hoover was an affable, genial, and gracious host; he was by nature sensitive and sentimental. Anyone who could inspire scores of intelligent men and women with an unswerving loyalty could not truthfully be called lacking in personal magnetism. Preoccupied with a succession of serious and enduring crises, he seemed to casual observers aloof, remote, and ill tempered, a man who wore an almost perpetual frown.

Old friends, veteran companions of many journeys and enterprises, found a warm welcome at the White House, where Mrs. Hoover presided as a quiet and gracious hostess. Among the most intimate of friends were old associates of globe-trotting days, Mr. and Mrs. Edgar Rickard; two couples from Stanford, the Ray Lyman Wilburs and the Vernon Kelloggs; and a close business associate and friend of long standing, Mark Lawrence Requa. A Stanford classmate and faithful defender, Will Irwin, wrote the best Hoover biography.

The President's exceptionally good health came at least in part from willing adherence to a regime of diet and exercise prescribed by his personal physician, Dr. Joel T. Boone. There was never any difficulty in assembling participants for the early morning medicine-ball tossing which usually lasted for twenty minutes or so. Cabinet members and their principal assistants, Supreme Court justices, favored members of the press corps, and nominees from the secretariat usually formed the circle.

Hoover had an uncanny ability, noted by many reporters, to keep many things moving at one time, to follow through with broad plans for subordinates to execute. In the White House, as in the Department of Commerce, he made the maximum use of his time. Lunches, dinners, receptions, and even weekends at his Rapidan retreat were rarely times of complete relaxation. Occasionally at the Rapidan camp he could get away by himself for short periods of solitude. This mountain outing place was a wilderness spot on the upper Rapidan near Cotoctin Furnace, Maryland. Lawrence Richey and Colonel Earl Long of the Marines selected the site. Hoover personally paid for installing utilities, building cabins, improving the fishing stream, and other embellishments, all of which he later gave to the Shenandoah National Park.

The anonymous public, supposedly, loves to think of little feet pattering around the White House that it might be thought of as a projection of the Great American Home. There were such feet but not for publicity purposes. Mrs. Herbert Hoover, Jr. brought her small children, Peggy Ann and Herbert 3d (affectionately nicknamed Peter) for extended visits while her husband was recuperating from a long illness. They could not, of course, be kept out of the news; but reporters usually avoided gurgly journalese in their feature stories.

2. *The Fourth Estate*

Much of Hoover's success or failure with the public would depend on his secretarial staff, who were dubbed the 'Vestal Virgins' by the authors of the *Washington Merry-Go-Round*: they complained that the presidential secretariat was baffling and bewildering. Members of this secretariat, with the exception of one man, were mediocrities unable to fulfill the impossible tasks assigned to them. Lawrence Richey, the former detective, who had been at Hoover's elbow for more than a decade, was an efficient, loyal, self-effacing secretary and friend. If Hoover had exercised the same excellent judgment in the selection of other assistants that he revealed in his appointment of Richey, his relations with the press would have been far better. He trusted Richey as he did no other man, and his confidence was never betrayed.

George Akerson, who worked so well for Hoover before his election, gave up in 1931, in part a victim of Richey's antagonism. Walter Newton, characterized as slow, clumsy, and dull, resigned his seat in the House of Representatives to become Hoover's political secretary; Richey still ruled. French Strother served the Chief as literary and research secretary until his resignation in May 1931. Then a professional press agent, George Aubrey Hastings, became Hoover's executive clerk. James Francis Burke left after a few months. Burke had authorized or inspired Mrs. Willebrandt's speeches to the Methodists in 1928; Mrs. Willebrandt received no thanks. Scorned, the lady became an attorney for a wine-brick company and wrote *The Inside of Prohibition,* which helped drive Burke from the White House, although he soon became General Counsel of the Republican National Committee. After Akerson left for Hollywood, Hoover made a blunder in selecting Theodore G. Joslin, correspondent of the *Boston Transcript,* to be his liaison with the press. Neither Hoover nor his secretarial staff established really good press relations.[13]

Not many newspaper reporters disliked Hoover when he was Secretary of Commerce; their attitude changed so fast that very few liked him after he became President.[14] Correspondents resented the canned handouts by secretaries, Hoover's refusal to take them into his confidence, and such tricks as the evasive summary of the Wickersham report. When one recalls the verbal drubbing administered to Hoover by newspapers that printed mordacious propaganda provided by Michelson on behalf of the Democratic party, the victim might be expected to be suspicious of anyone who smelled of printer's ink. Hoover was too sensitive to criticism; his feelings were too close to the surface; he was too busy to do battle with reporters who had a tremendously exaggerated idea of their own importance. He knew how correspondents worked, how they struggled for scoops, how they sought materials 'to satisfy the village gossips,' how they thought that the press—The Press—should have access to the most secret information. He paid tribute to journalists' ability to follow Washington's complexities; he raked reporters for reporting tales of exhibitionists.[15]

As Secretary of Commerce, Hoover had enjoyed good press relations because he talked freely, answered questions, volunteered information, and often was the source of leaks. His was not the supreme responsibility of the presidency; he did not feel any imperative need to weigh every word for its possible effect; and he had the help of George Akerson. Reporters were less interested in Hoover than in the news he had for them.

Washington correspondents consider a President as fair game. Everything a President does or says, everywhere he goes, everyone he sees—all are news. The press assumes that it enjoys an inalienable right to obtain news from the White House, not censored handouts; on several occasions during Hoover's Administration reporters were chagrined or angry upon discovering that even the handouts were either false or misleading. When Hoover tried to hold conferences in secret, reporters demanded to know what was going on. When Hoover issued a statement, reporters analyzed it mercilessly. When Hoover made a mistake, reporters pounced upon it gleefully with no charity in their souls. No President needed a good press more than did Hoover; no President in modern times had worse relations with the fourth estate. They were not improved by the requirement that all newsmen admitted to press conferences sign pledges 'that they were not connected with any brokerage tipping service.'[16]

The charge that Hoover did not understand the press is just as wrong as the assertion that he had no sense of humor. On 13 April 1929 he told the Gridiron Club of Washington what he thought of the manner in which reporters twisted his clearest statements and speculated wildly when he had nothing to say. And two years later, when newspaper columns were carrying so many stories about crackpot schemes, the President advised the same organization to start a crusade against the tyranny of bells, 'an issue of more human importance than a vast number of the reforms now agitating Washington.'[17]

One wonders, however, why Hoover was complaining. Allen and Pearson knew whereof they wrote when they condemned important newspapers for not printing the truth, for preventing their reporters from reporting the truth. The *Los Angeles Times, Chicago Daily News, Washington Star, New York Herald Tribune,* and even the self-righteous *New York Times* were among papers that could be counted on to do their best for the President. Among the Hoover press favorites were Mark Sullivan, Richard V. Oulahan, William Hard, Frederic William Wile, Leroy Vernon, Roy Roberts, and David Lawrence. These men would always report fairly, and some of them were valued political advisers.[18]

Mark Sullivan was a companion, friend, and confidant of the President, and his activities aroused jealousy in the press corps. This stalwart veteran of the Republican *New York Herald Tribune* accompanied Hoover to Latin America after the 1928 election and stood beside him to fish when the *Maryland* anchored off Cape San Lucas. Sullivan was a member of the medicine-ball cabinet and often stayed for regular breakfasts after the others had refreshed themselves with toast and coffee. On 16 December 1930 Sullivan had breakfast with Henry Ford and the President. In other words, Sullivan was ubiquitous.

Another important supporter was Richard Victor Oulahan, chief of the *New York Times* Washington bureau and dean of the press corps. Oulahan had filed many meticulously accurate stories about Hoover for more than a decade. No one knew Washington and the Congress better than this veteran and few reporters have been held in such high regard by more people with diverse political and economic views. On 30 December 1931, the day when Hoover visited briefly with some 500 newsboys on the White House lawn, Richard Oulahan died. The President and Mrs. Hoover had received daily reports during Oulahan's illness and they were among the mourners who attended the funeral on 2 January.[19] Hoover had lost an intimate friend and valued counselor.

The Associated Press, especially its Washington correspondents, was almost invariably kind. Writers for the United Press, Allen and Pearson believed, were generally more capable, more liberal, and far more independent. The Hearst services, International News and Universal, employed good journalists. Such outstanding reporters as Charles G. Ross, Paul Y. Anderson, Raymond P. Brandt, J. Fred

Essary, and Drew Pearson could be trusted most of the time; but Frank R. Kent's 'The Great Game of Politics' lost its impartiality and became a Hoover apology. Arthur Sears Henning, capable and urbane, reflected the policies of his paper, the ultraconservative *Chicago Daily Tribune*. Clinton Wallace Gilbert, employed by the rarely liberal Curtis publications, retained his personal integrity. Robert S. Allen, co-author of the *Merry-Go-Round*, could say little in his own praise, although the *Christian Science Monitor* found it convenient to discharge him after publication of the book.[20]

On the whole, newspapers were represented in Washington by very capable and intelligent writers. And, on the whole, most of the reporters were fully as friendly to Hoover as conditions warranted. The President failed to make the best use of powerful friends among the correspondents, as he also failed to obtain the best from his strong supporters in Congress.

3. *The Seventy-first Congress*

Republicans controlled the Seventy-first Congress when it convened in special session on 15 April 1929, and the Old Guard tried to control the Republicans. George H. Moses of New Hampshire became president pro tem of the Senate, with James E. Watson of Indiana as floor leader and Simeon D. Fess of Ohio as whip. Of Watson, despair of liberals, one keen commentator wrote: 'The cautious observer will wish to delve further in the past before he pronounces Mr. Watson's selection the nadir of leadership.'[21] This trio, with Reed Smoot of Utah, typified the Old Guard, whose antagonism toward Hoover, going back at least to 1918, was intensified during the Harding-Coolidge regime. Able men directed the Democratic minority. Joseph T. Robinson of Arkansas and Thomas J. Walsh of Montana were floor leader and assistant floor leader, while Key Pittman of Nevada was the whip.

Insurgent Republicans constituted a major threat to Hoover's leadership in the Senate. The President did not, at any time, have a united party behind him and in this fact lies the principal cause for his greatly overemphasized 'political failure.' In the Senate, where there were 56 Republicans and 39 Democrats, a baker's dozen of insurgents or liberals could and did co-operate with Democrats to exercise effective control.

The alliance of these rebels with Democrats of vaguely similar leanings, or just with Democrats, was referred to as 'the coalition.' Its membership varied. William E. Borah of Idaho was the nominal leader, but George W. Norris and Robert M. La Follette, Jr. provided the real leadership. Borah, a strong Hoover supporter in 1928, deserted the President during the 1929 tariff fight. Norris was a powerful and consistent political enemy. La Follette, who inherited his father's opposition role, constantly tugged manfully at a reluctant Congress in an effort to achieve a progressive program. James M. Couzens, Michigan's multimillionaire enigma, was liberal or conservative by fits and starts. He could never fit into the Hoover-Ford-Firestone friendship. Hiram Johnson, Smith Wildman Brookhart, and Peter Norbeck were consistent progressive champions. T. H. Caraway of Arkansas and Byron ('Pat') Harrison of Mississippi were Democratic conservatives who served with the liberals in the amorphous coalition. No wonder these 'sons of wild jackasses,' as Moses soon called them, annoyed the President!

Hoover had comparatively little trouble with the House of Representatives. Nicholas Longworth of Ohio, elected speaker by a comfortable party vote of 254–143, enjoyed more national esteem than his accomplishments warranted. J. Q. Tilson of Connecticut was floor leader and Bertrand Snell of New York ran the Committee on Rules. Among many staunch supporters were Will R. Wood of Indiana, Isaac Bacharach of New Jersey, C. William Ramseyer of Iowa, Carl E. Mapes of Michigan, Willis C. Hawley of Oregon, and Burton L. French of Idaho. They were 'helpful and amiable' but felt no personal devotion to the President. A bloc of independent Republicans followed New York's Fiorello H. La Guardia but the Longworth-Tilson-Snell leadership kept the House under control. Debates in the special and regular sessions of the Seventy-first Congress produced additional strains on party ties, intensified opposition to presidential policies, and created feelings of animosity that boded ill for smooth relationships between the White House and Capitol Hill.

There would, of course, be a large contingent of lobbyists waiting for Congress to start the legislative process. Joseph Grundy, vice-president of the American Tariff League (and a Quaker), was known as the greatest defender of high tariffs. Chester Gray, representing the American Farm Bureau, and Fred Brinkmann of the National Grange would keep tabs on agricultural interests. Dr. Clarence True

Wilson, secretary of the Methodist Board of Temperance, Prohibition and Public Morals, co-operated occasionally with Francis Scott McBride of the Anti-Saloon League to keep America dry. Bishop Francis J. McConnell represented the Federal Council of Churches and received aid from Frederick J. Libby (another Quaker) of the National Council for the Prevention of War, in efforts to promote disarmament. John Thomas Taylor represented the American Legion. There were many more special representatives present to bedevil members of Congress.[22]

Some members of Congress could be very annoying, especially in committee hearings. President Hoover in September 1930 appointed Eugene Meyer, Jr. to the Federal Reserve Board, and the Senate Banking and Currency Committee held hearings on the appointment some four months later. Louis T. McFadden, long a Republican member of Congress from Pennsylvania and chairman of the House Banking and Currency Committee, marshaled witnesses to challenge Mr. Meyer's fitness for the position. McFadden disapproved Meyer's record with various federal fiscal agencies, charged him with uncomfortably close association with international bankers, and warned that under his guidance the Federal Reserve System would become a securities bond market for international financing. Hoover had maneuvered the whole thing to give Meyer the job he wanted, McFadden insisted.[23]

The Seventy-first Congress was, on the whole, as high in quality as most of our national legislative bodies. There was in both houses a continuity of membership which fairly represented the United States of 1929. There were demagogues and political hacks; there were statesmen and others of lesser rank fully dedicated to the service of their country. For this Congress the President did provide so large a measure of leadership that its record, while controversial, was indeed impressive.

CHAPTER V

FORGOTTEN PROGRESS

1. *Conservation*

Although Hoover is remembered primarily as a depression President, concerned first of all with measures to fight that economic disaster, his administration was marked by achievements that endured. Many of the projects he had initiated as Secretary of Commerce came to fruition during his presidency; many others were carried to completion under the New Deal; and several reforms that he advocated are yet to be realized. One of Hoover's major achievements, accomplished despite depression handicaps, was to turn public attention once more to the conservation of public resources.

Americans have devoted more than three centuries to the careless exploitation of the land they stole, bought, or conquered. This indictment is the other and decidedly unpopular side of a coin whose resplendent face is generally turned to public view. We enjoy praising ourselves for living in a country settled by refugees from religious persecution; we repeat and embellish sagas of heroic deeds by brave and bold men. We think of ourselves as builders who have made nature serve our will. We girdle the trees, wrench loose the roots of prairie sod, kill off the buffalo, scoop ore from the Mesabi Range, blast out Pennsylvania's anthracite, sweep away the forests, and bind the country together with ribbons of steel and strands of wire. In the process, we have destroyed or squandered infinitely more wealth than we have gathered from the earth.

No one had to sell Herbert Hoover on conservation. As Secretary of Commerce he had taken a deep interest in developing and conserving natural resources; he was particularly concerned with wise use of water power, inland waterways, and irrigation and reclamation.[1] He was all too aware of the tragedy of waste going on in all parts of the country, and the presidency gave him an opportunity to promote projects which had been left unfinished.

As chairman of the Colorado River Commission, he had promoted settlement of a long-standing dispute over utilization of water resources in the Colorado River basin. Hoover proudly proclaimed the Boulder Canyon Project Act of 21 December 1928 effective as of 25 June 1929.[2] Work on the Hoover Dam in Arizona, one of the greatest engineering feats in history, began in September 1930 and was completed under the New Deal. Sale of electrical power and water were expected to repay the $400 million spent by the federal government.[3]

Why was President Hoover not bothered by this extension of government activity into an area of private enterprise? For one thing, private companies were as concerned to see the dam built as government authorities. The Southern California Edison Company was willing and anxious to develop Colorado River power; so was its great competitive rival, the City of Los Angeles. Indeed, it was the states which balked: only with the greatest reluctance had Arizona agreed to Boulder Dam, and Nevada had given grudging consent because it expected to get short-range benefits from the construction activities. The various states and competitive interests involved required that the federal government construct the dam. One reason why private power advocates kept so quiet was that the feasibility of the entire project was seriously challenged by competent engineers. The engineers raised such doubts about the project that private enterprise was content to let public enterprise take over: 'The subtle dividing line between public monopoly and private monopoly in the provision of essential services appears to be much more closely related to the prospect of profit than to care for the public interest.'[4]

Plans, surveys, and borings for the Grand Coulee Dam on the Columbia River in Washington were nearly completed by 1933 when the New Deal came in to carry on. Plans were also made for storage and flood-control dams in California's Central Valley, and the New Deal put them into effect. In the Tennessee Valley, the Norris Dam (then called the Cove Creek Dam) was being discussed; but, because Hoover would not agree to operating Muscle Shoals as a government project, nothing of consequence was done for the Tennessee Valley.

The system of inland waterways was expanded, and Hoover hoped for great interlocking water routes which would make use of canalized rivers and canals. Completion of the Ohio River Improvement Project, a nine-foot channel from Pittsburgh to Cairo, gave him a chance to praise a 'new instrument of commerce.'[5] On river projects alone, over $700 million was spent from 1929 to 1933. The St. Lawrence

Waterway seemed within reach when the treaty with Canada was signed on 18 July 1932; but the Senate, subjected to intense lobbying by railway and other interests, withheld its approval.[6]

The record in conservation of other resources was somewhat less spectacular. Hoover ordered the cancellation of permits to drill for oil in large areas of the public domain.[7] His efforts to promote oil conservation through an interstate compact failed, since the oil companies were interested in price fixing, not in conservation. A conference called to consider the problem endorsed federal control of oil production. However, Hoover and Wilbur did obtain state conservation laws and agreements from operators of fields on or near the public domain.[8]

In other areas, too, Hoover endeavored to promote conservation in the West. His favorite device was to appoint a fact-finding commission to make recommendations. A joint commission, appointed by the President and various governors, studied the western problem. This body, the Garfield Commission, considered grazing, reclamation, and conservation of oil, water, coal, and other resources. The Commission recommended enlarged reserves of oil and mineral lands, reclamation areas, national parks and forests, refuges, and defense areas. Lands of use primarily for grazing should be turned back to the states for regulation. These recommendations were largely an endorsement of Hoover's ideas.[9] Congress, deluged by other tasks, let the project die. Nevertheless, under Hoover's regime some 2,250,000 acres were added to the national forests by transfer or purchase, and the area of national parks and monuments was increased by 40 per cent. Included were the Shenandoah and Great Smokies parks, Carlsbad Caverns, Canyon de Chelly, and Death Valley.[10] In spite of the fact that Hoover was basically a states rights advocate, he did not believe in allowing individualism to be expressed through plundering the common heritage of natural resources.

2. *Public Works*

Hoover inherited a large backlog of badly needed public buildings, bridges, and other works. Since 1900, Hoover observed, only $250 million had been spent on public buildings. In his four years alone, more than 800 public buildings were completed or planned at a cost of $700 million. One of the first was the Department of Commerce

Building, for which the President laid the corner stone, using the trowel handled by George Washington in a similar ceremony for the Capitol. Most of the Reconstruction Finance Corporation loans for public works came under the New Deal, but many of the projects thus financed, including the San Francisco Bay Bridge and the Los Angeles aqueduct, had been planned before 1933. They could have been started long before 1933 had Hoover been more enthusiastic about public works as a means of fighting depression. Highway construction, stimulated by the depression and by increasing demands for better transportation, was promoted by raising federal aid to more than $260 million annually. The 16,000 miles of federal-aid highways built in 1932 were more than double the total built in 1929. All told, during Hoover's administration, some 37,000 miles of federal-aid highways were constructed.[11]

Hoover was skeptical about the effectiveness of public works as a means of ironing out troughs in the business cycle. He could not see the federal government spending up to $8 billion annually to take the place of private building. A program so gigantic in scope would require an appalling increase in taxation, since borrowing for such purposes was anathema to the President.[12]

This skepticism was hardly in keeping with his proposal late in 1928 of a $3 billion reserve fund 'to be used for public construction work, so as to ward off unemployment in lean years . . .' Labor leaders William Green and James O'Connell had hailed the reserve fund with high praise; some editorial writers called it all sorts of fine names, and some called it paternalism and socialism. Governor Ralph Owen Brewster of Maine, who later was a senator for many years, announced the plan in New Orleans on 21 November in a speech which accurately forecast what would happen in a depression. The Columbus *Ohio State Journal* chided Hoover for advocating 'a step toward State Socialism . . . The words State Socialism strike terror to the hearts of the conservatives and yet, when they see any advantage to themselves, they are ready enough to advocate another Federal bureau and another appropriation.' Needless to say, the plan was never implemented, since it required federal-state cooperation.[13]

Hoover had an excellent weapon that he refused to use adequately. Expanded public works paid for by taxation, which would take away excessive savings, might have prevented the depression from becoming prolonged disaster. But Hoover complained that there was a very limited field for nonproductive public works projects, such works often would be located far from centers of unemployment, little manufacturing would be stimulated, one just could not find more than $10 billion a year for public works needed to employ one-half of the unemployed, and it was just a drop in the bucket anyway. Public works absorbed 760,000 workers on 1 August 1931, and just see how many more were unemployed![14]

In spite of the President's misgivings, the federal government spent more than $2,358 million on nonproductive public works from 30 June 1930 to 30 June 1933. The Democrats, particularly in 1932, urged more and more spending to bring the annual total to nearly $3 billion. Hoover countered that the budget never could be balanced that way, and the evils stemming from an unbalanced budget would be awful. The bill backed by Garner in May 1932 appeared to Hoover as a terrific pork barrel. In addition to urging private expansion and improvement, the President did favor self-liquidating works like toll bridges, water power development, slum clearance, and municipal waterworks. He had asked that the Reconstruction Finance Corporation be empowered to loan for such purposes.[15]

3. *To Promote the General Welfare*

The President had an active program of reform which encompassed such areas as law enforcement, executive reorganization, veterans' affairs, tariff, business regulation, banking, stock exchanges, housing, reorganization of the Indian service, and various social problems. People have disagreed about whether all these plans belonged in the reform category, but most of his specific recommendations were in line with the highest traditions of American liberalism. At every turn he made both friends and enemies.

Hoover was proud of efforts directed toward better housing and child welfare. In each of these fields he followed his customary pattern of an investigation to determine facts, a conference to present recommendations, publicity to enlist public support, and request for legislative action. While Secretary of Commerce, he had created a Housing Division which attempted to promote better housing and slum clearance. After careful preparation, a national housing conference met in December 1931; its recommendations and special studies were of enduring value. Hoover, opposing federal housing construction, confined his activities to removing numerous handicaps in zoning ordinances, lack of credit, and other impeding factors. Slum clearance was financed by the Reconstruction Finance Corporation and was continued under the New Deal.

In the fields of child welfare, Hoover continued active in the Child Health Association, which he had founded in 1919. A committee appointed in 1929 began preparation for a national conference that met from 15–21 November 1930. Its reports and recommendations were followed up by state conferences and state and local legislation. In a message to Congress each year for four years the President recommended federal aid to match state funds for promoting rural health agencies; Congress failed to act.[16] The New Deal took up the welfare challenge and succeeded in establishing more adequate services. For origins of the New Deal's Social Security program, one needs to go far back into history. Hoover's principal contribution was in creating the privately financed Research Committee on Social Trends, which prepared monumental social studies. The President favored old-age assistance and outlined principles that read like a preview of the Social Security Act of 1935. He also favored unemployment insurance and old-age insurance, both primarily to be privately financed.[17]

To reform law enforcement, Hoover sought a favorable press and competent judges and federal attorneys. He referred to this problem in his inaugural address, emphasizing the need for moral support by citizens generally, and in several other speeches. But, beyond appointment of the Wickersham Commission and mild federal changes, the President could do little except to urge, to preach, and to exhort. To the Supreme Court he named Charles Evans Hughes, Owen J. Roberts, and the liberal Benjamin N. Cardozo. Attorney General William D. Mitchell drafted legislation for procedural reforms which were enacted. Reforms in bankruptcy legislation had been considered since early in the 1920's and were particularly urged because of the great increase in bankruptcies, from 23,000 cases in the federal courts in 1921 to 65,000 cases in 1931. Losses were averaging $750 million annually, and during 1928–29 a number of fraudulent receiverships in federal courts were revealed. Thomas J. Thacher and Lloyd K. Garrison devoted more than a year to studying bankruptcy problems and made their report in December 1931. The

President sent a bill to Congress on 29 February 1932 to reduce fraud, conserve assets, and save sound enterprises.[18]

The proposed legislation aroused opposition from beneficiaries of the unreformed practices. Appointment by the Attorney General of salaried administrators and examiners would deprive the legal fraternity of a lucrative practice. Jacob T. Weinstein, chairman of the Committee on Law Revision of the National Association of Federal Practitioners, at once charged 'gratuitous governmental interference and an unwarranted attempt to regulate the private relations between debtors and their creditors.' Just more bureaucracy, Weinstein cried, and he insisted that no changes were needed. Judge Max Isaac, editor of the *American Bankruptcy Review*, chimed in to protect the private attorneys and to protest creation of another army of bureaucrats. Failure of Congress to enact such legislation early in 1932 caused unnecessary distress, Hoover believed, since a large number of farm, home, and business debts could have been adjusted without resort to bankruptcy.[19] Lobbying by lawyers, not the political complexion of Congress, defeated bankruptcy reform until the very end of Hoover's term.

An important but little heralded reform was effected in federal prisons. Since this was not a controversial subject, Congress passed a series of acts in 1930 practically rubber-stamping bills sent over by the White House. This body of legislation created the Bureau of Federal Prisons and the National Board of Parole, built new reformatories and prisons, set up a probation system, and transferred medical services to the Public Health Service. 'No such extensive or enlightened reform in dealing with criminals had been accomplished heretofore in the entire history of the Federal government,' the President asserted.[20]

Despite the Republican party's rousing defense of Prohibition, Hoover had grave doubts about being able to enforce the law. In his inaugural he had urged law observance to prevent a breakdown in democratic government. Many states had given up, leaving the burden entirely to federal officers, who encountered steadily growing resistance and opposition. The Bureau of Prohibition was not above reproach. From February 1920 to January 1930 there were 1,604 dismissals for causes including bribery, manslaughter, dereliction of duty, intoxication, misconduct, perjury, robbery, theft, extortion, false reports, conspiracy, and bootlegging. In fiscal 1930 there were 85 dismissals, 32 of which were because of intoxication and misconduct! Sentiment in Congress against Prohibition kept pace with successes of the wet campaign. House Republicans and Democrats in 1932 voted in about the same proportion against an amendment to return Prohibition to the states; yet, on 20 February 1933 the same Congress passed S. J. Res. 211, the proposed repeal of the Eighteenth Amendment.[21]

Administrative reform or reorganization attracted Hoover's attention early. He believed that people would applaud efficiency; he discovered that dramatics had greater appeal. Unable to take from Congress all of its cherished patronage, the President refused to recommend postmasters for appointment until they had passed Civil Service merit examinations. Moreover, the number of civil employees declined from 573,000 in 1929 to 565,000 in 1933; six years later, under the New Deal, the number had nearly doubled. Of the 38 committees and commissions set up by Hoover, only four were permanent and only seven received public funds. This activity, so necessary in establishing facts as a basis for action, was far from excessive.

Executive reorganization, recommended by Presidents throughout our history, was one of Hoover's major objectives. His goals were to put related activities under one head and to separate legislative and judicial functions. All that the President obtained was creation of the Veterans' Administration in 1930, consolidation of Prohibition enforcement agencies under the Attorney General, and authority to consolidate by executive order subject to approval of Congress. This latter authority was granted in June 1932; but Congress, when it reconvened in December, blocked Hoover's proposed reorganizations.[22]

Chaos in the infant air transport industry led Hoover to bring about an orderly system of air lines serving the nation. Under the McNary-Watres Act of 29 April 1930, Congress set the maximum payment for mail at $1.25 per mile for nine pounds of air mail, required mail planes to carry passengers, and authorized the Postmaster General to consolidate or extend routes. Mileage flown steadily increased, service improved, and the number of passengers carried rose from 165,200 in 1929 to 550,000 in 1933. Not all of the improvements in commercial aviation could be credited to this one piece of legislation, but the McNary-Watres, or Air Mail, Act of 1930 did provide much of the impetus for orderly development.[23]

Hoover was less successful in his efforts to reorganize the merchant marine. Congress had voted large subsidies for carrying the mail, thus disguising grants to keep American ships at sea in competition with foreign carriers. When Hoover became President, mail subsidies amounted to $12 million annually. Since the United States Shipping Board was subservient to the shipping companies, Hoover wanted to abolish it and place the Board's functions in the Department of Commerce. Political pressures, however, prevented realization of this plan until after World War II.[24]

Spectacular events occurred during the years when Hoover was President, and toward them contemporary history has directed its major attention. Business failures and labor troubles commanded headlines; Ivar Kreuger and Samuel Insull competed with Japan's warlords for page one space; there were shocking crimes and hunger marches and Hoovervilles and the raucous clacking of Communist jackals. The world was too much with us, but the President did not lose sight of the goals he had fixed for the country under his guidance. That he achieved so many of them despite the rigors of an economic cataclysm is no small tribute to his wisdom and vision.

CHAPTER VI

HOOVER AND THE POWER QUESTION

1. *The Federal Power Commission*

Probably no major issue of Hoover's administration aroused more bitter controversy and brought on more serious investigation than the regulation of public utilities. In popular discussion, 'public utilities' meant primarily corporations engaged in the generation, transmission, and sale of electric power. These companies came of age in the postwar years, and the spectacular combinations of components under the direction of J. P. Morgan, Samuel J. Insull, and other 'tycoons' inevitably aroused the hostility of progressive Democrats and Republicans. Effective regulation of public utilities—that is, of the power companies—was impossible under the principles of government for which Herbert Hoover was a doughty champion. Regulation of rates, control over financing, inspection of records, prevention of pyramiding of holding companies, development of water power sites, and government competition with private industry were all involved.

President Hoover did not believe in unbridled competition by businessmen in any field of endeavor. As Secretary of Commerce he had urged the regulation of business in the public interest, and he believed in public encouragement of business in the private interest. Over and over he had repeated his warnings against government competition with business, and almost always he had accompanied those warnings with admonitions for regulation to protect the public. He clearly stated his case in his inaugural address, where he advocated 'the continued regulation of business to prevent domination in the community; the denial of ownership or operation of business by the Government in competition with its citizens . . .' [1]

President Hoover's interest in the whole power question was closely connected with his concern for conservation of the country's water power resources. Federal regulation of corporations engaged in the interstate transmission of electric power began timorously with the establishment of the Federal Power Commission in 1920. The work of this Commission was reminiscent of the Interstate Commerce Commission immediately after that body's creation in 1887. The Federal Power Commission simply failed to regulate, and state agencies were so powerless that holding companies in 21 states issued securities for more than $795 million on property worth about $441 million. Rates to customers, of course, would be based on the fictional values.[2]

The Federal Power Commission, through its power to issue licenses for the exploitation of power sites on navigable streams, had the authority amply to protect the public interest. However, the secretaries of War, Interior, and Agriculture, who made up the Commission, submitted readily to political pressure. Charles A. Russell, solicitor of the Commission, and William V. King, its chief accountant, made themselves obnoxious to power companies by endeavoring to enforce the law. Russell publicly accused Hoover of preventing the Federal Power Commission from deflating 'fantastically padded accounts of power companies occupying public sites.' And F. E. Brown, executive secretary of the Commission, said that Hoover acquiesced in the padding. Bloated values mean worthless securities, piratical rates, and outrageous prices if the United States decided to recapture the power sites through purchase of constructed facilities.[3] These charges against Hoover were never proved.

Designed primarily to control power development on navigable streams, as well as sites on public reservations, the 1920 law fell short of establishing adequate regulation of the power industry, a large portion of which felt no federal control at all.[4] President Hoover made the proper public gestures, and in his recommendations he was perfectly sincere; but he did not want an agency that would deprive the states of their regulatory powers, and, since only 10 per cent of the power generated moved across state lines, the problem did not seem one for much federal concern. He contemplated a commission that would co-operate with state bodies in controlling utilities engaged in interstate transmission of power. This objective could not win the approval of Senators James Couzens and George Norris. These public power proponents thus found themselves in a strange alliance with utilities companies in defeating Hoover's proposals. The President wanted the Commission to have 'authority to regulate all interstate power rates.' [5] Even this limited objective was not achieved in the act of 23 June 1930, which simply substituted a per-

manent commission of five members for the old ex-officio body.[6]
President Hoover did not make a serious effort to bring about effective control of all public utilities, and there was nothing but petulance
behind his accusation that Norris and 'other Socialists' were bent
upon creating such havoc in utilities that socialism would be the
only acceptable way out.[7]

There was an interesting squabble about membership of the new
Commission. President Hoover in July 1930 nominated Colonel
Marcel Garsaud, Claude L. Draper, and Ralph B. Williamson to the
reorganized body. Since the Senate took no action before adjourn-
ment, the President resubmitted their names in December, together
with George Otis Smith and Frank R. McNinch. Official sources
represented Smith, the chairman, as a capable geologist who had
served with the U.S. Geological Survey for thirty years. The public
was not told that Smith had supported cancellation of power-site
withdrawals by Richard A. Ballinger during the Taft Administration.
Garsaud was presented as a well-qualified engineer; he was also
identified with the Public Service Corporation of New Orleans, a
subsidiary of Electric Bond and Share Company. Although at the
time of his nomination he had no official connection with the company and had no financial interest in it, Garsaud had been solicitous
of power interests during his service as general manager of the Port
of New Orleans. There is no reason to doubt his devotion to private
power companies.[8] Draper, head of Wyoming's Public Service Commission for a decade, had done nothing inimical to private power
companies. All five of the new members were confirmed easily on
19 and 20 December 1930.

Smith, Garsaud, and Draper met on 23 December and notified all
employees of the old Commission that their services were ended by
the new law; they could apply for reappointment but final action
would be deferred until the full membership could meet. Charles A.
Russell and William V. King were among the dismissed employees.[9]
Disliked and feared by power companies, these two conscientious
public servants were accused of bickering. Thereupon the Senate on
9 January 1931 passed a resolution asking that the President return
the resolutions approving Smith, Draper, and Garsaud. The Senate
started a contest that it could not win and Hoover, on advice of the
Attorney General, indignantly refused to 'admit the power in the
Senate to encroach upon the Executive functions by removal of a

duly appointed Executive officer under the guise of reconsideration of his nomination.' [10] The issue, President Hoover said, was the Senate's attempt to dictate appointments to an administrative agency and not one of being for or against power companies. After all, the new Commission did not yet have power to regulate rates. The Supreme Court upheld the President on 2 May 1932; but the real issue was something else: Hoover had slipped one over on such watchdogs as Borah, Norris, and Thomas J. Walsh.[11]

2. *Muscle Shoals*

Reorganization of the Federal Power Commission and the quarrel over its membership were minor matters in public estimation when compared with the larger issue of Muscle Shoals, and this, in turn, was all but buried by even more pressing problems. Republicans and conservative Democrats were determined that no socialistic solution of the Muscle Shoals problems would creep upon them, regardless of the Great Depression that weighed so heavily upon the country.

Muscle Shoals is the name of several miles of the Tennessee River which falls rapidly in its course at the northwest corner of Alabama. Canals had been constructed near the end of the nineteenth century to provide passage around the dangerous shoals. Partly as the result of organized propaganda using the war emergency, Congress provided money to build the Wilson Dam, which would generate electricity for one of two nitrate plants. Current from Wilson Dam, however, could not possibly have been expected for years to come. The dam was completed in 1925 with facilities to house eighteen generating units. Power produced at Wilson Dam was sold to private companies for distribution.

The prospect of Muscle Shoals being operated publicly for public benefit attracted the full force of private utilities in opposition. For many years power companies had engaged in a vigorous and insidious campaign to discredit public ownership and effective regulation. The extent of this campaign was revealed by the Federal Trade Commission's six-year investigation begun in 1928. Privately owned utilities were determined to create a monopoly on how people should think and vote, even if it meant the complete destruction of free inquiry and criticism. Electric power had become one of the basic elements in modern life, so important that serious doubts arose about leaving it under private control.

Private utilities companies generally displayed uncompromising hostility toward all efforts to control or to regulate in the public interest. Problems involved included valuation, financing, organization, operating expenses, stock watering, managerial piracy, conservation and utilization of natural resources, and many more highly technical matters confusing even to experts. Private utilities defended their selfish interests by firing a terrific barrage of propaganda aimed at a bewildered public by 'information' committees. Samuel Insull, chairman of Middle West Utilities Company, had the first information committee in 1919. The National Electric Light Association began to serve as the overall director of propaganda in 1920; the National Utility Association, representing the American Street Railway Association, the American Gas Association, and the National Electric Light Association, set up a joint committee in 1921 to direct the national effort. The National Electric Light Association flickered out in 1932, and the Edison Electric Institute, organized on 12 January 1933, carried on the work.[12]

High-salaried public relations experts attempted to sell the people a wondrous array of truth, half truth, and overgrown lies. To be sure that future voters would have the truth as they saw it, utilities achieved textbook censorship, promoted university conferences, hired professors to teach the private utilities viewpoint or to perform other services, and contributed to endowments. These activities, directed by the National Electric Light Association, often cost upwards of $1 million a year, which was, of course, paid by the public.[13]

While this propaganda was going on, the whole problem of public utilities regulation and public power production received considerable attention in state legislatures. Forty-three of those bodies met in 1931; thirty-nine enacted legislation to strengthen regulation, regulate holding companies, investigate rates, provide for public ownership, promote rural electrification, and other matters. Many states authorized creation of public utility or power districts; New York created the Power Authority to control St. Lawrence River development. Municipal ownership was protected by laws in several states.[14]

This progress in state regulation was the more remarkable because of the strenuous propaganda barrage being thrown up by the utilities. The industry spared no expense and rejected no trick to tag public ownership as Bolshevism and strict public regulation as government interference in business. The houses of Morgan, Mellon, Insull, Sloan, Young, and others of the utilities hierarchy cheered their minions on in this gigantic effort so effectively directed by Merlin H. Aylesworth.[15]

In the midst of all this ballyhoo, the small consumer continued to be victimized. Figures from 1916 to 1931 showed that householders and other small users consumed 30 per cent of the current produced and contributed 61 per cent of the industry's revenues. Expert studies revealed that the cost of distribution was 'about twice what it should be . . . with an annual overcharge against the small consumer of between $400,000,000 and $500,000,000 a year.' [16] The industry refused to undertake studies looking toward a reduction of distribution costs. While the nation-wide average price of electricity fell from seven to six cents per kilowatt hour from 1926 to 1931, the reduction applied only to very large consumers; yet the revenue per domestic consumer increased from $29.70 in 1926 to $33.70 in 1931. This increased service was at practically no other cost than that of generating the current.[17] It was in this setting that the Muscle Shoals controversy raged for more than a decade.

The struggle over Muscle Shoals again brought out President Hoover's politico-economic philosophy. At Seattle in 1926 he had stated the need for a 'new and broad national program for the full utilization of our streams, our rivers, and our lakes.' Such a program involved development of water power, inland waterways, reclamation and irrigation, co-ordinated 'development of each river system to its maximum utilization.' Federal and local governments should improve navigation, flood control, irrigation, and reclamation. The federal government must not produce or distribute electrical power; electricity produced as a by-product of dams should be sold at the dams to pay construction costs. In other words, build the dams with federal money, repay the money with profits from sales, and let private industry reap all profits above cost of construction. This would, of course, prevent the demonstration that a federally owned power project could be a very profitable undertaking! Government should determine policies, not operate the great projects. Hoover's faith in the ability to achieve development of the various river basins should have been shaken by the long delays in developing the Colorado River basin, a project that involved seven states and Mexico.[18]

Development of the great river basins along lines best suited to each required a fine balance between statism or socialism and private enterprise; but Hoover had no fear of being able to maintain the balance. The major rules were to keep government from doing anything to compete with private enterprise, and to use governmental authority for regulation and restraint of private enterprise.

The Seventy-first Congress in its third session sent to the President a proposal to create the Muscle Shoals Corporation of the United States to maintain and operate the properties 'in the interest of the national defense and for agricultural and industrial development, and to aid navigation and the control of destructive flood waters . . .' The corporation would operate existing plants for experimental purposes, construct others for the manufacture of fertilizers, promote large-scale use of fertilizers, manufacture fixed nitrogen, and 'produce, distribute, and sell electric power' with preference to states, counties, and municipalities. The President was authorized to lease the nitrate plants and other facilities to private enterprise for manufacture of fertilizer. The measure was a victory for Senator Norris, indefatigable champion of public power.[19] President Hoover returned the resolution unsigned on 3 March 1931 and Congress sustained the veto.

There was no question about the President's attitude: 'I am firmly opposed to the Government entering into any business the major purpose of which is competition with our citizens.' Under emergency conditions such excursions might be justified; where public works are beyond private capacity, the government might step in. 'But for the Federal Government deliberately to go out to build up and expand such an occasion to the major purpose of a power manufacturing business is to break down the initiative and enterprise of the American people; it is destruction of equality of opportunity amongst our people; it is the negation of the ideals upon which our civilization has been based.' The power trust should be regulated, but it should not come through federal competition. Only the people of the Tennessee Valley, Hoover insisted, could develop the resources and industries in their area; interference by the federal government would undermine state and local government, deprive them of taxes, take away their liberty.[20]

Here was the President's basic philosophy again. Any deviation from it by Congress would meet with a certain veto; any refusal by Congress to agree with it would meet with petulant complaints. In the Muscle Shoals matter, as well as others, Hoover's attitude met with complete approval of spokesmen for private utilities. One of them could praise the President for his 'calm and resolute strength' of leadership in a time of crisis, glory in his Americanism, and discover a 'kindred spirit to Walt Whitman.' [21]

Seeking some solution, Hoover recommended creation of an Alabama-Tennessee Muscle Shoals Commission to consider disposal of the problem. The two states appointed their delegates, who presented a report on 14 November 1931. This Commission's recommendations were to lease the properties to private enterprise to produce fertilizers and chemicals, conduct experiments to promote agriculture, and sell surplus power with preference to public bodies.[22] The President made no recommendation for action on the basis of this report.

When the Seventy-second Congress convened, Senator Norris introduced another resolution to create the Muscle Shoals Corporation. Hostile witnesses at hearings on the proposal based their case on opposition to government ownership. Mercer Reynolds of Chattanooga objected to 'the Government ownership of any industry that can be financed by private capital. It is just an acknowledgment that we are gradually adopting the Russian form of government instead of our own. And if the Russian form of government is correct in one particular, it is correct in whole.'[23] The Committee on Agriculture and Forestry reported the resolution favorably on 14 March 1932. Its report observed that private enterprise for a decade had failed to make satisfactory bids for the lease of Muscle Shoals and had wanted only to get possession of the power facilities under guise of fertilizer production. Now advocates of private leasing, including farm organization officials, were challenged to prove their propaganda. If the President failed to negotiate a lease within twelve months, the Muscle Shoals Corporation would come into existence.[24] This resolution died in the Senate.

Lister Hill, Alabama Democrat, introduced a similar resolution in the House. Supporters and opponents once more went over the arguments so familiar to those who had followed the controversy since 1922. It was expansion vs. economy, public operation vs. private operation, socialized public utilities vs. private enterprise. Mr. Harry

C. Ransley, Pennsylvania Republican, begged the House 'to permit the business geniuses of this country to control all business enterprise.' Did not Mr. Ransley know what the geniuses had accomplished? Others, including William H. Stafford, Wisconsin Republican, cried 'Socialism!' and accused Democrats of playing politics and trying to increase the tax burden. 'The Government never went into a business yet that did not result in tremendous loss and that did not result in a scandal,' said Charles L. Underhill, Massachusetts Republican. J. Will Taylor, Tennessee Democrat, philosophically observed that Congress was 'in the midst of the ghouls and the ghosts, the weird and fantastic noises, and the bleak and grotesque shadows of the old Muscle Shoals cemetery.' Failure to do something with Muscle Shoals was 'a shining and outstanding example of the incompetency of the American Congress.' [25]

Like most debates, few if any votes were changed by arguments presented in the Congress. The House on 5 May passed the bill by 183 to 132, but refused to record the yeas and nays. And that was the limit of Muscle Shoals legislation in the Seventy-second Congress. President Hoover had won his battle against socialized power, but there could be no rejoicing, for even then one of the country's greatest utilities magnates was snatching defeat from the very jaws of victory.

3. *Insull*

The greatest single crash in American business history came on 14 April 1932. On that day the Lincoln Printing Company in Chicago filed a petition of receivership for Samuel J. Insull's top holding companies.

Insull, the genius of financial prestidigitation, had come from England to serve as secretary to Thomas Alva Edison. He rose rapidly. Ten years after his arrival he was president of the Chicago Commonwealth Electric Company. There is no gainsaying his vision and organizing ability. He brought Chicago's five generating companies together in 1907 to form the Commonwealth Edison Company. Three years later, he formed the Public Service Company of Northern Illinois to serve ten suburban towns, a company which was the prototype of superpower systems. The largest of the holding companies which he set up was the Middle West Utilities Company, organized in 1912 and floated on water. With this beginning, he expanded until he had created a tremendously complicated corporate maze which Owen D. Young could not understand, which Samuel J. Insull could not understand, which no one could understand. But while he was gaily creating holding companies and pyramiding them out of sight, Insull pioneered with turbine generators, high tension transmission lines, and other features of power generation and distribution which made him one of the great builders of America.[26] These facts are hard to remember in view of his shameless, uninhibited financial activities.

The Insull domain as it existed before the 1932 debacle was a wonder, indeed. Testimony before the Federal Trade Commission revealed that the empire contained 221 active and 27 inactive companies. At the very top were Insull Utility Investments, Inc. and Corporation Securities Co., both controlled by Samuel J. Insull and his son. Among the first subsidiaries were 16 companies, among which were such giants as Middle West Utilities Co., Commonwealth Edison Co., and Public Service Company of Northern Illinois. The top five holding companies controlled 156 subsidiaries with assets exceeding $2,500 million. Nearly all of the top 16 had subsidiaries of their own, and their subsidiaries in turn had still other subsidiaries. Following one company's connection through the maze is an interesting exercise: The Berwick & Salmon Falls Electric Co. was a subsidiary of the Twin State Gas and Electric Co., which was a subsidiary of the National Light, Heat, & Power Co., which was a subsidiary of the National Electric Power Co., which was a subsidiary of the Middle West Utilities Co., which was a subsidiary of Corporation Securities Co. and Insull Utility Investments, Inc.[27] Following the tribes of begetters through Genesis is a simple matter when compared with the Insull maze.

Samuel J. Insull was held in considerable awe throughout the United States. He was a potent political force in Illinois, used money lavishly to influence elections, and controlled public service commissions.[28] Samuel Insull built the Chicago Civic Opera House and enjoyed at least one good season before the financial dervishes whirled him off the stage. He was chairman of 65 and president of 11 of the 85 boards of directors of which he was a member; 72,000 workers were on the payrolls of companies he controlled; 600,000 investors had bought stock in Insull companies.[29]

Since it was profitable for outsiders to buy into the major holding companies and thus attempt to steal control, the Insulls were forced into operations that precipitated their downfall. The first major attack was by Alfred Loewenstein, a Belgian industrialist, in 1928. The battle for stock control hurt Insull but in the end his rival jumped from a plane and Insull celebrated by buying J. Ogden Armour's Mellody Farm near Lake Forest, Illinois, for $2.5 million.[30]

A far more serious clash occurred with Cyrus S. Eaton, the former Canadian Baptist minister. The struggle ended in 1930 when Insull bought Eaton's holdings at fantastic prices. From then on Insull was in trouble. He borrowed $2 million from Owen D. Young's General Electric Company (Young had been allowed to buy a large block of Insull stock at 12 when the public had to pay 30); Charles G. Dawes allowed his bank to loan about $12 million to various Insull companies; Melvin Alvah Traylor's First National Bank had also loaned heavily. By 16 April 1932 Middle West Utilities owed $21.9 million to banks, and its subsidiaries owed still more millions.[31]

The inevitable crash came with the filing of the bankruptcy petition on 14 April. In July 1929 Middle West Utilities stock sold for $570 per share; in April 1932 it was all but worthless. A conservative estimate of the debacle indicated to investors that their losses would exceed $700 million.[32] And 1932 was an election year, the year of intense Muscle Shoals agitation. Insull was a businessman and Hoover was a businessman. In public estimation, Insull's failure was linked to the Hoover regime, which had nothing whatever to do with it. The long fight over Muscle Shoals, the revelations of propaganda by utilities companies, and Democratic campaign charges all built up anti-Hoover sentiment.

Samuel Insull's failure revealed in all its ugliness the 'business ideal of power without responsibility or obligation,' which led to gold-plated anarchy. Insull was exceptional only in the scope, not the methods, of his operations. His career was a definite illustration of how a ruthless business giant could destroy basic social values. The very regulation against which he fought could have prevented his collapse.[33]

After months of investigation, auditors were still unable to present a clear picture of how the Insull companies sold, bought, loaned, and exchanged stocks, bonds, and debentures. Insull's activities were, indeed, 'a complicated piece of purposeful confusion . . .'[34] Insull escaped punishment for his political and economic sins. He served no jail terms for having wrecked the gigantic holding companies he created. A jury in 1934 acquitted him on charges of using the mails to defraud, as it acquitted more than a dozen other defendants whose lawyers buried bewildered jurors under tons of incomprehensible records.

The Insull crash was catastrophic for the Hoover Administration. It came only two months before the national nominating conventions and at a time when relations between Hoover and the Seventy-second Congress had reached a new low. The Reconstruction Finance Corporation had not yet appreciably halted the wave of bank closings, and breadlines lengthened in every great city. Hoover could be and was related to the Insull crash by use of the guilt-by-association technique, however unjust and unfair the charge might be. So far as the President was concerned, the system was correct although one practitioner within it might be wrong. The Insull debacle might have led Hoover to favor severe regulation; but nothing could have moved him from his firm conviction that government generation, transmission, and sale of electric power to the consumer was socialism; and that socialism would mean the death of American democracy.

CHAPTER VII

BATTLE OF THE TARIFF

1. *Fables and Facts*

The tariff has caused as much prolonged argument as any issue in American history. Economists have been found to support high tariffs and low tariffs and no tariffs; politicians generally have bowed to the demands of their richest and most powerful constituents; and the people have been bewildered. We have been told that our way of life is dependent upon a high protective tariff, that within such a framework wages are high, standards of living are maintained at lofty levels. Yet, with the highest protective tariff in our history we suffered the greatest depression in our history. Although economists do not agree on what connection there was between the tariff and depression, it is absolutely clear that the Hawley-Smoot Act did not start the depression that got underway in 1929; the tariff already was a high one, high enough to cause a depression if a tariff can have such a result. However that may be, the tariff alone is no guarantee of two cars in every garage, of a television set in every home, of a house for every family, and other American shibboleths.

We have been told that our economic advancement has been the result of tariffs. Too often we have forgotten the significance of a steadily increasing population exploiting a marvelous store of natural resources and exchanging goods within an expansive market. Regardless of arguments for and against protection, the tariff will be with us until that millennium comes when people in labor, industry, finance, and agriculture all realize that such price-fixing efforts contribute significantly to periodic depressions and chronic injustice to sectors of the economy not similarly privileged.

Hoover believed in a tariff to protect American industry, agriculture, and labor from the competition of low-priced foreign goods. He wanted to equalize costs of production at home and abroad.[1] In response to Senator Borah's prodding in 1928, he promised to call a special session of the Congress to revamp the Fordney-McCumber Tariff of 1922 along more scientific lines. He was particularly desirous that comparative costs should be determined by a bipartisan commission, and in this objective he clashed directly with pressure groups which were concerned only for their own immediate interest and indifferent to the national welfare.

Experience with a tariff commission had not been encouraging. Such a body was created in 1882 with the idea that it might be able to introduce a degree of objectivity in setting rates. The first commission was a complete failure, as was the Tariff Board of 1909, which Congress soon abolished. The Democratic Congress in 1916 created a six-man nonpartisan commission to act as a fact-finding body that would report to Congress. The Fordney-McCumber Act of 1922 gave the President the power to raise or lower duties up to 50 per cent when the Tariff Commission so recommended.[2] This was the flexibility that advocates of a scientific tariff demanded, but there was always a strong opposition to it in and out of Congress. Theoretically, the Commission would recommend tariff changes to equalize domestic and foreign costs of production to create a competitive tariff and not an embargo. There was, therefore, nothing fundamentally new in Hoover's proposals.

The idea of equalizing costs of production by a tariff levy is fantastic. Whose figures are going to be accepted as production costs? Every item, including bloated capital structures, padded expense accounts, useless advertising, administrative and labor featherbedding, would have to be examined in detail, and not by cost accountants employed by manufacturers. In determining foreign costs of production, the accountant would become involved in so many ingenious devices to obscure truth that even a mathematical genius would become lost long before valuations were decided at ports of entry.

Many manufacturers were not interested in an equalizing tariff but in an excluding tariff.[3] While proclaiming the fetish that competition is the life of trade, they were bending every effort to destroy competition by creating monopolies whose major purpose was to levy tribute on every consumer. Other governments responded to the demands of their own economic warriors and levied tariffs so high that American manufacturers resorted to building plants abroad in order to get behind the walls, thereby adding proof that the tariff was a barrier to trade, an unjustifiable interference with competition. In the two years ending in May 1932 American manufacturers built 259 factories abroad.[4] Thus did foreign tariffs achieve the unexpected result of attracting venture capital and equalizing industrial capacity.

Public interest in tariff revision probably was no higher in 1929 than in previous years. There was tremendous confusion within farm and labor groups; the mythical 'man in the street,' whom the popular radio commentator Boake Carter called 'John Q. Public' during the Great Depression, did not know what the tariff argument involved and he could not learn from politicians. Economists and businessmen argued in terms often incomprehensible to the bewildered voter.

Most economists would agree that goods and services must pay for goods and services, that countries will export goods in whose production they enjoy a comparative advantage, that absolute gains result from specialization.[5] Free traders would accept the argument that mass production does not require protection, that tariffs retard industrial growth. Some people, with little respect for abilities of politicians, saw no chance whatever for a scientific tariff because of the encyclopedic knowledge required to administer it.[6]

Regardless of what the economists might teach and the free traders preach, probably a majority of Americans took the protective tariff for granted. The vice president of the Bell Telephone Company of Pennsylvania stated the case well:

Although the precise formula of our national prosperity may be somewhat unintelligible to the man on the street or on the country road, he has a pretty good working idea of cause and effect. To him the fruits of American life appear not to be accidental. He has put the protection of his industry in the scales of his prosperity; and it will require tall talking to persuade him to take it out and start again.

Nor, he continued, should we worry about starting a tariff war since the battle already was in progress: 'Already Europe is taking a leaf out of America's book. Tariff walls are up, and trade wars are on with a vengeance. Our foreign salesman is not everywhere courted as he once was. Each westbound ship brings its group of observers, bent on studying not only our industrial methods, but our protective methods and measures.'[7]

Tariffs on agricultural products actually provided protection for a very insignificant proportion of farm production. Nevertheless, Senator Arthur Capper argued for higher agricultural tariffs: 'The farmer is as much benefited by the protective system as the manufacturer, notwithstanding impressions to the contrary.'[8] The politician could be more positive than the experts.

Agricultural imports in fiscal 1928 were valued at $1,880 million, of which about $647 million or about 4 per cent of domestic production, represented competitive imports. Asking if the home market could be increased significantly by raising tariffs, the experts gave a dubious answer. Higher tariffs would have little effect on the home market for domestic cotton, hides, sugar, and wool. Indeed, the increased sheep population after 1921, when wool tariffs were raised, was caused by higher demand for mutton. Tobacco imports would not decrease much; imports of eggs, butter, cheese, and milk could be stopped, but the total imports of $48 million in these products could not be considered crucial. Imports of beef and feeder cattle, worth only $26 million in 1928, could be stopped but only to the detriment of farmers who fattened the feeders and of people who bought meat. Pork and lard imports were insignificant. Altogether, by prohibitive tariffs, competitive imports could be reduced by about $225 million, lowering imports to 3 per cent of domestic production. Higher tariffs could, in short, put an end to some competitive imports; but there was little reason to believe that farmers as a whole would benefit much from higher prices.[9]

Farmer dissatisfaction with the tariff received impetus from research by the American Farm Bureau Federation. The net loss to agriculture was figured as $300 million a year after considering a $30 million gain from agricultural tariffs. Whether these figures were correct mattered little; politically it was important that farmers in traditionally Republican states were at last wary of tariff fallacies.[10] Few would agree with the bald assertion by Jerome Davis that 'Capitalism is directly accountable for the plight of the farmer because of its tariff policy.'[11] But capitalists need not worry: probably not one farmer in 5,000 had ever heard of Davis.

2. *Hawley-Smoot and Grundy*

Republican victory in 1928 was by no means a popular mandate to increase tariff rates, but, all the same, Hoover had promised a special session to consider limited revision. In response to the President's summons of 7 March 1929 the Seventy-first Congress met in special session on 15 April. Speaker Nicholas Longworth could see no reason why farm relief and tariff legislation should not be completed in a month or so. Farm relief had been thoroughly debated, so there was no sense in rehashing old arguments. Only limited revision of the tariff was needed, the raising of some rates and lowering of others. 'The line of cleavage between the two great political parties would seem to have crumbled in the past few years almost to questions of detail,' he told the House. 'I apprehend that under the leadership of the gentleman from Texas we will hear resounding from his party no clarion call that the American consumer shall be permitted to buy in the cheapest market.'[12]

The Speaker was optimistic as well as arrogant and presumptuous. The first session sweltered through the summer, cooled off in the fall, and adjourned on 22 November 1929 without passing a tariff bill. The introduction of 258 serious bills and 41 resolutions in the House on the first day should have been a warning. Opposition of such insurgents as Bronson Cutting and George W. Norris postponed enactment of tariff increases.[13]

Republican members of the House Committee on Ways and Means had been working since 8 January 1929 on revision of the tariff, and its chairman, Willis C. Hawley of Oregon, was well pleased with himself. Democrats wondered what was going on. Hawley told the House on 16 April that 'when the time comes that we have the new bill prepared we will take the Democratic members of the committee into our confidence and show them the whole thing.'[14] If this was intended as humor, the effort failed miserably.

Democratic leaders, stung by such cavalier treatment, accepted the challenge. Cordell Hull rebuked the Speaker for his impudence in assuming to speak for both parties on the tariff. Democrats had no intention of following the 'high tariff and special privilege leadership of Smoot, Mellon, Grundy, and their associate spokesmen of this small but powerful group.' He reviewed previous Republican tariffs, asked why there was need to raise the outrageously high rates of the Fordney-McCumber Act, and called the turn on the agricultural benefit dodge.[15] John Nance Garner followed with a denial that Democrats favored free trade, and asked for tariff revision to increase protection for agriculture and to decrease high rates on what farmers bought. He agreed that the present Tariff Commission was inefficient; he wanted changes in rates to be made only by Congress, not by the President and the Commission. Garner and Hull obviously had not studied the same text! Senator Borah on 13

June introduced a resolution to confine revision to agricultural schedules, but this intelligent proposal lost in the Senate by one vote.[16]

President Hoover followed the tariff-making process closely. Dis-
concerted and dismayed by the greed so baldly displayed by special
interests, he consoled himself with the thought that the flexible provision could be used to prevent excesses. Hoover had a long fight
with Congress in his effort to write a flexible provision into the
tariff bill, a provision that would enable the President, on recommendation of the Tariff Commission, to change tariff rates by as much
as 50 per cent. Progressives, led by Senator Borah, and Old Guard
reactionaries, led by Senator Watson, opposed the flexible provision.
This Republican hostility, aided by Democratic opposition, prevented the special session from completing a tariff bill.

The *Commercial & Financial Chronicle* reflected a growing impatience with Congress. There had been so many things happening
and here was Congress attempting to equalize agriculture and industry by means of tariff change, an obvious absurdity. There had
been the investigation of William B. Shearer in September; in October, Joseph R. Grundy was called before the Senate Lobby Investigation Committee. The *Chronicle* pooh-poohed such goings on. 'The
sharp edge of this Congressional farce has been blunted by the
sudden collapse of a "long bull market" which certain university experts and talking financiers said could never, never end. . . . What
is a party in power to a ticker that runs an hour and forty minutes
behind?'[17] Congress was even farther behind in its work. The special
session adjourned on 22 November, leaving less than two weeks before the opening of the first regular session of the Seventy-first
Congress. *The Magazine of Wall Street* was more charitable toward
Congressional investigations 'as an essential part of the process
whereby democracy maintains itself against the tyranny of the business world. They are ridiculous in detail but respectable in mass,
petty in method but large in effect.'[18]

President Hoover renewed his fight for a flexible provision when
Congress reconvened in December 1929. Senator Joseph R. Grundy
took his seat on 12 December to fill a Pennsylvania vacancy caused
by the scandal over William S. Vare's contested election. This notorious lobbyist frankly avowed that campaign contributors should
be rewarded with high tariffs.[19] He spoke with authority. As president of the Pennsylvania Manufacturer's Association, he had raised

nearly $2 million for Republican campaigns from 1924 to 1928. Senator Reed Smoot, chairman of the Senate Finance Committee since 1922, dictated Republican tariff and tax policies, and Smoot agreed with Grundy. Manufacturers thus had powerful champions in the Senate to fight their battle, and the coalition of Democrats and farm-bloc Republicans, led by Borah, was disintegrating. Its major success was the public interest it aroused. Grundy was for high rates and against the flexible provision. He and his cohorts finally accepted flexibility only because the President promised to veto any bill that did not include it.[20]

As the sorry spectacle of tariff making drew to a close in June 1930 a poll of newspapers revealed opposition to the bill from all but a small minority.[21] Although the country was sick of the bickering, opposing forces enjoyed a last round of charges and countercharges. Senator Norris paid his respects: 'It represents protection run perfectly mad. It is conceived and written in the interest of victorious business organizations who are using their power . . . to put through the Congress one of the most selfish and indefensible tariff measures that has ever been considered by the American people.'[22] Norris grieved over elimination of a consumers' advocate. He referred to the Senate's anti-monopoly amendment, under which corporations that had secured a monopoly would find the articles they made restored to the free list until the monopoly ended, which had been dropped in conference. This tariff bill, Norris insisted, made idle gestures of helping the farmer but in reality increased his burdens to benefit monopolists. Senator David A. Reed, the Pennsylvania Republican plutocrat who always favored high tariffs and low income taxes, believed agricultural rates were too high and industrial rates were too low! Unemployment, this sage remarked, was caused by low tariffs.[23]

That prince of lobbyists, Senator Grundy, was not satisfied with the Hawley-Smoot bill. He complained that it did not fill the party's 1928 pledge. Moreover, the bill had been written in secret sessions by committees which ignored expert advice! Grundy had other criticisms equally sensible; magnanimously, he agreed to vote for the bill which truly was his own. Without Grundy there might have been no significant tariff change.[24]

An editorial in the *Minneapolis Tribune* turned on Grundy with heavy sarcasm:

When the Grundyites begin to write an agricultural tariff bill, strange and wonderful things happen. The Grundyites are willing to go to any lengths to raise tariffs on the farmer's instruments for the deaf crop, his crutch crop, his oil crop, his shoe crop, his lumber crop, his hat crop, his cement crop, his brick crop, his pocketknife crop, his cartridge crop, his umbrella crop, and his doll crop. They visualize the modern diversified farm as one in which the proprietor looks out of the window and perceives not only a crutch orchard but a waving field of cement and, further along, a darker tinted field of waving brick. Cameras, umbrellas, and pocketknives go clucking about, and in the distance one hears the grunts of cartridges and the lowing of incandescent bulbs. . . . In fact there is nothing the Grundyites will not do for the farmer except to give him what he wants. All they wish to do is to tax him out of house and home—perhaps on the theory that the only way to solve the farm problem is to exterminate the farmer.[25]

The Hawley-Smoot Act, of course, provided some benefits for a few farmers, but nearly all of the tariff changes hurt rather than helped agriculture.

Senator Watson held the floor before the final vote and defended the tariff in a long, nimble speech that ignored all but the most palatable facts. Nevertheless, the Senate vote on 13 June found 31 Democrats and 10 Republicans opposing the bill, while 39 Republicans and 5 Democrats favored it. The one Farmer-Labor, Henrik Shipstead, voted with the opposition. By splitting the five pairs, the Senate stood 49 for and 47 against.[26]

President Hoover received plenty of advice from all parts of the country. Although he professed to place great faith in expert opinion, he declined the advice of 1,000 economists who urged him to veto the bill. In signing the measure he followed the wishes of some businessmen who wanted to end tariff agitation. His analysis played down the increased rates by pointing out that average duties on the value of all imports were increased from 13.8 per cent to about 16 per cent, that the proportion of duty-free imports was reduced by only 1.8 per cent, that rates were increased on some 890 items, reduced on 235 items, and left unchanged on 2,170 items.

Hoover's analysis disregarded the rates on dutiable imports and fell far short of providing an accurate evaluation. The duties collected under the Fordney-McCumber Act were about 39 per cent 'of the value of the protected imports.' Under Hawley-Smoot, the corresponding figure was about 59 per cent.[27] The President's 16 per cent figure was so misleading that an economist observed: 'Using that method of computation, if all the rates for dutiable commodities were so high as to be absolutely prohibitive, it could be argued that the average level of rates under the new law had been reduced to zero.'²⁸ If the President read such criticisms he gave no sign. To him the tariff was a reform measure designed primarily to benefit the farmer, but nothing other than granite stubbornness could have led him to such a conclusion. So he signed the bill and left for another day realization of his mistake in 'raising the tariff from its sleep.' A historian of the Republican party implies that the major reason for signing the bill was to get rid of Congress.²⁹

Probably nothing was so damaging to Hoover's reputation during his first two years in the presidency as his handling of the tariff. In the view of many competent observers, friendly and unfriendly, the Hawley-Smoot tariff making was a political disaster. The President intervened vigorously to preserve the flexible provision and to prevent the farm debenture from being slipped in, but on the matter of rates he was all but silent.³⁰

Whoever controlled the Republican party during the second session of the Seventy-first Congress, it was not Herbert Hoover. It is all but inconceivable that Hoover suddenly lost faith in himself, or found it impossible to make up his mind about what he wanted in a tariff measure, and so allowed the lobbyists to run wild. One could speculate on the influence of Andrew Mellon's tax pets, the great corporations and millionaires who were to finance the 1930 Republican campaign with driblets from the $3.5 billion in tax refunds, the abatements and credits received from a sympathetic Treasury Department in a decade of tenderness toward 'big money.' Legitimate, also, is the query: Did industrialists promise late in 1929 to hold the line on wages in exchange for a free hand with the tariff? The possibilities at least are intriguing. Whatever the answer, Hoover's performance with the tariff convinced a very large number of people that the President had failed in the first great test of his political leadership.

This increase in tariff rates came at a time when just the opposite course should have been pursued. At least two-thirds of American imports from 1919 to 1929 consisted of products used by our industries, and the physical quantity of imports 'followed almost exactly the same course as the curve of industrial production in the United States until 1929.'³¹ Curtailing imports, as a result of high tariffs and domestic depression, inevitably resulted in economic distress abroad, although this point has been greatly exaggerated by writers who are rarely able to focus their eyes on their own country; more important, higher duties decreased the ability of foreign nations to buy our exportable products, and widened the circle of distress in the United States.

'As a nation we normally spend a great amount of effort getting foreigners to buy our goods and then an almost equal amount of energy keeping them from paying for their purchases with other goods.'[32] The average value of American merchandise exports from 1926 to 1930 was $4,914 million annually, while imports averaged about $4,276 annually, leaving an annual favorable balance of about $638 million. This balance would have to be made up by charges against the United States for services, dividends earned on investments in American enterprises, outflow of long-term capital from the United States, and receipts from such other sources as the tourist trade and private cash remittances. In addition to paying the unfavorable trade balance, other countries would have to find dollars to make payments on the war debts, interest and dividends payable on American investments abroad, charges for services by Americans, and other accounts. They did not find the dollars and refused to use gold balances on deposit in the United States. From 1919 to 1929 other nations lacked $4,815 million needed to balance their accounts with the United States.[33]

The world economic structure was so closely interconnected that no unilateral major change could be undertaken without seriously affecting the entire structure. The manner in which members of Congress either ignored this fact or were ignorant of it was an amazing demonstration of irresponsibility. Equally amazing was failure to understand how vulnerable the United States had become in foreign trade. No longer could we ignore effects of foreign legislation on our own producers. Interesting, too, was the display of opposing efforts: on the one hand, President Hoover was doing everything possible to promote international peace and co-operation; on the other hand, he signed a measure productive of tremendous international irritation. There was no sense in talking about protection for agriculture—keen analysts had completely demolished that false argument; there was no sense in talking about equalization of costs—tariff advocates long since had ignored that principle; there was no sense in pointing to the flexible provision—experience had shown that rates almost always were flexed upward. With Europe in the trough of a severe depression, angry retaliation could be expected. Less apparent, but almost as certain to come, was an increased trend toward international cartels which might provide an even greater basis for an economic, and then a political, European Union.[34]

3. *World Response*

Repercussions resulting from the new tariff were prompt, effective, and often disastrous. Foreign countries retaliated by discriminating against imports from the United States, by intensifying impediments to trade which had been adopted in the immediate postwar years. The nature and extent of these effects were poorly understood in the United States, so thoroughly did friends and enemies of the Hawley-Smoot Tariff confuse the issue. High tariff advocates abroad argued for retaliation and charged the United States with engaging in economic warfare. By further curtailing imports, the United States was making it even more difficult for debtors to meet payments due the United States, and it also intensified the depression overseas.[35]

Angered by steadily increasing restrictions on exports to the United States and convinced that Standard Oil was party to a conspiracy against the peseta, Spanish officials were infuriated by the Hawley-Smoot Act. Spain's retaliatory Wais Tariff went into effect on 22 July 1930 with tremendously increased duties on major imports from the United States and correspondingly reduced imports thereafter.

Fascist Italy responded as did Spain. Arguing that the United States was trying to close its markets to Italian goods, the Italian automobile industry carried on a campaign against its American competitors and used the Hawley-Smoot Tariff to gain an advantage, at least in the Italian market. While the new American tariff was being made, Italy raised duties on imported automobile parts; under pressure from the Fiat Company, Italy raised its automobile tariffs as retaliation against both France and the United States. A large part of the Italian radio market had been captured by the United States in stiff competition from 1928 to 1930; in September 1931 prohibitive tariffs were levied. This delay in retaliation occurred to allow development of an Italian radio industry. Mussolini switched purchases of raw materials to other countries.[36]

Retaliation took different forms but occurred in Canada, Great Britain, Switzerland, France, Austria, and other countries. There were upward revisions in twenty-five countries in less than a year after passage of the Hawley-Smoot Tariff. In some cases retaliation preceded final passage of the act. The Australian tariff of 4 April 1930 embargoed imports of many articles without special permit of the Minister for Trade and Customs, raised rates by 50 per cent on a long list of articles and reduced them by 50 per cent on another list.[37]

Our tariff must not be condemned as the sole cause of decreased imports and hence of decreased dollar earnings abroad. There is a tendency to forget that increased tariffs and other trade barriers in many countries had reduced imports from the United States before 1930. Other nations, too, wanted the value of their exports to exceed the value of their imports; other nations, too, used tariffs to keep out competitive products. The European tariff war was so serious that all European countries except Russia attended the Customs Truce Conference at Geneva in February–March 1930. The Conference was a complete failure.[38]

Champions of the tariff denied that such cases as those just cited were retaliation, and they denied that the Hawley-Smoot Act interfered with the payment of war debts. Dr. Julius Klein, long Hoover's major assistant in the Department of Commerce, had to admit that many countries had increased their tariffs since Hawley-Smoot but denied any connection. In the four years before our 1930 act, forty-four countries had made major tariff alterations. The decline in imports and exports, he asserted, could not be traced to our tariff. Senator Smoot, reactionary Mormon elder, was still willing to argue that nothing calamitous had happened to our share of world trade. As to the war debts, Klein observed that the four major debtors owed payments of $228 million in 1930, while our imports and tourist expenditures amounted to more than $700 million. In other words, American funds were available for payments on the debt if the debtors wanted to use them.[39]

The Hawley-Smoot Tariff certainly caused retaliation, but all of the tariff increases abroad were by no means the result of resentment toward the United States. Impartial investigators concluded that 'it was not until after the financial crisis of 1931 that commercial policies everywhere turned sharply in the direction of violently restrictive action.'[40] When Great Britain abandoned the gold standard on 21 September 1931, many other countries followed her example. The gold standard disintegrated and with that catastrophe to old commercial methods came an avalanche of trade restrictions. Twenty-three countries raised their tariffs between 1 September 1931 and 31 December 1932, while other restrictions were even more common.[41]

Already hopelessly muddled, the world trade situation grew steadily worse after 1929. In that year American foreign trade had started its terrific plunge. The low point came in 1932, with exports at about $1,576 million and imports at $1,322 million. To find comparable lows, one had to go back to 1905! For the 1930–37 period, merchandise exports averaged $2,430 million and imports averaged $2,092 million annually, thus producing an annual favorable balance for the United States of $348 million. That would not have been so bad had it been possible for other nations to liquidate their unfavorable balance with the United States, but they could not.[42]

The more highly industrialized nations are under obligation to keep world trade moving. They cannot do so if at home they permit depressions that result in a catastrophic decline in imports, if their collective and mutually antagonistic policies create depressions. Discontent in the countries most severely stricken may take the form of warfare: 'The paths of the Mussolinis and Hitlers are made easy when men have nothing to lose but their humiliation.'[43] No nation is responsible for all conditions that may cause discontent and social inequalities abroad; every nation is responsible for pursuing a course that will not unduly aggravate such unsatisfactory conditions as may exist in countries with which it carries on economic intercourse.

The United States should have taken the lead in an effort to achieve multilateral reduction of trade barriers. However doubtful prospects for success may have been, Hoover should have called for an international economic conference to meet in 1930 and should have exercised his leadership to bring about a drastic reduction of tariffs. Many noted economists had presented unanswerable arguments against Republican tariff policy, but the President refused to heed them.[44] Hoover often argued that the Great Depression originated abroad; conditions abroad prevented recovery in the United States. Then why the emphasis on a unilateral tariff that could do nothing except to worsen conditions abroad? Why not exercise the leadership necessary to bring about co-operation in eliminating those foreign sources of depression?

Proponents of the protective tariff pointed to facts disturbing to free traders. With technology and management abroad on a par with our own, often in branch factories of our own corporations, labor costs per unit could be compared. If production techniques, management, taxes, raw material costs, and other items were roughly equivalent in the United States and Czechoslovakia, the lower wages in the latter might permit a shoe manufacturer to pay transportation costs and still compete in the American market. Either costs would have to come down in the American shoe industry or the market would be captured by the foreign goods. A protective tariff would preserve the market for domestic shoes without guaranteeing higher wages for labor. If the United States were to compete vigorously for foreign markets, it would have to allow competition at home. The logical course would be to become a free-trade nation, and let the more inefficient industries go into bankruptcy while only the most efficient survived. Free trade, the argument maintains, would tend toward a world-wide leveling of living standards. The United States had no intention of doing anything of the sort.[45]

Internationally minded members of the financial community urged the country to make the world its home market. Observing that a static population seemed certain, there would be less room for continued expansion of production without a world market. Theodore M. Knappen, a frequent contributor to *The Magazine of Wall Street*, advocated technological aid and a Point Four program long before there was official support for such ideas:

To do its part in keeping America moving swiftly, by means of waking up the backward parts of the world and quickening the commercial life of the modern countries, the surplus capital of this country must be used as fundamentally and as presciently as the automobile industry is now working. It must not be reluctant to undertake such prosaic things as sewers and canals, harbors and street improvements, water works and general sanitation.[46]

This intelligent answer to those who denied our need for foreign markets received little if any attention; but how many people would expect to find such a proposal for a bold, new program in the columns of a Wall Street organ?

Hoover had asked Congress for limited revision of the tariff and primarily in the interests of agriculture. Congress, in making the Hawley-Smoot Tariff, ignored the President's wishes in everything except the principle of flexibility. Loyal to his party, Hoover signed and defended the measure. The whole thing was a blunder significant in the hastening of economic collapse.

CHAPTER VIII

DEPRESSION INAUGURATED

1. *The Last Rush*

There were two inaugurations in 1929. Chief actor in the first, President Hoover was soon nominated to personalize the second. A depression does not start on the stroke of a clock, but there is no doubt that preliminary events reached a climax on 29 October and thus inaugurated the Great Depression. A convenient devil was not at hand, not a devil that could be flayed and scorned. The 'market' and 'Wall Street' were handy symbols, but long sustained emotion cannot be evoked by such impersonal entities. In the White House was the man who had become the symbol of prosperity; he became the symbol of depression.

In the late 1920's people the country over heeded Herbert Hoover when he spoke, perhaps more than any other one person. Hoover had said in his acceptance speech on 11 August 1928 that Republicans had reduced the national debt, Republicans had lowered taxes, Republicans had revived industry, Republicans had restored confidence in democratic government after regimentation during the war years. On 17 September he reminded voters that there were more than 5 million unemployed when Republicans took over in 1921, and Republicans had solved the problem in a year without 'doles, subsidies, charity, or inflation.' Of course, industrial leaders must be given much of the credit; but it was government that had provided the impetus needed to complete full employment, and Hoover did not let anyone forget who had been Secretary of Commerce during this great prosperity. At Boston on 15 October he gave Coolidge credit for adopting and applying the 'sound government policies' that brought prosperity; but no one forgot who was the strong man in the Coolidge cabinet. And one week later at New York he used up the last inch of a very long limb: 'I say with emphasis that without the wise policies which the Republican Party has brought into action during this period, no such progress would have been possible.' He could not believe that the voters would want to abandon principles championed by the Republican party, principles that had 'produced results so amazing and so stimulating . . .' To continue prosperity, voters must return the Republican party to power.[1]

There was no question whatever about Hoover's claim and promise. Republicans and Hoover had brought prosperity; Republicans and Hoover would continue prosperity. Even before the election, a wild boom began in the stock market. Immediately it was called the 'Hoover market.' While the President-elect was preparing for his famous South American good-neighbor tour, he made no public statement warning against such violent speculative activity. While Hoover was mixing good-will business with a greatly needed rest, he made no attempt to stop the market spree in celebration of his victory. He must have been worried even more than in 1925 when, as a cabinet official, he had protested vigorously against Federal Reserve easy money policies. But in the first stage of the 'Hoover market' he was not an official and he had too much respect for authority to assume prematurely the prerogatives he had won. Perhaps it was worry about the market rather than impatience for the coming of 4 March that caused Hoover to cut short his vacation in Miami, where his good friend and admirer, J. C. Penney, had provided his beautiful villa on Biscayne Bay for the Hoover party. No one seemed to be holding the reins in Washington.

The wild bull market of 1928–9, which came at the end of a period of feverish economic activity, has taken its place in history with other speculative sprees. Economists are still arguing about the relative weight that should be assigned to accepted causes of the speculative fever; politicians, occasionally, argue about governmental responsibility in such events. Whatever its causes, whatever the responsibility, the Great Bull Market was one of the most fascinating developments in an amazing century.

There were, in the summer of 1927, both foreign and domestic demands for credit inflation in order to prevent the well-merited economic collapse with which Europe was threatened. Beginning early in the year, an unusually large amount of gold flowed into the United States from foreign sources with the purpose of settling old debts and finding new investments. The Bank of France also began to pile up large gold holdings by repatriating capital and refusing to renew short-term credits. Bankers in Germany, Great Britain, and other countries became seriously alarmed lest they be compelled to abandon the gold standard.

After a preliminary conference, several major financiers appeared in the United States between 28 June and 1 July 1927: Charles Rist, deputy governor of the Bank of France; Montagu C. Norman, governor of the Bank of England, and Hjalmar Schacht, president of the Reichsbank. They came to confer with Benjamin Strong, governor of the New York Federal Reserve Bank from 1914 to 1928, who had led the Federal Reserve banks in helping to restore the gold standard in Europe by extending credit to countries in need. Ogden Mills attended the conference between the European and American bankers. They agreed that the Open-Market Investment Committee, of which Strong was chairman, would recommend easier credit—lower discount rates and open-market purchases of federal bonds. While these measures were being debated, a worrisome slump was under way in the United States.

Hoover, Secretary of Commerce and 'undersecretary of everything else,' apparently interposed no objections as he had in 1925. Then his earnest and spirited opposition had helped to prevent credit expansion by the Federal Reserve Board; but in 1927 the picture was different. Ogden Mills, to whom Hoover deferred in matters financial, favored credit inflation and that satisfied Hoover.

The process of credit inflation began slowly. After the Federal Reserve Board, against the advice of Adolph C. Miller, had approved the plan, Kansas City lowered its discount rate from 4 per cent to 3½ per cent on 29 July. Other banks soon followed, although Melvin Alvah Traylor of Chicago's First National Bank caused the Chicago Federal Reserve Bank to balk. By 13 September the lower rate was in effect and open-market operations went on apace, thus releasing bank funds. There is no proof that the speculative orgy which followed was the result of buying bonds in the open market and lowering the rediscount rate. Nevertheless, coincidence or not, these events must be considered in any attempt to explain the bull market.[2]

Happenings of the next few months are a familiar story to people in the middle-age group and older. Trading on margin increased rapidly as more and more people entered the market. Large brokerage firms opened numerous branch offices. Scores of issues made spectacular gains, frequently rising several points in one day. Banks and corporations with surplus funds loaned freely at high rates in the call money market. Foreign individuals and institutions enormously increased their trading. And while these things were going on, a presidential campaign took place. Who wanted to be a prophet of disaster? What political party would publicly warn of disaster ahead? What politicians would assume the responsibility for breaking the multicolored bubble? These questions are understandable. It is more difficult to explain why several professors, including Irving Fisher, made such positive predictions of ever-rising prices, permanent new plateaus of prosperity, and the end of poverty.

There were prophets and there were portents. On 3 February 1928 the New York rediscount rate went up to 4 per cent; twice more it was raised until it stood at 5 per cent in July, a rate posted by seven of the twelve Federal Reserve Banks. The stock market broke badly but soon recovered. Colonel Leonard P. Ayres, a Cleveland economic analyst of high repute, anticipated a serious decline in stock prices before 1928 ended; Melvin A. Traylor warned that it was time for a return to sanity. Bernard Baruch, the canny trader who never chased the greenhorn's dream of buying at the bottom and selling at the top, put his cash into tax-exempt state and local government bonds. Ogden L. Mills and Baruch advised friends to get out of the market; a few who heeded these private warnings were grateful.[3]

There was no general retrenchment as more money became available for speculation. Investment trusts were channeling funds into the market, bidding up the prices of available stocks, and the supply seemed ample. The number of shares listed on the New York Stock Exchange had increased from nearly 221 million in 1920 to more than 757 million in 1929. Shares listed on other exchanges, and those traded only over the counter, brought the total to an astronomical figure. Bank loans increased from $37,400 million in June 1927 to $41,500 million two years later. Stockbrokers' loans in New York stood at $3,560 million in June 1927 and at more than $8,500 million in September 1929. Charges have been made that the Federal Reserve Board, when it should have scotched the speculative fever, kept the boom going by refusing to permit member banks to raise discount rates from July 1928 to August 1929. This was the period of Hoover's election, inauguration, and honeymoon. As a matter of fact, the political implication is entirely unjustified. The Federal Reserve Board may not have done enough, but its actions through 1928 definitely were designed to be deflationary.[4] Its major error was in pursuing an inflationary policy in 1927 to help foreign banks.

Hoover could not have known that the gambler's beautiful ecstatic dream so soon would metamorphose into a hideous nightmare. His Committee on Recent Economic Trends, directed by Edward Eyre Hunt, made its long and optimistic report in 1929 after two years of investigation. The country on the whole, Hunt reported, showed steady progress. An effort has been made to prove that Hoover was genuinely alarmed and expected a crash, that he inveighed against speculation, supported the Federal Reserve Board when it attempted belatedly to put on the brakes, urged newspapers to editorialize on the evils of speculation, and pushed the Department of Justice after the outright gamblers. His defenders report that two days after the inauguration Hoover persuaded the Federal Reserve Board to prohibit member banks from providing funds for speculation. In the middle of March, Secretary Mellon announced at Hoover's request that bonds were the best buy. On 3 April 1929 the Federal Reserve Board warned that it would take even more drastic measures to reduce speculative credit.[5]

However, there is another version. The Board on 2 February had issued a plea to member banks to restrict speculative credit. This was the 'direct action' approach. Made public on 7 February, the request aroused immediate controversy. The New York Federal Reserve Bank on 14 February 1929 wanted to raise the rediscount rate to 6 per cent to restrict credit. The Federal Reserve Board disapproved and, after a long argument, Hoover—and Carter Glass, too—supported the Board. There is less discrepancy than appears to exist. It is one thing to raise a rediscount rate and another to forbid member banks to loan money on the call market. In any case, Charles E. Mitchell of the National City Bank defied the Board and pumped more credit into speculation.[6]

There were no major efforts by President Hoover, or by anyone with the power to do so, to stop the wild market. A few bankers, a very few editors, and still fewer brokers were willing to add their warnings to the feeble admonitions from Washington. There were far more who resented any implication that stock prices were too high, that the Federal Reserve Board should use its powers to halt inflation, or that the whole speculative insanity should be ended by raising margin requirements to about 90 per cent. Loring M. Black, Jr., a Brooklyn Democrat in the House, confidently asserted in the Congress on 17 April: 'We are at the economic peak of the world.'

He bemoaned extension of federal control into the field of capital. There was nothing wrong with the call-loan market; the New York Stock Exchange was a seasoned institution, 'a great contributing cause to the American economic development.' [7]

Much of the debate in Congress and in the press seemed far more important than later events proved it to be. Attracted by high interest rates, domestic private and corporate capital rushed into the threatened breach to finance another round of inflation. Companies with cash to spare loaned huge sums; soon companies even sold securities to obtain cash to loan to speculators. With interest rates up to 20 per cent for call money, loans from this source increased by a billion dollars in three months before the crash. The Federal Reserve Bank in New York advanced its rediscount rate from 5 per cent to 6 per cent on 9 August, causing a temporary decline in many issues. Recovery came quickly. Stocks mounted higher and higher until they reached their peak on 3 September. There was a bit of unpleasantness in the English stock market on 30 August when the so-called Clarence Hatry panic occurred and foreigners were deciding to end their American joyride.

In retrospect, it is apparent that the long slide of 1929 began on 6 September.[8] Still, there did not seem much reason for alarm as September passed. The Big Bull staggered into October and wobbled through the first two weeks. Somehow it had kept going for over five weeks. But then, in the third week of October, it crashed into the dust with a resounding bellow.

2. *Death of a Bull*

Warnings came from prophets of doom as certain stocks skyrocketed under brazen manipulation by operators of pools. There was no plateau in the market. The peak of 3 September was a sharp, narrow ridge with sides as steep as a cirque gouged by a giant glacier. Some stocks went even higher. Public utilities were at 259.3 on 3 September, fell to 250.4 on 13 September, then swooped to 267.3 on 24 September. The decline was the disturbance that later became known as the Babson Break. Speaking on 6 September, Roger Babson had said: 'Sooner or later a crash is coming, and it may be terrific. Wise are those investors who now get out of debt, reef their sails.'[9] In commenting on Babson's warning, a financial editor agreed that when the millions of investors, owners, projectors, workers, businesses large and small realize that the end is coming or has come to a fictitious 'prosperity' and change from prodigality to curtailment, from spending to saving, from gratifying wants to nursing needs, *then* the word finis will be written not only on the 'longest bull market in history,' but on a dream of 'perpetual' prosperity that has never had its equal in the annals of any people.[10]

Liquidation, already under way in September, gained momentum in spite of large dividend and interest payments on 1 October. The big drop of 19 October was called merely a 'technical correction' by the press. Prices trembled under selling pressures on 21, 22, and 23 October; on the next day, remembered as Black Thursday, stock tickers fell hopelessly behind and nearly 13 million shares were traded on the big board and another 3 million on the curb. Banks in large cities loaned recklessly to prevent collapse of the call market.[11]

The crash of 24 October developed when trading began at 10 A.M. There was an avalanche of selling orders, with prices going down so fast that it was impossible to find buyers. At noon Thomas W. Lamont of the House of Morgan called Charles E. Mitchell, William C. Potter, Albert H. Wiggin, and Seward Prosser for a conference. Potent bankers, these men represented more than $6 billion. Some cynics later charged that they hatched a scheme to save their own hides by bolstering the market until they could get out. They had, indeed. The immediate result of their meeting was the dramatic appearance of Richard Whitney, acting president of the New York Stock Exchange, on the floor at the Steel post offering (but not paying) $205 per share for 10,000 shares of U.S. Steel which was then quoted at $190. Soon there was a general recovery and brokers believed that Whitney 'had made himself a hero of a financially historic moment.' The bankers' pool had saved the market from collapse.[12]

Just what did these events mean? Irving Fisher pontificated on 23 October, the day before the first phase of the October panic reached its climax, that the slump was only temporary. On 25 October, when the first eruption had subsided somewhat, President Hoover said soothingly that business was on a sound and prosperous basis. On the same day, Roger Babson pressed his luck too far by assuring the country that only an orderly decline could be expected. Charles E. Mitchell, the banking wizard expert at avoiding income taxes, cheerfully announced that nothing was wrong. In the course of an excellent account of the 24 October crisis, the *Commercial & Financial Chronicle* observed:

The stock market this week passed through what may accurately be described as the worst panic in its entire history—barring the collapse which occurred in 1914 at the outbreak of the World War, when the Stock Exchange was kept closed for several months . . . Nor does it seem likely that a similar experience . . . at least in the magnitude and extent and widespread character of losses sustained will again be encountered for a long time to come.[13]

But Monday, 28 October, was coming. By noon of that day, with the sale of 3.5 million shares, it was apparent that 24 October was a mere warning. In spite of Hero Whitney's 'Horatio at Post No. 2,' steel fell to 186. Other stocks dropped disastrously, some by as much as 60 points. The bankers met in vain effort to stem the panic, or to decide how best to save their own skins. Then came 29 October with its 16,410,030 shares 'dumped as if they were so much junk.' Many of them were. There were plenty of bargains, according to past standards of judging a stock's value, and there were buyers who could afford to ride down or up, unaffected by price gyrations.[14] On the New York Stock and Curb exchanges, 23.5 million shares changed hands on 29 October, and at the close of trading the total value of listed stocks had declined by about $18 billion from 1 September values.[15] There was, of course, no suicide wave. Most of those who had been caught were too numb to raise a glass, pull a trigger, or leap from a window.

No one knows how much of those billions represented actual cash losses to some and gains to others. Catastrophe had visited the temple; high priests stole what they could and ran, trailing pious nonsense behind them. President Hoover, supremely confident that economic laws and a self-regulating economy could not go wrong, stubbornly clung to his belief that the country was basically sound. This adamantine refusal to become an alarmist made it easier for Democratic politicians to prefix 'Hoover' to every symbol of depression in the months to come.

A few weeks before the ides of October, that wizard of finance and politics, John J. Raskob, could see no reason why anyone could not be rich. Just save $15 a month, let dividends and rights accumulate, and within twenty years anyone could have $80,000 if he invested in good common stocks.[16] The brokers, at least, could be rich if they withstood the temptation to taste their own wares. Commissions on the New York Stock Exchange from 1 January 1928 to 31 August 1933 were more than $1,500 million.[17] How much of this came from the innocents is impossible to guess.

No one knew how many people were speculating in stocks. A well-reasoned estimate accepts a figure between one and five million, leaving a generous margin for error. Typical exaggerated statements assert that everyone was buying stock to get rich in a hurry and 'almost everybody borrowed money for the purpose of buying securities . . .'[18] An editor who surely knew better wrote: 'Everyone became seized with the idea that it was possible to get rich overnight by simply taking flyers in the stock market . . . and everyone participated therein.'[19] And a noted cynic wrote: 'This has been a children's crusade, not an adventure for a few hard-boiled knights; and no historian of the years 1924 to 1929 can afford to ignore the evidence that the butcher and the baker and the candlestick-maker have been in this market on an unprecedented scale.'[20]

Defenders of the status quo and apologists for financiers made these exaggerations in order to shift blame for the debacle from those who caused it. To say that 16 million Americans owned stock[21] does not mean that even a large percentage were gambling. Stuart Chase made the obviously inaccurate comment: 'Practically the entire literate population was running margin accounts and following tips and hunches.'[22] Still, there was so much feverish stock gambling that it is easy to exaggerate the number of speculators, to say 'the little men were buying by the million.'[23] A large part of this buying, in fact at least $3 billion of it, was by the 450 or more investment trusts organized in 1928-9.[24]

The big crash of 1929 was not caused by mad speculation of millions of common people, and very few of the literate population had margin accounts. The Senate Committee on Banking and Currency decided, after long investigation, that during 1929 there were 1,548,707 customers of member firms on 29 exchanges; of this number about 600,000 (38.69 per cent) were margin customers. Of the total, 1,371,920 were customers of New York Stock Exchange firms.[25] So much for the 'everyone-was-gambling' hyperbole.

3. *While We Were Asleep*

In general, people surely did not suspect what was coming. Newspapers and newsmagazines, faithfully reflecting daily froth or deliberately suppressing bearish stories, carried few if any warnings. The reading of *Time*, still less than a decade old and already the nation's diary, yielded few warnings. *Time's* editors, who soon were calling themselves 'the ablest historians of their day,' also wandered in the fog. In the first week of October 1929 consequential and inconsequential news was their fare. The Department of Justice began to investigate lobbyist William B. Shearer, who had sued three companies for $257,655 in back pay earned by working to prevent disarmament at the Geneva Conference of 1927. Walter B. Pitkin had published his *Psychology of Happiness;* a federal surplus of $229 million was expected; Senator Smith Wildman Brookhart of Iowa accused other senators of having liquor flasks at dinners given by Wall Street gentlemen. Senators quizzed Alexander H. Legge about the Farm Board, about why he was not using the $500 million appropriation faster; Ramsay MacDonald was expected from England on his trip to see President Hoover; and in Tokyo died Baron Giichi Tanaka, famed for the Tanaka Memorial blueprint of imperialism.

Further concentration of banking by consolidation and other means attracted attention. The automobile industry in eight months had turned out over 4.4 million units, with Ford alone reaching nearly 1.5 million. The railroads were thought to be prosperous. Pennsy had paid its 188th consecutive dividend, orders for new rails and new locomotives had been placed. Life insurance in force had topped $100 billion and companies were looking forward to the second hundred billion. A young daredevil aviator, Lieutenant Jimmy Doolittle, became the first man to fly completely 'blind.'[26] There was no indication of approaching disaster in Wall Street.

In the second week of October life went on much as usual. W. B. Shearer continued his Roman circus before the committee investigating lobbying against disarmament; the tariff battle went on in the Senate. At Marion, North Carolina, a sheriff and his deputies murdered striking workers, another episode in the anti-union drive of textile mills. There was a mad riot in Colorado's Canon City penitentiary. Stinson Aircraft Corporation sold out to Cord Corporation. E. A. Stinson and E. L. Cord, each thirty-five years of age, had cut quite a swath for their years. The cigarette war was over, prices going back to $6.40 per thousand. Then, careful readers of *Time* could have perused the single column labeled 'Break.' While Roger W. Babson, previously flayed for having predicted the break, kept mum, the market was not very encouraging. Walter P. Chrysler was reported as seeing no reason for the low prices of automobiles, and

Dun's Review wrote: 'Nothing has occurred to indicate that widespread trade recession is under way.' The Rock Island presented
'three superb new trains,' limiteds from Chicago west without extra
fare. Ernest Hemingway's *A Farewell to Arms* had just been published.[27]

During the third week of October, President Hoover named Irwin
B. Loughlin and Harry F. Guggenheim to be his ambassadors to Spain
and Cuba, respectively. Former Senator Albert B. Fall was back in
the news, on trial for allegedly accepting a bribe from E. L. Doheny.
The Senate debated censorship of obscene books, rejected independence for the Philippines which sugar senators were pushing. Hoover
and MacDonald had agreed on a naval reduction conference, and
Winston Churchill was just finishing a lecture tour in the United
States. The recent crash of Clarence C. Hatry's business empire still
had British financial circles agog over that swashbuckler's piracy.
Coffee brokers in New York had a mad time while futures crashed,
causing forecasts of ruin in Brazil's coffee states. S. W. Straus & Co.
ran a full-page ad: 'He invests his modest earnings in good sound
securities.' The public would remember S. W. Straus & Co. *Time*
announced that *Fortune,* at $10 per year, would appear in January
1930. Henry Luce, barely over thirty, was well on his way to something. Continental Can and Owens-Illinois Glass became units of
Continental Containers, Inc., a holding company. Texas Company
offered $100 million in 5 per cent debentures, and this 'biggest bond
issue since 1926' was sold in a few hours. And the Athletics won the
World Series from the Cubs.[28]

Letters to the editor of *Time* praised the *Fortune* prospectus almost
uniformly; but if any letter reached the editor about the market
jitters of 23 and 24 October with worries about what was in store
for the United States, they were not published in this fourth issue
of the month. President Hoover, 'all aglow,' went to Dearborn, Michigan, to help Henry Ford, Harvey Firestone, and Thomas Alva Edison
celebrate the fiftieth anniversary of the electric light and then on to
Cincinnati to dedicate the Pittsburgh to Cairo waterway, finished
at a cost of $18 million. The Senate investigated lobbyists who were
working for tariff revision. Harry A. Austin admitted that the United
States Beet Sugar Association had spent $500,000 since 1922 to off-
set propaganda of sugar interests abroad; Senator Hiram Bingham,
former Connecticut professor, was revealed as having smuggled a

lobbyist into the Finance Committee to work for higher tariffs to benefit Connecticut industries; and the senators prepared to go after Joseph R. Grundy like a pack of bears splashing fish in a mountain stream. At Charlotte, North Carolina, a jury convicted sixteen defendants charged with the murder of Gastonia's police chief, Orville F. Aderholt. Several Communists, including Fred Erwin Beal, were among the defendants who had led the Gastonia strike. The Interstate Commerce Commission decided to investigate extra fares by which some railroads increased their take by $10 million annually. The Senate confirmed the eight members of the Federal Farm Board over which Alexander H. Legge presided. Farmers soon could look back with nostalgia at quotations of the week: wheat at $1.42 per bushel, corn at $1.11, and cotton at 18 cents per pound.[29]

Turning to 'Business & Finance,' one learned of 'bear' William H. Danforth, who was supposed to have caused further market declines. Ivar Kreuger, whose financial crash and suicide were not far off, had gone to Berlin to tighten Kreuger & Toll's match monopoly in Germany. Southern Bell Telephone and Telegraph Company's $32 million bond issue through J. P. Morgan & Co. and other bankers looked like a good sign. [30]

But what of the market? Perhaps the first November issue would show some signs of warning about what was in store; at least, there would be plenty to record from Wall Street. For October, *Time* simply performed as a good reporter, a little sharper and more pert than many journals but certainly not gifted with the ability to dash ahead of time. There were no predictions of the great crash to come nor of disaster for years ahead.

4. *Prophets and Prognosticators*

Financiers, economists, statesmen, politicians, and journalists should have been able to assay economic conditions accurately. Their failure to do so revealed that they had something less than an adequate understanding of our economic system.

There were, in 1929, four major organizations that gave advice on the stock market: Standard Statistics Company, Babson Statistical Organization, Moody's Investors Service, and the Brookmire Economic Service. Not one of these agencies foresaw a panic, but the Babson service warned in August against buying inflated issues.

Moody's thought everything was wonderful; Brookmire warned against new commitments but advised sitting tight. At the end of September, only Standard Statistics advised retrenchment; a month later, on 28 October, Standard could see no reason for not buying. Brookmire and Moody's both advised buying on 28 October; Babson warned his subscribers to be wary. Thus, three of the four 'expert' services advised clients to buy on the day before 16 million shares hurtled from the heights and crushed the Dow-Jones index down 30 points! Anyone who took the advice of Standard, Moody's, or Brookmire stood to lose his shirt and suspenders overnight, with gravity taking care of the rest. All four services advised buying between 13 November and 7 December, none advised selling at the December highs.[31] The services continued to guess wrong time after time, demonstrating that investment experts lacked the knowledge to forecast market trends with reasonable accuracy.

A serene, confident Thomas W. Lamont gazed from *Time*'s 11 November cover. As if to demonstrate how unfounded all fears of the future might be, a Manhattan jewelry firm opened a new store and displayed a necklace of exquisitely matched pearls, priced at $750,000. A few companies declared extra dividends; some brokers were broke. There was a parade of men speaking confidently, as they tried to explain what had happened in October and what was going to happen.

The great Dr. Julius Klein, Assistant Secretary of Commerce, took to the air on 29 October to pass on Hoover's assurance of 25 October that business was sound, that only 4 per cent of the nation's families 'were affected by the break.' Irving Fisher and Roger Babson and Stuart Chase, who should have known better, issued reassuring statements. Fisher at once busied himself with writing a much too premature explanation of what caused the crash. Walter P. Chrysler, Walter S. Gifford, and K. R. Kingsbury endeavored to show that the empires of motors, telephones, and oils were not endangered. John J. Raskob of General Motors and William Wrigley, Jr. said they were buying stocks. Some daredevil businessmen guaranteed their employees' margin accounts. John D. Rockefeller, Sr. announced: 'My son and I have for some days past been purchasing sound common stock.' As Eddie Cantor asked, who else had any money left?

Confidence, opined *Time*, had won 'its subtle race against Panic.' The hero was not Richard Whitney after all, but the highly respected

Thomas W. Lamont, whose fantastic career had carried him to the top in Wall Street. Lamont had directed the forces of finance that stemmed the panic and cushioned its decline. Looking at some quotations, one wonders how much lower they could have gone in two weeks or less: U. S. Steel at 180, Radio at 43.75, and General Motors at 45.25 represented drastic reductions as of 4 November. These prices would, in less than three years, seem extraordinarily high. At least one industrialist would have fun: Pierre Samuel du Pont bought a $250,000 pipe organ for his estate.[32]

Carter Glass held Charles E. Mitchell, National City Bank chairman, more responsible for the stock crash than 'any fifty men.' That would depend upon selection of the fifty. More reasonable judgments explained that the 'Babson Break' of September had been ignored; corporations, by loaning on call, had encouraged speculation; and even cautious corporations, by not reporting full earnings, had caused speculators to overvalue some stocks. The idea that 'widespread distribution of stock to employees' had made too many people 'unduly stock-conscious' was untrue. Warnings of trouble, apparent in business indices, had been ignored. 'Slowly the Market began to realize that 1929 might be an abnormal year, a high-water year. . . . If this fear were well founded, what then of 1930, or 1931, of even more distant times, the anticipated prosperity of which had been already discounted?' Among predicted results were that people would work more and gamble less, more money would go into legitimate fields, and 'the constructive wizardry of Herbert Hoover . . . might soon be exhibited to a waiting and ready people.'[33]

One senator, Joseph T. Robinson of Arkansas, echoed a popular sentiment when he said that the Republicans, particularly President Hoover, had caused the crash.[34] Those who expected the President to pull a miracle from a magician's hat should have known that Herbert Hoover had not learned that he could snap his fingers, line up three letters of the alphabet, and send them charging forth to do his bidding. But the Democrats, smarting from a decade of Republican supremacy, quickly seized the opportunity for political capital gains. Solemnly the Democratic National Committee repeated Robinson's charge: Hoover caused the crash. Someone had to be the goat and Hoover was selected by popular acclaim of the Democratic party.

Newspaper editors, labor leaders, bankers, government officials, and economists poured out their assurances that business was sound.[35] As a matter of fact, labor relations were far from sound; agriculture was bankrupt, except for a few feudalistic, oppressive, and ruthless enterprises such as those that flourished in California's fruit and vegetable industries; the banking structure was unsound; mining still tolerated revolting conditions; sweat shops burgeoned in New York's garment industry; and in the South, hordes of workers, black and white, struggled along on starvation wages. One of the most important of all activities in the country, government at all levels, was grossly inefficient, and that inefficiency was causing a huge drain on the national pocketbook.

Nation's Business was not seriously worried about the market debacle. 'With satisfaction that a degree of sanity appears to be returning to our investment community and with sympathy for those whose losses have been the sacrificial instruments of restoration, we may view the matter as a manifestation of herd psychology . . . the mob was obsessed.'[36] The mob, only the mob! No word of condemnation for those cynical financiers who floated stocks so full of water that a good squeeze would leave little except the pulp of once gaudy certificates; no word about pools, preferred lists, inside speculation, market rigging. And not a word about corporation officials whose ethics would have exiled them from any jungle. Such practices, apparently, were unknown to Roy A. Young, governor of the Federal Reserve Board when the crash came, who explained the slump with the profound observation that the market 'went so high that it fell of its own weight.' [37]

Congress was available and so easy to accuse of guilt in causing the crash. After belittling, insulting, admonishing, and sneering at politics, politicians, and Congress through issue after issue, the editor of the *Commercial & Financial Chronicle* suddenly discovered that Federal Reserve policy had caused the bull market and the crash. Consequently, it was now the duty of Congress to prevent a repetition of such uncontrolled speculation.[38] He was asking for nothing short of revolution.

Congress did not cause the crash but its members were interested in finding out what had been going on. The Senate Banking and Currency Committee on 11 April 1932 belatedly and at Hoover's urging began hearings to which big operators from Wall Street were summoned to answer embarrassing questions. Revelations of these

hearings proved beyond doubt that 'The Street' and similar concentrations of economic power played a key role in precipitating the
economic debacle dramatized by the big blowup of October 1929.
The judgment of Ferdinand Pecora, the Committee's principal counsel, is indeed restrained: 'The testimony had brought to light a shocking corruption in our banking system, a widespread repudiation of
old fashioned standards of honesty and fair dealing in the creation
and sale of securities, and a merciless exploitation of the vicious
possibilities of intricate corporate chicanery.' [39]

Although the hearings continued into 1934, the shocking revelations that came in 1932 could not fail to discredit the Republican
party, the party of big business and prosperity and the Bull Market.
In the last days of Hoover's presidency, when the whole banking
structure was crashing in ruins, officers of the National City Bank
condemned themselves before an almost incredulous public, which
had regarded National City as one of the greatest, soundest, and
most respectable of banks.[40]

Under Pecora's questioning, financiers, brokers, and speculators
confessed to greed and ruthlessness unsurpassed in American history.
Pool operators manipulated prices—there was no free market. Bankers
made fortunes by trading in securities of their own banks. High
pressure salesmanship unloaded securities of questionable value.
Preferred buyers received bargain discounts on new securities.
Architects of business piled holding companies layer on layer to
siphon off every drop of loot. Persons with huge incomes defrauded
the government by evasion of taxes, and trustees betrayed their
trust.[41]

Major interest centered on such giants as J. P. Morgan & Co.,
National City Bank, Chase National Bank, and Dillon, Reed & Co.
They were big, they were prime targets for investigation. Activities
of hundreds of other bankers, industrialists, brokers, lawyers, politicians, and ordinary citizens were equally reprehensible. The Senate
committee was seeking information upon which to base remedial
legislation that finally came under the New Deal; but that was of
no aid to the country when Hoover was President.

CHAPTER IX

DEPRESSION POLICIES AND POLITICS

1. *First Aid*

Hardly more than a month was to elapse between the 29 October market crash and the first regular session of the Seventy-first Congress, but it was a month in which the President was a very busy man. His actions in those four weeks foreshadowed his basic policy throughout the depression: the federal government must help the people, but the people must bear the burden and not expect miracles. Hoover feared that federal aid might lead to federal mastery, something that he abhorred more than the mastery of concentrated wealth. Because of this fear, one critic charges, he was the greatest failure in our history as a crisis President.[1] This intemperate accusation gained wide credence largely through tiresome repetition.

Hoover never did believe that 'the irregular tempo' of economic activity could be eliminated in a free society. Recognizing that intricate economic relationships were not wholly understood, Hoover believed that combinations of events generated tides of optimism and pessimism which have considerable influence on business cycles. This is the key to Hoover's public cheerfulness, the explanation for the many optimistic statements not supported by fact. President Hoover's alarm was not concealed from the press nor from his associates. He told the Washington Gridiron Club on 14 December 1929: 'Fear, alarm, pessimism, and hesitation swept through the country, which, if unchecked, would have precipitated absolute panic throughout the business world with untold misery in its wake. Its acute dangers were far greater than we are able to disclose at the present time.'[2]

What did the President do to check these panic-making forces? A few immediate steps could be and were taken. The Federal Reserve Banks eased the credit situation through purchases of commercial paper and federal bonds and lowered the discount rate. Member banks increased their loans and investments by $1,600 million in October.[3] In the same month, wheat had fallen 17 cents per bushel, cotton was down by $7.50 per bale. The recently created Federal Farm Board loaned to co-operatives to cushion the price decline.[4] Farmers, already well calloused from previous falls, needed a prop instead of a cushion.

Hoover called leaders of business and labor to a series of meetings collectively called the Conference for Continued Industrial Progress. Preliminary conversations preceded the first formal meeting on 19 November when railroad presidents trooped to the White House. Then came the blue book of industrialists: Henry Ford, Owen D. Young, Julius Rosenwald, Alfred P. Sloan, Jr., Jesse I. Straus, Pierre S. du Pont, Walter Gifford, and others; and the labor leaders, among them Matthew Woll, William Green, and John L. Lewis. Unfair critics called them 'scout meetings.'[5] Hoover told the industrialists that the crisis went deeper than the market crash, that a severe depression had arrived which would see increased world-wide economic distress aggravated by dislocations of the World War.[6] Ignoring this 1929 warning, some Hoover critics say it was not until 1931 that the President appreciated the international nature of the depression.

Clearly the President had warned of difficult days ahead. He could not have foreseen either the duration or the seriousness of the depression. Readjustment was necessary, but in recognizing this fact Hoover did not want labor to bear an unjust burden; immediate problems were unemployment, distress, maintenance of social order and peace in industry, and prevention of panic. The President emphasized the need for maintaining wages, reiterating a belief expressed long before: 'The very essence of great production is high wages and low prices.'[7] There must be no drastic wage cuts. Industrialists agreed in principle, provided labor would be reasonable. Actually, wages were being cut in some industries, but Big Steel held the line until 1 October 1931. Green, Lewis, and the others were willing to let things ride for a time. Communist agitators called this nebulous no-strike pledge an outright betrayal by A.F. of L. leaders. Since wages were being slashed in unorganized industries, the no-strike agreement was a prelude to wage cuts of unionized workers. The agreement, said the Communists, was a Hoover trap.[8]

Leaders in the building industry arrived in Washington, conferred, and agreed to stimulate construction. Responding to presidential inquiries, governors and mayors indicated immediate public and private projects approximating $5 billion and a total private and public expansion program of $12 billion.[9] Public utilities magnates came to the White House on 27 November to pledge co-operation for full employment. The great, benevolent Samuel Insull could see no point to all the fuss. He would see it, a few years later.

These measures revealed Hoover's attitude toward the proper relationship between government and business. He had resorted to moral suasion to prevent unemployment and loss of wages. The federal government could help by expanding public works, reducing income taxes, restricting immigration, exercising great economy, and easing the descent of agriculture into new depths. Co-operation, not coercion, was to be the key to federal action.[10] Why shouldn't the remedies of 1921 work just as well in 1929?

More than three years later *Time,* which had not yet become the Republican newsmagazine, asserted that Hoover was asking for advice and that the 'swarms of bankers, financiers, businessmen, industrialists, railroaders, labor leaders, farm spokesmen' told the President to 'sit tight, keep smiling, let the tempest blow itself out.'[11] If that was their advice, Hoover did not take it.

Professor Galbraith has described the conferences as 'no-business meetings' which did not fail because they were not intended to do anything.[12] This view ignores the important fact that they stood as an urgent plea for business to solve its own problems in order to avoid federal intervention. Moreover, since it is generally agreed that adverse opinions expressed by persons high in government and business are deflationary in effect, would not expressions of confidence be steadying in effect?

The *New York Times* reported on 16 November 1929 that leaders of the financial district were convinced the storm had blown over. A large volume could be compiled of statements by prominent people who cited many reasons for optimism. The market was rallying and 'The most that can be done, and really the only thing to do, is to guard against men losing their reason and common sense.'[13] Flaunting a premature renunciation of caution, one writer intoned:

This generation has conquered the air and annihilated time and space. The young leaders of our business world have brought the nation to its current high position in international commerce and business. They have developed a banking system which has withstood the trials of a market cataclysm and our business structure is amply buttressed to meet its aftermath.[14]

At the end of November the *Commercial & Financial Chronicle* observed: 'The only thing that the President can do . . . is to prevent men . . . from yielding to unnecessary fear and cancel orders and scale down production to such an extent as to bring trade to an almost complete standstill, thereby paralyzing all the energies of the entire population.' [15]

Irving Fisher was optimistic in December. His was the voice of the industrialists, financiers, and their political allies who ruled the country. His philosophy was their philosophy. The crash, he declared, had been technical and artificial. Recovery, sparked by Hoover's conferences, had begun on 14 November, since the low point was reached on 13 November.[16] Although a large number of comments could be quoted in praise of Hoover's action, let one glowing tribute suffice:

They were right who said we had elected a business President. Our national government has come out of the clouds of politics and landed on the firm ground of business. No more abstractions about the rights of man, but a lot of thought about his well-being—practical thought and action. Less verbose philosophy and more jobs. . . . Thanks largely to Presidential leadership, the most interesting phenomenon of the day is not business depression but repression of depression.[17]

2. *Hope for Recovery*

While the market continued to act like a rubber ball bouncing down statistical stairs, the Seventy-first Congress was assembling for its regular session. Contemplating this dire event in the midst of Wall Street confusion, Roger Babson warned that Congress was the greatest hindrance to restored confidence: 'Here, while the stock market has crashed and business is declining, these men, without any regard for the nation or their constituents, are thinking only of themselves and their own political fortunes. . . . In behalf of the business men of America, I appeal to Congress to adjourn on the tariff and stay adjourned until business confidence is restored.' Groping blindly to recover lost bearings, Babson spoke of increasing exports without increasing imports, the soundness of the banking situation, and the bad condition of the political situation. Hoover should be made a dictator: 'Let Congress pass one bill giving certain necessary powers to President Hoover, as did the Democratic Congress of 1914, and then adjourn.' [18]

One must, perhaps, go back to the 1790's to find a Congress held in such low esteem. Then the heroic figure of Washington was a symbol of unity for the democratic faith. But these attacks on the Seventy-first Congress were based on feelings of guilt and apprehension lest the voice of the people clamor for reform. Many editorials in business magazines and newspapers ridiculed the whole process of democratic government. The ridicule was fairly well co-ordinated with investigations either in progress or in prospect. One editor, perhaps unknowingly, heralded a new era in government-business relations: 'It is plainly the duty of Congress and the Government that measures should be taken to guard against a repetition of the series of events that have marked the course of the unparalleled speculation of the last two years . . .' [19]

Conferences with business leaders were partly preparation for the opening of Congress. Hoover's four unhappy years with that body, despite failure to control tariff making, had started out well enough. He could not complain about the House, where a relatively loyal Republican majority under Nicholas Longworth supported most of his policies. But the Senate of the Seventy-first Congress contained 42 regular Republicans, 14 Progressive Republicans, 39 Democrats, and a lone Farmer-Labor. The Progressives, Democrats, and the Farmer-Labor senator could combine to hold a majority of 54 to 42. While not a legislating majority, this combination could cause tremendous embarrassment for a President who already was being regarded by a large part of the public as the Man who Caused the Depression.

In his message to Congress on 3 December 1929 Hoover recounted briefly what had been done in the November conferences with leaders of business and labor. He was convinced that confidence had been re-established. 'Wages should remain stable. A very large degree of industrial unemployment and suffering which would otherwise have occurred has been prevented.' He recommended legislation to remedy certain defects and to cushion the shock of reconversion to sanity: more public construction, reform of the chaotic banking system, regulation of utilities, railroad consolidation, and economy. Early in January 1930 the President advised appropriations of $60 million to start Boulder Dam, $75 million for highways, $500 million for public buildings, $150 million for rivers and harbors. This program, with additions such as a $160 million reduction in income taxes, cleared

Congress easily. By July, the President was concerned lest Congress succumb to various pressures to spend so much that a large tax increase would be unavoidable.[20]

Surveying the situation early in 1930, 'competent' observers again believed that the crisis was over. Mellon predicted a Treasury surplus, and on 7 March Hoover reported that the worst would be over in sixty days.[21] Optimism continued to prevail among all but the farmers and the unemployed. For the latter, Hoover continued to stress the need for public works by states and municipalities. They should follow the lead of the Seventy-first Congress which appropriated some $800 million for that purpose before adjournment in July. The Boulder Dam, greatest of all the individual projects, was begun on 8 July.[22]

Early in 1930, Senator Robert F. Wagner, New York Democrat, sought action on proposals that had been discussed for more than a decade. He presented an integrated program in three bills to provide for advance planning of public works by an ex officio Federal Employment Stabilization Board of cabinet members, creation of an effective federal employment service, and provision for adequate statistical coverage of unemployment. Wagner was exasperated when Hoover refused his support for all except for the last proposal.[23]

Hearings on Wagner's proposals brought out ideas incompatible with the President's individualism: public unemployment insurance, a guaranteed annual wage, and industry's obligation to provide employment. Moreover, Frances Perkins, who later became Secretary of Labor in the New Deal, and other witnesses before the Senate Committee on Commerce denied that prosperity had in fact been restored. James A. Emery, representing the National Association of Manufacturers, filed his organization's objection to creation of a strong federal employment service. Thinly masking its fears by an appeal to state rights, the N.A.M. saw in a federal employment service an agency that might gain effective control over the labor force.[24]

While contrary views were being aired in Congress and before committees, President Hoover delivered cheerful spring messages to the people. To the princes of kidders and critics gathered at the Washington Gridiron Club on 26 April, he observed that unemployment was being handled without resort to doles or unemployment insurance. The federal government had inaugurated 'one of the greatest economic experiments in history on a basis of nation-wide cooperation not of charity.' The experiment was 'voluntary coöperation of industry with the Government in maintaining wages against reduction, and the intensification of construction work.' [25]

To the United States Chamber of Commerce on 1 May 1930 the President voiced his conviction that the worst of the slump was over. This is what he had predicted on 7 March. The co-operative method had triumphed in mitigating ill effects of the crash and in shortening the period of adjustment. The major difficulty with the country's economy had been over-speculation, and in the past a train of destructive forces had followed boom collapses:

> Optimism swings to deepest pessimism; fear of the future chokes initiative and enterprise; monetary stringencies, security and commodity panics in our exchanges, bankruptcies and other losses all contribute to stifle consumption, decrease production, and finally express themselves in unemployment, decreased wages, strikes, lockouts, and a long period of stagnation. . . . I do not accept the fatalistic view that the discovery of the means to restrain destructive speculation is beyond the genius of the American people.

The President was optimistic in pointing out dangers that already were past, in assuming that the country was well on the road to full recovery, that measures already taken would be ample to complete the recovery process.[26]

Several important newspapers agreed that the President's efforts had been remarkably successful. The New York *Evening Post* rhapsodied: 'Mr. Hoover . . . gave the country the kind of anticipatory or preventative relief that has brought things to their improved position of today.' The *Herald-Tribune* referred glowingly to Hoover's 'cool and superlative leadership.' The President and other optimists were rushing the season. A slight spring upturn had occurred but the flurry was only in production and quickly ended. Bankers already were running for cover; the drought further diminished the almost invisible farm purchasing power.[27]

One needed no sensitive sphygmograph to determine the economic pulse: it did not quicken in response to presidential exorcism of depression. Events were to prove that confidence and courage had not been maintained, 'monetary panic and credit stringency' had not been avoided, and the danger of 'significant bank or industrial' failures most definitely lay ahead, not 'safely behind us.' When the President noted the absence of substantial wage reductions, one must wonder what he considered as substantial; when he said that the 'maximum point of depression was about the first of the year,' one is justified in asking how he could have drawn such a conclusion from such incomplete evidence.[28] If the President's speech reflected his genuine beliefs, and there is no reason to doubt it, he was convinced in May that the worst was over. After all, it was Herbert Hoover who in March had predicted that happy result.

Drought in the summer of 1930, slowness in industrial activity, Russian dumping of wheat in European markets, and other signs gave the President reason to wonder if he had not been too optimistic. Nevertheless, he clung to the belief that the depression was dying. He sought ways to reduce normal federal expenditures to meet declining revenues, established a National Drought Committee to provide relief in stricken areas, and urged speeding up of federal public works. Democratic propaganda kept reminding people that Republicans caused the depression, and new estimates of the number of unemployed promised another hard winter.

A note of caution appeared in Hoover's long address to the American Bankers' Association on 2 October 1930. Despite the severe economic shock, the nation's basic assets were unimpaired, resources were undiminished, science and inventions had progressed, equipment and organization were still in order. The problem was one of completing recovery, of preventing future depressions. Again the President observed that the depression was world-wide, that its causes lay only partly in the United States. Whatever the causes of depressions, Hoover was confident that 'the genius of modern business' could control them.[29]

There has been a suggestion that miniature golf contributed more than the federal government to recovery in 1930! Started by John N. Ledbetter and Drake Delanoy in New York in 1926, this fascinating recreation began to sweep the country in the spring of 1930. Garnet Carter, a hotel owner in Chattanooga, bought the southern rights in 1929 and started courses in Florida. 'Through the summer months, a million and a half people spent half a million dollars a day on some thirty-five thousand courses in a game which had hardly been known a year ago and which turned rapidly into an industry considered, by hasty observers, a proper ladder on which America might rise again to prosperity.'[30] Upward of $200 million was invested in this juvenile game before the fad died, and probably half again as much was paid in 'greens' fees.

3. Time Out for Politics—Election of 1930

Throughout the first phase of his campaign against the depression, President Hoover was haunted by increasingly frequent signs of Democratic resurgence. After his victory in 1928, Republican factions appeared to be waning in importance and the 'Hoover market' was hailed as a national seal of approval on Republican policies.[31]

Not all Democrats despaired. Al Smith recommended that the Democratic party develop a constructive program and not wait for a reaction from Republican incompetence. Jouett Shouse favored a permanent executive committee to keep party machinery alive, and National Committee Chairman John Jacob Raskob approved. Perhaps, stung by defeat in 1928, Raskob was laying plans to try Smith again in 1932. If Democrats expected to gain in the 1930 elections, it was high time they started. Early in June 1929, with Shouse safely installed as chairman of the Executive Committee, Raskob summoned leading Democrats to a dinner in Washington. Several prominent southern senators stayed away, refusing to give any semblance of support to the 'Smith crowd.' But Raskob, one of the few Democrats with money and the willingness to spend it, maintained his control.[32]

Prosperity was still in the air when the plans of Raskob and Shouse bore fruit. They rented space in Washington's National Press Building, engaged Charles Michelson as publicity director, and started collecting money to finance a superbly conducted 'educational campaign' by what one Republican writer called 'the most elaborate, expensive, efficient, and effective political propaganda machine ever operated in the country by any party, organization, association, or league.' Raskob pledged upward of a million dollars to finance the effort, although his ultimate contribution is reported as only $462,000. Pierre S. du Pont, Vincent Astor, and Bernard M. Baruch were among other contributors.[33]

Charley Michelson, brother of the famous physicist Albert A. Michelson, knew his way around, and a salary of several thousand a year would help keep him from getting lost. His many years of experience working for William Randolph Hearst and his twelve years as Washington correspondent for the *New York World* now bore acid fruit for Republicans, who interpreted that it was Michelson's job to smear Hoover with all the mud that could be flung in a 'mass production of misrepresentation and malice.' They charged him with being the sole author of hundreds of statements and speeches attacking Hoover and the Republicans. They complained that he had no regard for truth, that he was the mouthpiece of a diabolical plot to assassinate Republican character. Verily, as one wit remarked, 'the whispering campaign of 1928 has been succeeded by the whimpering campaign of 1930.' Democrats could derive grim satisfaction from adolescent expressions of outrage by Republicans, but the charges against Michelson were not greatly exaggerated.[34]

President Hoover was vulnerable to the Democratic publicity campaign. He was not universally popular within the Republican party, had never been the choice of professional politicians, and was notoriously thin-skinned. The party had done an over-selling job in 1928, being too eager to claim exclusive rights to prosperity. According to Michelson, the President was a promoter who took refuge in factual analyses to avoid facts and resented all legitimate criticism as a personal insult.[35] Occasionally the publicity bureau made blunders, but even the blunders helped. Such was the case in the flurry over Ralph S. Kelley's abortive attempt to create another oil scandal out of leases and patents to Colorado's oil shale lands.

The depression was just what the Michelson workers needed. Every mistake, every failure to take action, every over-optimistic statement by any Republican, could be turned to political account. As Mr. Kent observed, either the President would lose rapidly in prestige, become a one-term man, and be dubbed an inept leader, or prosperity would return and Mr. Hoover would confound his critics with claims to wise statesmanship. Prosperity did not return, nor did Republicans rally valiantly behind a leadership too many of them disliked. When James L. West was sent forth to clash typewriters with his fellow reporter, the campaign was already lost. Mr. Hoover squirmed, loftily refused to engage in mud slinging, and watched a legend die swiftly. By November 1930 a great many voters accepted the Democratic thesis: the Republicans, and particularly Hoover, were responsible for the depression and favored the rich over the poor; Hoover had no control over the party and provided no leadership for Congress. As the 1930 campaign progressed, these charges rankled so much that William Robert Wood, chairman of the Republican Congressional campaign, protested against Democratic slanders. Michelson then quoted an old *Congressional Record* to show that Wood himself had once sneered at Hoover's abilities.[36]

Confusion in the Republican high command occurred with the revelation that Chairman Claudius Hart Huston, hand-picked by Hoover to succeed Dr. Hubert Work, had used funds of a Muscle Shoals lobby, the Tennessee River Improvement Association, to support his stock market operations. Huston also was accused of welching on a poker debt of $80,000. This embarrassing political encumbrance finally resigned in August and was succeeded by Senator Simeon D. Fess of Ohio, with Robert Hendry Lucas as executive director.[37] Fess was either courageous or uninformed when he announced that President Hoover's vigorous measures had prevented an industrial depression! Before long Lucas was laying on with savage sweeps and saying that Democrats were afraid of a genuine business recovery. There were no statistics that foretold such a disaster for the opposition. Nor, apparently, could Republicans gain much advantage from the scandals in New York City, where Governor Franklin D. Roosevelt was treading warily over the noisome mess.

Americans began to eat apples in the fall of 1930 as they had never eaten them before. There was a surplus of the fruit and someone in the International Apple Shippers Association inaugurated street-corner marketing on credit, using unemployed workers as salesmen to put a shiny glow on red apple cheeks. Selling originally at $1.75 per crate to the unemployed vendor, who resold at 5 cents an apple, the price in less than two weeks rose to $2.25 per crate. Before election there were 'more than 6,000 apple peddlers on the streets of New York alone . . .'[38] It was a good marketing device which became another symbol of depression.

Republican leaders tried a crude, transparent trick in attempting to defeat George W. Norris for re-election in 1930. Norris, approaching seventy, would have been happy to retire from the national scene, but he refused to leave under fire. The Hoover-Norris feud, always smoldering, occasionally flamed high. Norris supported Smith in 1928, Norris championed the export debenture, Norris opposed the appointment of Irvine L. Lenroot to the United States Court of Customs Appeals, Norris snorted with disdain when Hoover named Samuel R. McKelvie, former governor of Nebraska, to the Farm Board. Norris was the major enemy of the power trust in America and the power trust struck at Norris through the Nebraska Press Association, the *McCook Daily Gazette*, and the Twin Valley Association of Commercial Clubs. Walter W. Head, chairman of the board of Nebraska Power Company, financed a secret poll to find a candidate to oppose Norris. William Allen White, sage of Emporia, protested the stupidity of trying to kill off the one man who gave the Republican party its aura of righteousness. The Ku Klux Klan and the Anti-Saloon League opposed Norris, but their efforts were nullified by labor's support.

While the enemies of Norris were bestirring themselves early in 1930, Hoover named Charles Evans Hughes as chief justice to succeed William Howard Taft. Norris was but one of twenty-six senators who opposed confirmation. When Edward T. Sanford died in March 1930, the President named John J. Parker, a North Carolina circuit judge, to replace him. Organized labor opposed Parker because he had in 1927 upheld an injunction that favored the yellow-dog contract. Norris, Borah, and Robert F. Wagner were among those who narrowly succeeded in defeating the Parker nomination.

The Republican Old Guard was grooming another George W. Norris to confuse the voters in the 1930 Nebraska primary. If two candidates by that name entered, neither could possibly be nominated because there would be no way to distinguish between votes for the senator and those for the grocery store manager from Broken Bow. The plot fizzled when a judge ruled that the decoy had filed his entry too late. Then came the fun to see who was back of the plot. Senator Gerald P. Nye conducted the investigation and concluded it after Norris had won overwhelmingly against Hitchcock in the November contest. The plot's trail led to executive director Robert H. Lucas.[39] The clumsiness of the plotters made them the laughing stock of the country.

The Republicans who went down to defeat in the primaries to the sound of apple munching in some instances blamed their failure on being too closely identified with Hoover. Friends of Wisconsin's Governor Walter J. Kohler thus explained Philip La Follette's primary victory. Even more serious was the support of Democrats provided by Republican schismatics. Gifford Pinchot's nomination in Pennsylvania caused a split in the Philadelphia machine, and its boss, William S. Vare, announced his support of the Democratic gubernatorial nominee. He was followed by William W. Atterbury, president of the Pennsylvania Railroad and member of the Republican National Committee. Almost the entire Republican machine in Philadelphia, together with leaders of industry and banking, ganged up on their party's 'radical' nominee. Support for Theodore Roosevelt in 1912 was not popular in 1930. More important was the fact that Pinchot was not a member of the finance-industry-politics alliance that preyed on the state of Pennsylvania.[40]

Although the Republicans used large sums of money to support candidates in key fights, the party received little dynamic leadership from President Hoover. With the elections less than a month away, Hoover strolled onto the jousting field. To bankers at Cleveland he reiterated his faith in American economic progress and counseled courage and optimism. To American Legionnaires at Boston he urged restraint in demands on the Treasury and praised the Republican foreign policy. To the A.F. of L. at Boston he cited increased public and private expenditures for construction and praised the record of co-operation between capital and labor. And in South Carolina he played the familiar record praising the American System.[41] There was little enthusiasm among his audiences.

Franklin D. Roosevelt, in accepting renomination as governor of New York, really opened his campaign for the Democratic presidential nomination in 1932. Going out of his way, he attacked the national Republican leadership. Hoover boldly accepted the challenge and sent Henry L. Stimson, Patrick J. Hurley, Ogden L. Mills, and F. Trubee Davison into battle. When these champions failed in their forays, Roosevelt's prestige mounted and the issue was joined for 1932.[42]

As political analysts followed the results of primaries, many were more interested in the wetness or dryness of a candidate than in any other attitude. A review of newspaper and periodical literature gives the impression that journalists were inclined to be anti-Prohibition. Their preoccupation with the wet-dry issue was not artificial—it was the big battle in 1930. After all, the Farm Board still had its supporters, the veterans had not yet made their greatest demands, Communists were leading hunger marches and were recognized as a nuisance rather than a menace, and a return of prosperity might eliminate enough unemployment to solve the relief problem. Economic issues were important in 1930; but no one economic issue, nor all of the economic issues combined, could arouse the emotional response called forth by the contest over Prohibition.

The prospect that the Seventy-second Congress, to be elected on

4 November, would kill Prohibition was of more interest to the rank and file of voters than the impending Republican loss of control. Republican candidates who dared express a wet preference were out of step with the President's dryness. Democrats could be what they wanted as local politics might demand. Some people turned from news of their own campaigns to read with wonder how a man named Hitler had catapulted his Fascist party into second place in Germany. Still more people were wondering what the National Law Enforcement Commission would have to say about Prohibition, or what success might be achieved by the Association against the Eighteenth Amendment.

The election on 4 November 1930 was practically a dead heat between elephant and donkey. After final counts had been made, Republicans and Democrats each had 217 seats in the House of the Seventy-second Congress, with a lone Farmer-Labor holding the balance of power; in the Senate would be 48 Republicans, 47 Democrats, and one Farmer-Labor. Jouett Shouse led prominent Democratic leaders on 6 November to pledge co-operation with the President 'in every measure that conduces to the welfare of the country.'[43] Barring a special session, the Seventy-second would not meet until December 1931. In the meantime the balance was due to change as death removed many of the representatives. Actually, 13 elected members of the Seventy-second died before Congress met. Among them was Ohio's Nicholas Longworth.

Drys shuddered when such Democratic wets as James Hamilton Lewis of Illinois, Marcus A. Coolidge of Massachusetts, and Robert J. Bulkley of Ohio defeated apparently well-entrenched politicians. Nevertheless, there would be an overwhelming majority for the dry phalanx in each house of Congress. Thomas (Tom-Tom) Heflin fell in Alabama; Huey P. Long promoted himself to the Senate from Louisiana's gubernatorial mansion; Dean Wilbur L. Cross of Yale frightened Puritan ghosts by becoming governor of Connecticut.[44]

Scar tissue was slow in covering political wounds suffered in 1930. The President enjoyed the 'high distinction paid to Democratic Party publicity' by the Washington Gridiron Club on 13 December 1930: 'I would not myself be so partisan as to have referred to it as a great factory of synthetic myth and legend. . . . The Democratic Party has a history of notable accomplishments in campaign strategy and gangster tactics of this sort, and it would appear from a long-view study of the results that it is an admirable method of retaining their position in opposition.' Hoover noted what he thought to be fear of what the Seventy-second Congress might do: 'It is an extraordinary thing in the history of the United States that the whole Nation should shudder with apprehension and fear at the possibility of an extra session of its great legislative body.' [45]

The best one can say about this wild exaggeration is that it was pardonable hyperbole. Hoover was frankly serving notice that he would get along without Congress just as long as possible. Hoover promised presidential co-operation to the Democratic Senate leader, but Congress would be hard to control: 'He and the country will, I am sure, expect me, in the performance of my obligations, to resist with vigor visionary schemes which would expend billions, result in increased taxes and which, in the meantime, fill the country with fear and apprehension that daily intensify this depression.' The lame-duck Seventy-first Congress would meet for its third session; but for the Seventy-second there would be no special session—that, at least, the President could prevent. And that, too, became a major objective of Republican leadership. Representative Bertrand Snell promised that Norris could have his way on Muscle Shoals and the lame-duck amendment if only the Progressives would not hold up routine business and thus force a special session of the Seventy-second Congress.[46] Republicans were not going to allow Democrats to enjoy the fruits of victory any sooner than necessary.

4. *From Phase One to Phase Two*

When the Seventy-first Congress convened for its short session on 2 December 1930, the President could say that the major causes of continued depression lay outside the United States, that depressions cannot be cured by laws or executive action. Mr. Hoover's confidence was based on unprecedented measures to relieve distress, expand public works, support farm prices, provide drought relief, and reduce expenses.[47]

There were too many minus signs on the ledger to support the President's official optimism. Lower wholesale prices, lower production, lower stock prices—in fact, almost everything was lower except the numbers of unemployed, bankruptcies, bank suspensions, and demands for relief. The Bank of United States, a state bank in New

York City, closed its door on 11 December 1930, tying up $180 million in deposits and causing fear for other large banks. Poorly informed Europeans confused this bank with the Federal Reserve Bank of New York.[48] At the year's end there were more than 5.5 million unemployed. A.F. of L. estimates were 2 million larger.

Some economic prophets were optimistic in spite of unfavorable statistics. Public and private construction under way amounted to more than $8 billion, representing a depression increase of $3 billion or more stimulated by Hoover's policies. At the end of 1930, the federal government had committed itself to spend more than $1.5 billion to relieve the depression, most of which was to go into construction work. But the rate of new building was decreasing rapidly because long-range plans had not been prepared.[49]

After the Republican disaster in the 1930 campaign, John N. Garner returned to the tax 'scandal' charge he had made in March. His evidence was devastating and should be remembered in connection with later publicity of Reconstruction Finance Corporation loans. Contributors of large sums to the Republican coffer had received an aggregate of at least $100 million in tax favors. Seventeen of these beneficiaries had given $10,000 each. Their names were well known to Robert Hendry Lucas, for it was Lucas who had handled the business while he was a commissioner in the Bureau of Internal Revenue. Mellon and his associates profited greatly from Secretary Mellon's generous policy.[50]

When Democrats organized the House in December 1931, numerous investigations were launched into other matters, and somehow they never did get around to carrying out Garner's threat to 'look into Uncle Andy's books.' However, Wright Patman of Texas had sought Mellon's impeachment for violation of an old statute against active participation in business. The House Judiciary Committee was considering these charges in February 1932 when Hoover decided that he should 'call upon one of our wisest and most experienced public servants' to serve his country abroad.[51] So Mellon was hustled off to London, the brilliant Ogden L. Mills, who had done most of the work since 1927, became Secretary of the Treasury in name as well as in fact, and refunds continued but on a vastly diminished scale. If President Hoover saw anything wrong in this unsavory business of tax refunds and abatements, his reprimands were so gentle as to be inaudible.

As the new year 1931 opened, senatorial opposition to railway consolidation promised failure for one of the President's pet proposals. Congressional attacks on Hoover's relief policies continued, and the President replied by repeating his story of what was being done and reiterating his insistence on local responsibility, with the federal government standing back ready to lend a hand only when states and municipalities no longer could handle the problem. The Congress pushed through a bill to permit veterans to borrow up to 50 per cent of the face value of their bonus certificates. Hoover argued in his veto message of 26 February 1931 that 'we cannot further the restoration of prosperity by borrowing from some of our people, pledging the credit of all the people, to loan to some of our people who are not in need of the money.' If the bonus could promote return to prosperity, then 'we should make government loans to the whole people.'[52] Congress promptly repassed the bill by large majorities.

As Phase One closed and merged imperceptibly into Phase Two, how did the record look? To Arthur Krock, whose analysis of Hoover's first two years is by far the best in print, the record was not very good. Sold to the public as a miracle man, the President had no miracles to unveil. The Seventy-first Congress had done well enough in passing laws requested by the President, but its failures in dealing with railways, the tariff, Prohibition, and immigration were serious. The bonus legislation, a big blunder, was not a presidential error; for the tariff and the Farm Board, Hoover must share responsibility.

On a numerical basis the total of the President's achievements, with Congress and with the social problems of American life, is far greater than the number of his failures. But his failures are conspicuous. Although he will most certainly be renominated, Mr. Hoover thus far has failed as a party leader. He has failed as an economist, although thus far he has had no chance to succeed. He has failed as a business leader because of his fatal economic inheritance. He has failed as a personality because of awkwardness of manner and speech and lack of mass magnetism. In his party there is no passionate loyalty for him such as animated the group which went to Kansas City bent upon his nomination in 1928. In the country, always unfair to a President who is in office when times are hard, there is steady magnifying of his shortcomings.[53]

Failure or not, the President continued his struggle, confident that the measures he had taken would at least halt the downward trend. Instead of improving, economic conditions continued to grow worse and the President could not conceal his worry. Stimson noted in his diary that a feeling of gloom ran through the whole administration, and Hoover had no time for good cheer.[54]

Prominent in Hoover's philosophy was the conviction that free enterprise, socially conscious individualism, and benign government, working within the framework of the fundamental law, eventually would solve all problems. When, as the leader of benign government, he had taken the permissible measures to reactivate free enterprise and socially conscious individualism, he fully expected that the economic order would right itself. When it did not there was only one place to look for the reason—abroad. The domestic system was correct; the remaining difficulty must lie with malign influences coming from abroad.[55]

Whether the prime cause lay abroad is immaterial because there is no 'abroad' in finance. Our banking structure, our entire credit system was inextricably linked with Europe and Latin America through the war debts, short-term and long-term credits, bond issues, and a veritable labyrinth of less obvious economic ties. The depression lay upon the European world, and the United States was an integral part of that world regardless of official reluctance to admit it. Two of President Hoover's finest achievements were his vigorous actions to meet the crises in international and domestic finance.

CHAPTER X

RESCUE FOR THE MONEY CHANGERS

1. *Moratorium*

Throughout Hoover's Administration, Europe passed from one economic crisis to another. The causes, of course, were closely connected with the terrible destruction wrought by the World War. Every economic crisis was also a political crisis, and each had international repercussions. The failure of Austria's largest bank, the Credit-Anstalt in May 1931, precipitated a general panic in central Europe that reached catastrophic proportions in June.

People on our side of the Atlantic were hopefully studying charts and indexes, looking for indications that the depression was being whipped, trying to find some justification for the President's assurance that the worst of the storm had passed a year earlier. Some signs were encouraging in March 1931 but they were not impressive, even to people eager to believe in reasons for confidence. There was no general knowledge that short-term international debts were more than $10 billion and that $6 billion of this indebtedness would be liquidated in 1931. Nor was there any indication that soon there would be a flight from the gold standard, and that a whole galaxy of economic devices would be tried as each nation attempted vainly to go it alone.

People who put great stock in a balanced budget were shocked when first installments on 1930 income taxes were off about 40 per cent from the previous year. Appropriations for fiscal 1932 were $518 million more than for 1931 and declining revenues promised a billion dollar deficit. To add more gloom, the Secretary of Commerce admitted in April that there had been 6 million unemployed in January, compared with the President's figure of 2.5 million. Many employers reported impending wage reductions. Workers' incomes had fallen off by $10 billion in 1930 and were to be reduced even more.[1]

Faced with conflicting economic data, President Hoover was cheerfully pessimistic as he put up a bold front that bespoke a confidence he did not feel. In his address to the Gridiron Club of Washington on 27 April 1931 the President referred to 'this depression' and refused to offer prophecies. Two months later he was more bold and felt that the auguries were favorable: 'We will prevent any unnecessary distress in the United States, and by the activities and courage of the American people we will recover from the depression.'[2] But note that the President talked of depression. He was in the second phase period, the months of waiting for the economic order to correct itself during the spring and summer of 1931. He knew that Europe was in serious trouble, as all the sins of postwar militarism, extravagance, market dislocations, unbalanced budgets, overproduction, cartelization, excessive foreign loans, and speculation came home with a rush like a flock of teal swooping in for a night's rest.[3]

Unfriendly critics spread the word that French policies were a primary cause of the central European economic collapse. An Austro-German customs union was proposed on 21 March 1931. French and British protests were prompt and vigorous. At the time this union was being discussed, French bankers held some $300 million in German and Austrian short-term securities. The French demanded payment. Germany and Austria both were insolvent. Their failure to obtain loans to meet French demands and the subsequent withdrawal of French funds helped to force the Credit-Anstalt into bankruptcy in May.[4]

German economic distress was caused by war losses and by postwar reparations and extravagance. During the four-year conflict, Germany lost some $3 billion in foreign investment, exhausted a large proportion of accumulated capital goods, and drew heavily upon natural resources. Immediately after the war, Germany lost another $6 billion in cash and goods in reparations. Under the Dawes Plan (1924–9) Germany paid $1,904 million in reparations—borrowed abroad at interest rates of 7 per cent to 10 per cent. The approaching economic crisis, including diversion of funds to stock exchange gambling, brought a great decline in funds available for lending to Germany. The Young Plan of 1929 then reduced payments, but Germany found it impossible to meet even the revised schedule. By September 1930 the Reich owed $2,510 million in short-term credits and $2,213 million in long-term credits; some $1,428 million of foreign capital was invested in German business and real estate. Foreign bankers had little confidence in German stability. There were the fear of French intervention, the growth of Nazi and Communist

strength, and the proposal of a customs union with Austria to undermine confidence. The French then began to withdraw short-term
credits, forcing a drain on German and Austrian gold supplies.[5]

Heinrich Bruening, the German Chancellor, visited London in
June 1931 but obtained no aid; German bankers also failed to get
help in Paris. Foreign capital began to flow swiftly out of Germany
until some $238 million in gold was lost by mid-July. A repetition
of the 1923 inflationary debacle was imminent and more gold was
withdrawn by hoarding. A credit of $100 million on 15 June, ex-
tended by the World Bank at Basle and by London, New York, and
Paris banks, helped for the time being.

Americans, of course, were well aware of the long drive to link war
debts with reparations. Most of us were by no means willing to accept
the thesis that debts, reparations, and our tariff policy were prime
causes of international economic distress. But these issues figured
prominently in the discussions of 800 delegates from 35 nations who
met in Washington on 4–9 May 1931 as the sixth congress of the
International Chamber of Commerce. When President Hoover addressed the conference on its first day, he ignored the major issues
and lectured the delegates on the need for arms reduction.[6]

This conference started directly after the White House had
avoided a crisis in protocol arising from a royal visit. The cause of
the difficulty had been a frank, wholesome lad who had gone around
the White House grounds snapping pictures with a box camera.

A late winter blizzard had swept across southeastern Colorado at
the end of March and caused the driver of a school bus to run off
the road. Twenty children were trapped. While the driver went out
into the blizzard to die in search of aid, thirteen-year old Bryan
Untiedt took charge. Despite his efforts, which included giving them
nearly all of his own clothes, some of the children died of exposure.
Resting later in a Lamar hospital, Bryan was happy to learn that his
hands and feet would be saved—and he had been invited to visit the
President. In Washington the White House staff was perturbed.
Bryan would arrive on 30 April and on that same day, with pomp
and proper protocol, Siam's King Prajadipok and his queen would
make a visit of state.

There were no complications. The royal couple's welcome was
proper and brief. Bryan, scheduled to stay overnight, completely
captivated the President and Mrs. Hoover. After four days they said
good-by to their young guest. Untroubled by gold crises and crash-

ing banks, Byran Untiedt toted his new luggage, heavy with gifts, back to Colorado and left lighter hearts behind him.[7]

President Hoover had been watching the European situation closely. He knew that European conditions were seriously affecting American business by depressing securities and commodities prices. His thinking led to the moratorium idea, which apparently emerged from conferences with Frederic M. Sackett, his ambassador to Germany, on 6 May. Hoover then summoned officials to provide an accurate review of European economic conditions. According to another version, Owen D. Young worked out the details of the plan which Stimson urged upon Hoover. The President, however, needed a month's prodding by Dawes, Mellon, Morrow, and several other bankers. Whatever the origin of the idea, the President on 5 June 1931 suggested to some of his cabinet that inter-governmental debts should be put into cold storage for a year. During the next two weeks he discussed the proposal with various prominent people but hesitated to take action that might fail.[8]

Hoover took the European problem with him on a crowded trip into the Middle West. He addressed the Indiana Republican Editorial Association at Indianapolis, dedicated the Harding Memorial at Marion, Ohio, dedicated the remodeled Lincoln tomb at Springfield, Illinois, and spoke briefly to a joint session of the Illinois legislature. But his major concern, and the principal topic of conversation with politicians who boarded his train, was the European crisis. Hurrying back to Washington, Hoover received an appeal from President Hindenburg to do something to save Europe. He had already consulted, personally and by telephone, with leaders of both parties in Congress. The famous moratorium announcement came on 20 June: all payments on intergovernmental debts were to be suspended for one year. Except for French resentment, immediate reactions to the moratorium were favorable. Panic was averted, prices increased, and trade picked up. The danger of economic collapse and domestic revolution, however, was still present. Except for William Randolph Hearst, few if any important critics of the moratorium called attention to the well-concealed fact that only public debts were affected. Since the moratorium actually became cancellation of the public debts, it was a great boon to holders of private debts. In the United States, there was another wave of intense interest in the whole debts-reparations question and a growing conviction that the war debts never would be paid.[9]

A considerable amount of international bickering followed the Hoover proposal, but no nation dared to refuse its support. British, Scandinavian, Dutch, Swiss, and American bankers held some $4 billion of German securities, and default would ruin many a bank. The French cure was for the United States, France, and England to take equal parts of a $500 million loan to Germany, a loan that would be used to pay Germany's current debts without reducing the actual debt at all. It was a proposal to transfer the bag from private bankers to the American taxpayer, who already was juggling a fine collection of bags. President Hoover had little difficulty in penetrating this scheme to siphon off more American and British money. He insisted that a creditors' meeting should be held in London to consider the problem. This meeting, the London Financial Conference, which opened on 20 July, accepted Hoover's 'Standstill' proposal that short-term bills would not be presented for payment until after February 1932. It was also agreed to renew the $100 million credit for three months and to set up a committee to study Germany's needs.[10]

2. Cancellation by Default

The London Standstill Agreement eased but did not cure the central European economic crisis. Pierre Laval, who later achieved infamy as a Vichy collaborator, came from France to consult with Hoover in October. Before talking to Laval, the President conferred with Senator Borah, and they agreed that there would be no consideration of debt reduction unless France would move to reduce reparations and settle the Polish Corridor issue.

Laval and Hoover conferred at various meetings with all the confidence of 'two crap shooters who each sit down with loaded dice.'[11] They discussed disarmament, German reparations, and the international gold standard. Laval wanted a guaranty of French security. Hoover assured him that the United States would guaranty no nation's security, that real security lay in collective action. Laval suggested an international conference to consider the matter of war debts and reparations. He wanted a promise that the United States would scale down French debts in exchange for a French reduction of reparations. This request was somewhat brazen in view of the reduction from $4,230 million to $1,680 million by the Mellon-Berenger Agreement ratified in July 1929, an agreement which canceled all but the post-Armistice debt. What France owed was for reconstruction and other purposes.[12] With these facts in mind, Hoover refused to link the two matters.

All of the European countries that received reparations payments from Germany insisted that war debts and reparations were inseparable. If Germany paid them, they could pay part of the receipts to the United States; but they could not pay on any other basis. Hoover refused to admit that the debts and reparations were connected; the debt agreements had been made on the basis of each country's ability to pay, not on Germany's ability to pay reparations. And at that very time, when Laval was urging a reduction, French deposits in American banks were about $600 million, enough to meet payments for several years. Laval, of course, was trying to escape from a financial obligation, just as other debtors, including France, escaped by default.[13]

The Hoover-Laval discussions raised suspicions in many minds that some secret agreement had been made. A joint communiqué stated that an agreement on intergovernmental debts 'may be necessary covering the period of the business depression,' and that Europe should take the initiative. Europeans took this statement to mean that the United States would reconsider war debts.[14] But there was no secret agreement. The anguished cries were those of Democratic propagandists who mixed truth and fiction with such abandon that not even they could separate one from the other.

The moratorium on intergovernmental debts was a *fait accompli* when Hoover on 10 December asked Congress to give it its legislative blessing. Approval of the arrangement was a foregone conclusion, but sanction did not come before many congressmen delivered remarks for the record. Several members did not like the arrangement that granted a moratorium to foreign governments while American citizens were being forced into bankruptcy. Deferment quite properly was regarded as a prelude to default and unilateral cancellation, and feeling was widespread that the United States was being played for a sucker. During the debate, destined to be the congressional farewell to the World War debts question, Senator Hiram Johnson argued most strongly against the moratorium. Johnson introduced the resolution which was aimed at investigating the sale of foreign bonds and securities in order to determine whether international bankers were exerting pressure for cancellation so as to protect private loans.[15] The Senate adopted the resolution on

10 December, and hearings began on 18 December, the day when the House approved the moratorium.

Argument in the House was rancorous, even though members had little choice. Oregon's Willis C. Hawley defended Hoover's action and denied any link between debts and reparations. Harold McGugin, a Kansas Republican, admitted that the debts would never be paid, excoriated international bankers, and called for bipartisan support of Hoover's financial program lest industry and finance be reduced to agriculture's level! Democratic opponents denied any need for the moratorium and echoed charges that it was a plot by international bankers to save themselves. Nevertheless, the House approved the resolution by 318 to 100, and the Senate added its consent on 22 December by the nonpartisan majority of 69 to 12.[16]

While Congress was debating approval of the moratorium, the Young Plan Advisory Committee was concluding its work. Its report was very discouraging; the German currency system was in peril, unemployment had increased dangerously in Germany, agriculture was in serious trouble, and tax collections had decreased alarmingly. The Committee concluded that Germany probably would not be able to meet the deadline date of 1932 for the conditional annuity. A general 'adjustment of all intergovernmental debts' was necessary for 'economic stability and real peace.'[17] The Germans on 9 January 1932 agreed that they could not pay.

In general, Americans made little attempt to stay abreast of Europe's desperate moves to restore financial order. They viewed the moratorium as a magnificent gesture which would provide the debtors with time to discover how to meet their obligations. In contrast the European view on the reparations-debts question became more bitter. Germans were insistent that no more political impositions should be paid; the French saw an end to reparations if the moratorium continued, and feared that the end would come before the United States could be persuaded to cancel the war debts; the British believed that 'in demanding her full pound of flesh the United States was wounding herself, preventing world economic revival, and committing a harsh moral injustice.'[18]

The result of the Europeans' deliberation was that Germany's creditors were determined to join war debts with reparations when they met at Lausanne on 16 June 1932 to consider revision of the Young Plan. Ramsay MacDonald and Edouard Herriot were chief architects of the agreement, signed on 9 July 1932, which canceled

German reparations and reduced other obligations by 90 per cent. The agreement hinged on the expectation that the United States would reduce the debt payments. However, there was no change in American policy. Hoover believed that the debtors could pay. Stimson, who held the opposing view, unsuccessfully tried to persuade Hoover to support cancellation in an effort to face the economic facts of international life. Stimson held that the debts had been incurred in a common struggle, they could not be repaid in view of American tariff policy, and any attempt to force payment would merely serve to compound international bitterness.[19]

The moratorium certainly helped Europe temporarily. It led Hoover to believe that he had averted a catastrophe by his bold action. There is no reason to suppose that he knew there would be almost no war debts payments after 15 December 1932. Hoover fully expected that at least partial payments would be continued. The President wanted to revive the Foreign Debt Funding Commission, for the obvious purpose of considering further reduction of the debts, but Congress was opposed. After the 1932 election, Governor Roosevelt refused to join the President in this proposal. Opposition to further payment of war debts produced mob action in France and the formal resolution by the Chamber of Deputies to default. Press reports from European and Latin American countries revealed a growing conviction that further payment was outrageous and that the United States was guilty of crass materialism in demanding payment. It was no surprise when Belgium, France, Hungary, Poland, Jugoslavia, and Estonia defaulted on 15 December. Great Britain and five others paid, most of them for the last time.[20] So ended the great attempt to secure equitable liquidation of war debts.

3. *Phase Three and the R.F.C.*

At the same time that he was establishing the moratorium to deal with the foreign monetary crisis, President Hoover was acting to keep the domestic financial structure from complete collapse. Investors in foreign and domestic bonds suffered not only from the general strangulation of business, but also from an epidemic of defaults, particularly in Latin America and Europe. By the end of 1933, the interest on some $2,493,600,000 of dollar loans was in default, and an incomplete tally showed that more than $6 billion of domestic industrial, public utility, and real estate bonds were in default in the United States.[21] These defaults meant some readjustments within the country, but they did not necessarily affect the sum total of national wealth seriously. During this readjustment, domestic financial institutions were subjected to additional strain.

The Bank of England proved that it was no Gibraltar when French depositors began to withdraw gold from British banks. During August large American and French credits held off catastrophe for a few weeks; but the Old Lady could not stand the strain, even with this $250 million transfusion. England went off the gold standard on 21 September 1931. There were repercussions throughout the world. Prices again rushed to a new bottom in the United States. Our banks became weaker, there were 298 bank suspensions in September, and foreigners increased gold withdrawals. We were in the transition to Hoover's Phase Three of the depression, a phase already reached when Eugene Meyer warned in December that 'the political and financial disaster in Europe is a fundamentally important factor in our country, entirely apart from the question of investments . . . or bank loans . . . or reparations or intergovernmental relations.' [22]

In the first week of October, the President called in bankers, insurance men, and members of Congress to let them know how serious financial conditions had become. One year earlier he had praised 'the soundness of the credit system [and] the capacity of our bankers in emergency.' The reluctant bankers finally agreed under the President's prodding to set up a $500 million National Credit Corporation, also called the National Credit Association, to take up paper ineligible for rediscount with the Federal Reserve Banks.[23]

The important fact to remember is that in this financial crisis the banking fraternity revealed no ingenuity, no leadership, no collective genius. Everything they did collectively was the result of presidential leadership. The new agency so reluctantly organized, held its first meeting of directors on 17 October 1931—perhaps to forestall a special session of Congress—and was ready to make loans three weeks later. Although there was skepticism in many quarters, most commentators were hopeful that this co-operative effort would impart new strength to the banking structure and instill new confidence in worried depositors. Mortimer M. Buckner, president of the New York Clearing House Association and chairman of the New York Trust Company, was president of the Corporation. Bankers generally, and the public as well, believed that the N.C.C. would last only until Congress could create an agency to save the banks. The N.C.C. made loans over a period of about three months. In all, 575 banks borrowed $153 million, 17 of which had suspended operations.[24] The National Credit Corporation relieved the banking crisis as an aspirin relieves the pain of a smashed finger.

During the first week in November 1931, President Hoover told newsmen that he was happy. His joy proceeded from only the most modest of economic improvements. A few million dollars had returned to banks; suspensions were averaging only seven daily instead of the former twenty-five. Wheat, which had been less than 44 cents per bushel at Chicago on 5 October, had risen to about 61 cents; cotton had soared like a wingless dinosaur up to $6 more per bale; and other timid increases could be found. Actually, the economic headache was getting worse. Business failures, unemployment, hoarding, and gold withdrawals increased markedly.[25]

The President might have found at least a chuckle in the suggestion of Lloyd Raymond Smith, Milwaukee industrialist who was also a member of his Committee on Unemployment Relief. Among other equally brilliant ideas, Smith fathered the suggestion that every family should 'buy $79 worth of merchandise over normal needs for three months.' As the National Credit Corporation prepared for business, one even higher in the economic pecking order revealed similar wisdom when asked how to prevent depressions. Albert Henry Wiggin of Chase National Bank could only suggest that the Sherman Act should be liberalized.[26] And in October there were 512 bank suspensions.

Still the President could take pleasure in little things. Wheat rose to 67 cents by the end of November, steel operations increased from 29 per cent to 30 per cent of capacity, and carloadings increased slightly. Automobile production, however, was less than one-half that of a year earlier. Not even the prospect of Santa Claus ringing bells on windy streets could start a buying boom. The economy skidded in December and Hoover once more had Congress on his hands. It was this Congress which, in creating the Reconstruction Finance Corporation, started the agency that deserves credit for the recovery in Hoover's Phase Three. Had the National Credit Corporation been anything but a dismal failure, the R.F.C. probably would not have been created when Hoover was President.

In casting about for a way to put government into business as the depression deepened, some rugged individualists remembered the

War Finance Corporation, which had been effective during and after the World War. The W.F.C., created in April 1918, was designed to finance enterprises essential to the war effort. Congress revised the agency in March 1919 to enable it to make loans to finance foreign trade and thus established a precedent for the Export-Import Bank begun by the New Deal. Carter Glass of Virginia was chairman of the W.F.C., Eugene Meyer, Jr. was its managing director, and Louis B. Wehle was general counsel. After successfully promoting foreign trade for more than a year, the agency's functions were practically ended by David F. Houston, who succeeded Glass as Secretary of the Treasury in May 1920. From August 1921 to its liquidation in 1925, the W.F.C. financed agricultural co-operatives, loaned to country banks, and aided greatly in preventing a serious postwar depression.

Ten years after he left the agency, Louis Wehle suggested to Eugene Meyer that a similar institution would be handy in the depression. Meyer then asked Walter Wyatt, general counsel of the Federal Reserve Board, to draft a bill to create such a corporation. 'Ike' Hoover believed that the R.F.C. was concocted by Meyer and Ogden Mills, 'whose policies have directed all attempts to alleviate the depression,' an opinion that merely reflects White House gossip. President Hoover, of course, was familiar with the old W.F.C. and had thought of creating a similar organization before he received Wyatt's draft bill. Melvin Traylor had suggested it in September 1931, and Hoover had promised in October to use such an agency if needed.[27]

Hoover hoped that the National Credit Association would be strong enough to meet the banking crisis. Its creation was an example of his philosophy of individualism: government would help citizens to help themselves. But the crisis was too serious. Eugene Meyer and Ogden L. Mills persuaded him that the time had come for direct federal action in banking, that a federal agency would restore confidence. Even Mills, upon whom Hoover depended so much and who generally spoke for the President before congressional committees, underestimated the need when he testified:

I do not figure this corporation as one that is going to be called upon immediately to lend vast sums of money, in order to put the whole credit structure of the United States on its feet. I think that the credit structure, generally speaking, is sound; but it is the loss of confidence to-day which is resulting in the very deflating movement, and fear plays a very large part in it.[28]

President Hoover's willingness to undertake the drastic measures needed for recovery was definitely limited by an apparently infrangible philosophy. None of his ideals must be violated. Federal acts must fit in a scheme of things that Hoover wanted to exist, although too often the ideals were not facts. The President, however, could be flexible to a certain degree. One of his most cherished principles was that government must not compete with citizens in economic activities. Loaning money is an economic activity carried on by private enterprise; government, therefore, should not loan money. The bankers proved that they could not or would not loan enough money to prevent a general financial collapse. In this situation the President was willing for the federal government to perform the loaning function for a limited time; but he would not agree to what some bankers wanted, which was an agency that would buy bank stock and thereby provide banks with new capital. The result would have been a tremendous encroachment on private enterprise.

What Hoover contemplated in his message of 8 December 1931 was 'an emergency Reconstruction Corporation' primarily to restore confidence, and he thought that it would not be needed for more than two years. After considerable senatorial opposition, Congress passed the bill with unusual dispatch and the President approved it on 22 January 1932. The new Reconstruction Finance Corporation began to function on 2 February. Here was an agency, Hoover said, that would shore up credit, banking, and the railways, stop deflation, and increase employment. It was not intended to bolster the big industries and the big banks, institutions well able to take care of themselves. These were brave words, but many big banks were not able to take care of themselves and many people believed that the primary aim of the R.F.C. was to prevent bank failures.[29]

4. *Record of the R.F.C.*

The newly created agency received power to loan to a large number of corporations. Its resources were available to 'any bank, savings bank, trust company, building and loan association, insurance company, mortgage loan company, credit union, Federal land bank, joint-stock land bank, Federal intermediate credit bank, agricultural credit corporation, livestock credit corporation . . .' Banks closed or in the process of liquidation could borrow, but not more than $200 million of the original R.F.C. appropriation could be used for this purpose. Railroads could borrow with approval of the Interstate Commerce Commission. Thus began an institution which was to use about $10.5 billion in fighting the depression, although its original resources were only $2 billion. So well was the corporation managed—primarily by Jesse H. Jones, according to Jesse H. Jones—that it recovered all of its original stake and made a substantial profit for the Treasury.[30] At the very time that spokesmen of big business were shouting 'Keep the Government Out of Business!' the R.F.C. loans were keeping many of them in business. And, at least until 1945, there was little or no fraud, although no one could honestly deny that there had been favoritism.

Self-appointed guardians of the Treasury watched eagerly for signs of tenderness toward big business. There was a peculiar feeling that R.F.C. loans should not be made for the purpose of enabling a corporation to repay a loan to a Wall Street giant. President Hoover was very sensitive to criticism of loans to wealthy persons and corporations. In the presidential campaign of 1952, he defended the R.F.C. of twenty years earlier: 'Far from "bailing out" the rich, as one orator says, 90 per cent of the loans under Republican Administration went to saving building and loan associations, savings banks, insurance companies, small country banks and farmers' loan associations. These were not the institutions of the rich. They represented the small savings of the people.'[31] Still smarting from the 1932 defeat, Hoover had never stopped campaigning.

There is considerable truth in this description of how the R.F.C. operated, but it is far from being the whole truth. There is a very big difference between 90 per cent of the loans and 90 per cent of the money loaned. Actually, of course, the R.F.C. did begin its work by loaning to many small banks; but of the first $61 million loaned to 255 banks, $41 million went to three banks and $15 million of that went to the Bank of America; and shortly thereafter $90 million was loaned to one bank. Of the first $264 million loaned to railroads, $156 million went to the Van Sweringen, Morgan and Pennsylvania groups.[32]

What really happened when Hoover was President is a matter of record and not subject to political argument. Using Hoover's basis of comparison, 70.8 per cent of the authorizations to banks and trust companies to 31 March 1933 were made to institutions in places under 5,000 in population; 92.6 per cent of the authorizations were to institutions in places under 100,000 in population. This is very impressive when one is talking about saving the little fellow, assuming that the little fellow lives in the smaller urban communities, an assumption that is obviously false. It becomes less impressive when one observes that this 92.6 per cent represented only 46.5 per cent of the total amount authorized. In other words, 7.4 per cent of the borrowers received 53.5 per cent of the money loaned.[33] Nor should it be forgotten that loans to small financial institutions generally went through them to the big-city banks. Thus, R.F.C. funds generally filtered into the large centers; the R.F.C., instead of the large banks, became the creditor. Under Republican administration, most of the loans went to small institutions but most of the money went to big institutions.

Through clearing house associations and deposits in metropolitan banks, financial institutions in large areas were closely tied to one another. Difficulties in one large bank quickly affected the solvency of others, especially when 'smart money' was withdrawn for hoarding or for deposit elsewhere. Even Cincinnati banks, which had been more conservative in their loaning policies than many others, were compelled to limit withdrawals. Failure of one or two large banks in a major center like Chicago would have serious results in several states, so the R.F.C. was fully justified in aiding its first president, General Charles Gates Dawes.

When the banking crisis deepened in mid-1932, General Dawes resigned from the R.F.C. to resume charge of Chicago's Central Republic National Bank and Trust Company. The Insull crash, collapse of the real estate market, closing of many suburban banks, and heavy runs on Loop banks had created a tense situation in Chicago, on the eve of the Democratic National Convention, almost duplicating the near panic of a year earlier when Chicago's big five saved the Middle West banking structure. Runs on the Central Republic, Hoover suggests, were inspired by Communists; but Communists had not caused Chicago banks to advance $150 million for Samuel Insull's mad whirl into the eye of a financial hurricane. Faced with a complete drain of cash, Dawes decided to close his bank; but Jesse Jones of the R.F.C., Hoover, and other officials feared that such a course might well have a snowballing effect that could close all of the nation's banks. The result was a loan of $92 million, which was almost as much as the bank's total deposits.³⁴

The loan did not end the Central Republic's troubles, and Dawes soon decided to liquidate and start another bank. The bitter denunciation of the R.F.C. and big bankers that resulted from these circumstances was not justified. The R.F.C. recovered all of its loan with about 2 per cent interest, and no institution was deprived of help because of the loan.

The statistical picture of R.F.C. activities from 2 February to 30 June 1932 was so impressive that one wonders what sort of debacle would have ensued without it. In this period, 4,196 different institutions received 5,084 loans for a total of $805,150,006.³⁵

President Hoover vetoed a bill on 11 July 1932 which would have authorized the R.F.C. to make loans 'for any conceivable purpose on any conceivable security to anybody who wants money.' He feared a tremendous centralization of financial power in the federal government would result. He also objected to allowing the states and an untold number of the 16,000 municipalities to 'dump their financial liabilities and problems upon the Federal Government.'³⁶ After elimination of the objectionable blanket loan provision, the President signed a bill on 21 July which extended R.F.C. activities into loans for relief.

The R.F.C. by 31 March 1933 had assisted 7,411 institutions with $1,785,315,120 in loans. Of this amount, railroads borrowed $331,197,888 and banks and trust companies $1,055,060,418. Of the total loans, $418,316,605 had been repaid. In addition to these activities, the R.F.C. loaned money under the Emergency Relief and Construction Act of 21 July 1932. Its actual disbursements under this act were $223,709,778 by 31 March 1933, although it had authorized $496,025,337 for loans and projects. Relief loans disbursed were $201,374,181.³⁷

No one can know what would have happened had a much more vigorous R.F.C. been created as early as 1930. Hoover, indeed, was reluctant to take the original step, and in the first act there was no provision for loans necessary to revive business at the grassroots level. In spite of its heroic activities, the agency did not stop the downward trend of business activity, although it made the descent less agonizing.

President Hoover's principal contribution to recovery was the R.F.C. This agency definitely put the government in business in a very big way. By using the nation's credit to rescue institutions in distress, a long step toward some form of statism or socialism was taken by an administration which viewed such words as just a trifle below communism in their horrendous implications. In asking for and accepting R.F.C. aid, rugged individualists had confessed the emptiness of their own sacred credo. But the R.F.C. was a failure as a device for stopping the depression; it was a palliative that failed to get at basic causes of disequilibrium. In providing emergency resuscitation, the agency succeeded. The glorious opportunity to rebuild the banking structure was recognized by a few observers, but the Republican leadership was unequal to the task.[38]

CHAPTER XI

HOOVER AND THE SEVENTY-SECOND CONGRESS

1. *Skirmishes*

More than two years had passed since Hoover had been inaugurated. Shock waves from the collapse of the ticker-tape empire continued with unabated intensity. There were, indeed, sectors of the economy so moribund that revival appeared hopeless. Already, journalistic historians were laying on with savage sweeps, chiding and scorning the President for his professed optimism. They were so positive, those men like Frederick Lewis Allen! They had no responsibility other than to interpret current events as they saw them, and they poured out their frustrations and exasperations in columns and volumes condemning the President.

Herbert Hoover was approaching his fifty-seventh birthday. Two days before that occasion, on 8 August 1931, Mrs. Hoover christened the *Akron,* then the world's largest airship, by releasing 48 pigeons, which wheeled above the nearly 100,000 spectators who had gathered to witness this American triumph. There was something satisfying to the national ego in being able to beat Germany and Great Britain in creating such a beautiful but vulnerable behemoth of the skies. News that Russians were patiently poking around in the Arctic gathering scientific data caused no worry; we could beat them, too. The Hoovers were together at the White House on 10 August but there was no celebration. Two days later the President entertained at dinner the ten surviving members of Stanford's champion football team of 1894. Hoover had been the treasurer and financial manager for the team coached by Walter Camp.[1]

Such moments of relaxation were all too infrequent as foreign and domestic crises competed for attention. Confusion was growing in foreign and domestic financial circles. Released from its bondage to gold, the pound sterling plunged to successive new lows. World trade suffered from uncertainties created by Japan's war against China. As civilization seemed to be shattering itself to bits, the President increased his efforts to prepare for Congress a program that would enable the United States to stand firmly in the midst of these man-made storms.

There was cause for pessimism. A third depression winter lay upon the land. Local relief resources were being strained and exhausted under the steadily growing need. In New York City, more than 100,000 unemployed registered with Harvey D. Gibson's Emergency Unemployment Relief Committee, which was conducting a drive for funds. White collar workers already were compiling a city directory, an early example of work relief. Governor Roosevelt, by now very much a candidate for the Democratic nomination in 1932, publicly announced his opposition to a dole and endorsed public works as a means of relief. The Gold Dust Corporation, famous to generations for its black Gold Dust Twins on boxes of granulated soap, donated and improved a six-story building in New York to house 2,000 men for the Salvation Army.[2]

While President Hoover was struggling with problems of international finance and worsening domestic depression, Senate committees also were preparing for the opening of Congress. The Committee on Agriculture and Forestry examined the workings of the Federal Farm Board, Hoover's great effort to solve the farm problem; and a subcommittee of the Committee on Manufactures compiled a huge volume of testimony on the question of national economic planning.

Senators not noted as enthusiastic Hoover men conducted the Agricultural Conference and Farm Board Inquiry. Charles L. McNary, Oregon's champion of the equalization fee, George W. Norris of Nebraska, Peter Norbeck of South Dakota, Lynn J. Frazier of North Dakota, and John Thomas of Idaho were less than consistent supporters of the President. Democrats John B. Kendrick of Wyoming, Burton K. Wheeler of Montana, and Oklahoma's Elmer Thomas would go along with their Republican colleagues. The committee had a strong anti-Hoover majority and more than a score of reporters covered its sessions. 'I have not,' Senator McNary admitted, 'attempted to bring those here who are wholly in sympathy with the Farm Board or the marketing act. I have invited anyone to express his opinion who is opposed to the actions of the Farm Board or who desires a repeal of the marketing act.'[3]

The probe revealed little that was not already known. James C. Stone, chairman of the Farm Board, and other officials were candid and defended the Hoover farm relief effort. Heads of the great national farm organizations gave grudging approval but wanted amendments. Co-operatives generally found much to praise, but many commission merchants and brokers agreed with the indignant protest of C. L. Poole, president of the New York Mercantile Exchange: 'We feel that the fundamental principles of the Constitution have been overlooked. . . . We do not feel that it is all right to create discriminatory legislation against one group or in favor of another.'[4]

President Hoover needed no one to read him lectures on the American system, particularly when he was preparing to ask Congress to make a huge appropriation for a gigantic fiscal agency. But Jouett Shouse, anxiously waiting for 1932, commented shortly after hearings on the agricultural situation ended: 'The Farm Board has resulted in the most ghastly fiasco in the country's history. . . . It is unthinkable that Republican ineptness along these lines should be permitted to inflict the country with further failures of that sort and magnitude.'[5] Shouse, of course, did not need to read committee hearings to come to such a conclusion; nor did Republican senators need to conduct an investigation so obviously intended to discredit Hoover's major plan for farm relief.

Demands for economic planning built up to a minor crescendo as the depression continued. The President was well aware of the more obviously socialistic plans championed by leftist writers, combinations of reform measures lumped together in various 'plans,' and proposals of business leaders to eliminate competition under the guise of planning. Senator Robert M. La Follette, Jr. had introduced in the last session of the Seventy-first Congress a bill to establish a national economic council of fifteen members to represent industry, finance, agriculture, transportation, and labor. The council's duties would be to investigate economic conditions and propose remedies for problems. The press faithfully reported hearings on this proposal, which began in October and concluded in December 1931. They produced nothing especially spectacular.

Perhaps someone knew the right answers, but there was no agreement. Paul M. Mazur, partner in Lehman Brothers, observed that there were as many explanations and as many remedies 'as there are people who give the opinions. That is really astonishing, and it is simply an evidence of the fact that we do not know; and when we measure that ignorance against the cost of not knowing, again I think that the discrepancy between the need and the available in-formation shrieks for some agency that at least will make an honest effort to find out what the facts are.'[6] This was a logical conclusion to draw after hearing witnesses from business, labor, finance, agri-culture, government, foundations, and universities. Some of them, like Henry I. Harriman, New England utilities executive, wanted to relax the antitrust laws and promote gigantic trade associations; others, equally potent men of affairs, were dubious about trying to change anything. The consensus was in favor of an advisory fact-finding council, but there was little support either for economic planning on the Russian model or for the benevolent concentration of industry as advocated by Gerard Swope, president of General Electric Company. Albert H. Wiggin, chairman of the board of Chase National Bank, had only a counsel of despair: 'Nothing will prevent the recurrence of business troubles at intervals.'[7]

These hearings had no immediate result in legislation. However sternly such labor leaders as Sidney Hillman and John L. Lewis might assail the lack of political and economic leadership, the President could not in honesty be accused of doing nothing. His program for the Seventy-second Congress was comprehensive and, in the light of traditional conservative attitudes, even daring.

2. *Houses Divided*

The many hearings and investigations were proof enough that Hoover would have difficulty with the Seventy-second Congress. Party factions and coalitions, rivalries of politicians hopeful of being dark horses in 1932, and the lack of control in either chamber of Congress compounded the President's troubles. For a while in the fall there was a faint hope that Republicans might have a slim ma-jority in the House, but Democrats won three of five seats filled on 3 November and held a precarious dominance in the House with 218 to 214. There were still two vacancies, which also went to Demo-crats in January, and it mattered little how the lone Farmer-Labor, Minnesota's Paul J. Kvale, might vote. Senator Fess was so blandly cheerful in the face of a very obvious anti-Hoover trend that he held a 'virtual monopoly of the existing store of Republican hope' for 1932.[8]

Knowing that Democrats would control the House, administration leaders prepared carefully for the opening of Congress. The President's insistence on economy was under attack by many pressure groups, including the Navy League, whose president, William Howard Gardiner, accused Hoover of 'abysmal ignorance of why navies are maintained.' The Navy League fracas sputtered for weeks, but Hoover held his ground, ably assisted by Senators Borah and Capper and Representatives Wood and French. A big navy meant big spending, so Patrick J. Hurley, Ogden L. Mills, Reed Smoot, and James E. Watson all made speeches or gave interviews to drive home the need for more taxes and less spending.[9] Hoover was fighting desperately to head off demands for spending before Congress could meet.

A dependable Republican minority would have been a great solace, at least. Here, too, the President was to be frustrated. For many years the House had been controlled by Nicholas Longworth, Bertrand L. Snell, and John Q. Tilson. Longworth's death precipitated a struggle between Snell and Tilson. Widely known as the President's personal friend and political ally, Tilson had been majority leader in the Seventy-first Congress. In the party conference preceding the opening of Congress, Progressives swung their support to Snell simply to strike at Hoover. Although he had kept out of the struggle, Hoover lost prestige with Tilson's defeat. Snell hurried to the White House for a conference and announced his unqualified support of the Hoover program. There were also Hoover enemies among the Old Guard Republicans and none was more unrestrained than Louis T. McFadden, representative from Pennsylvania, who saw in the moratorium a diabolical conspiracy by Hoover and the international bankers. McFadden's attack against Hoover in a speech on 15 December stunned his colleagues, and it was significant that a Tammany Democrat, John J. O'Connor, was first in defense of the President.[10]

Democrats organized the House for the first time since 1919. John Nance Garner of Texas won the speaker's gavel and Henry T. Rainey of Illinois, for whom Hoover had nothing but contempt, was majority leader. Fiorello H. La Guardia and other Republican insurgents acted more like Wilsonian Democrats than Republicans of any variety. They would co-operate in every effort to enact those 'socialist' measures Hoover feared so much. La Guardia, indeed, attempted to organize a small bloc to control the House, an effort supported by Minnesota's Paul J. Kvale. While promising co-operation to promote recovery, Garner refused to define a political truce as support for every Hoover proposal.[11]

Theoretically, Republicans controlled the Senate with 48 seats, after having won the vacancy that existed when Congress met. With party forces so evenly split, President Hoover made the petulant suggestion to Watson that the Democrats be permitted to organize the Senate and 'convert their sabotage into responsibility . . .'[12] But Republicans enjoyed their leadership prerogatives and refused to abdicate. Anyway, Jouett Shouse warned that Democrats would not accept the responsibility.

The President's worst fears were realized when a fight developed over the election of president pro tempore on 8 December. Insurgent Republicans refused to support Senator George H. Moses of New Hampshire for that important post. He had called them 'sons of the wild jackass,' but their resentment probably was directed more against Hoover. Weeks before Congress was to meet, political gossip predicted a showing of heels. Moses hinted that if the insurgents contrived to defeat him for his accustomed post, he would vote with Democrats when it came to elect committee chairmen, and all committees would thus be thrown under Democratic control. Undeterred by this empty threat, insurgents worried Watson and Moses by not voting or by voting for other candidates. Democrat Key Pittman, silver champion from Nevada, received 42 votes and Moses only 33 on the first ballot. In successive ballots, a group of fourteen insurgent Republican senators refused to vote for the Old Guard's candidate. The rebellion ended in January, though, and Moses won the position.[13]

Hoover's break with the insurgent Republicans was irreparable. His failure to support Borah's resolution to confine tariff revision to agricultural schedules and his feeble defense of the Hawley-Smoot Tariff opened the breach that grew steadily wider. The insurgents spoke for a great part of the G.O.P. in the West; they dominated the Republican party in the Middle West. They represented middle-class Republicans, the social stratum to which Hoover so obviously belonged, and without them he was lost.

President Hoover had little respect for the leaders of Congress, and they both knew and reciprocated his attitude. He disliked Watson and regarded Snell as little more than a party hack. Joseph T. Robinson, minority leader in the Senate, he would admit revealed considerable statesmanship; but he despised Rainey, whom he called a purveyor of filthy smears. The Democrats, however, were not unreasonable men and admitted the need for a working agreement with the President. Hoover could push nothing through Congress, having no party whip to crack; the Democrats could expect small success in efforts to override a presidential veto. The session would be filled with politics and the major objective of both parties would be the election of 1932.[14]

Two hunger marches converged on Washington during the first days of the Seventy-second Congress. Interesting phenomena, they accomplished nothing. Herbert Benjamin and Carl Winter, Communist leaders in the Unemployed Councils of the United States, were prominent organizers of one well-publicized group that called itself the National Hunger Marchers. Benjamin had brazen plans for gaining admission to the Senate floor, but he changed his mind after a conference with Senator Borah on 4 December. The 1,670 'delegates' who reached Washington paraded behind communistic banners. Benjamin, permitted to testify before a Senate committee, presented their demands for cash payments and unemployment insurance.[15]

Father James R. Cox, priest of Old St. Patrick's Church in Pittsburgh, led an army of some 15,000 to Washington during the first week of 1932. The group was well behaved and no extra White House guards were posted, although 1,341 policemen remained on call. Father Cox had his picture taken with Pennsylvania politicians and called on the President, who informed him that he was fighting the 'final campaign against the depression.' Father Cox apparently was unconvinced. Ten days later he addressed some 55,000 men and women in the Pitt Stadium and promised a national convention for a new party that would be concerned with troubles of the unemployed.[16]

3. *Hoover's Program*

The most pressing problem before Congress obviously was relief of economic distress. There may have been a 'small burst of recuperation' early in 1931, but by December no signs of recovery were apparent. Comparative statistics revealed unmistakable losses during the year. Business failures had increased, imports had declined by 40 per cent, and the index of business activity had fallen about 35 per cent in one year. The country had found new lows; but there were many who agreed with Laurence H. Sloan, vice president of Standard Statistics Co., that October 1931 probably would 'be the lowest month in the depression.'[17]

Hoover's full program for meeting the crisis consisted of nearly a score of proposals intended to remedy specific weaknesses. There is by no means any certainty that the presidential prescription would have been sufficient to end the depression. President Hoover's program was revealed in several of the sixty-three messages he sent to Congress, and only part of it was contained in his annual message of 8 December 1931.

In this communication the President noted 'a remarkable development of the sense of co-operation in the community . . . absence of public disorders and industrial conflict . . . enlargement of social and spiritual responsibility among the people . . . The country is richer in physical property, in newly discovered resources, and in productive capacity than ever before.' He observed gains in public health, education, science, and invention. He repeated that major causes of our economic distress were foreign in origin, that panics, restraints on banking, and abandonment of monetary standards affected markets and prices, increased unemployment, and damaged our financial structure. In relieving distress, the government had kept out of the economic field; but public and private construction had provided employment, industry had spread work among employees, immigration had been curtailed, and the President's Organization on Unemployment Relief had mobilized public and private relief agencies. 'The evidence of the Public Health Service,' the President reported with obvious satisfaction, 'shows an actual decrease of sickness and infant and general mortality below normal years. No greater proof could be adduced that our people have been protected from hunger and cold and that the sense of social responsibility in the Nation has responded to the need of the unfortunate.'[18]

Hoover's program emphasized relief for financial institutions and measures to liberalize their policies while reforming some of their practices. This broad program was tied in with more public works, railway reorganization, and international co-operation.[19] These proposals hardly justify the intemperate language of critics who pretended to see desperation in the presidential program. One such critic was Paul Y. Anderson, a contributor to liberal journals, who charged that Hoover has lapsed into utter panic. The condition of the man is really pathetic. . . . After refusing for nine months to call Congress into extra session, he now plies it with frenzied entreaties to enact all manner of legislative panaceas. . . . There is an abundance of skill and intelligence in the country, but he avails himself of none of it . . . while his economic ideas are derived from a succession of financial adventurers and industrial sweaters, most of whom helped to precipitate the present situation.[20]

Had the President included an urgent demand for appropriating up to $2 billion to relieve distress, such critics as Anderson might well have found much to praise. More temperate in his criticism was Rexford Guy Tugwell, brilliant Columbia University economist and New Dealer-to-be, who admitted that the President's plan might well restore confidence and stem the downward trend of prices.[21]

After the preliminary business of organization had been disposed of, Democrats proceeded to attack the President's message and embarked on a course not designed to promote the general welfare. Charles L. Underhill, Republican representative from Massachusetts, challenged the Democrats to present their own program if they did not like the President's. And his Republican colleague from South Dakota, Royal C. Johnson, called the Democrats 'the most disorganized group politically that has ever yet been disorganized.' Nevertheless, Republican support in the House was far from vigorous. If the Democrats were not disorganized, they at least lacked strong leadership. Most of the work fell on three committees, and House leaders moved as rapidly as possible to consider major items in the President's program.[22]

Patrick J. Hurley's cabinet position might well have been re-named Secretary of Political War. On many occasions he served as the President's voice at political rallies; frequently, Hurley and Ogden L. Mills, with an occasional assist from Ray Lyman Wilbur, 'went to the people' for Hoover. When the President's program was under attack, the Republican National Committee was meeting in Washington. After the Committee had met with Hoover in the White House, Hurley spoke: 'The President's program is altogether the most outstanding economic program ever presented to any Congress. . . . The Democrats have offered nothing in lieu of it. The Democrats have no program. They are probably waiting to get all the President's ideas to use them in an attempt to set up a program of their own.' Senators Robinson and Harrison immediately charged Hoover with undermining the harmony plan: every nonpartisan effort was being hailed as a Hoover achievement.[23]

After this sputtering from both parties, Hoover summoned rival leaders to the White House for a conference. The President maintained that they could not agree on nonpartisan legislation and believed that Rainey was determined to wreck his program.[24] Other reports, as well as action in Congress, indicate that there was an agreement on expediting the President's eight-point plan of critical legislation, most of which he had discussed with leaders of both parties on 6 October. This was the 'harmony plan,' which included more capital for the Federal Land Banks, creation of the Reconstruction Finance Corporation, establishment of Home Loan Discount Banks, more flexible discount regulations for the Federal Reserve, aid for depositors of closed banks, strengthening the railways, revision of banking laws, and drastic economy. The leaders did not promise passage of bills to accomplish all of these things, but most of them were achieved with as little partisanship as could have been expected.[25]

Both Houses began their labors promptly, although most of the important bills were held up until after the holidays. This delay annoyed the President; but, if he was in such a hurry, why had he not called a special sesssion?

The Hoover family was united for the Christmas season. Herbert, Jr. and his wife came with Peggy Ann and 'Peter.' Allan, too, was home for the holidays. Reporters who accompanied the family on a shopping tour emphasized the visit to a five-and-ten, where toys common to every American family that could afford them were purchased for the grandchildren. On Christmas Eve there were ceremonies at Sherman Square to light a giant Christmas tree, and a dinner for the President's personal and official household.[26]

The New Year's Day reception brought a crowd of some 3,000 callers to the White House, less than half the number who had greeted the President and Mrs. Hoover at the start of 1930 and 1931. Justice Oliver Wendell Holmes, Jr., long recognized as one of America's greatest citizens, at last bowed to the inevitable on 12 January and resigned his position on the Supreme Court. The President replied for the nation: 'I know of no American retiring from public service with such a sense of affection and devotion of the whole people.'[27]

When the Congress reconvened on 4 January 1932, President Hoover sent his message containing the eight-point program agreed to on 18 December and urged Congress to speed its work.[28] Speaker Garner, with a slim Democratic majority of six, managed to push emergency measures through the House by April. There was still the Senate, where real and nominal Republicans had exactly one-half of the votes. Through nearly all of the first session, the Senate was much more unmanageable than the House; and after April the House, too, got out of hand. A proposed manufacturers' sales tax, favorably reported out of committee, was defeated by a vote of 223 to 153, and no revenue bill was passed until June. Except for the revenue bill, various hearings, and routine matters, Congress might well have adjourned in April. After all, Hoover himself was author of the truism that the country could not legislate itself out of depression.

4. *Battle of the Budget*

With such people as Eugene Meyer, Jr., Ogden L. Mills, and Henry M. Robinson, a banker friend from California, available to offer advice, it is logical to assume that the President would have sent to the Congress a budget with accurate estimates of receipts and expenditures, provisions for economies, and tax revision necessary to balance the books. Not that there was any real sense in trying to balance the budget in 1932, but among conservatives respect for 'balance' had become a fetish. Some journalists ignored the balancing act long enough to accuse Mills of deliberately confusing Congress with conflicting statements and estimates. Walter Lippmann, ever ready with a revelation from Delphi, scolded the President for not showing definitely how to balance the budget.[29]

Mr. Hoover must have been greatly pained by this criticism if he read it. The fault for deficits greater than those anticipated would lie with Congress, which displayed a tendency to enact measures calling for expenditures without providing revenues to meet them. Organized pressure groups sent 'locust swarms of lobbyists who haunt the halls of Congress seeking special privilege,' the President observed.[30] Nearly every pressure group paid lip service to the balanced budget, but then went away to obtain increased appropriations for its pet interest. As neither the President nor party leaders could offer vigorous and sustained leadership, pressure groups enjoyed unwonted success. A balanced budget became a legislative impossibility when there was an effective lobby against every tax and against every economy. 'The forgotten man was completely forgotten by every Senator whose constituents desired a special privilege.'[31]

The battle of the budget began in December and continued to June 1932. Hoover's message on 9 December informed Congress that there would be a net debt increase of over $3.2 billion for fiscal 1932 and 1933. Taxes must go up and expenses come down. The government could not borrow much more without destroying confidence, denuding commerce and industry of their resources, extending unemployment, and demoralizing agriculture. The deficit for fiscal 1933 was estimated at $1.4 billion in a total budget of $3.9 billion, which was a decrease of $369 million under the previous budget.[32]

Mills painted a gloomy picture to the Economic Club of New York in another attempt to lecture Congress on the need for economy. Huge federal expenditures and deficits would endanger the whole financial structure; the gross debt already was $17,310 million. How much higher could it go? He also implied the need for enlisting more taxpayers, since some 382,000 income tax returns in 1928 yielded $1,128 million, while 3,689,000 returns yielded only $36 million.[33] Mr. Mills did not mention that several of the country's richest men had discovered ways to avoid paying any income tax at all.

Hoover favored moderate estate taxes to prevent accumulation of inherited wealth that would not be used for public benefit; he would exempt estates under $100,000 and impose graduated taxes against the heirs rather than against the estate. Income taxes should be raised in the upper brackets and collected at the source where possible. He was considerably worried by lobbies that proposed expenditures of $40 billion and asked for a reduction of $669 million in expenses.[34]

The President also asked for power to reorganize executive departments, a project Republicans had been toying with for a decade; but Democratic leaders blocked bills that would permit that form of economy. Representative Joseph W. Byrns, a Tennessee Democrat, discovered what happened to consolidation proposals. As chairman of the Committee on Appropriations, he introduced a bill to put the Army, Navy, and Air Force together in a Department of National Defense, only to encounter adverse lobbying by the Army and Navy League.[35]

Congress was deluged by public demands for increased expenditures and decreased expenditures, with proponents of economy being somewhat more vocal. While some spokesmen of business called for large construction programs, others demanded the reduction of federal operations to the threadbarest minimum. While a very few enterprisers called for new taxes, most of the business owners, operators, and managers called for tax relief. The gap between normal receipts and expenditures in fiscal 1931 was a great shock after the 1930 surplus. By 30 June 1931 some $3,317 million had been received for the year and about $4,220 million had been spent. In December 1930 Mellon had announced that the deficit for fiscal 1931 would be $180 million. He missed by $723 million! Calvin Coolidge reported that 'a cold shiver went down the financial spine of the public' when the deficit for 1931 became known.[36] With the financial spine already frozen, the shiver was hardly noticeable.

In an attempt to lift the public works program out of its red tape tangle, Senator Robert M. La Follette, Jr. introduced a bill to create an Administration of Public Works with an emergency $5.5 billion appropriation. Testimony revealed a great drop in construction despite state and federal efforts. The hearings on this bill were going on while the House Committee on Ways and Means was preparing its controversial revenue bill. One witness urged that the federal government stop 'being merely the cheerleader for business' and break the deadlock with a bond issue for construction.[37] But this was another attempt to unbalance the budget, raid the Treasury, and avoid the requirement that public works be self-liquidating. President Hoover could not approve this deviation from his basic principles. This was not the kind of Public Works Administration he had proposed when Congress opened.

The Committee on Ways and Means had a revenue bill ready for debate on 10 March. Leading Democrats and Republicans, expecting little trouble in the House, were amazed when rebels in both parties combined on 16 March to oppose the bill. Senator Watson in November had warned Hoover that Congress would not accept a sales tax, and now this tax drew fire from champions of the forgotten man. Fiorello H. La Guardia was at the front of this opposition, but the Democratic leaders—Garner, Rainey, and Crisp—absorbed the blame. Charles R. Crisp 'beat his breast until it resounded like a kettle-drum' in arguing for the sales tax. Crisp, indeed, so faithfully served the interests of a balanced budget that Hoover appointed him to the Tariff Commission when he was defeated in his bid for the Senate. The

Democratic majority melted away as ranks broke against the sales tax. John J. Raskob and Jouett Shouse, party executives outside of Congress, exhorted in vain for a closing of ranks. The revenue bill was forced back into committee by La Guardia's 'allied Progressives' and nearly three-score Democrats led by R. L. Doughton of North Carolina and aided by an Iowa Republican, C. W. Ramseyer, who had been a Hoover stalwart in the Seventy-first Congress. La Guardia, Doughton, and Ramseyer were at once dubbed leaders of the House soak-the-rich bloc. Speaker Garner finally won enough co-operation to get the bill through on 1 April without the general sales tax. In the Senate, renewed chaos threatened when coal, copper, oil, and lumber interests worked for including higher tariffs, camouflaged as excise taxes, in the bill.[38]

These efforts toward writing a tax bill took place in an atmosphere of rapidly increasing tensions. Hitler's rise in Germany, arguments about war debts and reparations, futile attempts at disarmament, and ever-deepening economic distress kept Europeans in turmoil and Americans in the grip of fascinated apprehension. Japan's war on China entered a new phase with the attack on Shanghai on 29 January, and Americans were exasperated by the cynical disregard for supposedly sacred obligations. Communist-led demonstrations increased in the United States as the jagged descent of charted lines showed no economic improvement. The quality of the Senate experienced no visible improvement when Huey Long blew in from Louisiana to take his self-appointed seat on 25 January 1932.[39]

While the Committee on Ways and Means struggled with a revenue bill, Hoover attempted to persuade Congress to make cuts in the budget as presented in December. On 19 February Garner appointed an Economy Committee of four Democrats and three Republicans to seek ways to reduce expenditures. This committee wanted to attack the problem item by item, but Hoover wanted the omnibus bill which he sent to the group on 15 April. The President anticipated saving up to $250 million by salary cuts, reduced veterans' benefits, and other measures.[40] The Economy Committee recommended cuts of $263 million; but when the House finished with economy on 3 May, the saving was down to $38 million.[41]

Observing that his frequent statements on the need for economies and for a balanced budget were making no impression on Congress, the President gave the legislators a verbal lashing with a message on

5 May. Again he asserted that restoration of confidence was indispensable for recovery, but Congress by its actions was arousing fear throughout the country.[42]

Conservatives took heart, and some of them hailed Hoover as a leader who had at last found himself. A National Economy Committee and a National Action Committee, both made up of wealthy conservatives, were organized hurriedly. Heartened by the flood of telegrams and telephone messages that followed his rebuke, the President issued a press statement excoriating lobbyists and claiming to speak for the people 'against delays and destructive legislation which impair the credit of the United States.' Response in the House was immediate. Joseph W. Byrns, chairman of the Appropriations Committee, was so excited that he pounded the leg of Connecticut's E. W. Goss as he took Hoover to task for not having cut his own estimates in December. Republicans, including members of Hoover's official family, had done as much as Democrats to prevent sweeping economies.[43]

The Revenue Act of 1932 which went to Hoover for his signature on 6 June 'provided for the largest peacetime tax increase in history.' There were several innovations that have since become commonplace: collection of some income taxes at the source, new manufacturers' excise taxes, luxury taxes, the three-cent rate on first class mail, and gift taxes. Excise taxes were levied on oil, gasoline, toiletries, jewelry, tires and tubes, refrigerators, sporting goods, candy, chewing gum, soft drinks, electric energy, admissions, bank checks, yachts, and other items that made the good life good to live for those who could afford it.[44]

President Hoover disliked the Revenue Act. He complained that Speaker Garner had permitted stultifying delays and that its passage on 6 June was too late to reassure the public and to balance the budget. Nevertheless, it was Garner who soon was blaming Republicans for not balancing the budget. Perhaps the Texan had some reason for doing so, since Republicans had wanted the sales tax and it was that feature of the bill that caused Garner to lose his precarious control over the slim Democratic majority. After all, the poor who wanted to soak the rich were far more numerous than the rich who wanted to go on soaking the poor. Ogden L. Mills and the President himself must bear a large share of the blame for delay because of their frequent revisions of estimates.[45]

5. Banking and Credit

Perhaps President Hoover's greatest disappointment was in the area of banking reform. He could complain about the peremptory way that Congress handled his recommendations and also object to its annoying predilection for managed currency, inflation, and other spine-chilling heterodox proposals. On the whole, however, the President received essentially what he asked for: revision in the Federal Reserve credit requirements, expanded capital for the Federal Land Banks, and creation of the Reconstruction Finance Corporation, Agricultural Credit Associations, and a Home Loan Bank. In no case did Congress give him exactly what he wanted, but Herbert Hoover surely would not have liked a rubber-stamp Congress!

Practically nothing was accomplished by the Seventy-second Congress in necessary banking reforms. The Senate Committee on Banking held hearings through 1930 and 1931 on a measure to accomplish reforms. Bankers opposed the bill, appealed to Hoover to prevent its passage, and were aided by the Federal Reserve Board in lobbying against it. When Hoover did become seriously interested in pushing bank reform in late 1931, his activities aroused the bankers' ire. The President wanted all commercial banks included within the Federal Reserve system and subject to its control, separation of long-term financing from commercial banking, and branch banking by national banks.[46] The failure of Congress to enact reform legislation cannot be called a Democratic conspiracy to discredit the Hoover Administration. Bankers themselves were responsible. They had not yet been whipped, shamed, exposed, and bankrupted into submission to reform demands.

President Hoover and most of the business community regarded departure from the gold standard as a calamity too awful to contemplate. Three things might bring about the catastrophe: hoarding, the gold reserve requirement, and foreign withdrawals. Hoarding reflected an entirely justified lack of confidence in banks. A sudden increase in the amount of money in circulation without a corresponding increase in business activity is a clear indication of hoarding. The amount of money in circulation increased by about $1 billion in the year ending 31 October 1931. This hoarding withdrew about $10 billion from the credit system, since $1 in cash supported about $10 in credit. People who withdrew cash from banks deposited some of it in Postal Savings accounts. Many, with no faith at all in government credit, hid specie and bills in walls, holes in the ground, privies, linings of coats, horse collars, coal piles, hollow trees—any place except a bank.[47]

The Federal Reserve system was required by law to back every $100 in Federal Reserve notes with $40 in gold, a reserve of 40 per cent. As hoarding of Federal Reserve notes increased, gold in reserve had to increase. The other 60 per cent was backed by eligible paper, and any shortage of eligible paper had to be made up by more gold. In February 1932 the Federal Reserve Banks were required to pledge $930 million of their excess reserves as collateral and had only $416 million available as 'free gold' to meet demands from abroad.[48] Foreign balances accumulated in the United States amounted to about $800 million, and foreign owners of American securities were selling and converting the proceeds into gold balances. If this gold were demanded by its foreign owners, the United States might easily be forced off the gold standard.

Hoover attacked the problem on two fronts. Announcing on 3 February 1932 that hoarding had withdrawn $1.3 billion, he castigated the practice as un-American and assured the public that the R.F.C. was initiating a campaign for reconstruction and recovery. But on the same day three banks closed in Pennsylvania. The President induced Colonel Frank Knox, owner of the *Chicago Daily News,* to become chairman of the Citizens' Reconstruction Organization, which was to spearhead an anti-hoarding publicity drive. To aid in this effort to hold back the sea with a screen, the President appealed to patriotic sentiments. Representatives of 42 national organizations with a membership of 20 million met with Hoover at the White House to pledge co-operation in the campaign. Will Rogers, who called at the White House on 11 February, admitted that hoarding was discussed and confessed that 'the President looked directly and most severely at me when we were on the subject.' For six months or so the situation improved somewhat, although there was no demonstrable connection with the anti-hoarding campaign. When hoarding increased sharply after the brief respite, Congress' political activities were blamed.[49]

The anti-hoarding campaign failed; the amount of gold earmarked for foreign account fluctuated widely in 1932. There was, moreover, a great movement of gold back and forth across the Atlantic for no good purpose. During 1931 there was a net inflow of gold of

$135,325,000; in 1932 there was a net export of $446,214,000, all of which came in the first seven months.[50]

There was a crisis, beyond doubt, particularly if one held the gold standard in far higher esteem than it deserved. One way to meet the crisis was to increase the amount of gold that could be exported on demand, and one place to get that gold was from the reserve against Federal Reserve notes. The President urged Congress to liberalize the collateral requirement, and Congress responded with the Glass-Steagall Act, which permitted Federal Reserve notes to be backed by 40 per cent gold and United States Government obligations purchased in the open market. Thus, a shortage of paper eligible for rediscount would not require additional gold to be held as collateral. Some $700 million in reserve gold was released. The act also liberalized credit by permitting members to borrow from Federal Reserve Banks on their promissory notes.[51] This was a strange role for a sound money man to play! The President had sanctioned the use of a promise to pay as partial backing for Federal Reserve notes.

Congress responded with reasonable promptness to the President's request for enlarging credit facilities. Passage of the act to create the R.F.C. obscured other important measures, particularly those to relieve agriculture and home financing. There were several federally sponsored agencies that provided agricultural credit—a hopeless operation which treated the symptoms of the farmers' troubles rather than the disease. Federal Land Banks loaned to National Farm Loan Associations, which in turn loaned directly to farmers; and Intermediate Credit Banks loaned to farmers' co-operatives and discounted agricultural paper.

Hoover had two proposals to improve agricultural credit facilities and Congress enacted both into law with little delay. The first measure added $125 million to Land Bank capital, and provided that $25 million could be used to extend overdue mortgages. The President approved the act on 23 January 1932 but was disappointed that so little was done to relieve mortgage distress.[52] A second act, in March 1932, created Regional Agricultural Credit Corporations which could loan to various agricultural associations. What the farmer really needed was a general moratorium on mortgages, then a realistic adjustment of mortgage obligations to the level of agricultural prices.[53]

One of Hoover's sound complaints against the Seventy-second

Congress was that it had not taken prompt action to relieve home owners: 'Had we been able to get a general mortgage discount institution established at the time I proposed, it would have saved thousands of homes, farms, and holdings of city real estate from foreclosure, and prevented many bank failures.'[54] Mr. Hoover first proposed a system of mortgage discount banks to thirty-two leaders of Congress who met with him on 6 October 1931. He wanted a system similar in organization to the Federal Reserve, with a central mortgage bank and twelve discount banks, which would enable banks and loan associations to unload their frozen assets. The leaders of Congress did not take to this proposal. On the next day Hoover tried the idea on insurance men and bankers. Only the building and loan people and some representatives of savings banks gave their support. Consequently, Hoover decided to ask for a system of Home Loan Banks instead of the general mortgage discount system.[55]

Congress was dilatory, to put it charitably, in meeting the President's request. Hoover had informed the country on 13 November that he would propose the Home Loan Banks to help mortgage institutions, and optimistic observers thought that upward of $30 billion in mortgages might be affected. Senator Watson and a House colleague started the measure through Congress early in the session, but it was not until 22 July that the President was able to sign the bill. Rabid Republicans accused Democrats of deliberately delaying relief for home owners until after the election,[56] although it was banker and not political opposition that was responsible.

The act created a Federal Home Loan Bank Board and authorized the creation of eight to twelve districts with a Federal Home Loan Bank in each district. Members of the district banks were to be institutions making long-term loans; home owners could not borrow directly from the Home Loan Bank. Lending institutions could discount mortgages on homes worth not more than $20,000; mortgages in arrears for six months, or which had more than fifteen years to run, were ineligible. Since mortgages were to be limited to 50 per cent of the property value, the Home Loan Banks could hardly lose money.[57]

The Home Loan Bank Board moved into action so quickly that the Home Loan Banks were operating before the end of August. Their activities provided the basis for further federal aid to housing under the New Deal, but the general paralysis already creeping through the country's economic system was too far advanced to be affected seriously by the Home Loan Banks.

Although its legislative enactments constituted a relatively small contribution toward relief of economic distress, positive measures of the Seventy-second Congress are impressive. These measures were revolutionary in nature, breaking sharply with the past and revealing Hoover's analytical and planning ability at its best. Bad as the Seventy-second may have been in the President's view, it enacted most of his important recommendations. Of the twelve defeats detailed by Hoover, several bills enacted his ideas in general outline, but differed in detail. Other defeats were more important: incomplete reform of bankruptcy laws, failure to reorganize the railroads, refusal to permit regulation of interstate power rates, lack of banking reform, and refusal to resurrect the war debts commission.

The Seventy-second Congress served when crises occurred so rapidly that they merged in a common catastrophe. To hunt them out and to apply specific remedies was the task to which Herbert Hoover bent his genius. That he 'permitted his legislative program to become entangled in the meshes of congressional politics'[58] should cause no wonder. A Republican president with a different philosophy might have accomplished somewhat more with the Seventy-second Congress, but it is doubtful. Democrats smelled victory in 1932. Why try to make Hoover look good? Nevertheless, there is no sense in attempting to portray Democrats generally as lacking in patriotism while ascribing to Republicans a monopoly on that elusive quality.

Herbert Hoover, for all his brilliant organizing ability, his selfless devotion to his country, his faith in the American way as he saw it and as he wanted it to be, could not command. Confident that his analysis was correct, confident that his proposed actions would meet the crises as they arose, he was defeated by the refusal of his party to close ranks behind him, and he could not summon the mass of people to his support. He lacked that one spark necessary to stir men's hearts. The people en masse do not follow reason, but only emotion. John Quincy Adams, Woodrow Wilson, and Herbert Hoover all discovered that a President must not put too much faith in offering steadily glowing embers, however bright, to people who want fireworks.

CHAPTER XII

FAILURES IN FARM RELIEF

1. *Genesis of the Farm Board*

In his dealings with agriculture President Hoover suffered from two misfortunes. He was exposed to a battery of farm experts who could agree neither on the statistical portrayal of agricultural troubles nor on programs for relief. An even greater misfortune was the President's belief in his own competence to prescribe a remedy, a belief that made him adamantine in opposition to McNary-Haugenism. Perhaps that favorite remedy of farm groups in the early 'twenties would have failed, but its failure could not have been more pronounced than Hoover's Farm Board.

Hoover did everything his conscience would permit to seek farm relief. That he stopped short of rigid crop controls and a bold, drastic land-use revision program showed that he refused to violate the tenets of American individualism which he held so firmly. Farmers generally expected from Hoover far more than he or anyone could deliver. They wanted nothing less than a solution to problems which had been accumulating for decades. To carry out their program a whole series of historical trends would have had to be reversed and American society would have to be realigned. Hoover had no intention of doing this job.

Most of Hoover's program was acceptable to conservative Republicans. Higher tariffs on agricultural products, promotion of co-operatives, improved marketing, and better credit facilities—none of these could go very far to deprive the business community of profits garnered by farming the farmers. But Republicans accepted the co-operative movement reluctantly. It was the least obnoxious of a series of proposals that included price fixing, currency tinkering, domestic allotment, export debentures, compensated dumping, freight rate reductions, inland waterways, tax reduction, and a general moratorium on mortgages. For Hoover to give his blessing to a federal agency that would actively enter the market seemed like rank heresy, a departure from his basic philosophy of government.[1] Such departures were all right, but only when Hoover himself defined them and set their limits.

Hoover's interest in farm problems dates back at least to 1917. Three years later he published a number of articles on agriculture. As Secretary of Commerce, he believed that farm marketing was his concern, and Coolidge made him his farm adviser instead of Henry C. Wallace, the Secretary of Agriculture. In the early 'twenties, Hoover developed a plan for promoting agricultural co-operatives as a corollary to the industrial associations he was advocating. In order to counteract the socialism that he saw in McNary-Haugenism, Hoover proposed a federal farm board whose major functions were to aid co-operative marketing associations. The result was the Capper-Williams bill of 1924, of which Hoover was co-author. Wallace, already nearing death, opposed the bill and so did advocates of McNary-Haugenism. Hoover's plan sought price stabilization through co-operative marketing associations; McNary-Haugenism, which most farmers wanted, supported price stabilization by selling surpluses abroad and making the tariff effective on domestic sales.[2]

The remedies that Hoover advocated, and which the Seventy-first Congress enacted, were planned to operate in a generally prosperous economy. The Federal Farm Board was never intended to launch a 'crash program,' although it was fated to operate entirely within an economic depression of unprecedented severity. This very important fact has been universally ignored in judging Hoover's efforts for farm relief.

True to his campaign promises, the President summoned Congress into special session on 15 April 1929 to consider agricultural relief and 'limited' tariff revision. Briefly he reviewed the causes of farm distress: heavy indebtedness resulting from the 1920 deflation, disorderly and wasteful marketing, seasonal market congestion or occasional climatic surpluses, increased freight rates, competition in world markets with products of low-cost labor, overexpansion into marginal lands, increased local taxes, decreased consumption on the farm resulting from mechanization, and other factors. No one plan or principle could be found that would solve all of these problems. They could be met 'by the creation of a great instrumentality clothed with sufficient authority and resources to assist our farmers to meet these problems, each upon its own merits. The creation of such an agency would at once transfer the agricultural question from the field of politics into the realm of economics . . .'[3]

That, of course, was mere wishful thinking. The tariff had never removed protection from the field of politics to the field of economics, nor would farm legislation ever take farm problems out of politics unless that legislation completely satisfied a very large majority of farmers, processors, and industrialists.

Objectives contemplated by the President, while not meeting with general approval of farmers and their organizations, certainly marked a tremendous break with former treatment of agriculture by the federal government. Hoover wanted a farm board to reorganize the marketing system by 'creating and sustaining farmer-owned and farmer-controlled agencies'; advancing funds for purchasing, storing, and marketing products; creating and supporting clearing houses; and eliminating wastes. W. J. Spillman, Principal Agricultural Economist in the Department of Agriculture, believed that the Board could render the most important service by simplifying marketing and reducing costs to benefit both farmer and consumer.[4]

These proposals threatened to tread on the sensitive toes of private marketing agencies. The Board should furnish production guidance, devise means for withdrawing marginal lands from production, and develop by-products for industry. But there must be no stifling bureaucracy, no tax or fee, no governmental buying, selling, and price fixing, no duplication of facilities available at reasonable rates under private ownership, no increase in surplus production. Co-operative marketing already embraced about two million farmers and distributed farm products worth about $2.5 billion. Upon these co-operatives Hoover based his case for more efficient marketing. These proposals, the President anticipated, would 'lay the foundations for a new day in agriculture, from which we shall preserve to the Nation the great values of its individuality and strengthen our whole national fabric.'[5]

Co-operation was a basic principle in Hoover's philosophy of government. Democracy, he believed, rested upon co-operative action on a national scale. The role of government should be to reduce conflicts among organizations, to emphasize the area of common interest; government should interfere only when co-operative action failed.[6]

Hoover's faith in co-operatives as a means of aiding agriculture was well placed. Marketing co-operatives could reduce charges made for use of terminal facilities, and for bridging the gap between producer and processor. Processing and manufacturing co-operatives could distribute the profits of business enterprise to their producer members. Purchasing co-operatives could save members large sums in distribution of such items as fertilizer, seed, and petroleum products. Credit co-operatives could pool resources and take advantage of low interest rates provided by federally sponsored lending agencies. These three basic types of co-operatives grew rapidly in number during the 1920's and continued in healthy condition. The nearly 11,000 co-operatives of 1925 were a significant economic force.[7]

In 1929 agricultural leaders tried once more to put the export debenture scheme into the farm relief bill. They succeeded in the Senate, despite Hoover's disapproval, but the House refused to undertake an experiment widely assailed as being an outright subsidy which would not reach the farmers. It has been charged that the President encouraged a group of senators to believe he would accept the export debenture, then repudiated their efforts after the Senate Agriculture Committee had reported favorably.[8] The charge is not true. Senators Capper, Heflin, Norbeck, and Ransdell called on the President on 12 April to ask his opinion. Hoover promised to get advice from three departments and to study the question himself.

There is no reason to suppose that Hoover gave any additional study to the export debenture scheme; his mind was already set on that point, and his reply to the senators on 20 April merely repeated stock arguments against the plan, arguments which are formidable but hypothetical. The export debenture, Hoover believed, would stimulate overproduction, cause increased taxation, invite foreign retaliation, and yield no benefit to the farmer. Borah's work in the Senate in favor of the device aroused many of the Old Guard and served to warn Hoover that the man from Idaho, one of his strongest supporters, was no man's lackey.[9]

The Agricultural Marketing Act, approved on 15 June 1929, solemnly proclaimed its purpose 'to promote the effective merchandising of agricultural commodities in interstate and foreign commerce, so that the industry of agriculture will be placed on a basis of economic equality with other industries, and to that end to protect, control, and stabilize' marketing of agricultural commodities by minimizing speculation, preventing waste and inefficiency in distribution, encouraging co-operatives, preventing and controlling surpluses 'through orderly production and distribution . . .'

The law directed the Federal Farm Board, made up of eight members and the Secretary of Agriculture, to invite co-operative associations handling a commodity to establish a non-salaried advisory committee for that commodity. Upon these advisory committees, obviously, would fall the principal burden of gaining farmer co-operation in production control. The theory was that producers, once told what they should do for their own good, would act individually and without coercion. The Board had ample authority to investigate, to report, to recommend—but no authority to compel. When an advisory committee should recommend, the Board could designate any corporation as a stabilization corporation to act as a marketing agency, its activities financed by the revolving fund.[10]

The Board's operations were to be based on the premise that prices could be raised on crops sold at home if the surplus could be temporarily removed—that is, pending its disposal either at home or abroad. To aid in reducing the surplus, Hoover wanted 'the Farm Board to withdraw the excessive acreage of marginal lands which had been brought into cultivation during the war.'[11] At the same time, we should observe, Hoover was attempting to increase agricultural acreage by reclamation and irrigation. At the same time, also, a veritable host of agencies and scientists were doing everything in their power to increase and to improve agricultural production. And at the same time, every intelligent farmer was trying frantically to increase production per acre in order to raise his total income.

2. Billion Dollar Failure

Hoover appointed a Farm Board of recognized 'farm' leaders, with Alexander Legge, president of International Harvester, as chairman. The President expressed his high hopes for the Farm Board at its initial meeting in the White House on 15 July 1929. The Board must discover facts and find solutions for 'a multitude of agricultural problems,' and create permanent marketing institutions to be owned by farmers. For these purposes the President solemnly invested the Board with 'responsibility, authority and resources such as have never before been conferred by our government in assistance to any industry.'[12]

The Board went to work with great enthusiasm. Hoover confidently turned his attention to other problems. The Farm Board was his brain child, his triumph over champions of compulsory production controls and export corporations. Farmers were skeptical as the Farm

Board brought several national co-operatives into existence by forming federations of local and regional co-operatives. The Farmers National Grain Corporation, over which Clarence E. Huff of the Farmers Union presided, was organized in October 1929 and operated from Chicago. Allen Northington directed the American Cotton Co-operative Association, formed on 13 January 1930, from New Orleans. There were similar national marketing co-operatives for wool, beans, livestock, pecans, and other products. Farmers marketed their crops though the local co-operatives, which were agents for the nationals. If the nationals ran into difficulty, the Farm Board would create stabilization corporations to take over unmanageable surpluses.[13]

Commission houses could hardly view with equanimity this threat to their very existence. Hoover, the champion of keep-the-government-out-of-business, had done his best to destroy them; but they could be cheered by observers in and out of agriculture's ranks who freely prophesied failure for efforts of the Farmers National Grain Corporation to raise prices. A. S. McDonald, president of the Grain Dealers' National Association, protested that there was plenty of private capital ready to buy and sell farm products—which was exactly what farmers did not want. Nevertheless, brokers howled too soon. In its operations the Grain Stabilization Corporation worked through 54 Chicago agencies and three score in other cities in addition to the Farmers National.[14]

A storm of protest from special interests met the offer of the Farmers National to buy wheat on 21 December 1929. Within a few months, farmers' marketing agencies had acquired several million bushels of wheat, the mere presence of which might have a depressing effect on the market. Prices went down, the Farm Board's agency kept on buying. Then the Grain Stabilization Corporation was created in February 1930 to support wheat prices by buying stocks already accumulated by the co-operative and by dealing in futures.[15]

World prices of wheat dropped sharply late in the summer of 1930. The Farm Board attributed the disaster in part to forced exports by Russia, Argentina, and other countries. Many country bankers had made loans on the basis of dollar wheat; when the price fell below 80 cents per bushel, there were many country bank failures—so many, in fact, that a banking crisis was created. When the Chicago price fell to 70 cents in November, the Board ordered the Grain Stabilization Corporation to step up its buying. The result was a Chicago price of 81 cents, in January 1931 compared with a Liverpool price of 58 cents. Normally the Chicago price would have been 15 cents to 20 cents lower than the Liverpool price because of shipping costs from Chicago to Liverpool. Buying continued until by 1 July 1931 the Corporation had increased its bag by 257 million bushels of cash wheat and futures, for which it paid an average of about 82 cents per bushel. Then the Board decided to liquidate gradually. No longer supported by Corporation purchases, the price fell to less than 40 cents per bushel on 15 July. With wheat selling for 30 cents per bushel or less in Dodge City, where many a farmer might have envied the peacefulness of Boot Hill's residents, merchants began to offer 50 cents per bushel in trade for cars, furniture, and other merchandise. When Senator Arthur Capper wanted to know what was causing the debacle, the President telegraphed that a large part of the trouble came from paralysis in European markets. Once the European situation improved, so would wheat prices. But they went on down, and Senator T. H. Caraway of Arkansas called Hoover 'the worst guesser that ever occupied his exalted position.'[16]

The Corporation's stocks of wheat were disposed of by 29 April 1933. In the process of liquidation, the Corporation traded 25 million bushels to Brazil for about a million bags of coffee, sold 15 million bushels to China on credit for a little over $9 million, sold 7.5 million bushels to Germany on credit for nearly $4 million, gave 85 million bushels to the Red Cross, and sold the balance in domestic and foreign markets. The Corporation lost about $154 million in its operations to 30 June 1932; farmers apparently received about $160 million more than they would have without the Corporation's activities. But the final accounting reduced the loss.[17]

Failure in wheat stabilization operations was paralleled in the cotton market. The Cotton Stabilization Corporation, created in June 1930, had relieved co-operatives of 1.3 million bales by 30 June 1931. The Corporation also loaned the two national cotton co-operatives funds sufficient to withhold 2.1 million bales from the market. Prices continued to fall: from 18 cents per pound in September 1929 to less than 12 cents in July 1930, to 8.5 cents a year later. There was too much cotton—not too much to wear if it could be converted into cloth for clothes, but too much for domestic and world markets held in the paralyzing grasp of depression. Exasperated, one observer suggested that 'The cotton might be disposed of in one grand conflagration, by the light of which the Government could ask the American people to read large posters containing the words: "The End of One More Governmental Attempt to Fix Prices." '[18]

Confronted with a new crop of 15.5 million bales in 1931, the Farm Board saw a carryover of 24.5 million bales. Desperately James C. Stone, harassed chairman of the Board, wired governors of cotton states that they 'immediately mobilize every interested and available agency . . . to induce immediate plowing under of every third row of cotton now growing.' A thundering chorus of indignant opposition, tempered by only slight approval, met this proposal, which the *New York Times* called 'one of the maddest things that ever came from an official body.'[19]

The third row remained to be harvested in 1931, and the price slid to 4.6 cents per pound before the 1932 harvest. The result was that a surplus of 6.5 million bales was added to the 3.4 million bales held by co-operatives and the Corporation. The latter began to liquidate its holdings in August 1932. At that time it had paid $127,575,389 for cotton then worth $42,523,912. All of the cotton held by the Corporation was sold in the market or donated to the Red Cross by 15 June 1933. The net loss was less than $16 million, not counting some 850 thousand bales worth over $78 million given to the Red Cross.[20]

In attempting to explain the Farm Board's failure, some critics could find nothing good in the whole scheme. It was, they maintained, merely 'a process of involved speculation,' a conspiracy 'to deliver the co-operative movement into the hands of the private grain trade.' That, the critics said, was why Legge offered James H. Murray, president of the Chicago Board of Trade, the job of managing both the Farmers National Grain Corporation and the Grain Stabilization Corporation. The $500 million fund was used as a club to force producers to submit to dictation by professional promoters:

Republican politics, personal favoritism, and outright corruption, to say nothing of the naive attempt to stabilize prices by gambling in grain and cotton, marked the activities of the Farm Board for two and a half years. At the end of that period the board had gambled or given away virtually all of its assets, a few men had enriched themselves at the expense of the taxpayers and producers, farm prices were at or near the lowest points in history, and thousands of farmers were in open rebellion.[21]

These charges were widespread. Regardless of favoritism, politics, or corruption, there is no question about the Board's abysmal failure to perform the impossible by the measures it followed.

The Federal Farm Board did lose money, but not as much as popularly supposed and it was not the most expensive operation in American history. For all purposes, the Board made net commitments of $1,158,089,950 from 1 July 1929 through 26 May 1933. Its actual advances from the revolving fund were $1,148,906,533; repayments were $777,410,041, leaving $371,496,492 outstanding.[22]

A large crop of farm relief bills emerged from the Seventy-second Congress. Republican and Democratic senators joined in attacking the Farm Board, and none of these advocates of change was a Hoover stalwart. Several bills concentrated on devices to guarantee prices that would meet production costs. Senator Brookhart attempted to introduce the equalization fee and to broaden co-operative activities; Senator James F. Byrnes would abolish the Farm Board but retain the promotion of co-operatives; Senator Lynn J. Frazier would carry on a gigantic refinancing of farm debts; Senator Elmer Thomas would abolish the Farm Board and inaugurate domestic allotment; Senator Charles L. McNary returned to his familiar equalization fee, and Senator Burton K. Wheeler proposed a Farmers' Reconstruction Finance Corporation.[23]

In testifying for the Frazier proposal, C. C. Talbott, president of the North Dakota Farmers' Union, struck hard at the Hoover policies:

The people in my territory . . . feel that especially since the socialistic bill [R.F.C.] was passed a few days ago by the House and the Senate to rehabilitate the big bankers, the railroad companies, and the big insurance companies—and no doubt they need it; we will accede to that—but the same people who have cried, 'Socialism' against us Bolsheviks out on the farm, have gone to the United States Government and asked for the most socialistic program that has ever been put over in the history of this Government. We feel that, without any blush of shame, we can come and ask for the same thing.[24]

Ogden L. Mills vigorously assaulted the Frazier bill by declaring it was 'ruinous to the Federal land bank system and the Federal reserve system and would imperil the monetary standards of the country.'[25]

Administration spokesmen were much too busy to bother with bills which had been introduced primarily to worry the President or to air new schemes. No matter what the House might pass, even if the Senate did follow, a Hoover veto was almost certain to be upheld. Talk about domestic allotment, therefore, was more significant for the future. Dr. M. L. Wilson, agricultural economist of Montana State College, presented a lucid explanation of what was to be the heart of the New Deal farm relief effort.[26] There may have been a little malice in bringing Paul Moore from West Branch, Iowa, to testify on farm relief. He did not disappoint the President's enemies: 'I think the time will come . . . when we will have what may be called a farmers' strike; that they will take that peaceful mode first before they will enter into a mob action or revolution or anything else.'[27]

Neither Congress, which established the Federal Farm Board, nor farmers, for whom it was created, were friendly to the Hoover farm relief effort. Confusion, fragmented counsels, resentment, and exasperation characterized Republican farm relief measures from their inception. Most farmers were less coherent than William Gordon Stuart, a New York dairyman, but most of them were just as bewildered, just as frustrated, just as angry: 'We farmers have been the under dogs too long. We have been humbugged by the politician, cheated by the railroads, imposed upon by the unionization of other forms of labor . . . and now we are going to get justice or know the reason why!'[28]

3. *Black Blizzards*

Nature conspired to confound farm experts and to give searing comfort to the irreconcilable critics of any effort for aiding agriculture. 'The worst drought ever recorded in this country prevailed during much of the 1930 crop-growing season and greatly reduced production.'[29] Even the weather set a new disaster record when Hoover was President!

Rainfall in fifteen states east of the Rockies was one-half of normal from June to August, and thirty states, from Virginia to Texas and from Pennsylvania to Montana, were hard hit. Streams dried up and rivers idled past cracked mudbanks. The long green leaves of corn shriveled, turned brown, curled up in despair, and rustled mournfully while burning winds swept the plains. Cattle wandered through eddies of dust in search of food, and stockmen saw their stacks of hay disappear. From the valleys of the Potomac, from the Ohio, the Mississippi and the great Northwest, came a stream of dreary reports, as a million families and twenty times as many animals faced the worst drought of the century.

Wheat baronies in the Great Plains harvested a good crop in the summer of 1930, since the drought came too late to do much damage.

War demands for wheat had accelerated expansion of sod-busting in semiarid regions west of the 100th meridian. Here, in western Texas and Oklahoma, southwestern Kansas, northeastern New Mexico, eastern Colorado, and southwestern Nebraska, were vast expanses of fertile soil that lacked nothing but water. Aside from providing grazing for herds of cattle, much of this land appeared to be good for nothing except to provide a bridge between East and West. A few years of fairly ample moisture coincided with war demands. The use of increasingly efficient machinery so reduced cost of production that bonanza farmers of the plains felt little distress during the 1920's.

Even these last pioneers, whose plows raped the virgin soil, should have been disturbed by the surplus crop harvested in 1930 and by the severe drought. But farmers in newly plowed wheat country owed money for land and machinery. Only by making another crop and still another could they hope to escape foreclosure. They planted good seed in dry ground in the fall of 1930. The year was not too bad, although yields fell off drastically. In the fall of 1931 they planted more good seed in still drier ground. As winter came there was no rich cover of green to be blanketed with snow. The ever-present winds dried up the scanty winter moisture, whirled the dry soil into eddies of dust, and filled the sky with black blizzards. The drought of 1930 and 1931 on the Great Plains was but a preliminary to the main tragedy of dust that cast its pall over the country in the spring of 1932.[30]

Decreased production might have been expected to cause increased prices, but there was no general decrease in agricultural products in 1930. The wheat crop was 840 million bushels, up 34 million over 1929; rye increased from 40.8 million to 46.7 million bushels. Buckwheat, caught by the 1930 drought, was off 24 per cent from 1929. Rice and peanuts were down in volume, while sugar beets and beans increased considerably. Cotton fell off slightly, and corn production was down by 22 per cent. Statistics varied from state to state, with Colorado, Arizona, Oregon, and California showing much higher yields than in 1929. The gross farm income fell to $9.4 billion in 1930, off about 20 per cent from 1929.[31]

Few states were stricken as badly as Arkansas in the summer of 1930. Conditions were so bad that the Red Cross was providing driblets of food, clothing, and other aid in 73 of 75 counties by January 1931. During the preceding summer, the thermometer reached or exceeded 100° for 42 of 43 consecutive days; rainfall for 100 days was not enough 'to wet a man's shirt.' Normal precipitation in June and July was nearly 8 inches, but in 1930 it was only 1.5 inches. Cotton in 1929 brought $119 million to the state, but only $41 million in 1930; corn averaged a miserable 14 bushels per acre in 1929 and approached nullity in 1930 with an average of 4.1 bushels per acre. There were 143 bank failures in the last six months of 1930, most of them in rural areas where banking and agriculture were intimately related. No one, not even the people of Arkansas, realized how extensive was the calamity. There were authenticated cases of hardworking families to illustrate disaster. One family of eight had nothing to eat except unseasoned turnips and turnip greens for a week; another was better fed with one meal daily of bread, molasses, and occasionally beans or 'white lightning'—salt pork with no meat in it. Arkansas tried to help itself. Harvey C. Couch, well-known utilities executive, headed a drought committee which sparked local relief efforts. The Red Cross broadcast quantities of turnip seed which provided greens and 'pot likker' in the fall. Mr. Heartsill Ragon, representative in Congress, bitterly commented on appropriations to provide 29-cent meals for federal convicts, yet Congress hesitated to provide 3-cent meals for starving Arkansans.[32]

Hoover attacked the drought emergency with an eagerness akin to pleasure. Here was a problem that would yield to his experience, one that could be solved with emergency measures. Resorting to his favorite technique, the President summoned a conference of governors to meet on 14 August 1930. These gentlemen agreed to set up drought committees in the afflicted states which would receive reports of relief needs from county committees. Secretary Hyde presided over the Federal Drought Relief Committee, which could draw on a pitiful $500,000 left over from the disaster appropriation of $6 million—a fund set up to provide loans for farmers in the Southeast who had suffered from storms and floods. A similar appropriation had become available at the end of March 1930, just in case of need. The National Association of Commissioners of Agriculture, which met in Washington on 20 October, appointed a committee to work with Secretary Hyde to draft drought relief legislation.

Chairmen of state drought relief committees presented a gloomy picture of conditions but displayed no desire for charity. The general tenor of their reports revealed grim determination to get along through hard work if credit could be made available. Numerous bank suspensions had dried up customary sources of credit and contributed to increased distress; bankers in some states were generally hostile to agricultural credit corporations, yet they either could not or would not make crop loans in sufficient volume to meet the demand. Careful estimates revealed that 330,000 farm families in fifteen states would need about $85 million in loans.[33]

President Hoover persuaded the railroads, their freight revenues seriously threatened, to haul feed to the stricken areas at half rates under specified conditions. Red tape in acquiring freight-rate reductions on hay handicapped that part of the program. Reduced rates were effective only until 1 October, but the period of real need came after 1 January. The Federal Farm Board offered loans to enable the Grain Stabilization Corporation to sell feed grains in car lots to special corporations of dealers, farmers, or businessmen if such corporations would guaranty payment by the individual farmers. This offer, like the timid and ineffectual freight reduction gesture, made practically no dent on the mass of suffering farmers. As one Nebraska farm woman put it, most of the farmers could get through the winter if only they could have a moratorium on taxes and mortgage payments, but they could not buy feed and pay other obligations from practically exhausted resources. 'To sum up,' she wrote, 'drought relief to date amounts to this—from the railroads, a gesture; from the government, nothing.'[34]

By the time the Seventy-first Congress convened in December 1930 for its final session, the federal government had accomplished very little in the area of drought relief. The harmony conference of party leaders discussed the problem before Congress met, and members believed that the President would support an appropriation of $60 million that would provide food for families, feed for workstock, fuel and oil for tractors, seeds, and fertilizer—all on a loan basis. Joint resolutions were presented in both houses in the first days of the session with these objectives in mind. These resolutions were neither an attempt to deal with unemployment nor a step toward a dole. Then an administration measure, providing only $25 million and excluding loans for food, was introduced. Democrats and liberal Republicans were amazed at what they considered a doublecross engineered from the White House. Mr. Hyde, faithfully supporting the President, called food loans dangerously close to a dole.[35]

Much of the President's opposition to the increase was caused by fears that there would be the tremendous raids on the treasury which he had warned against in his December message. Bills introduced in Congress would cause an expenditure of $4.5 billion, Hoover estimated. He had recommended appropriations of up to $150 million to enlarge the public works program to relieve unemployment throughout the nation; he was unwilling to go beyond that, for he felt strongly that the nation could not squander itself into prosperity. If he let the bars down and permitted appropriations to buy food for farmers in the drought area, there might be an irresistible flood of demands for federal appropriations to put the unemployed on a dole. One of the basic principles of rugged individualism was at stake. Nevertheless, Congress insisted and, after quibbling over the sum, finally agreed on $45 million. The President gave his approval on 20 December.[36]

Why had Hoover let himself be maneuvered into a position so vulnerable to opposition attacks? Partly because he was depending on the Red Cross, which, as of 30 November 1930, had $14,626,000 in its general funds, of which some $10 million was committed. Chairman John Barton Payne assured Hoover that the Red Cross was 'prepared to relieve actual distress in the premises.' Whatever Payne meant, the Red Cross was not at all prepared to provide significant relief. By the end of 1930, the Red Cross had provided food, clothing, and other relief to nearly 50,000 families at a cost of more than $500,000. An average of $10 per family could make no impression on the desperate situation, but in the first week of January 1931 Mr. Payne believed that the $4.5 million left in the disaster reserve fund would carry through the winter! Secretary Hyde was equally unrealistic when he assured the press that Payne and the Red Cross could handle the problem of drought relief. Then, on 10 January 1931, Mr. Payne must have remembered some very elementary arithmetic. He asked Hoover to support a public plea for $10 million for farm relief in the drought area. Hoover, as president of the Red Cross, approved the appeal.[37]

In Congress there were charges that Hoover had supported this plea in order to kill a $15 million amendment that would provide loans for food. The President appealed to the nation for contributions, formed a nation-wide committee to help the Red Cross meet the national emergency, and made a radio appearance to promote the cause. By the end of January, with the aid of Will Rogers, Calvin Coolidge, and other prominent people, the Red Cross had raised some $5 million. Senator Joseph T. Robinson, in whose state of Arkansas the Red Cross was very active, led a fight to add $25 million to an appropriation bill for the Red Cross.The Senate voted in favor on 19 January, but Payne announced that he would not accept the money because it would seriously diminish voluntary contributions. The House, therefore, rejected the Robinson amendment, and President Hoover approved heartily. In February, Congress did provide $20 million for rehabilitation in the drought area, and Secretary Hyde ruled that the money could be used for food. The rehabilitation money, however, was for loans, and only farmers with some sort of security could obtain it. As a source of genuine relief, this fund was woefully inadequate.[38]

To people willing to read even as they ran, the problem of drought relief revealed starkly the woeful state of agriculture. Millions of farmers were absolutely bankrupt; so long as they were not dispossessed and nature continued to behave normally, farmers might at least have something to eat. But in the face of any natural disaster, few if any farmers had any reserve.

The fight over adding a few millions for food to the drought relief measure cost the President an incalculable loss of prestige. A relief expert with world-wide fame, Hoover could have played a leading role with full popular support. Sufferers from drought were just as hungry as victims of floods in China or in the Mississippi Valley. The drought, too, was an act of God requiring prompt remedial action, which might have come if someone else, Woodrow Wilson for example, had been able to say: 'You get relief to the people, we'll provide the money!' But Hoover had to make the decision and he feared 'wholesale raids on the public treasury.' He seemed to forget the long history of federal appropriations to supplement private contributions in disaster relief. He feared that approval of even $15 million for food to drought sufferers would open the way for appropriations to feed victims of the depression. To acknowledge failure of voluntary giving might lead people to draw the logical conclusion that only the federal government could provide the necessary assistance to deal with the depression. When critics of food relief called it a dole, they were thinking beyond the drought victims, most of whom were not unemployed, to the millions of jobless victims of depression. It was easy for relief advocates to picture the President as being indifferent to human suffering, however unfair such a charge might be. Hoover clung with wonderful stubbornness to the idea that local resources should be able to take care of hunger and misery regardless of their causes.

Relief funds voted by Congress were pitifully small in view of the need and were soon exhausted, as farmers borrowed over $47 million for seed, fertilizer, fuel and oil, and that vague thing called 'rehabilitation.' With gross income off as much as 46 per cent in some states, the loaning of about $150 apiece to some 385,000 borrowers was meager help indeed.[39]

Unemployment relief and increased road building aided the few farmers who were able to get in on local or national projects. For the year ending 30 June 1931, $135.6 million was spent on federal-aid highways. An average of 100,000 men were kept at work on road construction from January to September 1931, but very few of them were farmers. Those who from incurable optimism, habit, inertia, or animal instinct remained on their dessicated farms, returned to their work early in the spring. Their prospects were indeed poor: gross farm income had been $9.4 billion in 1930 and fell to $6.9 billion in 1931.[40] On this sum, the average net return was $342 for the year's work!

4. *Unsolved Problems*

Hoover's estimate of the farm problem was entirely sound, regardless of the Farm Board's failures. His analysis of causes was correct, but he was unwilling to take the bold coercive steps necessary to remedy the troubles that he saw so clearly. A short-range program to relieve immediate distress had to be accompanied by a long-range program to remove causes of distress. As economic difficulties increased, the short-range program needed to be intensified. There is ample evidence of worsening conditions. Farm prices in 1930 were 88.3 per cent of the 1926 level, 64.8 per cent in 1931, and 48.2 per cent in 1932. No other major indices fell so low. In terms of gross income, this meant a decline from $12 billion in 1929 to $5.3 billion in 1932. Net cash income of all farmers in 1932 was less than $1.5 billion, an average of less than $250 per family for the year. Between 1930 and 1934, nearly a million farms passed from owner-borrowers to mortgage holders.[41]

What happened to farm prices is dramatically portrayed by values of agricultural products, exclusive of livestock, in Kansas from 1913 to 1932. In the first of these years, aggregate value of Kansas farm products was about $241.5 million. This figure, after a 300 per cent rise in 1919, fell to about $351 million in 1921. After fluctuating but generally rising until 1929, it plunged to $203.9 million in 1932. There was, of course, considerable variation in production. Especially significant are such facts as these: Some 138 million bushels of winter wheat in 1929 were worth more than $1 per bushel; but 106 million bushels were worth less than 30 cents per bushel in 1932.[42] Farmers might well have repeated the jingle of earlier days: 'In God we trusted, in Kansas we busted!' God and Kansas were not to blame, nor were the farmers who trusted in both.

Not even in their rear-guard action against the Democrats in 1932 could Republicans claim success for their Farm Board experiment. The Farm Board had recognized the futility of its operations in July 1931, when it stopped trying to hold up wheat prices. In January 1930, Alexander Legge had warned against crop supports without production controls and his warning had been entirely ineffective. By early 1932 the $500 million revolving fund was gone, exchanged for 'twin leaning towers of wheat and cotton which threaten to overhang the market for several years . . .'[43]

In that election year of 1932, the largest national farm organizations could agree on condemning the Farm Board. They could not agree on policies, though: the Grange wanted an export debenture; the Farm Bureau a return to the equalization fee; and the Farmers Union urged price fixing. Farmers generally were no more in favor of regimentation in 1932 than they had been in 1922. Rugged individualists themselves, most of them were in favor of eliminating the rugged individualists who controlled marketing and dictated prices.

Some people who had little status as agricultural experts struck out boldly for a solution to the farm problem after the Farm Board's failure became evident. Among them was Walter B. Pitkin, enamored of the super-farm. Hickman Price in Texas and J. S. Bird in Kansas demonstrated what could be done with super-farms. Competition from Russia and other potentially great producers, Pitkin warned, would force abandonment of the 'quarter-section half-wit.' There were two roads: the way of the coolie and the way of the corporation. Owners of small farms should exchange their titles for stock in a super-farm which would then rip out the fences, burn the shacks, sell obsolete equipment, and proceed to large-scale production. Of the 390 million acres in cultivation in 1930, about 70 million should be given up as submarginal; about 5 million adults and children should be moved to urban centers to replace the low-grade unskilled immigrants, who would be shipped back home; huge public works programs would care for displaced farmers unable to find other employment. But the Great Dirt Conspiracy, supported by the small farmers and countless parasites, would oppose this plan for agriculture.[44] This mixture of wisdom and foolishness was typical of what most critics had to offer.

Proceeding from the assumption that the law of supply and demand operated in the case of agricultural prices, many farm economists attacked the farm problem on the basis of land use. President Hoover had emphasized the need for withdrawing marginal lands from cultivation, but he had not proposed a practical plan for doing so. Secretary Hyde called a national conference on 24 November 1931 to consider land utilization. The problem, he informed the conference, was to obtain 'voluntary control of production through farmer-owned, farmer-controlled, co-operative associations.'[45] He understood the problem posed by farmers trying to make a living from land unfit for cultivation. He could point to the millions of acres sold for taxes or abandoned by their owners.

Mr. Hyde may have been relaying the President's ideas; whatever their paternity, they were sound and are still applicable to large areas where private enterprisers are ruining soil resources. The Secretary proposed sound measures:

The answer to the problem of submarginal lands is purchase and reforestation by the Government. There probably are areas which possess so high a value for national uses that they should be acquired. National uses, under our present policy, include watershed protection, national forests, parks, and game preserves. Possibly sound policy would include acquisition to stop erosion and to conserve the soil for future generations. [Mr. Hyde was right, but was he not advocating socialism?] Our traditional national policy of planless agricultural development should be replaced without delay by a program based upon such a utilization of our land resources as will yield greater economic and social values, will stay erosion and soil depletion, will preserve and conserve our land inheritance, and limit our agricultural plant to such size as will supply the nation's needs, without the ruinous blight of overproduction.[46]

What were the solutions that would have helped the majority of farmers? Hoover was correct in denying that any one remedy would be a panacea; he made a serious mistake in not insisting upon the diversified attack which he knew was needed. He was correct in believing that a restoration of urban prosperity was necessary for farm prosperity; but it had to be a broad urban prosperity, with high purchasing power available to the masses of people and not alone to the fortunate few. He was correct in emphasizing the need for world recovery; he was terribly mistaken in signing the Hawley-Smoot Tariff. Agriculture would not prosper unless urban areas prospered, and the United States could not prosper indefinitely unless the world economy recovered. Rural and urban, national and international relationships were too close to permit any other outcome.[47]

Specific measures could be taken. Lower taxes were desirable, but higher prices would erase that inequality. Better credit facilities for long and short term loans were needed. The Hoover Administration provided them. Definitely submarginal lands should have been retired from production and a reservoir of marginal lands set up to be drawn upon when needed. These steps were not taken, although the problem of what to do with the people who would be displaced was not unsolvable. This solution would be socialistic—but was it any different in principle than federal construction of Hoover Dam?

It was essential that the government halt reclamation and irrigation projects which would contribute to surplus production, but such a measure, although greatly needed, was certain to be politically unpopular. Standby facilities might be constructed as public works projects; but the land thus added to agricultural acreage should have been kept out of production until domestic and world demand required its cultivation. Marketing processes could be controlled to prevent racketeering practices which would rob the producer; exchanges could be regulated to prevent gambling without interfering with legitimate economic services provided by brokers; farmer-owned co-operatives could be supported, guided, and protected. Some of these things the Republicans attempted, but they refused to lower tariffs on major items farmers purchased. Lacking domestic and international competition, manufacturers charged monopoly prices.[48]

Planned production—which means controlled production—was necessary to keep farmers from turning themselves into peasants. We could continue to have no controls and a permanently depressed agriculture; we could resort to federal control and thus impinge upon traditional and revered rugged individualism. Hoover recognized the need for control, and as President he went as far as he could to promote voluntary control through integrated co-operatives.

Solution of the farm problem, in so far as government could solve it, lay in creating conditions under which the intelligent, industrious farmer could prosper through his own competitive enterprise. No price fixing, market support, stabilization, or subsidy schemes could make any permanent contribution to anything except further chaos. All such schemes simply postponed inevitable readjustments. But this kind of free competition for agriculture is impossible unless it is enforced in all other sectors of the economy. That means an end to excessively high protective tariffs, to transportation and other rates based on bloated capitalization, to monopoly prices through conspiracies in restraint of trade. Since the powers that were refused to surrender their cherished special privileges, or to relinquish their control of political parties, legislatures, and courts, the only way that the farmers could be kept moderately satisfied was through subsidies. And such measures only postponed further the day of reckoning which will have to come sometime if mankind is ever to give substance to the ideas of justice and right.

CHAPTER XIII

STRUGGLE FOR RELIEF

1. *The Mounting Crisis*

Unemployment and relief problems were nothing new in American history. Before 1850 humanitarians of the transcendentalist school had concerned themselves with ways to abolish poverty; their successors had persisted in devising measures to aid the unemployed, the unemployable, and the poverty-stricken members of society. The belief persisted that relief should be taken care of by organized charity and local governments; but the burden had become increasingly severe during the 1920's, so severe that the entire structure of private and local efforts broke down under the tremendous demands of the Great Depression.

Distress was felt first in the industrial areas, in the cities where people were concentrated and where there were no groups organized to cope with worsening conditions. People in these cities saw their jobs disappear, their savings frozen in closed banks, and their investments melting away. There were many people who never had saved anything, either because of extravagance or because of low earning capacity, persistent illness, or other good reasons. By April 1930 there were 'about one million families without breadwinners.' Or, if one takes other figures, there were 4.5 million unemployed plus the usual quota of unemployables. The number grew from more than 8 million in 1931 to perhaps 13 million or more in 1932. State and local governments did not possess the machinery, funds, and experience to cope with a problem of such magnitude. President Hoover stubbornly fought against expansion of federal functions in providing direct relief, but he was doomed to lose the battle.[1]

Month after month, in any city, tragedy born of economic disaster blighted the lives of proud Americans. 'We didn't know that one of the fathers in our neighborhood was out of work until we wondered why his small son's legs grew thin.' That was in Detroit, where Joe Raymond, fifteen years old, supported a family of nine on $7 a week; his father earned $13.80 in four months. And Thomas Karekin 'stood in line all night for seven weeks outside the factory gates at the Ford plant.'[2] There were thousands upon thousands of Joe Raymonds and Thomas Karekins.

Private and local relief agencies felt the increasing pressures of economic distress several months before the market crash formally inaugurated the long depression. The expected seasonal drop in unemployment did not occur. Persons on relief increased in number with each passing month until the market catastrophe confirmed the worst fears of social workers. Bread lines, already fixtures in out-of-the-way streets before the Big Crash, lengthened in the winter of 1929–30. Every city had them, except for a very few that ignored the growing need. Existing relief agencies soon were overwhelmed, but federal and state officials continued to be optimistic. There was no quick and adequate response to the needs of the unemployed; there was nothing to match the moratorium on intergovernmental debts in 1931, nothing so bold and determined as the Reconstruction Finance Corporation in 1932. To be sure, drought in the summer of 1930 caused Hoover to create the National Drought Committee in August; but this was disaster relief, and the federal government had not yet entered the realm of general public relief.

Winter, striking early in 1930, emphasized the need for action. There had been no significant seasonal increase in employment. Public and private efforts over the country revealed a growing uneasiness, a growing appreciation of the need for heroic measures. John D. Hunter, head of the United Charities of Chicago, accurately assayed the situation in October with a terse comment: 'We are face to face with the worst winter the United Charities has known since 1866.' Toward the end of October, Boston appropriated $1 million for relief and started a campaign to raise $2 million; New York City added $1 million to its relief funds. Seward Prosser of Bankers Trust Co. enlisted fellow financial leaders to form an Emergency Employment Committee to finance boondoggling. They would raise $150,000 per week to hire 10,000 men at $15 per week to do made work. In Illinois, where 400,000 were unemployed, public charities planned to spend $12 million; in Detroit, Mayor Frank Murphy encouraged job rotation, and four potent financiers and companies gave $475,000.[3]

As the nation prepared to go to the polls on 4 November, more reports were available from the relief front. Governor Roosevelt prepared to shelter several thousand unemployed in armories; New York City planned to feed 15,000 persons daily; Pittsburgh raised a pitiful $100,000 fund, supplemented by a $300,000 construction program.

Milwaukee was ready to spend $200,000 on work relief for 13,500 men using hand tools. Samuel J. Insull in Chicago taxed his employees one day's pay to raise $100,000 per month. In the midst of all this activity, Vice President Charles Curtis announced the wonderful news that 'Good times are just around the corner.'[4] Erroneously attributed to Hoover, this uninspired prophecy was a lethal political boomerang.

Following his general practice in crises, President Hoover appointed a committee, the Emergency Committee for Employment, on 21 October 1930, and persuaded Colonel Arthur H. Woods to be its chairman. Woods, then an official of the Rockefeller Foundation and the General Education Board, had served on the President's Conference on Unemployment over which Hoover had presided in 1921. Hoover now assigned to him responsibility for developing 'a program for dealing with the unemployment emergency.' Woods and his thirty-two fellow committeemen had a threefold program: develop job opportunities, provide 'effective direct relief measures when needed,' and carry on a propaganda campaign to arouse general interest in the unemployment problem. The Committee was very active in distributing information about how states and small communities were trying to make jobs and spread the work; it circulated ideas on sprucing up the home, buying low-cost foods, caring for the transient unemployed, persuading young men and women not to hit the road, and growing gardens for food supplies.[5]

The Committee confessed that it was impossible to discover how many were unemployed, or how many needed direct relief. While trying to get a good estimate, Woods sought an immediate increase in appropriations for public construction. Despite increased federal building, public and private construction showed in 1930 a decrease of 11 per cent from 1929. Woods confidentially advised Hoover to ask for $840 million for roads, public works, and other projects. Hoover considered this proposal imprudent. The President also dealt his Committee another blow when in March 1931 he vetoed the Wagner bill to create an effective Federal Employment Service. Woods favored the bill and urged Hoover to accept it.[6]

2. *Labor Policies*

Hoover had no concise program or plan to deal with labor as an economic group. He saw labor as an indispensable part of the entire industrial process and whatever made for full production and elimination of waste would benefit labor. Unemployment was an emergency problem to be handled by private, local, and state resources with federal assistance through public works. Social security measures, particularly unemployment insurance and retirement benefits, would be quite proper if provided by private enterprise.

Hoover believed that a community of interest existed between labor and industry, that neither could be served through industrial warfare. Government should make available facilities for voluntary arbitration but there should be no compulsion.[7] He favored unions, collective bargaining, abolition of child labor, maintenance of high wages, and a shorter working day. He opposed the closed shop as being an interference with equality of opportunity; on the same basis he opposed the yellow-dog contract and excessive use of injunctions in labor disputes.[8] Hoover's attitude toward labor may be described as positive, but most of his actions were negative or indirect.

Hoover fought hard and successfully against Senator Wagner's proposal to strengthen the ineffective United States Employment Service. This agency, begun in 1907, had never been important in bringing jobs and workers together except in very limited areas. Wagner's bill aroused intense employer opposition, but the Congress passed it, only to encounter a presidential veto on 7 March 1931.[9]

Labor's friends had more success in their attack on the use of injunctions in labor disputes. The Norris-La Guardia Anti-Injunction Act went through Congress with little numerical opposition. In framing the bill, Norris sought advice from Felix Frankfurter and other widely respected legal authorities. In general, the law declared that labor should have freedom of association and organization, outlawed the yellow-dog contract, drastically curtailed the use of injunctions in labor disputes, and relieved union officers of responsibility for acts of members.[10] This type of legislation had been under consideration for more than a decade.

Hoover was not pleased with the sweeping provisions of the bill, but he interposed no serious objections. Earl C. Michener, Michigan Republican who had led the fight in the House against the Wagner bill to strengthen the United States Employment Service, believed that labor deserved a reward since the A.F. of L. had 'done more than any other group or class of our people in maintaining peace and order during this depression.' [11] Representatives joined in a paean of praise for labor's docility and its opposition to communism, but James M. Beck anticipated industrial anarchy should the bill be passed. Opposition was insignificant and the bill cleared the Senate on 1 March by a vote of 75 to 5; then a week later it sailed through the House by the impressive margin of 362 to 14. Hoover signed it on 23 March 1932.[12]

The Norris-La Guardia Act was a major step toward releasing labor from shackles that had bound it so long. To make possible a mature and effective labor movement, to protect labor from cyclical economic disaster, several other acts were needed. President Hoover would agree to none of them and so passed on to the New Deal both the responsibility and the prestige of providing compulsory collective bargaining and compulsory social security measures. Voluntary collective bargaining and voluntary mediation fitted perfectly into Hoover's American system; compulsion would mean a tremendous expansion of federal power and an invasion of state rights. So, too, any form of federally controlled social security would mean swollen bureaucracy, competition with private insurance business, and a weakening of American individualism. Despite numerous hearings on bills that proposed such radical measures, Hoover was not seriously challenged by social security agitation.

Sober recommendations of the Woods Committee received little publicity, while Edward L. Bernays, its public relations director, poured out reams of copy that infuriated social security experts. One of them, Abraham Epstein, was exasperated with the unrealistic optimism generated by the Committee, ridiculed the sloganeering approach, and jeered at the 'luxurious growth' of futile organizations. Instead of wasting time in medicine-man incantations, Epstein urged the Hoover Administration to obtain facts about unemployment, set up employment exchanges, stabilize industries that could be stabilized, expand public works, provide old-age pensions, raise the working age of children, establish the 48-hour week, raise wages, start a huge housing program, and provide for unemployment insurance.[13] Throughout the depression the principal champions of social security were professional social workers.

3. *Federal Relief—Almost*

A false optimism, based on failure to assess needs accurately, dominated Hoover's thinking at the end of 1930. He was not alone, of course; but plans should have been prepared for drastic measures to deal with the situation should the storm increase, despite the cheerful admonitions of reckless prophets. Had the relief crisis been concentrated or overwhelming like a massive Russian famine or a flood-ravaged valley, the President would have visited the scene of disaster to initiate vigorous action. Distress was dispersed throughout the country, although more acute in urban centers, and Hoover relied upon inadequate reports. However exact, statistics could not impart the sense of urgency that followed from standing on a Mississippi River levee and watching the flood pour through a crevasse. Unemployment was not a swift disaster certain to disappear quickly; it was a continuing catastrophe. Hoover tried to treat it as an emergency limited in duration; he refused to see it as a condition to which no end was in sight.

The President's message to Congress on 2 December 1930 took as its text: 'The fundamental strength of the Nation's economic life is unimpaired . . .' Depressions were only temporary, the golden glow would return:

Economic depression can not be cured by legislative action or executive pronouncement. Economic wounds must be healed by the action of the cells of the economic body—the producers and consumers themselves. Recovery can be expedited and its effects mitigated by cooperative action. That cooperation requires that every individual should sustain faith and courage; that each should maintain his self-reliance; . . . that the vast majority whose income is unimpaired should not hoard out of fear but should seek to assist his neighbors who may be less fortunate; that each industry should assist its own employees; that each community and each State should assume its full responsibilities for organization of employment and relief of distress with that sturdiness and independence which built a great Nation.[14]

Basically, this was the same line Dwight Morrow followed in his senatorial campaign in 1930: 'There is something about too much prosperity that ruins the fibre of the people. The men and women that built this country . . . were people that were reared in adversity.' Edmund Wilson, then beginning his notable career as essayist and literary critic, commented: 'It is a reassuring thought, in the cold weather, that the emaciated men in the bread lines, the men and women beggars in the streets, and the children dependent on them, are all having their fibre hardened.' [15]

The President's optimism came from interpretations that refused to consider fundamental facts. He noted that employers had agreed to maintain wage standards and labor leaders promised to avoid industrial strife. 'The index of union wage scales shows them to be to-day fully up to the level of any previous three years.' But what of total wages received? What of part-time employment? What of displacing high-priced with low-priced labor? Mr. Hoover mentioned none of this. Construction work would total $7 billion in 1930, up $700 million over 1929. 'We have as a Nation a definite duty to see that no deserving person in our country suffers from hunger and cold.' This objective was being achieved by the President's Emergency Committee for Employment by promoting co-operation. The government's public works program called for $520 million in the current fiscal year, more than double that for 1928. But there was a limit imposed by financial prudence: 'To increase taxation for purposes of construction work defeats its own purpose, as such taxes directly diminish employment in private industry.' Therefore, the President disregarded his Committee's recommendation of $840 million and asked for only a maximum of $150 million in new appropriations for public works.

There were many in Congress—liberal Republicans and Democrats —who believed that the President underestimated the seriousness of unemployment. Members of Congress began to worry Hoover by introducing relief measures, at first for effect on home opinion, then seriously. These measures 'bobbed up persistently like apples in a tub of water and kept the Administration leaders busy slapping them down.' [16] Every time they slapped, they knocked votes into the Democratic column for 1932.

The wide variations in estimates of how much money should be made available for various kinds of relief were a clear indication of prevailing confusion and ignorance. No one knew exactly what the situation was and no one could find out, because there were no reliable statistics and no immediate way to obtain them. The fumbling, erratic proposals so annoyed President Hoover that he released a general blast to the press on 9 December 1930. Measures introduced in Congress, he observed, would cost $4.5 billion in the next eighteen months. He had already recommended the maximum that could be appropriated without increased taxes. 'No matter how devised, an increase in taxes in the end falls upon the workers and farmers, or alternatively deprives industry of that much ability to give employment and defeats the very purpose of these schemes. . . . Prosperity can not be restored by raids upon the Public Treasury.' Sponsors of some schemes were 'playing politics with human misery . . . and they are all mistaken as to the ability of the Federal Government to undertake such burdens.' [17]

Senator T. H. Caraway, the eloquent defender of the Democracy from Arkansas, accepted the President's challenge. In scathing oratory he denounced Hoover for having ignored the unemployment problem in 1928, thus playing politics with misery; for excoriating people and organizations vitally concerned with relief, thus revealing a callous attitude. Senator David I. Walsh succinctly phrased what was to become a familiar accusation against the President: 'Whatever the emergency, whatever the appeal, whatever the cry that comes up from the suffering people of this country, he does not propose to levy one dollar more in increased taxes.' [18]

A few Republicans tried to calm their indignant Democratic brethren by saying that Hoover had not singled out any one person for attack, that the whole Congress was included in the December explosion. But their efforts were weak. No one arose in the Senate as a doughty champion of Hoover economy, or as a defender of his peevish summation of bills obviously introduced to satisfy demands of constituents. A more perceptive politician would have known that thousands of bills are introduced with no serious intent whatever; a more skillful politician would not have accused Congress of irresponsibility in a time of national crisis. Roosevelt and his managers already were warming up for the 1932 campaign, and Hoover could ill afford to antagonize any more people in his own party.

A few states began to assume more responsibility for unemployment relief but most of them did little if anything to aid private charity and local governments. With 8 million or more unemployed in the first months of 1931, such seers as Myron C. Taylor and Charles M. Schwab piously told people to take whatever work was at hand or just grin and bear it. President Hoover at last accepted the Census Bureau's guess that there were 6,050,000 unemployed as of 2 January 1931,[19] but he did not believe that there was any serious threat to public health through starvation.

The President clung tenaciously to his belief that 'The humanism of our system demands the protection of the suffering and the unfortunate. It places that prime responsibility upon the individual for the welfare of his neighbor, but it insists also that in necessity the local community, the State government, and in the last resort, the National government shall give protection to them.' The last resort, apparently, had not been reached. Again he thought, in the spring of 1931, that the worst was over. Chairman Woods resigned at the end of April from the Emergency Committee for Employment, fully aware that more heroic measures were required. The Committee struggled on with Fred Croxton at the helm, while alarm bells rang with increasing clamor. Worried though he was, Hoover stubbornly insisted that state and local government should care for the unemployed.[20]

Something had to be done to head off the expected flood of 'socialistic' measures in Congress. Staunchly refusing to summon a special session, the President assured the country that he would have a 'concrete program for relief of the unemployment situation when Congress meets.' Officials of Chicago's great fair, the Century of Progress, announced that the giant star Arcturus instead of the President would start the fair's machinery in 1933. Unconcerned by this eclipse, Hoover conferred with his close economic advisers, Silas H. Strawn, Julius Barnes, and Walter S. Gifford. He also received welcome assurance from Allen T. Burns, executive director of the Association of Community Chests and Councils, that private and local agencies could take care of relief in the approaching winter.[21]

Hoover grasped eagerly at this good news and revamped his relief committee in order to provide greater support for Burns and his community chests. He changed the committee's name to the President's Organization on Unemployment Relief on 19 August 1931 and named Walter S. Gifford as its chairman. There was no break in continuity with the old committee, and most of the organization and personnel continued to function as before.

Gifford blandly ignored the possibility that the federal government could or should do anything effective to relieve suffering. He did put out a lot of advertising which promised that 'Between October 19 and November 25 America will feel the thrill of a great spiritual experience. In those few weeks millions of dollars will be raised in cities and towns throughout the land, and the fear of cold and hunger will be banished from the hearts of thousands!' [22]

Mr. Gifford was abysmally ignorant about the entire relief problem. Profoundly he observed: 'I think that what we need is that everybody go back to work and have full pay for all jobs.' And on relief needs: 'I think, by and large, the money spent is the money needed.'[23] On the same day that Gifford made this comment, Edward L. Ryerson, Jr., chairman of the Governor's Unemployment Commission in Illinois, showed that Cook County lacked about 60 per cent of what it needed for the year.

The President's Organization on Unemployment Relief nagged state officials, insisted that unemployment was a local problem, urged industrialists to spread the work, strove manfully to back up the President's philosophy, and minimized facts as to actual distress. Gifford's committee quite properly was called one of ballyhoo for 'private enterprise in relief on a scale no city or community chest or individual charity agency could afford.'[24] The organization probably helped in raising the funds of 130 community chests by more than 14 per cent over 1930. Needs, however, in several large cities were from two to four times as great as in 1930, and only a small part of chest funds went for relief.

4. *The Lost Opportunity*

The question of federal aid dominated relief talk in the fall of 1930. A new Congress was about to meet, a new opportunity was at hand for a display of what massed political wisdom could do. Gifford Pinchot, governor of hard-hit Pennsylvania, which had one-twelfth of the country's population and one-sixth of its unemployment, raised his voice to oppose the hands-off policy clung to by President Hoover. After two years of acute depression, there was no doubt about the need for federal aid instead of 'gentle bedside language.' If federal aid would be a dole, what were state and local disbursements? Pinchot struck directly at the root of the problem: 'Industry and business are not giving men the chance to work. Nor are they feeding the unemployed. We must feed them if they are to live.' To Pinchot, opposition to federal relief was caused by 'fear lest the taxation to provide that relief be levied on concentrated wealth—fear lest the policy of years, the policy of shielding the big fortunes at the expense of the little ones, should at long last be tossed into the discard.' This noted conservationist outlined briefly public works projects to which federal funds could be applied. The list is almost a blueprint for the New Deal's Public Works Administration.[25]

This was not the kind of talk that conservatives wanted to hear. Nor could they gain comfort from the pointed questions of the prominent journalist Anne O'Hare McCormick and the blunt remarks by humorist Will Rogers. Why, asked Mrs. McCormick, does American intelligence seem paralyzed before the great issues of the day? 'Are we to go on waiting for something to happen until it does?' On a radio program to aid the drive for relief funds, Rogers drawled that our only problem was to make it possible for men to get work and 'if our big men in the next year can't fix that—well, they just ain't big men, that's all.' With more of everything than any nation in the world ever had, 'we are starving to death. We are the first nation in the history of the world to go to the poorhouse in an automobile.'[26]

President Hoover again revealed his dogged optimism in the message to Congress on 8 December 1931. Again he expressed his basic philosophy and struggled manfully to call attention to the good things in life. He noted that immigration had been curtailed, industries had spread work. The President's Organization on Unemployment Relief had mobilized public and private agencies to prevent suffering and would do the same in the months ahead. Improved health, shown by statistics on sickness and mortality, proved that there was protection from 'hunger and cold, and that the sense of social responsibility in the nation has responded to the need of the unfortunate.'[27]

Time after time Hoover cited vital statistics to prove that 'there was no widespread undernourishment,' that the volunteer committees were doing a magnificent job. Mr. Hoover's frequent denial that large numbers of people were starving resulted from dependence on completely unreliable statistics. Surgeon General Hugh S. Cumming provided figures to prove that the country had never been in better health than in 1931. The year's record was so heartening that Cumming practically gloated. However, the facts were quite different, as can be seen from the following illustration, which could be multiplied many times. The Bureau of Vital Statistics showed two deaths from starvation in New York City in 1931; but an investigator found 95 cases listed in the records of four hospitals, and 20 of the 95 had died in hospitals.[28] Since numerous diseases accompany starvation, deaths often were attributed to the wrong cause. Policemen on their beats, social workers, reporters, teachers, and ordinary citizens knew thousands of cases of starvation and deaths from starvation, malnutrition and unmet illness problems. People who are not starving do not rummage through garbage cans and line up to wait for the latest batch to be piled on a city garbage dump. Yet such lines did form on the edges of many cities.

Many criticisms of relief stemmed from prevalent attitudes toward any sort of aid to the disadvantaged. Very persistent was the conviction, inherited from the days of a limitless frontier, that work could be found if one wanted it. This concept ignored fundamental facts in American history, including disappearance of the frontier, growth of business monopoly, commercialization of agriculture, unprecedented urbanization, technological changes, and many other factors. There were exceptions, of course; some people would not work if led by the nose to a good job. But to generalize from such cases for the whole labor force reveals no respect for logic. Refusal to work was actually rare in the American economy.[29]

The 'undermining' argument also ignored facts. Reliefers were supposed to lose their self-reliance, self-respect, and initiative. If they lost such qualities, the cause was the conditions that made them reliefers, not the receipt of relief which all but a small minority would accept only as a last resort.

In the Congress that met in December 1931 there was considerable support for federal aid. Senators Edward P. Costigan of Colorado and Robert M. La Follette, Jr. of Wisconsin introduced bills providing for federal aid, bills that were consolidated in January into one measure asking for $375 million to supplement state efforts. One-third of the amount could be spent before 30 June 1932. A Federal Emergency Relief Board would allocate the funds and the Chief of the Children's Bureau would administer the act.

Costigan, less prominent than his younger colleague from Wisconsin, was well educated, urbane, cultured, and had a thorough grounding in economics and political science. His long record as champion of progressive and reform causes was almost as distinguished as that of the senior La Follette or George W. Norris.[30] Now he argued that federal aid was necessary in view of the dismal failure of state and local governments to meet the need. The best estimate of total relief costs in 1931 placed the bill at $450 million, or about 2 per cent of labor's annual loss in wages and salaries. A much larger sum must be provided from some source for 1932. Overwhelming testimony came from social workers, senators, labor leaders, clergy-men, and other informed persons about the helplessness of charitable organizations to prevent appalling deterioration throughout society.[31]

Decay and deterioration in the middle class threatened one of the major foundations of society. The white-collar class of lawyers, doctors, clerks, teachers, skilled laborers, writers, and artists all felt the sting of depression and the pains of poverty. They lost their homes and savings, many lost the struggle to retain their pride and self-respect. Communism was making inroads in this group, particularly among the young intellectuals. Several of them joined the party, wormed into federal service, and provided a slim basis of fact for the mad anti-intellectualism known to another generation as McCarthyism. He could not foresee this result, but William Hodson of New York City's Welfare Council, testifying before a Senate committee at the end of 1931, warned of the danger to society when 'the great middle class is hit.'[32] They needed help that did not come.

The plight of great cities could not be ignored. One-third of the possibly gainfully employed population of Illinois was out of work, and three-fifths of the unemployed were in Chicago. State and local funds, supplemented by private donations, could not keep up with the demand as more and more people, their savings exhausted after many months of unemployment, were forced to ask for aid. The Jewish charities in Chicago established a minimum sum of $1.50 weekly to support a child between two and five years of age; a work-ing man was allowed food worth $2.40. But these paltry sums, which had been set in 1930, were reduced by 25 per cent a year later. On an average day in the Cook County renters' court, 250 eviction cases were being heard. Chicago had no funds in sight to carry beyond 15 February 1932.[33]

Pennsylvania had nearly one million unemployed in the fall of 1931. The State Department of Health reported a general increase in malnutrition, a higher general death rate, and increasing trends in communicable diseases. 'In many Pennsylvania counties families receiving relief from poor boards average grants of from $8 to $12 a month for food,' one social worker testified.[34] 'Where relief is in-adequate you often have our clients starving while they are being "helped." They do not die quickly. You can starve for a long while without dying.'[35] The American Friends Service Committee fed children of miners in several states without making much headway.

Walter West, executive secretary of the American Association of Social Workers, accurately summarized the national situation: 'It is my conviction that there are no amounts in sight from public or private sources now which would come anywhere near meeting the necessary relief amount for the winter or for the next two years.' [36]

Walter S. Gifford's testimony before the Senate Committee on Manufactures marked him as the President's spokesman. If federal aid were available, he asserted,

The sincere and wholehearted efforts of the hundreds of thousands of volunteers engaged both in raising and administering relief funds would doubtless be materially lessened. Individuals would tend to withdraw much of the invisible aid they are now giving; private funds raised by popular subscription would become less; efforts to spread work and to provide work that would not be done except for the emergency would be lessened; business organizations would tend to do less for former employees. Communities, counties, and States undoubtedly would appropriate less public moneys. The net result might well be that the unemployed who are in need would be worse instead of better off.[37]

This was Hoover's philosophy, but Mr. Gifford was not a good witness for the President. He did not know the extent of relief needs anywhere in the country, but he did know that many states had refused to enact legislation necessary to meet the crisis.

Donald R. Richberg, noted Chicago liberal and counsel for the Railway Labor Executives Association, was an eloquent spokesman for federal aid projects:

There has been project after project presented to this Congress for the relief of capital; and men of high position and vast influence seem to think it sound doctrine to urge that the full resources of the Federal Government should be invoked to relieve the distress of all men who have frozen assets. . . . We would like to ask what frozen asset is more deserving of sympathy and relief than the asset of a a capacity and willingness to work, which is frozen in a man who can not find a job? . . . It is intolerable even to consider that throughout a third long winter of want and privation the best available means of furnishing food and clothing and shelter for millions of suffering Americans should remain unused. Somewhere in human nature there is a limit to the injustice and misery to which men will voluntarily submit.[38]

After the Senate Committee on Manufactures had concluded its hearings, the House Committee on Labor provided a repeat performance. Benjamin C. Marsh, professional reformer and social worker, appeared as the major champion and co-author of the La

Follette-Costigan bill and its counterpart in the House, the Lewis bill. Mrs. Marsh, Mrs. Florence Kelley, and Miss Grace Abbott, Chief of the Children's Bureau, had on numerous occasions attempted to obtain federal funds for children's relief. Bills introduced by La Guardia and Burton K. Wheeler in 1928 and 1929 contained provisions similar to those in the La Follette-Costigan-Lewis measure. The principal supporting lobby was the Joint Committee on Unemployment, a council made up of officers from fourteen social welfare and labor organizations. John Dewey, president of the People's Lobby, was chairman of the Joint Committee; Benjamin C. Marsh, a vice chairman of the Joint Committee, was also executive secretary of the People's Lobby. There was no connection between the various welfare groups and Representative George Huddleston of Alabama, who introduced a bill to provide $100 million for the President to dispense as he saw fit to meet the need for relief.

Witnesses brought by Marsh painted a picture of hunger, despair, and hopelessness. Particularly hard hit were the coal mining areas and the textile towns. In Allegheny County, Pennsylvania, 'There are families who have not even salt in their homes. It is a matter of beans, week after week. . . . I have known babies who have not gotten any milk since last spring,' declared David Rinne of the Miners' Relief Association.[39] Several counties in West Virginia had no relief facilities whatever: 'Babies are actually starving, especially in cases where they live in isolated territories back from the highways. There are no private stores there, only the coal company stores. They are up the creek and hollows, and sometimes they are 15 or 50 miles from a town and there is no other place to get food only what is brought in or what they get from the company camps.' [40]

Marsh managed his witnesses like a general directing a battle. He opened with laborers, eloquent and emotional; then came professional social workers—Lea D. Taylor, president of the National Federation of Settlements, Frank D. Loomis, secretary of Chicago's Joint Emergency Relief Fund, and Helen Hall, officer in the National Federation of Settlements; then more laborers. Oscar Ameringer, editor of the *American Guardian*, warned: 'The job before you now is to avoid, eventually, a revolution in the United States.' [41]

Speaking for the People's Lobby, Marsh overplayed his hand:

We have got to face the fact that our entire economic system has broken down. This little relief bill for which we are asking, calls for only $375,000,000 to be expended to keep people from starving and to prevent a revolution. I do not mean a widespread revolution, but upheavals such as officials were fearing here when nearly 100 extra police were put in reserve only yesterday when it was thought that communists might make trouble. We ask that this Costigan-LaFollette-Lewis bill be considered a stop gap while we are revamping our entire economic system as we have to do and as the world has to do.[42]

Members of the committee were not revolutionists, not even mild upheavers, and did not approve these revolutionary objectives.

James A. Emery, counsel for the National Association of Manufacturers, expressed a belief widely held and difficult to deny: the states had not 'vigorously employed, much less exhausted, their resources of taxation or private contribution.'[43] Frank L. Peckham, vice president of the Sentinels of the Republic, sympathized with 'the undertakings of cities, towns, localities, and industries to avert suffering and to tide over these unhappy times' and believed 'they are able and willing to meet this grave responsibility.'[44] Mary G. Kilbreth, speaking for the Woman Patriot Corporation, condemned taxation for relief as a communist principle and ridiculed reports of malnutrition. She quoted Dr. H. E. Barnard, director of the White House Conference on Child Health and Protection, who discovered that 'American children are not undernourished. They are just as healthy to-day as they were in the boom days of 1928 and any one who denies this fact is either ignorant of his facts or is guilty of spreading 'red' propaganda. . . . Foods are plentiful and they are cheap, hence there is no legitimate reason for any child in this country to be undernourished.'[45]

While the House Committee on Labor was preparing its report, senators debated the La Follette-Costigan bill at length. All of its sponsors' great forensic skill could not prevail against the combination of regular Republicans and race-conscious Southern Democrats. The opposition used the pork-barrel, states-rights, self-respect, unbalanced-budget, historical-precedent, morale-weakening, it's-a-dole arguments, none of which made much sense in the presence of unprecedented economic disaster.

Champions of relief thought that Senator Joseph T. Robinson had promised to help defeat the bill in exchange for a nomination to the Supreme Court.[46] Robinson stayed in the background while Senator Hugo Black voiced the Southern fear of bureaucratic interference with 'social habits and social customs.' The bill was defeated on 16 February 1932 by a vote of 35 to 48. Only 7 southerners were among the 18 Democrats who joined 16 Republicans to vote yea. Among 21 Democrats voting nay were 13 from Southern states.[47]

Thus the Senate managed 'to save starving Americans from the humiliation of being fed by their government—and to protect the payers of large income taxes from annoying increases in rates.'[48] So it appeared, but the victory was Hoover's and his forces had no difficulty in 'slapping down' Wagner's bill to appropriate $2 billion for public works, Black's bill for a bond issue of $1 billion for public works, and Cutting's proposal for a program costing $5 billion.

In defeating relief legislation in February, President Hoover and the Republicans took a long step toward disaster in November. Lines between Progressives and the Old Guard within the Grand Old Party were drawn more sharply than they had been since the Bull Moose split in 1912. Theodore Roosevelt, expert in the art of assuming leadership of popular movements once someone else had started them, would not have missed such a grand opportunity. Hoover, by taking his own 'dire necessity' escape route, could have made tremendous political capital. He did give ground five months later.

5. *Too Little, Too Late*

The battle for federal aid did not end with defeat of the La Follette Costigan bill. After noting sentiment in the Senate, the House Committee on Labor reported a greatly changed Lewis bill, a key provision of which was $300 million for relief loans to states. The House took no action. Several state legislatures increased aid to local agencies. Riots and hunger marches occurred as relief became thinner and thinner. Congress on 7 March 1932 authorized the Farm Board to provide the Red Cross with 40 million bushels of its surplus wheat for distribution to the needy; in July another 45 million bushels of wheat and 500,000 bales of cotton were made available. To more and more observers it became increasingly apparent that a relief crisis had arrived and only federal aid could prevent wholesale disaster.[49]

Opposed as he was to federal aid for the unemployed, President Hoover could not resist combined and accumulating pressures. Insull's crash, continued bank failures and increased hoarding, mounting relief rolls and hordes of migrants, veterans in Washington and Japanese in Manchuria—there was trouble everywhere. Senate and House committees continued to hold hearings on the many bills that sought billions for relief. These hearings hammered with maddening persistence at the inadequacy of private and local efforts to meet the fact of unemployment. The threat was especially strong from the Wagner and Rainey (or Garner) bills, each of which was a composite of proposals brought together in the hope of creating a measure that could get through Congress and, possibly, override a veto. Congress might pass these bills in some form, and Hoover would have to veto them on the eve of the national nominating conventions. Only by providing some kind of substitute could the Administration hope to avoid the incubus of complete indifference to widespread suffering.

Major interest centered on H.R. 12353, the Rainey or Garner bill. Title I was the Huddleston proposal to provide the President with $100 million to be used in direct relief at his discretion. Title II would authorize the R.F.C. to make loans 'to any person,' and to finance the sale abroad of agricultural surpluses. Title III was Garner's pet pork barrel, or bread basket as La Guardia called it, and provided for constructing federal buildings in every state and territory, extensive flood control projects, and river and harbor improvements. The total appropriation would be $2.2 billion, and service on the debt thus contracted would be met by a gas tax of ¼ cent per gallon. This was not pork, Garner protested: 'Do not put one single ham in this bill; not a slice, nor even a smell.' [50]

As hearings began on the Rainey bill, Hoover sent a protesting message to Congress that provided a program he would endorse, a program already published after a conference with Senators Robinson and Watson. He held fast to the principle of individual, community, and state responsibility for relief, but was willing for the federal government to loan up to $300 million to states for relief. The R.F.C. might buy bonds from local governments to finance public works, loan to 'established enterprise,' finance the sale abroad of agricultural products, and help the Farm Board give further aid to co-operatives. But there must be no gigantic pork barrel of public works.[51] This was Hoover's testimony to the nation.

Again came the witnesses to present familiar testimony, but this time unexpectedly strong opposition developed. Railway associations objected to improving waterways, cotton shippers complained about competition and ruining of foreign markets, and opponents generally challenged the wisdom of a 'crash' program of public works which could not possibly provide immediate employment.[52] Secretary of War Hurley again protested against putting Americans on the dole, but Ogden L. Mills presented the Administration's case. The expanded lending power of the R.F.C., he said, would create a gigantic federal bank to compete with all commercial banks, one that would 'lend to any individual for almost any purpose on almost any security . . .' When Hoover vetoed the Wagner-Rainey bill, his message closely paralleled the Mills testimony.[53]

Senator Wagner introduced a much milder bill, one that embodied enough of Hoover's proposals of 31 May to arouse the President's interest as a way out of the relief impasse. In testifying on the Wagner bill, Mills finally approved loans to financially exhausted states, but he wanted to be convinced that they were exhausted. As finally combined for passage in the Senate on 9 July, the Wagner-Rainey bill contained too many of Garner's proposals to be palatable. Hoover's veto was inevitable.[54]

Observing the battle over relief in Washington, Paul Y. Anderson predicted that a bill would be passed after each party had used it for vote-getting purposes. And so it happened. In a hurry to complete its session, the Seventy-second Congress passed the Emergency Relief and Construction Act on 16 July and Hoover approved it five days later.

This version of the Wagner-Rainey bill was an omnibus measure that avoided direct relief but met in part the desires of many lobbyists. States financially exhausted might borrow from a $300 million fund in the R.F.C., and the R.F.C. would be repaid over a period of five years, starting in 1935, by reducing appropriations for federal-aid highways. The R.F.C. could loan up to $1.5 billion for publicly or privately constructed self-liquidating public works, and $200 million on the assets of closed banks to assist in liquidation. For specified public works, $322,224,000 was appropriated. Hoover disliked the requirement that the R.F.C. report its loans to Congress, but he could not afford a veto.[55]

This was the Hoover Administration's first significant step toward direct federal aid for relief, but it was a step forced by circumstances and public demand over which the regular Republicans had no control. President Hoover signed the bill while Bonus Expeditionary Force troops were still encamped on Anacostia Flats, the Farm Holiday Association was displaying its exasperation, the public was still gossiping and gasping about Kreuger and Insull, most economic indexes had at last reached bottom, and politicians were steaming up for the 1932 campaign.

Almost at once governors of twelve states asked for about $175 million in direct relief loans. By 29 May 1933 some $280 million had been loaned to 42 states, Hawaii, and Puerto Rico; another $20 million had been loaned to 20 counties and 13 cities. The local governments repaid their loans, but the states were relieved of that responsibility. Six states—Connecticut, Delaware, Massachusetts, Nebraska, Vermont, and Wyoming—received nothing from the $300 million fund. Seven states—California, Illinois, Michigan, New York, Ohio, Wisconsin, and Pennsylvania—obtained 60 per cent of the total. Generally, the big industrial states, the ones with great concentrations of industrial and finance capital, were those with the poorest records in meeting relief needs. True, their needs were proportionately much greater than other states with smaller populations; but it is also true that their resources were proportionately greater.

The ineffectual President's Organization on Unemployment Relief ended for all practical purposes when the R.F.C. began to carry out its assignment under the Emergency Relief and Construction Act. Fred Croxton went over to the R.F.C. and performed brilliantly as director of its Emergency Relief Division. The organization was simple, with six regional representatives appointed to aid states in setting up better relief machinery. The R.F.C., a reluctant partner with the states, had no control over how the money was spent.

Private agencies continued to function, and the President continued to promote reliance upon local efforts. A National Citizens Committee for the Welfare and Relief Mobilization took shape in July and August 1932. The President summoned a Welfare and Relief Mobilization Conference to meet at the White House on 15 September. Under the direction of Newton D. Baker, this committee carried on a fund-raising campaign through November.[56] The Association of Community Chests and Councils pushed its campaigns in the winter of 1932–3, cut down on non-relief budgets, and thus raised private relief spending to a high point of more than $57 million. This was less than one-fifth of all expenditures that winter, which reached a total in excess of $308 million. Thereafter private funds decreased rapidly until in 1935 only 1.4 per cent of the nearly $841 million spent on relief came from private sources.[57] What President Hoover had constantly predicted came to pass: let government enter the relief business and privately financed relief would practically end. Of course, the resources of many people not on relief had been exhausted, and they could no longer contribute to community chests.

If any one attitude lost the election in 1932, it was Hoover's refusal to use federal resources in direct relief. Only industry could solve the unemployment problem, only state and local governments should deal with relief except as a last desperate resort, the President said. To these ideas Hoover clung with an obstinacy worthy of a better cause. Despite his great faith in the Surgeon General's statistics, had Hoover never seen any of the scores of Hoovervilles? Was he blind to the thousands and millions who had exhausted their savings, were doubling up with relatives, were burning their furniture because they had no other fuel? Did he not know that thousands of children, for whom he had promulgated the verbose Children's Charter, were going to school, if they went at all, with inadequate clothing, unattended diseases, and undernourished bodies? Did he not know that the fine reports of how well relief problems were being met ignored realities? No matter how often he denied it, people were starving in the midst of plenty. They were starving physically, and a dry rot had set in which could provide an excellent seed bed for communism.

CHAPTER XIV

NOBLE IN MOTIVE

1. *Dry Decade*

The whole complex known as the liquor problem existed in all of its ramifications when Hoover became President. Bootlegging and smuggling rings, corruption in all enforcement agencies, speakeasies and illegal brewing and distilling, smart-aleck drinking by adolescents and adults, stupid drinking of bay rum, canned heat, Jamaica ginger, perfume, vanilla extract, and medicated wines—all were well established before 1929. The fantastic, bizarre, and wildly exaggerated fact and fiction that flooded newspapers and periodicals became plots of motion pictures and undisguised fiction. Wet and dry propaganda agencies fought an increasingly bitter battle, a conflict in which the wets slowly gained ground.

The Senate passed the Eighteenth Amendment on 1 August 1917, and the House gave its approval on 17 December. The states completed ratification on 16 January 1919, and the National Prohibition Act, better known as the Volstead Act, went into effect one year later. Billy Sunday, still a popular hell-fire evangelist, solemnly buried John Barleycorn at Norfolk, Virginia, while William Jennings Bryan, Wayne B. Wheeler, Andrew J. Volstead, and Morris Sheppard devoutly celebrated in church the demise of an old enemy.[1]

With hope and skepticism the United States entered upon a thirteen-year experiment which was to divide the people, if not the country, into opposing camps as had no major issue since the abolition crusade before 1860. All of the problems of administration and enforcement, all the characteristics of the dry decade, appeared during the first few months of Prohibition. As the years went by, propaganda agencies were able to crack their whips so effectively that a majority of politicians were afraid not to vote dry. Eventually the whip had been swung so often that no crack was left.

During most of the years when the experiment 'noble in motive' was going on, Congress attempted to avoid coming to grips with problems of enforcement. Funds voted for administration of the Volstead Act were never sufficient to finance more than a gesture toward enforcement; nevertheless, several hundred thousand American citizens were arrested and a few hundred were killed by state and federal Prohibition agents. Courts were congested with Prohibition cases, and convicted violators took up space in overcrowded federal prisons.

Professional prohibitionists maintained a steady pressure on governments at all levels, although they encountered increasing indifference among the general public. The Anti-Saloon League of America, with such propagandists as Bishop James Cannon, Jr., Wayne B. Wheeler, and F. Scott McBride, thumped the tub, rang the welkin, and flayed the air in behalf of Prohibition. Dr. Clarence True Wilson directed activities for the powerful Methodist Board of Temperance, Prohibition and Public Morals. The Methodists attempted to equate Prohibition with Christianity and Democracy and by so doing alienated many whose natural inclination was to support temperance if not Prohibition.[2]

The Volstead Act could have been enforced much more efficiently. Probably a majority of people favored the experiment when it began, but general corruption, mismanagement, and indifference at the federal level in the years up to 1927 destroyed public confidence. Noisy propaganda by its opponents convinced a great many people that Prohibition could not and should not be enforced. The battle for Prohibition was lost before 1929, and President Hoover's efforts to enforce the experiment were neither inspired nor exceptionally vigorous. He refused to retreat from his endorsement of the experiment, but he had the good sense not to waste energy in trying to enforce something that could not be enforced without wholesale co-operation from the people in their state and local governments.

Official Washington—that is, social Washington—had set the standards for violation of the Volstead Act from the very dawn of Prohibition. Cocktail parties at the White House during Harding's short tenure were notorious. Wet-voting and wet-drinking senators and representatives were no more prominent than dry-voting and wet-drinking colleagues; both species were known to gather in offices where an elbow could be bent to strike a blow for freedom. The diplomatic corps was wet and very popular. The Curtis-Longworth parties were always wringing wet . . .'[3] No matter how often denials were made for public consumption, the facts were well known. There was no lack of alcoholic beverages at the majority of Washington society functions. Parties were successful when made up of senators, diplomats, journalists, cabinet people, H.B.V.'s (High Bosomed Virgins), and smuggled Scotch. White House parties given by the Hoovers were dry. At least there was no leak at the top; but the lower echelons of high society dripped.

Prohibition did not prevent drinking, but no one knew how much drinking was being done. Wild exaggerations, backed by synthetic statistics, were offered with a vehemence whose intensity varied inversely with their truth. The Bureau of Prohibition in 1931 guessed that there was a tremendous decline in beer and wine consumption compared with 1914, and a New York City police commissioner said there were 32,000 speakeasies in that city alone; but Detroit could report no more than 1,561 'speaks' in April 1931.[4]

Before and during Prohibition, the dry forces claimed fantastic economic benefits. Increased consumption and production, larger capital accumulations, and a generally higher standard of living seemed to be apparent during the dry decade; therefore, these things were caused by Prohibition. After the Great Depression settled down to a long run, wets claimed that repeal was the magic wand to restore prosperity. The American people would drink the farmer into prosperity; taxes on liquor would make the income tax unnecessary; revival of the legitimate liquor industry would prime the dead economic pumps.[5] There is no evidence that President Hoover believed any of this nonsense, but he was committed to do something about Prohibition.

Congress apparently spent a tremendous amount of time debating and worrying about Prohibition when Hoover was President. Wet propaganda reached its height and would not be pushed into the background by unemployment or the farm problem or the bonus or relief or the war debts or anything else. This propaganda flood began to mount during the second session of the Seventy-first Congress, 2 December 1929–3 July 1930. Members introduced more than sixty bills and resolutions, all of which died in committee.[6] The Republican party had promised to enforce Prohibition, and Congress was entirely willing to permit President Hoover to make good on the promise.

Hoover saw the Prohibition problem as merely a part of the greater challenge to law enforcement. Let state and local officials accept their responsibility to enforce the laws, let all good citizens rally to the support of their government:

Our whole system of self-government will crumble either if officials elect what laws they will enforce or citizens elect what laws they will support. The worst evil of disregard for some law is that it destroys respect for all law. For our citizens to patronize the violation of a particular law on the ground that they are opposed to it is destructive of the very basis of all that protection of life, of homes and property which they rightly claim under other laws. If citizens do not like a law, their duty as honest men and women is to discourage its violation; their right is openly to work for its repeal.[7]

Time and again the President was to return to this inaugural theme.

Herbert Hoover was never a strong advocate of Prohibition; he was never a strong supporter of the Anti-Saloon League. He upheld the Volstead Act not because it was concerned with Prohibition but because it was a federal law. Never in the campaign of 1928 did Hoover pose as a fanatical dry.[8] Prohibition was politically expedient, so he called it an experiment noble in motive. Never did he announce categorically that he thought the Eighteenth Amendment and the Volstead Act were the combination needed to promote temperance. The President fully realized that Prohibition could not be enforced by federal effort alone, that organized crime and violence would increase unless state and local governments co-operated with federal officials.[9] The President was not hypocritical, as Oswald Garrison Villard charged, and he most certainly was not 'oblivious to growing corruption, growing defiance of the fundamental law and the Constitution itself.'[10] In linking Prohibition to law enforcement, the President was adopting the official Anti-Saloon League line: Prohibition had to be defended not because it was Prohibition but because it was law. Therefore, an attack on Prohibition was an attack on law.[11]

2. *Congress and the Wickersham Battle*

For the purpose of discovering the facts about failures and needs in law enforcement, the President announced in his inaugural that he would appoint a special commission. The promised agency, the National Commission on Law Observance and Enforcement, began its labors with a meeting at the White House by hearing a brief message from the President, who spoke at, if not to, the entire country:

A nation does not fail from its growth of wealth or power. But no nation can for long survive the failure of its citizens to respect and obey the laws which they themselves make. Nor can it survive a decadence of the moral and spiritual concepts that are the basis of respect for law, nor from neglect to organize itself to defeat crime and the corruption that flows from it.[12]

Members of the Commission were Chairman George W. Wickersham, Henry W. Anderson, Newton D. Baker, Judge William I. Grubb, Judge William S. Kenyon, Monte M. Lemann, Frank J. Loesch, Judge Kenneth Mackintosh, Judge Paul J. McCormick, Roscoe Pound, and Ada L. Comstock. Perhaps Hoover had taken the advice of Bishop Cannon, who sent a cable from Cairo urging the appointment of an outstanding wet, an ardent prohibitionist, and a woman. He did, at least, confer with Charles Evans Hughes before making the appointments.[13]

While the Wickersham Commission was at work, President Hoover recommended to Congress proposals often made before. In order to expedite reorganization and concentration of responsibility for enforcement of Prohibition, he asked Congress on 6 June 1929 to appoint a joint committee to recommend measures to the next session. The President would appoint an interdepartmental committee to co-operate with the congressional committee, and John McNab of San Francisco was appointed in October to make a special study of enforcement. This appointment should have mollified dry leaders who were disgruntled because the Wickersham Commission's activities were to be so broad. In his annual message on 3 December the President advised Congress that detection and prosecution should be the duty of the Department of Justice, leaving to the Treasury Department control over industrial alcohol and legalized beverages. By simplifying procedure, congestion in federal courts could be avoided. The more than two dozen statutes on Prohibition should be codified and rectified, and the border patrol should be reorganized under the Coast Guard.[14]

The President's message set off a typically rambling debate during which members of Congress added little to what was already known. Representative Louis C. Crampton, Michigan Republican, spoke glowingly of the great improvement in enforcement. Fiorello H. La Guardia retorted that the law was not being enforced and never could be. In Idaho, La Guardia jibed at Borah, 'there is more drinking per capita . . . than there is in the city of New York.' Representative Loring M. Black, Jr., New York Democrat, chided drys for not showing more enthusiasm for Prohibition. Crampton received frequent applause when he replied that the House would give the President whatever he asked for to enforce Prohibition. La Guardia challenged the drys to show their strength, and John C. Schafer, Wisconsin Republican, cried: 'The whines and wails of the dry leaders to-day are comparable to rats leaving a sinking ship.'[15] In the midst of this foolish chatter, the Wickersham Commission dropped a preliminary report.

Mr. Wickersham reinforced the President's recommendations in his preliminary findings on 13 January 1930. The President's suggestions and those of the first Wickersham report had been urged periodically for a decade without result. The Anti-Saloon League had opposed transferring the Prohibition Bureau to the Department of Justice. There was one new proposal to permit trials of petty cases before United States commissioners without juries in order to relieve congestion in federal courts.

The proposal attracted far more objection than support, especially in Congress. In the House, Mr. Loring M. Black, Jr. sneered: 'The mountains have labored and all they have brought forth is a ridiculous mess, a ridiculous legal mess. How can you enforce a law that requires 50 per cent of the people to keep the other 50 per cent in jail all the time?'[16] Senator Robert F. Wagner took the President to task for having talked about abuses in 1928 only to forget them in 1930. People were not worried about a little court crowding, and lost motion between departments was insignificant. They were worried about wanton killings by Prohibition agents, unlawful searches and seizures, wire tapping, corruption and hypocrisy of officials and citizens, the rise of a new criminal class, the increasing tide of intemperance, 'the obvious failure of the law to find a place in the popular conscience.' The Wickersham Commission had brought forth a mouse. Its plan to try petty cases before commissioners, with right of demand for jury trial if convicted, gave the district attorney too much power to decide if the offense were petty or felonious. The whole idea, Wagner snorted, was as preposterous as it was unconstitutional.[17] The Senate then went on to consider such matters as control of the pink bollworm, crime in the District of Columbia, and tariff revision.

Debate on the question during the remainder of the second session of the Seventy-first Congress was uninspiring. On numerous occasions wets and drys in both houses returned to the fray, adding almost nothing except fresh details.[18] Nevertheless, Congress passed the Prohibition Reorganization Act, and Hoover signed it on 27 May.

The major feature of this act was to transfer the Bureau of Prohibition from Treasury to Justice, leaving control of industrial alcohol under Commissioner J. M. Doran in Treasury.

George W. Wickersham presented his final report to the President on 7 January 1931. The Commission had made use of special reports prepared under its direction, statements of federal officials, surveys prepared by the Commissioner of Prohibition, testimony of expert witnesses, and much more printed and oral information. Albert E. Sawyer, working for the Commission, prepared a monumental *Report on Federal Prohibition Enforcement*.[19] On the whole, the President observed in transmitting the report to Congress, the Commission believed that enforcement had improved after the Department of Justice had taken over the task in 1930. That was about the only encouraging thing he could find, but he was not on very solid ground in concluding that the Commission did not 'favor the repeal of the eighteenth amendment as a method of cure for the inherent abuses of the liquor traffic.'[20]

The President was entitled to interpret the report as he pleased, but two commissioners favored immediate repeal, five favored revision and adoption of a national and state monopoly, two favored revision and further trial, and two opposed revision or repeal. The Commission as a whole did not, as Hoover stated, favor repeal; the Commission as a whole did not favor anything! A majority did oppose repeal of the Eighteenth Amendment, restoration of the saloon, government in the liquor business, and manufacture of light wines and beer; a majority agreed that state co-operation and public support were needed for enforcement, present enforcement agencies were inadequate and needed more money, and certain statutes should be improved. It was, indeed, difficult to discover exactly what the Commission recommended. To illustrate: In Conclusion 1, 'The Commission is opposed to repeal of the Eighteenth Amendment.' In Conclusion 10, 'Some of the Commission are not convinced that Prohibition under the Eighteenth Amendment is unenforceable. Others of the Commission are convinced that it has been demonstrated that Prohibition under the Eighteenth Amendment is unenforceable and that the Amendment should be immediately revised . . .'[21]

No one was satisfied with the Wickersham Commission's report. Journalists generally had a field day satirizing the report and the

Commission. In the House, Thomas L. Blanton, a Texas Democrat who had been a staunch defender of Wickersham, was extremely embarrassed, and Emanuel Celler and La Guardia needled him unmercifully. Celler also reprimanded the President for having sent out a completely misleading summary before the whole report was available.[22] A few members of Congress with opinions to express did so by extending their remarks, a device to please the home folks without boring yawning colleagues.

The real debate, or attack, on the Wickersham Report was precipitated on 31 January 1931 in connection with H. J. Res. 477, introduced ten days earlier by Frederick R. Lehlbach, New York Republican, and referred to the customary cemetery for such proposals, the Committee on the Judiciary. The House, considering the appropriation bill, resolved itself into the Committee of the Whole House on the State of the Union. Lehlbach then offered a sober analysis of the Wickersham Report which provided two irrefutable conclusions: the Eighteenth Amendment 'is not observed and not enforced,' and a majority of the Commission believed it 'can never be adequately enforced.' Congress should at once place before the people an amendment that would repeal the Eighteenth Amendment and aid any state that wanted to retain Prohibition. This resolution was nearly identical with the Twenty-first Amendment as proclaimed on 5 December 1933. The House applauded assertions that Congress must not temporize, that 'The party that refuses to face the facts and refuses to meet the issue with firmness, courage, and wisdom will be overwhelmingly repudiated at the next national election.' The Prohibition issue should be removed from the 1932 presidential campaign. Apparently this reasoning failed to move Don B. Colton, Republican from Vernal, Utah. Only one state had asked for repeal, Colton remarked, so why the fuss? But to keep from going stale, Heartsill Ragon changed the subject to conditions in Arkansas, where people were starving.[23]

The third session of the Seventy-first Congress had fun with the Wickersham Report but did nothing significant to change the Volstead Act. A measure to provide light punishment for first, mild offenses was approved on 15 January 1931. No other proposed change cleared the legislative hurdle in spite of the great amount of talk. A Senate bill to enforce Prohibition in the District of Columbia got plenty of talk but no votes; a measure to enable physicians to prescribe malt liquors, a proposal for a national referendum on repeal, a bill to divest alcoholic liquors of their interstate character—all were buried in committee. Such, too, was the fate of numerous joint resolutions: a constitutional amendment to allow use of intoxicating beverages in homes, for referendums on the Eighteenth Amendment, to use the armed forces to suppress smuggling, to prohibit issuance of liquor permits to foreign diplomats, to suspend enforcement in any state that failed to appropriate funds for aid in the general effort.

Although far more important business was pending, the Senate spent precious hours in debating a bill (S. 3344) to tighten enforcement in the District, a bill that had been before the Senate for a year. Senator Robert B. Howell, Nebraska Republican, described unbelievably bad conditions in the District. Senator Tydings heckled Howell through several pages of the *Record,* but the persistent dry won his attempt to have the bill considered. Most of the fireworks occurred over the provision for search of a home if liquor were delivered to it for sale. The debate continued with little sparkle or purpose. Senator Harry F. Ashurst, Arizona Democrat, led his colleagues through early English history as he sought to protect the home. He sailed with Hengist and Horsa from Jutland to Thanet in A.D. 449 and sat on the banks of Runnymede in 1215. With swift strides he reached 1931 in a dextrous performance. Although Senator Howell plaintively hoped for passage, the Seventy-first Congress adjourned and left Hengist and Horsa masters of the field.[24]

The Senate enjoyed contemplation of wine-grape concentrates on 6 February 1931. Dr. Clarence True Wilson, General Secretary of the Board of Temperance, Prohibition and Public Morals of the Methodist Episcopal Church, had written to Senator Tydings to denounce Vine-Glo and similar enticing commodities. Dr. Wilson wanted Congress to stop the home-wine leak. Senator Tydings referred to Amos W. W. Woodcock's estimate that in five years before Prohibition the country produced less than 230 million gallons of wine; in the period 1925–29, wine production was about 679 million gallons. This home light-wine industry was perfectly legal when carried on for home consumption, and the Federal Farm Board had loaned more than $19 million to California grape-grower co-operatives, much of it to produce grape concentrates. Senator Sheppard doggedly insisted it was all illegal, but the courts were against him and the Wickersham Commission was against him. Section 29 of the Volstead Act prohibited the sale of non-intoxicating fruit juices made in the home except to persons who had permits to manufacture vinegar. Why? Because such juices automatically became wine; and it was not illegal for nature to go on being nature. Wayne B. Wheeler himself had written Section 29.[25] The Senate finally could do nothing about grape concentrates, and the industry continued to thrive.

Dry forces could find little comfort in the Wickersham Report but not all of them gave up in despair. Mrs. Henry W. Peabody, who had fled from wringing wet Massachusetts to dripping Florida, rallied a hypothetical 12 million women supposedly affiliated with the National Woman's Democratic Law Enforcement League. She organized the National Commission of Twenty-one Women on the Eighteenth Amendment, a group studded with important names. Mrs. Jesse W. Nicholson presided over a convention of the League in mid-April 1931 and led 200 delegates to shake President Hoover's hand. As if in answer, Mrs. Charles H. Sabin and members of the Women's Organization for National Prohibition Reform moved into Washington as Mrs. Peabody and Mrs. Nicholson moved out. There was the usual round of buttonholing and conferring and pressuring, but the presidential hand was too tired for another round with hundreds of women.[26]

3. *Victory for the Wet Crusade*

No one can say with certainty just when the big swing toward repeal sentiment took place, nor can the change be attributed to anything except a combination of circumstances and arguments. Apparently valid evidence could be assembled to support each side of every argument on the question of repeal. Probably the major reason for the increase in repeal sentiment was the growing conviction that Prohibition could not be enforced by democratic means. Plausible arguments that great economic benefits would follow repeal had a cumulative effect as the Great Depression deepened.

The last real battle in Congress over Prohibition was fought in the first session of the Seventy-second Congress from 7 December 1931 to 16 July 1932. Nearly six columns of fine print in the *Record* were required to index references to 'Alcoholic Liquor Traffic.' Members introduced seventy joint resolutions to amend or to repeal the Eighteenth Amendment, in addition to proposals for referendums, 3 per cent beer, permissive home manufacture and consumption of alcoholic beverages, use of federal forces to suppress smuggling, and numerous other purposes. There were 56 bills to amend or to repeal the Volstead Act and 34 other bills dealing with liquor or the liquor traffic. Not one of these scores of resolutions and bills cleared the legislative obstacle course.

The reason for all the ferment was perfectly apparent. Congress would do nothing until after the November election. An International News Service poll of the Congress early in the session correctly forecast no changes in the Volstead Act, although wets had made significant gains. There might be support for a referendum, but a two-thirds majority could not be mustered for an amendment. On the question of submitting a referendum on Prohibition, the House would show 155 votes in favor, 96 against, and 183 on the fence; in the Senate the comparable figures were 32, 29, and 34. One vote in each chamber was undetermined. Outcome of legislative proposals would depend on the attitude of the noncommittal members, many of whom echoed Senator James J. Davis of Pennsylvania, who 'awaited the arrival of his convictions.' The party split in the Senate was almost squarely in the middle. Some of the 187 members of Congress who favored a referendum would vote against legalizing light wines and beer. The wets, however, had enough votes in the House to rescue bills from the customary burial in the Committee on the Judiciary.[27]

There was a time when the Anti-Saloon League of America could cause a member of Congress to hiccup backwards, but there is no reason to believe that the Seventy-second Congress was bothered seriously by the League convention held in Washington during January 1932. Dr. A. J. Parton, chairman of the League's executive committee, predicted that the southern vote would turn on the Prohibition issue, that the South would not accept a Tammany man and would vote for a Prohibition candidate regardless of party. Some members of Congress might have heeded this thinly veiled threat, but there was no reason why they should unless they believed Senator Sheppard. The dust-dry Texan scoffed at the repeal movement and wondered why some people could be so naive as to believe that beer was returning: 'I can conceive of a man building a hotel at the present time to catch the tourist trade from Mars when communication with that planet begins but my imagination and my dreams stagger at the erection of a brewery in anticipation of the return of beer.' Sheppard continued this assurance to the League's convention with a pulsating tribute to women:

All in our civilization that is permanent and pure, all that induces peace and faith and hope and progress may be traced to the exhaustless fountain of a woman's sacrifice, a woman's love. To-day that love endures, unshaken through the ages, the shield of the modern as well as the ancient home. In return for that affection we shall continue to protect its chief beneficiaries, the home, the child, from the destructive influences of alcoholic drink. In return for that affection and in behalf of the purity and welfare of our institutions we shall continue to sustain and guard that hope of freedom, that light of progress, that radiance of the ages—our dry United States.[28]

Sheppard's emotionalism made as much sense as the increasing emphasis on the economic effects of repeal. Just be rid of Prohibition and new sources of taxation would appear, thousands of jobs would open, farmers would sell their surplus grains, the depression would end. These arguments, sincerely believed by supposedly intelligent people, reached their nadir in a speech by Senator Hiram Bingham: 'Repeal is the one thing that will restore prosperity; it is the one thing that will put hundreds of thousands of men to work; it is the one thing that will furnish a market for 100,000,000 bushels of grain; it is the one thing that will furnish a market for 7,000,000 tons of coal . . .'[29]

Each chamber made one serious effort to do something about Prohibition. The House attempt preceded the Chicago conventions, and the weak Senate gesture came at the end of the session. In the House, James M. Beck, Pennsylvania Republican, and J. C. Linthicum, Maryland Democrat, presented a proposal on 15 January 1932 that in effect would return liquor control to the states. Referred to the usual burying ground, the Beck-Linthicum resolution failed to be reported out of committee by a vote of 14 to 9. The House on 14 March voted 187 to 227 against the motion to discharge the committee. For the first time since its adoption, Prohibition had been tested in the House. Senator Sheppard in June gleefully interpreted the vote as showing a solid front of 23 states still opposed to repeal: 'Prohibition will continue to survive every whirlwind and to ride out every storm.'[30] But the country as a whole paid no attention. In that same March, Charles Augustus Lindbergh, Jr., less than two years old, had been kidnapped from his crib. The news of this horrible crime was still fresh when on 12 March, less than two weeks later, the Swedish match king Ivar Kreuger committed suicide.

Members of Congress who remained in Washington during the Chicago conventions followed Prohibition developments with keen interest. Although Prohibition had been a major issue in the campaigns of 1928 and 1930, neither party had officially approved repeal. By 1932, conventions or party committees in 25 states called for either repeal or a general referendum. A majority of delegates to each convention decided to take the plunge. Such long-time champions of temperance as Oswald Garrison Villard urged both parties to adopt repeal planks.[31]

The Republicans, who met first, made it easy for the Democrats to write a better Prohibition plank. After wandering, squirming, and weaseling, the Republican platform declared:

We . . . believe that the people should have an opportunity to pass upon a proposed amendment, the provisions of which, while retaining in the Federal Government power to preserve the gains already made in dealing with the evils inherent in the liquor traffic, shall allow the States to deal with the problem as their citizens may determine, but subject always to the power of the Federal Government to protect those States where prohibition may exist and safeguard our citizens everywhere from the return of the saloon and attendant abuses.[32]

If Hoover did not write this plank, his ghost had acquired the presidential style.

The Republicans' stand was really a blow to the drys. Walter Lippmann, writing from Chicago on 16 June, the morning after, reported the wet victory was so concealed by 'a smoke screen of dry slogans . . . that it may take some time before the drys realize how complete was their defeat and the wets how imposing was their victory.' Frank R. Kent called the Republican plank 'the most striking political milestone of a decade. It marks the definite end of the noble experiment, the turn of the country against it.' The rising tide of wet sentiment had at last swamped the drys, who had 'browbeaten and cowed every convention of both parties for ten years.'[33]

Less than two weeks later, the Democratic convention adopted a repeal, beer-and-wine plank:

We advocate the repeal of the Eighteenth Amendment. To effect such repeal we demand that Congress immediately propose a constitutional amendment to truly representative conventions in the States called to act solely on that proposal. We urge the enactment of such measures by the several States as will actually promote temperance, effectively prevent the return of the saloon, and bring the liquor traffic into the open under complete supervision by the States.[34]

In the House, John C. Schafer of Wisconsin challenged the Democratic leadership to act at once on repeal, promising enough wet Republican votes to make up for the dry southern Democrats.

The Prohibition Party met in convention at Indianapolis early in July. Its keynoter called the Democratic plank 'perforated with corkscrews and bungholes.' Now, he cried, is the time for the southern Democrats to prove that they rejected Smith in 1928 because he was a wet, not because he was a Catholic. The Republicans were especially damned as the 'wringing wets and the wobbling wets.' He condemned their stand: 'The Republican ambidextrous, amphibious, and porusplaster plank . . . is the most pitiful example of ducking, dodging, and duplicity in the history of American politics. It is the most stupendous, titanic, colossal, calamitous, crimson, consciousless [*sic*], barbaric, and cataclysmic fraud ever perpetrated upon the American people.'[35]

Since both of the major parties had succumbed to the wet crusade, Senator Carter Glass tried to get hasty action on submitting an amendment to the states. The Glass resolution provided for repeal of the Eighteenth Amendment and abolition of the saloon. The state and federal governments were to have concurrent power to enforce the amendment. But it was too late in the session for Congress to achieve anything except to show that the principal argument in the next session would be over granting to the federal government any control over the liquor traffic other than to help keep liquor out of dry states.[36]

Not repeal of the Eighteenth Amendment but the manner of repeal concerned most people in 1932. The voters were so completely sold on the failure of Prohibition that none but irreconcilables like Sheppard, Borah, Norris, Cannon, and Wilson would refuse to acknowledge defeat. Relief, banking, agriculture, and public power far overshadowed Prohibition in the 1932 campaign. Both parties favored drastic change, a clear recognition that the controversial amendment was doomed. The Roosevelt-led Democratic landslide in November did not necessarily mean that the majority preferred the Democratic to the Republican plank, but Senator John J. Blaine's resolution attempted to gain congressional approval for the Republican proposal.

Senator Blaine, Wisconsin Republican, introduced on 6 December 1932 S. J. Res. 211, which was destined to become, in greatly modified form, the Twenty-first Amendment. The Committee on the Judiciary, of which Blaine was chairman, reported the resolution favorably on

6 January 1933. Two powerful wet groups together objected to all of the proposed amendment except the section to repeal the Eighteenth Amendment. Both the Constitutional Liberty League and the Association Against the Prohibition Amendment objected to writing into the Constitution any power to prohibit importation of liquor into states in violation of state laws. Congress already had the power.[37] The proposed amendment would have provided in Section 3 'concurrent power to regulate or prohibit the sale of intoxicating liquor to be drunk on the premises where sold.' Most of the argument centered on this proposal to use federal power to prevent return of the saloon, and on the provision for ratification by legislatures.

There was only a short debate in the Senate on the resolution. Even Senator Borah, who announced his opposition to repeal, was favorable to a referendum on Prohibition; but he wanted Congress to act on more pressing matters. Senator Norris was willing to let the new Congress handle Prohibition. Most of the debate on 15 and 16 February revolved around wording the amendment so as to remove the last vestige of federal control in states that wanted liquor. Senator Wagner led the successful fight against giving Congress such control, and Senator Borah prevented elimination of the section giving the federal government power to aid in keeping liquor out of states that wanted Prohibition. A few senators cried out against repeal with warnings that the saloon was returning. But the people had spoken, or so the senators thought. On 16 February by a vote of 63 to 23, the Senate passed S. J. Res. 211. The House rejected the last solemn warnings of irreconcilable drys as it proceeded on 20 February to pass the resolution by 289 to 121.[38]

Even the mournful sounds of bank doors closing failed to drown the cheerful noises of breweries and distilleries preparing to go into open production.

CHAPTER XV

1932—B.E.F.

1. *Hunger and the Bonus*

The United States of America, reputedly the richest nation in the world, shuddered under the impact of economic disasters in 1932. Economic distress produced social confusion, but still it would be wrong to say that the United States was on the verge of revolution in that year. Violence and riots, just beneath the surface in many communities, flared dangerously in coal mining sections of Kentucky and in the textile towns of the South and New England. The Iowa Farmers' Holiday, the Bonus Expeditionary Force, various 'shirt' movements, and numerous hunger marches were all protests, surface manifestations of organized anger. These were disconnected phenomena. There was no acceptable body of revolutionary social or political philosophy behind them. Communists had a philosophy, but they were completely unrealistic as a party. Advocates of various planning schemes were developing a creed; but how can an economist or an engineer generate wild enthusiasm by waving a blueprint? American radicalism failed to gain widespread support partly because of intellectual aridity but more because the mass of Americans had not lost faith in the doctrines of democracy.

Hoover certainly had every opportunity to know how urgent were demands for action. Despite the favorable interpretation he gave to gloomy facts, the comprehensive program he presented to the Seventy-second Congress was a measure of his understanding. The prospect of riots, even of revolution, could not have escaped his thoughts; but, except for a few references to the peaceful condition of the country, there is little evidence that he expected political chaos. He paid little attention to the fourteen rain-soaked pickets who paraded before the White House as the Seventy-second Congress was gathering in December 1931; but someone was extremely nervous about the 1600 Communist-led hunger marchers who milled around the Capitol a few days later. There were special guards and machine guns just in case they might be needed. There were special precautions to protect the White House. Hoover talked briefly with the leader of the next hunger march, Father James R. Cox of Pittsburgh; but the priest was very respectable and his marchers arrived in a motorcade and left promptly.[1] These were faint warnings and of little significance when compared with that phenomenon known to history as the Bonus Expeditionary Force.

Payment of a federal bonus to veterans of the World War was opposed by every President from Harding to Roosevelt. In 1917 Congress had enacted a comprehensive program of life insurance, family allotments, compensation for injuries, hospitalization, and education to benefit men in service and to continue after the war. Theoretically, there would be no pensions. This vain expectation Congress itself exploded in February 1919 by voting a bonus of $60 to each man mustered out. As veterans' organizations worked to obtain all they could from Congress, a general bonus became their major objective.[2] The goal was won when Congress passed the bonus bill over Coolidge's veto on 17 May 1924. Attempting to postpone the day of reckoning, this act provided a bonus certificate for every veteran according to days in service. The certificate was, in effect, an endowment policy for which the Treasury paid the premiums until due in 1945.

This indirect method of paying a bonus did not end agitation. In one form or another, the subject appeared at each session of Congress. Demands for immediate payment were prominent in the second session of the Seventy-first Congress and became insistent in the third session. There were proposals to increase the loan value of the certificates, to pay 50 per cent of their face value, and to pay the full face value at once. A proposal to loan up to 50 per cent of face value received Owen D. Young's approval, and Republicans prepared a bill to accomplish that purpose.[3]

With more than 700,000 veterans and dependents receiving about $900 million in federal aid in 1931, Hoover protested against the proposal to permit any veteran to borrow more on his certificate. Originally, a veteran could borrow up to 22½ per cent of face value, paying 6 per cent interest, after he had held the certificate for two years. If a veteran did so borrow and failed to repay the loan with interest, he would get nothing in 1945. About $330 million had been loaned as of February 1931, when Congress passed the bill to permit borrowing up to 50 per cent. Since the face value of the certificates was

$3,426 million, it was apparent that well over a billion dollars might be borrowed by the 3,478,956 holders. The average loan could be about $500, although about one-fourth of the loans would be for less than $200. Hoover was correct in his analysis of the bill, of its objectives, and of the motives of its sponsors. He observed, in his veto message of 26 February 1931, that 387,000 veterans already were receiving 'some degree of allowance or support from the Federal Government.' A great many more did not need assistance; several hundred thousand were employees of the federal, state, and local governments. It was not a question of justice for veterans: 'The breach of fundamental principle in this proposal is the requirement of the Federal Government to provide an enormous sum of money to a vast majority who are able to care for themselves and who are caring for themselves.'[4]

The veto was a foregone conclusion, and the National Commander of the American Legion urged Congress to override the President. Congress did so on 26 February, the day it received the veto message. None of the President's objections met even the semblance of serious consideration. Veterans availed themselves of the new source of funds by borrowing $1,386,828,621.[5] How much of this sum was injected into the economic stream and what effect it had are matters impossible to evaluate accurately. Beyond doubt, thousands of veterans needed the help; to these needy veterans, the loans were so much manna.

President Hoover understood the political implications of his veto as well as Congress; he was made of sterner stuff than most of the people's servants, or he was less easily affected by veterans' demands. Agitation for full payment of the bonus, planned before the increase in loan value went through, steadily increased in volume as the depression worsened and unemployment increased. President Hoover consistently opposed any liberalization of treatment for veterans and displayed his courage by appearing at the American Legion's Detroit convention on 21 September 1931 to condemn not only the proposal for immediate payment of the entire bonus but also every other proposal to increase federal expenses. The convention voted, 902 to 507, not to endorse legislation for immediate payment, although it is very doubtful if the delegates accurately represented prevailing sentiment among veterans.[6]

At least twenty bills providing for some sort of immediate payment were introduced in the Seventy-second Congress. Similar demands, such as one endorsed by Senator Arthur Vandenberg as 'an act of justice,' had been made in the Seventy-first Congress. Representative Wright Patman was a major champion of this legislation, most of which suffered adverse committee reports. Bonus boosters obtained 2,240,030 names on petitions for immediate payment, and more than 1,200 veterans gathered at the Capitol on 8 April to present the mammoth plea for action.[7]

The second of Patman's bills, H.R. 7726, eventually reached the House floor after leisurely hearings before the Committee on Ways and Means. Henry T. Rainey, Democratic majority floor leader, reported adversely because the bill would require $2.4 billion in fiat money to pay the bonus. With a daily deficit of $7 million, and in view of heroic measures needed to balance the budget, payment of the bonus would be suicidal. Moreover, adding $2.4 billion to money in circulation would cause a tremendous inflation. Fred Vinson of Kentucky defended the bill in a minority report. After the unfavorable report, Patman introduced a resolution to make the bill special order of business. The resolution went to the Committee on Rules on 10 May[8] and there it was buried until B.E.F. lobbying forced a vote. Had the Patman resolution been voted on promptly, there might have been no Bonus Expeditionary Force.

2. *B.E.F.*

The Hoover prescription of local responsibility and old-time American individualism as medicine for the unemployed on relief caused resentment and bitterness among jobless veterans. They ignored such facts as an increase from 367,000 to 853,000 destitute or disabled veterans on the benefit rolls from 1929 to 1932; they ignored the 25 new hospitals with 19,000 additional beds; they ignored increased efficiency in the reorganized Veterans' Administration. More and more the sentiment grew among veterans that they had fought in 1917–18 to defend a place to starve in. The bonus was not a gift in the veteran's eyes but a small part of a debt owed by the nation. It was inadequate additional compensation to narrow the gap between pay received by service and non-service men. Veterans generally would hardly agree with Nicholas Murray Butler, who pontificated: 'It is absolutely essential that the organized raids on the Treasury in the name of war veterans . . . should, despite the cowardice of Congress, be resisted and repelled.'[9]

Continued unemployment consumed the veteran's savings, sent his valuables to the pawnshop, left him hungry, ill clothed, unable to care for his family, and on the verge of panic born of despair. Of course the bonus was not due until 1945; but the country could afford to pay, could afford it if the R.F.C. could make such huge loans to financial institutions. Veterans, like the majority of people on relief, wanted jobs above everything else. Many of them did not need the bonus and some would squander their money; but surely the great majority would use it to meet current debts, bolster credit, and finance the continuing search for nonexistent jobs. If undercover lobbies could work so well for special interests, why not a giant lobby for veterans?[10]

Bonus marchers were organized locally and spontaneously for the most part. In Portland, Oregon, Walter W. Waters broached the idea in March 1932 to a group of veterans but aroused little enthusiasm. Others took up the idea as hope for the passage of bonus legislation faded. When the Patman bill was pigeonholed in the House in May, larger meetings were held in Portland. Veterans signed up for the trip to Washington, elected officers, and 'three hundred men, with less than thirty dollars among them all,' began a 3,000-mile march on the capital. It was, like other contingents, a respectable group. The percentage of criminals 'in the whole Bonus Army . . . was far less than the percentage of convicted criminals in the Harding Cabinet, of which Mr. Hoover had been a member.'[11]

Early in May the Portland marchers set out. Washington officials followed their progress with an apprehension that increased as the unwelcome petitioners approached the capital. President Hoover was too busy with his superhuman tasks to show much concern as he read about the marchers in the newspapers he scanned regularly. The public, generally, was more concerned with revelations of banditry in the New York Stock Exchange, in the latest efforts to track the murderer of the Lindbergh baby, and in Amelia Earhart Putnam's solo flight across the Atlantic.

Bonus marchers converged on Washington from every part of the country. On 29 May Waters and his 330 men were in Washington where the Major and Superintendent of Police, Brigadier General Pelham D. Glassford, prepared a friendly welcome after having sought instructions that the District Commissioners failed to give. Other bonus marchers, attracted by the publicity given to Baltimore & Ohio efforts to keep the men off their trains at St. Louis, had arrived two days earlier, making a total of 1,300 men in the District. The number increased rapidly; for many weeks there would be more than 20,000 veterans petitioning Congress by their presence. On 31 May Waters became commander of the entire group camped in parks and empty buildings. When more than 8,000 marchers had reached the city early in June, Glassford set up a B.E.F. camp on Anacostia Field. Eventually there were twenty other billets in the District. All through the B.E.F. story the name of Glassford stands out boldly as friend, provider, counselor, treasurer, and defender.[12]

Communists, too, were preparing to march on Washington. Earl Browder, leading American Communist, recognized the tremendous revolutionary potentialities revealed by the B.E.F., but he claimed no credit for the march. Communists had no part in the origin of the B.E.F., an oversight which earned a stinging rebuke from Moscow. This lapse was remedied on 19 May with the formation of the Ex-Servicemen's League. Emmanuel Levine, a former Marine, was put in charge of making plans for the march on Washington that was to culminate on 8 June. The peaceful B.E.F. was to be infiltrated and captured, and the whole movement turned into an uprising that would force Hoover to call out the troops.[13]

The first Communist move came in Detroit where Joseph Kowalski, a notorious maker of riots, prepared to follow orders brought by Jack Stachel. Quickly organizing a bonus march committee under John T. Pace, a bankrupt contractor who had become a Communist in 1931, the Reds recruited bogus and bona fide veterans from their Unemployed Council in Detroit. With four other Communists, Pace led some 400 marchers to Washington. Communist-led contingents, often ignorant of their leadership, began to arrive from various cities. Pace is credited with having 'seized complete control of the embittered veterans' and was able, it is claimed, 'to proclaim himself the undisputed head of more than ten thousand veterans.' Actions of the B.E.F. testify that the Communist estimate of Pace's power is greatly exaggerated. The simple fact is that Communists did not at any time dominate the B.E.F.[14]

Since lobbying was their only purpose, leaders of the B.E.F. appointed a legislative committee to force debate on the Patman bill.

Veterans haunted House members so effectively that by 13 June the bill was called up for debate the next day. The move pleased General Glassford, who thought that the B.E.F. would dissolve as soon as Congress took action. Heartsill Ragon of Arkansas directed debate in favor of the bill, while Willis Hawley of Oregon led its opposition. Veterans followed the arguments closely and continued the debate in their billets.

The B.E.F. inevitably became a topic of widespread concern and even anxiety. One member of Congress feared that Washington would be swamped by the unemployed if the federal government fed the bonus army. Numerous reporters visited the billets and their stories, while by no means always friendly, reassured the public that the bonus marchers were normal, hungry, unemployed Americans. The marchers, like many who stayed home, were convinced that

> Mellon pulled the whistle,
> Hoover rang the bell,
> Wall Street gave the signal
> And the country went to hell! [15]

Stories of what bankers were getting out of the R.F.C., of Mellon's tax refunds, or R.F.C. loans to railroads, of utilities services cut off for nonpayment of bills, of people slowly starving to death without hope—typical depression stories and complaints went the rounds among men who could not understand how high officials could minimize suffering among the unemployed. Their criticisms were voiced in the *B.E.F. News*, a paper published weekly for five cents per copy.

Passage of the Patman bill in the House was practically certain without any debate. It was also certain that the Senate would vote overwhelmingly against it, and that President Hoover would veto the measure should the Senate surprise itself with a favorable vote. Basically, the Patman bill called for immediate payment in greenbacks of the face value of adjusted compensation certificates. The debate swirled around two points: payment of the bonus in any form at that time, and how it should be paid.[16] When the vote was taken on 15 June there were 211 yeas, 176 nays, and 43 who were paired or refused to vote. The vote crossed party lines, although major support was Democratic and major opposition Republican.

In the Senate there had been no such flood of bonus legislation. Senator Elmer Thomas, Oklahoma Democrat, introduced what was practically a duplicate of the Patman bill on 1 March. Various senators, including Royal S. Copeland of New York, Thomas D. Schall of Minnesota, and Robert F. Wagner, presented petitions for the bonus. Thomas had been a doughty champion of the B.E.F. He defended the veterans against vilification, described their plight, and needled various committees in a futile effort to get action. The Senate made no attempt to bury the Patman bill but debated it promptly on 17 June, following an adverse report by the Committee on Finance. The 22 senators who spoke pro and con probably changed no one's mind. The vote on that day was 18 for, 62 against, and 16 not voting.[17]

So far as Congress was concerned, the bonus bill was dead and the B.E.F. had better disperse. During the Senate debate, some 8,000 men sat around the Capitol waiting for the defeat that nearly all felt was certain. Officials were worried. 'Washington in general and the Capital in particular never has been as nervous as today,' one reporter wrote. General Glassford had the drawbridges to Anacostia raised in order to prevent recruits from joining the watchers on Capitol Hill. When Waters announced the vote to the B.E.F. lobbyists, he wondered just what the men would do. At the suggestion of Elsie Robinson, a Hearst reporter, he told them to sing 'America' and go back to their billets. They did. Behind them in the Senate there was a flurry of argument over a senator's right to speak if nothing was before the Senate, and a feeble attempt to gain reconsideration of the vote. Senator Peter Norbeck had inserted into the *Record* reports on the grasshopper situation in South Dakota.[18]

3. *The Colossal Blunder*

The campaign to get the B.E.F. out of Washington was intensified on 18 June; at the same time B.E.F. leaders began to recruit more men to increase pressure on Congress. Hoover, who had refused to receive Waters, at last recognized existence of the bonus army and asked Congress to appropriate $100,000 to pay transportation home for any veterans who would ask for it. The appropriation became law on 8 July and the time limit, set first at 15 July, was extended later to 25 July.[19] The sums advanced were to be deducted from the adjusted compensation certificates when due in 1945.

The major motive in this move was not charity but to relieve Washington of an embarrassing group. By midnight 10 July only

590 veterans had obtained 'free' tickets; on 11 July a thousand more marchers joined the B.E.F. The Administration reported that about 6,000 veterans had departed, leaving between 5,000 and 7,000 'mixed hoodlums, ex-convicts, Communists, and a minority of veterans . . .' *Time,* more accurate, referred to 500 Communists among nearly 20,000. Many of the tickets were sold for cash and others were issued for destinations far from the veteran's origin. No one knows how many veterans actually left, either for home or on a junket, although the Veterans' Administration provided funds for 5,160.[20] Except for this transportation, the Hoover Administration did nothing about the B.E.F. except to abuse it and then drive it away at bayonet point.

Congress adjourned on 16 July. In spite of the transportation offer, Waters claimed that more than 20,000 veterans were still in Washington. Seventeen thousand went to the Capitol, some hoping to see the mysterious Mr. Hoover when Congress closed; but the President stayed at home behind a doubled White House guard. When a group of thirty men assembled near the White House, Hoover ordered the area cleared for two blocks. There was no rioting. The B.E.F. began to break up slowly, with Waters advising the men with homes to go to them. By 26 July B.E.F. figures showed fewer than 15,000 remaining; one estimate placed the number at 10,000.[21]

Plans for eviction were being formulated, but it is difficult to fix responsibility other than to ascribe them to the District commissioners, President Hoover, Ogden Mills, and Secretary of War Hurley. On 21 July the Treasury Department issued an order giving the B.E.F. until 24 July to evacuate occupied buildings that were to be demolished. Work was to begin on 25 July. This flimsy excuse was so lame that most of official Washington limped in sympathy. Waters expected trouble, but none came and no eviction took place on 24 July. An interview with Hurley revealed nothing except the determination to drive the B.E.F. away and to brand it as a gang of Communists and hoodlums. The District commissioners extended the time limit to 1 August, knowing all the while that the next eviction order would be issued on 28 July. The idea was to goad the B.E.F. into causing disorders; then the commissioners, headed by Luther H. Reichelderfer, would tell Hoover that they could not handle the situation, and Hoover would call out the troops. At least, that is the way things went.[22]

Police surrounded a building at Third and Pennsylvania on 28 July before the veterans had a chance to evacuate it, and led the men out. *Time's* reporter wrote: 'Four times 200-odd veterans were ordered out. Four times they refused to budge.' Only one, a Negro not registered with the B.E.F., resisted. Then hundreds of veterans from other camps wandered into Pennsylvania Avenue. There was no riot at the time. Then came the Communists.[23]

A small group of Reds carrying an American flag tried to break through police lines around the building. About forty veterans, nearly all of them Communists, struggled for six minutes with twenty police. Glassford, in the midst of the melee, stopped the 'riot,' and one of the men ran off to a car, which drove away at once. There was not, according to Waters, any other rioting on 28 July. Again, one can only guess at what happened. Another eyewitness reported:

Three men, one carrying a large American flag, started a march across the block, followed by several hundred. When the leaders encountered a policeman he grabbed the flag. There was a scuffle, and one of the marchers was hit on the head with a nightstick. He wrested it from the officer and struck back. Other policemen rushed toward the spot, and there was a shower of bricks from the marchers in the rear.[24]

Early in the afternoon, Glassford and a few policemen started to climb to the top of a vacant building to see what was causing a melee among a small group of veterans. Some of the men followed, pushing close to the police. One of the officers, without warning and without provocation, except that he stumbled on a step, whirled and fired three shots into the crowd. Another policeman fired once. Two veterans, William Hushka and Eric Carlson, were mortally wounded. This version by Waters is contradicted by another account: During 'bloody battling' in which 800 police reenforcements were rushed in, two policemen were cornered on a second floor. In response to the cry 'Let's get 'em!' the police fired 'a half dozen shots' that killed Hushka and Carlson.[25]

Waters expected that this was the 'riot and bloodshed' Hurley and Hoover would use to bring in the Army. There were men, lots of them, milling around on Pennsylvania Avenue; but a crowd is not a riot. The Communist contingent had been reinforced by some 200 non-veterans from New York whom Levine had directed Pace to quarter in unoccupied government buildings. That the Communists would endeavor to make trouble was certain; intervention by the

Army would be excellent propaganda stuff. The official and too simple explanation of the 28 July trouble is that groups led by Communists swarmed into Pennsylvania Avenue when police tried to dislodge the men from their billets. The police were badly mauled in the 'riot,' Glassford asked the District commissioners for help, and Hurley followed Hoover's orders in calling out the troops.[26] Glassford definitely did not ask for troops and did not want them.

The Army moved in after five o'clock with six tanks, cavalry, machine guns, and General Douglas MacArthur. Resplendent in a hastily donned uniform, the general was a dashing figure at the head of about 700 troops. Present, too, were Dwight Eisenhower and George B. Patton as junior officers. Methodically the soldiers ferreted veterans out of their billets and scattered them with cavalry charges and tear gas .Veterans, Communists, and soldiers participated in setting many small fires. The dispossessed fled to Camp Bartlett on private property outside the District, and the gallant troops prepared to conquer Anacostia Field.

As yet there were no troops at Anacostia, which certainly did not need to be evacuated under the flimsy construction pretext. Early in the evening Anacostia's water supply was cut off. Urged by a reporter, Senator Borah called the White House to recommend that troops be kept out of Anacostia the night of 28 July. The promise was given and broken. An hour before midnight, MacArthur's men were at Anacostia with tanks, tear gas, and fixed bayonets. The only reported casualty in the midnight attack was Bernard Myers, a baby two months old who died from inhaling tear gas from a bomb thrown at his father's feet. Soldiers started fires in the billets, then the B.E.F. set its own fires. The veterans offered no resistance.[27]

Communists were not quite ready to give up. James Ford, Negro candidate for vice president, endeavored on 29 July to persuade his colleagues to resist the Army. Police raided the meeting, arrested Ford and 42 others, and effectively ended the Red menace. Early in August, when Pace was still directing White House picketing, orders came to call off the dogs. Pace went on to New York, where he attended a meeting with Browder, William Z. Foster, a Russian representative, and others of the hierarchy. The leaders commended Pace and sent him on a speaking tour to damn MacArthur and Hoover.[28]

Meanwhile, the B.E.F. reached the anticlimactic end of the road.

A straggling band of some 7,100 men, women and children arrived at Johnstown, Pennsylvania. The town's mayor was not quite certain about what to do with them. Billeted at an amusement center renamed Camp McClosky, the bonus marchers were a pitiful group. Baltimore & Ohio officials and community leaders arranged for free transportation out of the city. Uncertain of himself, sick of efforts to turn the B.E.F. to selfish advantage, Waters played with the idea of starting a 'shirt' movement before he gave orders to disband and the great protest ended—until November.[29]

The full story of the B.E.F. could not be of any value to the Republicans in 1932. Communists zealously spread the most malicious lies they could concoct, and Republican orators in reply painted the whole B.E.F. as a mob dominated by Communists. Even later, writers with more facts available found little excuse for Hoover's action in calling out the Army. The official explanation was that Hoover either had to honor the request for troops or surrender the capital to mob rule. Critics attributed the use of the Army to Hoover's jumpy nerves, made jumpier by Communist demonstrations.

Official statements helped matters not at all. President Hoover believed that a challenge to the government had been met 'swiftly and firmly.' General MacArthur opined that not one-tenth of the B.E.F. were veterans; but General Frank T. Hines, the Veterans Administrator, said that 94 per cent of the B.E.F. were veterans. F. Trubee Davison, Assistant Secretary of War, called the B.E.F. 'a polyglot mob of tramps and hoodlums, with a generous sprinkling of Communist agitators.' The Secretary of War, Patrick Hurley, offered a peculiar explanation: Red agitators had caused an organized attack of several thousand men against the police, B.E.F. billets had not been fired by the Army, and the military operation had been conducted with 'unparalleled humanity and kindness.' [30]

President Hoover had been unduly frightened by the B.E.F. No matter how strongly he insisted that a serious threat to the government existed, there was no such threat. The small contingent of Communists could not start a revolution among the middle-aged veterans already thoroughly whipped by economic forces of the depression. A sympathetic observer wrote: 'There is about the lot of them an atmosphere of hopelessness, of utter despair, though not of desperation ... they have no enthusiasms whatever and no stomach for fighting.' The veterans resembled, in large measure, the other unemployed who drifted aimlessly over the country to escape misery at home. The Bonus Army, Mauritz Hallgren correctly judged, was 'simply a minor manifestation of the unrest spreading through the country.'[31] Conditions that caused the bonus march should have scared Mr. Hoover; the B.E.F. itself was no threat to cherished American traditions. General MacArthur's statement that the government was in peril from the dispirited B.E.F. should be allowed to fade away. If 8,000 or 10,000 unarmed veterans could have overthrown the national government in one week, what might they have done with arms?

Just what influence the B.E.F. affair had on the November election is something no one can estimate accurately. Paul Y. Anderson called the forcible eviction Hoover's opening move for re-election: convince the people that the B.E.F. was a threat to the government, move decisively, then pose as a savior after provoking conflict.[32] Use of the Army may have cost Hoover a few thousand votes, but his attitude toward the bonus was far more costly. One lesson should have been learned: a petition presented in person by a group of several thousand citizens must be taken with dead seriousness. No government, however well entrenched, can ignore the demands of a well-organized and determined minority if it wishes to remain in power. Minorities have a way of becoming majorities.

CHAPTER XVI

1932—BACKDROP FOR POLITICS

1. *Bottom at Last*

The campaign of 1932 was the most dramatic political battle since William Jennings Bryan had assaulted the citadels of privilege. While by no means rebellious in a military sense, the masses of people were seething with a raging discontent that no serious person ignored.

Economic activity was woefully low in 1932. No matter how favorably one interprets the slight movements upward after July, they were not enough to bear out the widely believed assertion that business improved when, and therefore because, Congress had adjourned. What Congress did or did not do, what it threatened or failed to threaten, had no demonstrable effect on business.

Practically all major indexes showed at last that bottom had been reached, but this was apparent only in retrospect; in 1932 one could see only that new lows, followed by slight improvements, had occurred. These slight increases Hoover called a 'turn toward recovery.' The President praised the Reconstruction Finance Corporation for having saved financial institutions. Now, the President said, we need confidence in the future and the government can promote confidence by reducing expenditures, balancing the budget, reforming the banking system, and co-operating with other governments in economic matters.[1]

If one drew conclusions from stock market behavior, there were reasons for moderate rejoicing. Stocks listed on the New York Stock Exchange on 1 July had a nominal value of $15.6 billion, off about $74 billion from the 1929 high. The market advanced spectacularly during the next two months.[2] But this advance did not reflect a marked improvement in economic activity. Compared with 1929, statistics for 1932 showed declines of 45 per cent in lumber production and 75 per cent in steel ingot production, while automobiles fell from 5,358,420 to 1,426,960. Employment figures revealed 45 per cent of factory workers unemployed. Contracts for residential building were 86 per cent less than in 1929.[3] Statistical evidence of depression was comparatively easy to obtain. More difficult was the task of measuring intangibles in 1932. While Congress was debating and Hoover was struggling, public confidence received a series of terrific blows. Chief among them were the failures of Ivar Kreuger and Samuel Insull.

Kreuger was a Swede whose financial adventures were such magnificent swindles as to defy imagination. With less than $3,000 in capital, Kreuger and his partner, Paul Toll, started a business in 1907 that eventually cost American investors some $250 million. They dominated the match business in many countries, owned real estate and forests, iron mines and banks, and tied it all together in a corporate maze that Insull would have admired. Lee, Higginson and Company sold their securities without really knowing anything about Kreuger and Toll and without bothering to find out. Net earnings were reported in 1931 as about $23.5 million when actually the corporation was bankrupt. Caught by the depression, Kreuger resorted to forgery to meet commitments; but there was no escape. When exposure was unavoidable, Ivar Kreuger put a bullet in his heart. The day was 12 March 1932.[4] A month later the country was shocked again when the Insull utility empire collapsed.

The problem of destitute and starving citizens became steadily worse during the fall and winter of 1932. While the presidential campaign was under way, a powerful protest against spreading disaster suggested that both candidates should serve alternate terms of three months during which Sherwood Anderson offered to take them into places they had never seen so they could know what was going on in agriculture, in the streets, in slums, in alleys, in Hoovervilles all over the land.[5]

With such a tremendous amount of hunger, malnutrition, and economic injustice in all parts of the country, the wonder is that people remained so calm. Except for sporadic incidents and a few places where turmoil was chronic, the general aspect was one of uneasy peace. The American Civil Liberties Union, while reporting a long list of official and unofficial violations of individual rights, believed that increased tolerance for minorities could be observed. Official lawlessness as well as mob violence increased, partly because of protracted labor struggles in such places as the mines of Kentucky and Illinois.[6]

The B.E.F. was, in large measure, a hunger march. Its fate did not discourage similar demonstrations equally futile if less alarming to the Republican high command. The reaction of most conservatives was that expressed by the Troy, New York, *Record*, which observed that there probably were no genuine hunger marches but just a bunch of Communist trouble makers. In September, Carl Winter, a notorious Red, led a reported 5,000 Communists to New York City Hall to demand direct relief for the unemployed. Mayor Joseph V. McKee, who had taken over when Jimmy Walker resigned under Governor Roosevelt's penetrating questioning, could only protest: 'I'm not here to be heckled by you!'[7] Indeed, there was little more that he could do.

Chicago's only big hunger march occurred near the end of October, when a united front of protesting groups staged a parade estimated to have included 20,000 shuffling marchers. Apparently upward of 200,000 people saw the march as it progressed from Randolph Street through the Loop and debouched on Michigan Avenue. A driving rain in part accounted for the lack of enthusiasm among marchers. The most prominently displayed placards carried understandable demands: 'We Want Bread!' 'We Want Food!'

Onlookers were both curious and puzzled. Although there were 700,000 dependent on relief in Chicago, although thousands of families were trying to exist on $3.15 worth of food a week, people not on relief simply did not understand the misery that existed behind the lake-front façade. Demands presented to City Hall included the novel proposal that 'all unemployment funds . . . be administered by elected representatives of organizations of the unemployed.'[8] That would be one way to turn relief funds over to Communists!

Worried officials in Washington kept watch on reports of a disintegrating society. Major E. W. Brown, who had succeeded General Glassford, heard that numerous groups were planning to descend on the capital. All over the country, city after city confessed its inability to care for the destitute. St. Louis turned 13,000 families adrift, and Detroit did the same with 18,000 families. New York City had 180,758 destitute families receiving no relief. Many qualified observers began to think in terms of multi-billion-dollar relief programs.[9]

One more Communist-inspired hunger march converged on the capital in December to demand a cash payment of $50 for each unemployed head of a family, $10 for each dependent, and unemployment insurance. Police herded the group into New York Avenue, sealed off both ends, and had 1,200 officers, 700 firemen, and a force of militia available to use machine guns, tear gas, or whatever was necessary to subdue the 'unarmed, weary, wan, and undernourished men and women.' Anti-Hoover congressmen who visited this street camp were indignant over conditions. Less disturbing was the Farmers' National Relief Conference, which demanded $500 million in immediate relief for agriculture.[10]

Incidents such as these drew acid comment from some quarters. Proceeding from the assumption that the worst was over and people who wanted to could obtain jobs, an editorial writer advised:

There is reason for congratulation that chaos was avoided as the entire civilized world was adversely affected. The trying ordeal having passed, the survivors should take hope, stop quarreling about wages, grit their teeth, put their shoulders to the wheel and *work*. It is time to cease talking about a living wage and the 'high standard of living' when many fellow citizens have been compelled to rely upon organized public aid for food and shelter. . . . Work and thrift will accomplish more than may possibly be achieved by profligate distribution of private and public funds which may tend to undermine self-reliance and create a false and temporary prosperity, whereas the old-fashioned method has often been tried and never found wanting.[11]

Work and thrift and self-reliance and sound principles and the American Way of Life and Go-West-Young-Man and everybody ought to be rich—never did so many people reveal so little so often! The *Commercial & Financial Chronicle* returned to the same theme in advising the farmers: 'The time has come when it is necessary for the farmer to show resourcefulness in meeting changes in world economic conditions. He needs to adopt every economy of production. He needs to recognize handicaps, natural and economic, that foredoom him to failure.' But, as usual, the editor blamed much of the farmer's plight on the convenient devil, politics: 'It looks as if the farmer has again been made the victim of politics, and somehow it seems a miracle that he is managing to get along in spite of the fact that the agricultural dollar is reported as only worth 51 per cent of what it was before the war.' [12]

2. *Farm Holiday*

Farmers did not need to read the statistics to know that they were in bad shape in 1932, even worse than they had been at any time since 1921. However one read the statistics, it was difficult to find anything encouraging. Farm prices by June 1932 were only 52 per cent of the 1909–14 average; but prices farmers paid were 106 per cent of the prewar average and taxes were 166 per cent higher than in 1914. Dairy farmers everywhere were restless under a regime of surplus production and low prices, a situation they shared with nearly all agricultural producers.[13] The stream of farm bankruptcies increased, and thousands of farmers lost their land through mortgage foreclosures. Auctions disposed of livestock and machinery at give-away prices. Farmers began to defy the law. They threatened to lynch judges who sanctioned foreclosures; they bid a penny, a nickel, or a dime for valuable property and returned it as a gift to the bankrupt owners; they threatened and attempted marketing strikes.[14]

Farmers continued to suffer from drought, surpluses, and Republicanism throughout the Hoover Administration. They gave Hoover's Farm Board a chance to solve their ills; when the Board failed, agricultural discontent flared into angry denunciation and direct action in the Middle West, where continued distress assumed hysterical proportions. It was in Iowa, one of the most richly endowed agricultural areas in the world, that resentment was first translated into desperate action. In that great cornucopia of hogs, corn, chickens, and cattle, Milo Reno raised an exhorting voice. This native of Iowa, born to parents who had been active in lost causes, first won notice in 1920 as a delegate to the Farmers' Union state convention. During the Age of Normalcy, Reno combined a prosperous insurance business with demands for radical farm policies. President of the Iowa Farmers' Union and of the Farmers' Holiday Association, Reno recalled the bumptiousness of 'Sockless' Jerry Simpson and Mary Lease of Populist days. Reno's major weakness lay in striking out blindly against everything in sight that might possibly be connected with the farmer's troubles. He appealed to passion, ignorance, prejudice, and superstition; occasionally he appealed to reason. He had an audience in farmers all over the country but particularly in those Iowa counties where anger and desperation were mounting, where farmers agreed that an embargo on food for such centers as Sioux City would be a good idea.[15]

Depression prices, Farm Board failures, and the 'cow war' of 1930–31 set the stage for a farmers' strike. The National Farmers' Holiday Association was born at Des Moines in May 1932 while the B.E.F. was converging upon Washington. Milo Reno and John Chalmers, vice president of the Iowa Farmers' Union, provided the leadership.

Reno, in addressing several thousand farmers at the Des Moines fair grounds, offered to lead the association for a salary of $5 per day to be paid from membership dues of fifty cents. Each member was to sign a pledge not to ship goods to market until reasonable prices were obtained.[16] The Farmers' Holiday Association on 30 July decided to set 15 August as the date for its strike.

In the meantime, and entirely independently, milk producers had begun to picket roads leading into Sioux City in order to force a rise in prices from $1.70 to $2.17 per hundred pounds of raw milk. The dairymen's pickets received reinforcements on the morning of 15 August. Farm-made barriers appeared on highways leading into Sioux City, Des Moines, Council Bluffs, and other cities. Farmers, hired hands, and drifters manned the barriers with clubs, sticks, and pitchforks. In some cases young fascists of the Khaki Shirts joined the farmers until sheriffs ordered the roads cleared. The sheriffs were gentle; although bankrupt, farmers still voted. On 17 August some 450 farmers tried to empty Sioux City stockyards but were turned back by deputy sheriffs and the police. The old laws of supply and demand seemed to have been suspended: hog receipts at Sioux City fell from 2,000 to 500 daily, but the price dropped. The price should have risen with the decreased supply, since there could not have been an immediate decrease in demand. The milk producers did win an increase of 10 cents per hundred pounds; the dairies, as usual, gouged consumers by raising prices one cent per quart.[17]

Republicans could take little comfort in observing farmers moving farther and farther from the Grand Old Party just as the presidential campaign was getting under way. The Iowa situation was dangerous, and farmers in neighboring states were picking up the cue. In Nebraska, South Dakota, and other states farmers armed with pitchforks dumped trucks of milk and other produce into ditches; neighbors who refused to participate in the strike program sometimes were handled roughly.

The Farmers' Holiday movement did not spend itself barricading roads and dumping milk in ditches. The movement became one to stop foreclosures and tax sales; it agitated strongly for reduced interest rates on mortgages, an end to deficiency judgments, a decrease in taxes, a moratorium on farm debts, and other measures of relief. In the year ending 1 March 1932 forced sale of farms had reached 41.7 per thousand and could have been far worse had creditors insisted on their legal rights. By the end of 1932 foreclosures had reduced the farm mortgage debt from $9,347 million in 1930 to about $5 billion. By the end of 1932, officials of insurance companies and other financial institutions that held mortgages were seriously alarmed. Such institutions in the East held farm mortgages worth $1,250 million in Iowa, $560 million in Nebraska, and $350 million in South Dakota. The stability of all major life insurance companies was threatened. Farmers in Iowa, Nebraska, Wisconsin, South Dakota, Indiana, Kansas, and other states swarmed through legislative halls with their petitions. In Nebraska they threatened, with pardonable hyperbole, to tear the beautiful skyscraper capitol to pieces and scatter it over the prairies like buffalo chips.[18]

There were some temporary results. Laws were enacted to provide grace periods, to increase the number of years for redemption of property lost by tax sales, and to drag out proceedings almost interminably. Some insurance companies, including the largest, adopted a rule of reason and displayed both leniency and good judgment in refusing to foreclose on property in default. Some governors declared a mortgage holiday. On the whole, the strike was a miserable failure, but it did dramatize the farmer's plight.[19]

There was plenty of cause to worry about the future when farmers armed with pitchforks took the law into their own hands. As William Allen White wrote, 'When the American farmer comes out to the road with a club or a pitchfork, the warning flag is out. There may be danger ahead.'[20] No greater law-abiding group, no stauncher foundation for democracy, existed in America than the farm population. While deploring the futility of a farm strike, the *Christian Century* accurately editorialized: 'The chaos of our economic system could not be more vividly portrayed than in the sight of a rich agricultural state like Iowa, in the midst of a good season, finding itself in such distress that such extra-legal and disorderly methods are adopted by conscientious and responsible men.'[21]

Hoover might lecture the farmers on the duties of citizenship, but he could not dismiss them as a bunch of hoodlums and Communists. They were exasperated capitalist-producers, overflowing with that rugged individualism Hoover had written about with such fervor at the end of the World War. Caught in a ruthless squeeze play by urban capitalists and historical legacies, they had lost their respect for the law of institutions that denied them the fruits of their labor. Daniel

Shays, who led the rebellion in Massachusetts in 1786, would have been at home among them. So would Nathaniel Bacon, leader of Virginia's frontier uprising in 1676.

3. *The Lord Helps Those . . .*

What happened to the unemployed? How did they weather the depression? There are so many variations to the story that volumes would be required to do justice to this great tragedy. Those with no savings to fall back on and with families to support eventually found themselves on relief rolls of private and public agencies; people with any kind of property usually disposed of it at sacrifice rates before applying for relief. Men and women constantly moved here and there in cities investigating rumors of jobs to be had. Families doubled up, tripled up in some cases; single men and often fathers took to the highways and the railways looking for jobs, or just looking. People past forty-five frequently discovered that they had lost the last job they ever would have a chance to fill. Some were able to eke out an existence through odd jobs; some resorted to begging and petty thievery; some went back to the farm, if they had been country-born, back to live with a relative who at least might have food and shelter. For the most part, workers generally stayed where they were, sharing the work, tightening their belts, hoping for the best, and cursing the Republican party.

Sharing the work was merely another way of sharing unemployment, of making labor bear an outrageously high share of relief costs. A great many corporations resorted to this device and gave employment to thousands who otherwise would have been entirely idle.[22] Corporations were by no means soulless monsters; hundreds of examples could be given of corporate efforts to aid the victims of economic distress.[23] However, all of their aid fell far short of meeting the need.

Desperate times fostered desperate measures. The unemployed resorted to various emergency self-help schemes in an effort to provide themselves with goods and services denied them by the industrial system. One organization, perhaps the first, was the Unemployed Citizens' League of Seattle, which was formed by unemployed students and instructors at Seattle Labor College in July 1931.[24] A barter and exchange movement was begun by Benjamin Stringham in Utah in August 1931, when he bartered the truck loads of potatoes he had brought from Idaho to Salt Lake City and had been unable to sell. The barter idea caught on and was organized into the Natural Development Association in January 1932. Eventually there were units in four other states engaged in manufacturing, retailing, and exchanging occupations.[25]

The Unemployed Citizens' League of Denver began on 23 June 1932. Within a few weeks 34,000 people enrolled in 25 local groups. Working for farmers who could not hire labor, the League salvaged 2,000 tons of food by December. Borrowing a closed bakery for two months, it turned out 500 loaves of bread daily. Meals were served at several kitchens; apartments or homes were found for some 200 families. A wood camp provided cordwood for fuel; some supplies were obtained from the Red Cross and other agencies. So successful was the League that units were organized in eleven other Colorado cities.[26] Similar enterprises existed in Ohio, where Dr. Arthur E. Morgan, president of Antioch College, organized the Midwest Exchange. In New York the Emergency Exchange Association, formed by prominent citizens, promoted the Mutual Exchange System. In this, as in other self-help groups, the basic modus operandi utilized a barter-token-scrip system.[27]

Self-help activities included planting of gardens. Railroad systems had encouraged gardening for many years, even going to the extent of renting garden plots. The steel industry in northern Indiana was enthusiastic in promoting this new competition for the farmers. The 'plant-a-garden' movement spread into every state and occasionally, as at Ventura, California, was the nucleus for much broader cooperative activities.[28]

Gardening and self-help activities helped those who remained relatively immobile, but there were thousands who refused to 'stay put.' Accurate statistics of the transient unemployed were impossible to obtain, but samples indicated what a serious problem was created by these wanderers. Many small towns in Texas, New Mexico, and Arizona reported 200 men and boys passing along trains of the Southern Pacific every day. That popular railroad ejected 683,457 trespassers in 1932. The Volunteers of America at Phoenix, Arizona, fed and lodged 1,529 boys in about 100 days. At Yuma, Arizona, 30,000 men and boys were fed at soup kitchens in four and one-half months. In New York City, minors were referred to the Childrens' Aid Society's

Newsboys' House. The Salvation Army provided help for many in scores of communities.[29]

The best any community could do was to provide food and lodging of some kind for a limited period, often for only a day. Elliot Chapman, seventeen years of age, was one of the wanderers of 1932. Unable to make a living in Detroit, where he had been a radio salesman, Chapman joined the transients. In Chicago he worked briefly as a caddie, returned to Detroit, then left for California after Labor Day. Pickings were slim and competition keen on the coast, so Chapman took the southern route to glamorous New Orleans. Everywhere it was the same story:

They do not like you to stay there, especially in New Orleans and a few places where they arrive a couple of hundred a day. The Salvation Army places will feed you for a night, or rather let you sleep there. In the morning they will give you a bowl of beef broth or something. In the other places they give you coffee, soup, and bread. But the soup, as one fellow put it, is just some hot water with a little cabbage dipped in . . . Most of the fellows, young fellows that start out, will not panhandle. They have a pride and are sort of scared to go up to a person. But you soon lose that, and there is just a feeling when you are tired and hungry you do not care much what happens to you.[30]

Chapman met the professional bums, rode boxcars and blind baggage, passed through jungles, and was chased out of city after city. He was fortunate in having a grandmother in Washington, D.C., who gave him a home.

This evidence of social disintegration worried the Children's Bureau and thoughtful citizens everywhere. Thousands of homes were broken and upward of two million migrants or vagrants wandered over the country. A very large proportion of them were young men from 16 to 21 who thumbed rides on the highways, boarded freight trains, slept in jungles and railway cars, lived precariously and generally in bad health. Newton D. Baker, chairman of the National Welfare and Relief Organization, guessed that more than 200,000 boys were wandering over the country in the winter of 1932–3.[31]

The idea of work camps for young men, a natural solution to the hordes of transients, was considered seriously by a Senate committee. The few state labor camps already in existence provided a model, and General Pelham D. Glassford, his interest aroused by the plight of the B.E.F., favored a semi-military organization to operate federally supported camps.[32] Thus the New Deal's Civilian Conservation Corps was in part a result of experience during the Hoover years, but work camps were never a Hoover project.

Surely no candidate seeking re-election ever had a more dismal backdrop for a political campaign. The B.E.F. in Washington, hunger marches in many cities, farmers defying courts of justice, citizens turning to communal societies, bread lines growing longer, banks continuing to close and breweries waiting to open—against all of this and even more would Herbert Hoover fight as he stood before the people for their judgment.

CHAPTER XVII

1932—CRUSADE FOR RECOVERY

1. *Hoover Again*

Nineteen thirty-two was a year of decision, a year of despair, a year of confusion. By chronological accident it was also the year of a presidential election. There was a feeling of jubilation in Democratic ranks, a conviction that any acceptable nominee could defeat Herbert Hoover. There was also a stirring of hope among the left-wingers that 1932 might be their year to register political gains if not to capture the major prize of the political lottery. And there were honest and earnest men who hoped for the appearance of a party with ideals, a party impervious to opportunism and dedicated to the proposition that the United States could truly become the greatest nation on earth. Perhaps the leading Democratic hope lacked some of Galahad's purity but he was a good facsimile of a gallant champion.

Franklin Delano Roosevelt was one of the greatest campaigners in American history. This phenomenal success he owed to extraordinary personality and character traits combined with a general run of superb political luck. His voice was golden, his smile infectious, his presence magnificent. He was an optimist, confident of his own ability, superbly courageous, mentally alert, and well educated.[1] He possessed the power of leadership, and his instinctive humanitarianism bridged the gulf between Groton and the alley tenement.

After three years of unremitting labor and unsuccessful efforts to halt the depression, President Hoover had no overpowering desire to run again in 1932. He was fully aware of both insurgent and Old Guard opposition, of the moves to gain support for Calvin Coolidge, William E. Borah, Hiram Johnson, and several others. When his secretary broached the subject early in the year, Hoover brusquely stated his indifference to another nomination. The President did not want politics to interfere with the program he was trying to shepherd through the Seventy-second Congress.[2]

Hoover may have regretted the compulsions of his position but he had no intention of refusing a second nomination. If for no other reason, he must make the fight to be true to himself. Postmaster-General Walter Folger Brown, political hatchet man extraordinary, worked with quiet efficiency to line up delegates for Hoover in the approaching convention.

The pace of domestic politics quickened as the time for choosing approached. More than 2,000 Democrats assembled in Washington on 8 January to eat in honor of Andrew Jackson, raise money, and talk politics. Al Smith said: 'I believe that this is the time when we should forget party lines entirely.' And in the same speech: 'It is up to the Democratic Party to give not only to our country but to the world that leadership in which they are lacking.' Arthur M. Hyde replied for Hoover: 'He makes vain search who seeks a plan or a coherent suggestion among the followers of Mr. Raskob.' [3]

In spite of such sniping, the Senate voted overwhelmingly for the Reconstruction Finance Corporation bill, and General Charles G. Dawes discovered that 'this country generally has started on the upgrade; we have passed the bottom.' [4] Two days later, on 14 January, Brown announced that Hoover definitely was a candidate for renomination. There was no political truce and could not be.

A flood of oratory on Lincoln's birthday linked Hoover with the savior of the Union. Even Senator Watson was lavish in praise and defense. Although there was practically no possibility of stopping his well-organized machine, the President kept his aides busy. In April campaigners emphasized European causes of continued depression, and Hurley claimed for the President successes that simply had not occurred. The fighting Secretary of War went to Oklahoma City to answer Roosevelt's 'forgotten man' speech and later repeated the message in New York: 'There are no forgotten Americans in the President's program. . . . Basically, the question before the American people today is individualism against some form of collectivism.' W. Irving Glover, Second Assistant Postmaster General, told Missouri postmasters 'to get out on the firing line' for Hoover or resign. 'As long as you do that,' he assured his listeners, 'you are filling the job of postmaster.' [5]

The Republican nomination for 1932 was settled on 27 April when Kentucky's votes were pledged to Hoover. But the campaign did not end and Hoover undoubtedly felt new strength as he prepared his May message scolding Congress for not having balanced the budget. In spite of the result in Kentucky, the President's enemies refused to admit defeat. Too blind to realize that Hoover was their best hope to maintain the system that profited them so greatly, twenty industrialists and financiers met in New York on 20 April and sent an emissary to ask Coolidge to be a candidate. The taciturn New Englander knew when he was well off. Harold L. Ickes, the Old Curmudgeon who became a staunch but reluctant New Dealer, tried to persuade Hiram Johnson to seek the Republican nomination. Bronson Cutting and Gerald P. Nye agreed that Johnson could beat Hoover, but the California isolationist was not interested. He knew a losing thing when he saw it. Gifford Pinchot, old enough to know better, wanted the nomination, and Ickes wasted $3,500 in sounding out sentiment.[6]

Many Republicans shivered, physically and editorially, when they contemplated the 1932 campaign with Hoover again as nominee. The party was terribly embarrassed by collapse of the superman myth that had been put over by years of effective publicity. Severe critics within the party called Hoover a hesitant, vacillating, confused leader who avoided issues as long as possible and then presented 'hastily devised expedients.' Unable to dictate, as he had when he headed war agencies, the President could not provide the confident leadership needed to 'strengthen the moral fiber of the nation' while he summoned the mass intelligence of the country to point the way toward 'economic recovery and stabilization.'[7]

Altogether too glib and pontifical, Walter Lippmann voiced a widely held conviction that the Republican party could not escape considerable responsibility for the depression. The party was isolationist and had undermined the peace settlement; the party had championed economic warfare. Hoover as President had opposed necessary readjustment through his program of wage maintenance, agricultural price supports, reduction of taxes, and increase in expenditures. Not until June 1931 did Hoover acknowledge his error in trying to hold the line. Then, Lippmann continued, when it was too late, he threw over the war debts, withdrew his objection to wage reductions, and advocated higher taxes and lower expenditures. It did not matter how unfair this picture was; too many people believed it. Other critics could complain that Hoover refused to use enough experts, that he ignored competent advice and demanded that his hirelings assure the people that 'there is nothing fundamentally wrong with the existing economic order.'[8]

Casting up accounts was a popular game in 1932, a game in which historians indulged along with people without professional reasons for being cautious. Allan Nevins, who enjoyed high favor as a historian, could find little to praise except Hoover's industry and his conduct of foreign affairs. President Hoover had inherited a stable of wild horses from Coolidge; instead of riding them, he had perched on the mangers, whence he read lectures on good manners. Professor Nevins believed that Mr. Hoover was a poor policy maker, a poor leader who could neither direct a political party nor lead a parliamentary group.[9]

No matter how much of this criticism was justified, no matter how much was nonsense, practical politics made Hoover's nomination in 1932 a foregone conclusion, since Republican repudiation of the President would have been an open confession of defeat. Not since 1880, when Rutherford B. Hayes felt the axe, had Republicans discarded a President in office. Nevertheless, Hoover and his organization worked carefully to prevent a recurrence of that phenomenon. Edwin Emerson wrote his reversed biography, *Hoover and His Times;* Lewis Corey chimed in with *The Truth about Hoover,* a hasty rebuttal to Hamill's mud-slinging *Strange Career of Mr. Hoover Under Two Flags,* which had been published in 1931. Thousands of political appointees depended on Hoover's re-election to hold their jobs; two-fifths of the delegates to the Republican convention were federal employees.

2. *Two Conventions*

Proceedings in the Republican convention at Chicago, which began in apathy on 14 June, were desultory and dreary. Hoover's secretaries, Walter Newton and Lawrence Richey, manned a private wire from the Congress Hotel to the White House command post from which the President managed proceedings. Public interest in the Chicago convention was synthetic; even the delegates acted as though the day of execution had arrived, and displayed great concern lest the fatal hour find them sober. Observers who expected economic insurgency expressed surprise that there was none; conservative Republicans explained that the country was moving to the right, that the Progressives had shown their sterility. Delegates acted as though defeat in November was inevitable; anyway, what they did would not affect the outcome. The Prohibition question had caused an irremediable party split, leaving the only sane course one of holding on to the wets, striving to keep the party together, and waiting hopefully for 1936.[10]

The temporary chairman, Lester J. Dickinson of Iowa, delivered a loud, boring and platitudinous canned speech. Bertrand H. Snell, the permanent chairman, did better with a rousing condemnation of the Democrats which reminded the delegates that they needed enthusiasm, even if it were synthetic. In praise of the President, the orator stretched truth somewhat: 'He solidified labor and capital against the enemy. He avoided the deadly pit of the dole. He rescued the drought victims. He beat off the attacks upon railroads, agriculture, banks, and public securities. He warded off the stealthy approach of panic by the way of Germany. He preserved the integrity of the gold standard.'[11] Hurley had already said all of this in Oklahoma, and in nearly the same words.

The platform, dictated by Hoover and Ogden Mills, contained little that could arouse anyone's enthusiasm for another four years of Hoover in the White House, even though Calvin Coolidge did praise it highly. Only the Prohibition plank set off fireworks. The convention accepted a straddle plank in spite of valiant efforts by Senator Hiram Bingham and Dr. Nicholas Murray Butler. Mills, whom Mencken called 'one of the wettest wets in Washington,' defended the majority plank.[12]

President Hoover generally is given both credit and blame for the Prohibition plank, 'a masterpiece of evasion,' which, after needless verbiage, finally advocated submission of an amendment to conventions. The plank contained self-praise for the Republican party as a bulwark of the Constitution, insisted that Prohibition never had been a partisan issue, and so concluded that the party could cover both wets and drys. Hoover definitely refused to champion Prohibition in the 1932 campaign and hoped desperately that other and more important issues would decide the election. Hoover had rejected the majority recommendation of the Wickersham Report in January 1931 but accepted it eighteen months later.[13]

An overwhelming majority that lacked only 28 votes of being unanimous nominated the President for another term on 16 June. Immediately after this not unexpected result, Charles S. Hutson of California directed a carefully planned demonstration that created a completely synthetic pandemonium for thirty minutes. Hutson managed the uproar like a cheer leader at the Big Game. Former

Senator Joseph I. France of Maryland rushed to the platform to nominate Calvin Coolidge, but police hustled him away before he could do any damage by injecting a trace of democracy into the proceedings. The nomination of Charles Curtis to run again for the vice-presidency was practically automatic when Charles G. Dawes refused to be considered.[14]

After Hoover's nomination, Progressive Republicans had no place to go except into the Democratic party, which welcomed them eagerly. Hoover had condemned the Progressives in definite terms. He had vetoed liberal legislation they sponsored. To him these 'Sons of the Wild Jackass' were socialists or something worse. They had co-operated in the Senate with the Democrats, making Republican control purely nominal. They had voted against the Administration's candidate for majority leader when the Seventy-second Congress convened. George W. Norris, Bronson Cutting, Donald Richberg, Harold L. Ickes, Robert M. La Follette, Jr., Hiram Johnson, Smith W. Brookhart, and Gerald P. Nye either voted for Roosevelt or worked against Hoover's re-election. Ickes, who sniffed the historic scent of moose, headed a Western Independent Republican Committee for Roosevelt with $10,000 from the Democratic National Committee. In addition to better known Progressives, such political laymen as Henry A. Wallace and George N. Peek climbed on the Roosevelt calliope. There was also a National Progressive League for Roosevelt which absorbed an earlier committee headed by Norris.[15]

Not since 1896 had a national convention attracted the attention that centered on Chicago when the Democrats began to assemble. There was widespread confidence that this convention, which opened on 27 June, would nominate the next President of the United States. Delegates arrived keenly aware of their party's opportunity, and the public anticipated the climax of the Smith-Roosevelt fight. Here was the last chance for anti-Roosevelt men to stop the champion campaigner, whose astute managers had come so close to winning the necessary two-thirds vote in pre-convention maneuvering.

The historic convention opened at noon with Alben W. Barkley as temporary chairman and keynoter. Solemnly the Kentucky senator intoned: 'We meet to fulfill an appointment with destiny.' Very properly he pointed with alarm and promised with pride. But most of the interest settled on Roosevelt's ill-advised effort to abolish the two-thirds rule.[16] After the end of this scrap, Farley strengthened his hand by winning two contested delegations. In preliminary balloting on 1 July, it became apparent that John Nance Garner must be won to Roosevelt's side. Many men undoubtedly played a role in Garner's fateful decision. Byron Patton Harrison, Cordell Hull, Daniel C. Roper, William Gibbs McAdoo, and even William Randolph Hearst were busy. Their efforts were not needed. Garner, having no desire to see the Democratic party debase itself by another Madison Square Garden debacle as in 1924, threw his votes to Roosevelt. Happy days were here again and soon the victorious Roosevelt was flying to Chicago to accept the nomination.[17]

As he stood on the platform at Chicago on 2 July 1932, Governor Roosevelt had few if any positive ideas about what he was going to do after he won the election. Then his task was to start the campaign with a stirring call to battle. As an oration, his acceptance speech was far inferior to Bryan's Cross of Gold in 1896; but, as was to happen so often, Roosevelt's forensics and superb confidence imparted to commonplaces a significance innately lacking.

The Democratic nominee accepted his party's platform in its entirety. He promised real progress, real justice, in the spirit of Woodrow Wilson. He praised the people for not succumbing to radicalism and promised a constructive program made for all the people. He jibed and jeered at Republican leadership but invited Republicans to join the true faith. There were promises of action for everybody, and he concluded with a rousing summons: 'I pledge you, I pledge myself, to a new deal for the American people. Let us all here assembled constitute ourselves prophets of a new order of competence and courage. This is more than a political campaign; it is a call to arms. Give me your help, not to win votes alone, but to win in this crusade to restore America to its own people.' [18]

3. *Of Mice and Men*

A comparison of the two principal candidates is not any easier now than it was in 1932, so complex were their personalities. President Hoover had been standing in the glare of spotlights for nearly two decades; although not always the principal actor, not always in the center of the stage, he had been in the cast since 1914. Roosevelt, too, had become a familiar figure behind the footlights. Major attention would naturally go to the challenger who sought to play the leading role in the old play but with a new cast.

Franklin D. Roosevelt was a flexible, receptive man with a fluid philosophy. One of his greatest assets was the willingness to experiment, to try one thing and if it failed to try something else. He did not have, as did Hoover, a relatively inflexible ideology against which all things must be measured. Thus, he would argue convincingly in favor of balanced budgets, then adopt policies that would unbalance the budget to a degree that struck fear into the hearts of orthodox economists. He could talk about sound money and countenance adventures into monetary tinkering. This does not mean that he lacked basic standards. He was passionately devoted to the principles of fairness and equal justice; he believed in conservation of natural resources, in government regulation, control, and even production and distribution of electric power. He believed in low tariffs without defining the lowness of low. As governor, he had consistently fought for social security measures, child labor legislation, equal justice to workers, shorter hours, improvement of labor conditions, regulation of financial institutions, administrative reforms, slum clearance, regional planning, and other measures later identified with the New Deal.[19]

Above all, Roosevelt was a leader highly competent in picking men's brains. He dominated his aides, often played them against one another, and did not hesitate to make continued service impossible for those who could no longer serve best his interests or his policies. 'Roosevelt liked men around him who would act like tutors.'[20] He was a skillful politician whose belief in his own mission he took for granted. Always he presented to the public the aspect of a supremely confident, serene man whose faith was unswerving, who could appeal to members of both parties to renounce bad leadership. Compared with Hoover, he appeared warm, cordial, sociable—a good fellow who greatly enjoyed just being alive. Hoover's knowledge was both broad and deep; Roosevelt's was broad and deep enough to grasp fundamentals. Both were very sensitive; their feeling for people and their problems was sincere and intimate. Hoover, when he wanted facts, would appoint a commission to make a survey and present a report, summon experts to aid him, or get his own material. Roosevelt listened to a procession of experts, formed his decision, then acted boldly without worrying. Hoover believed that government should point the way to reform, serve as a fact-finding agency, encourage application of remedial measures, and use its police powers sparingly. Roosevelt, as one keen observer stated, was quite ready to employ governmental authority 'to redress the balance of the economic world.'[21] Both Hoover and Roosevelt were Progressives. But Hoover was a terrapin Progressive; Roosevelt was an impala Progressive.

President Hoover gained little advantage from being in the office he wanted to hold. He began his campaign in a defeatist mood but doggedly, courageously met every attack and ended far stronger than he was at the start. The badgered and bedeviled President, tired and worn, was so soundly whipped politically by the depression that almost anyone, with the possible exception of Al Smith, could have beaten him by exuding confidence. He was too busy, too conscientious, to feel that he could spare much time for campaigning. He wrote practically all of his speeches and could have used a clever ghost to good advantage. His major role was that of defending his record and searching for weaknesses in his opponent's pronouncements. His defense was masterful, his revelation of Roosevelt's vacillations was merciless. On several issues impartial judges would have to decide that Hoover won or at least came out even in the debate. He seemed to lose on very few issues—except at the polls. At first planning only three major speeches, Hoover was forced by reports from the country, especially from Maine in September, to deliver nine major addresses and many minor ones.[22]

Republicans generally expressed little genuine enthusiasm either for the candidate or for the platform. Hoover's supporters, engulfed in pessimism, often omitted any reference to the party leader. As Oswald Garrison Villard observed, a very large number of the politicians who praised Hoover in their speeches did so with utmost reluctance. And William Allen White, great among political sages, recalled: 'Whatever flings and gibes the Progressives in Congress may have aimed at the President's face were confetti beside the javelins which the regulars hurled when his back was turned. So, in the campaign, literally, he walked alone.'[23]

Hoover's cabinet provided indifferent support. Only Patrick J. Hurley and Ogden L. Mills spoke strongly in the Republican cause, although Walter F. Brown, Ray Lyman Wilbur, William N. Doak, and Arthur M. Hyde made a few ineffectual forays. Henry L. Stimson suddenly discovered that it would be beneath a Secretary of State's dignity to engage in the rough and tumble of a political campaign.

He made a few speeches and helped Hoover assemble campaign ammunition. People of property generally favored Hoover's election but without enthusiasm. They were motivated primarily by fear of Democratic radicalism.[24]

Hoover selected Everett Sanders of Indiana to replace Senator Simeon D. Fess as his campaign manager. Sanders knew his way around in politics. A lawyer practicing in Washington, he had served Coolidge as private secretary and was a veteran of three terms in the House. The Republican campaign committee represented the usual mixture of politicians, financiers, and public relations personnel. None of them had any good advice to offer the President. Chicago's Palmer House was the headquarters but there was also an eastern headquarters in luxurious rooms at the Waldorf-Astoria.

James A. Farley directed Roosevelt's campaign from quarters at the Biltmore and 331 Madison Avenue. Politicians and braintrusters managed to keep out of one another's way. While the Hoover organization failed to integrate or to control state efforts adequately, the closest liaison was maintained between Democratic headquarters and state organizations. An accurate account of costs is impossible. Judging by reports made to Congress, the Republican National Committee received $2,649,554 in 1932 and spent $2,900,000. The Democratic National Committee received $2,378,688 and spent $2,245,975.[25] Unknown amounts were spent by individuals and organizations. Regardless of funds, Republicans didn't have much of a chance.

Hoover's relations with the press became steadily worse in 1932, a condition that at least contributed to his defeat.[26] Press conferences became even rarer than before and ceased altogether after the election. During the campaign a few faithful correspondents stayed with the sinking ship, although there was far more excitement to be had by mingling with Roosevelt's buoyant crew.

Several anti-Hoover books appeared during the campaign to defame the President. Those that pretended to a degree of impartiality, like Walter W. Liggett's *The Rise of Herbert Hoover* (H. K. Fly Company: New York), failed to provide sufficient documentation to satisfy critical readers. Liggett aroused the President's indignation but probably did little damage with his strange concoction. Robert S. Allen, in *Why Hoover Faces Defeat* (Brewer, Warren & Putnam: New York), argued hopefully that the President had failed and collapsed because of incompetence, pettiness, deviousness, 'shocking callousness to tragic suffering,' timidity, plain ignorance, and 'blind reactionism.' Such drivel could be offset by drinking at the spring of brotherly love bubbling through Walter Friar Dexter's *Herbert Hoover and American Individualism: A Modern Interpretation of a National Ideal* (Macmillan: New York). Although gushy, uncritical, and often silly, Dexter offered a good analysis of Hoover's philosophy. It is doubtful if any of these volumes or others like them had a significant influence on voters.

Students of politics knew that the presidential campaign was going to be different from the previous postwar contests. Even after the platforms were announced, the only clear division appeared on the Prohibition issue, and even that difference practically disappeared before November. Sensing a popular revolt against Republican policies, Walter Millis found a strange parallel with 1912. Then the dynamic T. R. had championed the New Nationalism for the people; his distant cousin in April 1932 had restored the Democratic party to the people with his 'forgotten man' speech, which Al Smith had so sharply denounced because it might create class warfare! Restlessness and doubt prevailed throughout the country; a cataclysm obviously was building up in Europe, and again Americans refused to look. Taft and his regulars in 1912 were devoid of ideas; in 1932, the Republican platform revealed that neither Hoover nor his party had any new ideas. Neither Taft nor Hoover understood the profound economic problems of his day, Millis contended, and each directed his efforts to shoring up and maintaining the status quo of people with status.[27]

Roosevelt's campaign speeches were composites of ideas and writing. The Brain Trust prepared drafts of each major speech. The farm policy speech, for example, was prepared after hearing about the domestic allotment plan from Professor M. L. Wilson of Montana State College. Wilson conferred with Henry A. Wallace and prepared memoranda. Henry Morgenthau, Jr., Hugh Johnson, and many others made contributions to it. Other speeches were the work of scores of men who were, Hoover remarked, 'experts in semantics but grievously undernourished on truth.'[28] Roosevelt revised, added, interpolated, and often extemporized. In some cases, as with the tariff, Roosevelt plainly did not know what he wanted. Cordell Hull and Charles W. Taussig prepared a draft speech calling for a general 10 per cent reduction of tariffs; but Roosevelt wanted to win pro-tariff votes, and Raymond Moley opposed the Hull program. Moley, Johnson, Key Pittman, and Thomas J. Walsh were the major architects of Roosevelt's tariff speech at Sioux City on 29 September, which proposed little change in the Hawley-Smoot rates.[29] The tariff gave Roosevelt a bad time. His discomfort came from a belief that he could bring opposite poles together into a compromise at the middle. Instead of a compromise solution, what often resulted was self-deception.

Roosevelt exploded the rumor that he could not stand strenuous exertion. His campaign itinerary carried him 13,000 miles, during which he delivered 16 important speeches, 67 minor ones, met countless people, rode in parades, attended banquets, and exhausted his companions.[30] On the first major tour, from 12 September to 3 October, Roosevelt traveled 6,900 miles and delivered speeches at Topeka, Denver, Salt Lake City, Butte, Seattle, Portland, Chicago, and Detroit. This trip, together with the Democratic victory in Maine in September, shook Republicans out of their paralytic coma. To these extensive trips and the major effort by Roosevelt were added hundreds of speeches by big and little politicians, endorsements by prominent people, and campaigning by hundreds of other candidates who hoped that Roosevelt's coattails would be broad and sturdy.

Although many observers were misled into thinking that the voter approached November 1932 with great indifference, feeling on many issues was intense. Republicans would try to convince the voters that they had done everything possible to solve major economic problems. The columnist Jay Franklin believed that political leadership had degenerated into producing civic morons who praised bankers, industrialists, business leaders, and unclassified persons of wealth. Business leaders had smeared and vilified politics and politicians in an effort to kill liberalism before it could be translated into tangible programs. However, the American people were so calm, in spite of the B.E.F. and farm holidays and hunger marches, that conservatives of both parties found it impossible to excite the electorate with radical scares.[31]

4. *The Things They Said!*

A large part of the Democratic strategy in the campaign of 1932 was to persuade voters that the Republicans, and particularly Hoover, were responsible for the country's economic ills. Democrats argued that the depression was domestic in origin: Republicans had encouraged speculation, promoted foreign lending, fostered overproduction, destroyed foreign markets, started the chain of defaults and trade reprisals, and capped it all with a strangling deficit. Instead of boldly attempting to correct these terrible mistakes, Hoover had minimized the market crash with reassuring noises, tried to blame the depression on external conditions, and ignored the need for reform.[32]

Hoover's replies in general developed the chain-of-circumstances argument: prosperity caused excessive optimism, which caused overexpansion, which caused reckless speculation, which caused waste, exploitation, and crookedness. Democrats, Hoover emphasized, continually ignored the effects of the World War in loss of life and property and the inheritance of debt and heavy taxes; overproduction of many products in many parts of the world; trade barriers erected by succession states; maintenance of burdensome armaments; the Chinese and Russian revolutions, agitation in India, and political instability that paralyzed economic activities in many countries. These exogenous causes of depression could not be ignored.[33]

A political campaign is indeed conducted to win votes, but that purpose should not be incompatible with truth and restraint. In his Baltimore speech about the four horsemen of Destruction, Delay, Deceit, and Despair on 25 October Roosevelt said: 'The Horseman of Destruction came likewise from the false policy of lending money to backward and crippled countries.' The Hoover Administration had been guilty of trying to 'open markets in foreign lands through the lending of American money to these countries . . .' And that policy, Roosevelt so confidently proclaimed, 'was utterly and entirely unsound.'[34] Compare these statements with Roosevelt's Export-Import banks, his Lend-Lease program, and both Democratic and Republican policy after World War II! This was one issue that Roosevelt should have ignored, and Hoover's reply at Indianapolis on 28 October was devastating. But how many voters paid any attention to it?

Hoover also outpointed his opponent on the question of economic overexpansion, but the matter was too complicated for hot pursuit in a political campaign. Republicans were more vulnerable on their depression record, not because they were guilty of donothingism but because the depression continued. Roosevelt's major speeches in October hammered hard at this vital weakness. He accused the President with being indecisive, incompetent, and lacking in leadership.

He characterized Hoover's efforts to relieve unemployment as a policy of denying its existence.[35]

President Hoover was very touchy on this point, and in several speeches he recounted at length what Republicans had done to fight the battle against depression. Much of this battle had to be a silent one lest panic ensue. It was too dangerous to reveal what was being done, even to counter the blasts of misrepresentation. Now, in spite of Democratic opposition, remedial measures were working.[36]

The do-nothing and not-enough accusations also touched public works. Roosevelt charged the Republicans with doing too little and that too slowly. As he was to discover, it is one thing to make vast appropriations for public works and quite another to develop the plans for projects. Starting with more than $356 million in 1929, Republican appropriations for public works increased to nearly $656 million in 1932, making a total of almost $2 billion. Roosevelt's pledge to keep all unemployed on self-liquidating public works was properly labeled as fantastic unless socialism was the ultimate goal.[37] Actually, there was only one distinction between the candidates on the issue. Hoover emphasized that public works must be productive or self-liquidating; Roosevelt wanted public works with no proviso.

Hoover complained that Roosevelt ignored or scarcely mentioned constructive measures taken to strengthen the financial system. He defended aid to institutions at the top of the structure.[38] The assertion that these measures were giving 'to the whole system a new breath of life' was somewhat inaccurate. The new breath was fluttering weakly in October 1932 despite some improvement in various index numbers.

The two major candidates solemnly went through the sacred ritual of obeisance to that economic deity named Balance-the-Budget. Roosevelt called for a 25 per cent reduction in expenses, a budget balanced annually, taxes based on ability to pay, and consolidation of offices. He asked for courage to stop the deficits and to insist on a sound currency. The country simply could not stand $625 per year per family in government costs. He was shocked to an exclamation point by an increase of $1 billion in ordinary federal expenditures from 1927 to 1931.[39]

From the historian's vantage point, this budget-balancing and smaller-government talk by Roosevelt is the most ludicrous part of this strange campaign. President Hoover, champion of organizational efficiency, sound money, and balanced budgets, actually was on the defensive! Hoover met the attack squarely. Extraordinary expenditures, in spite of Democratic efforts to raid the Treasury, had been held to a minimum; ordinary expenses and services of government had been reduced to the danger point. The country's credit, as evidenced by securities sales, was perfectly sound.[40] On this issue, any fair debate judge would have to award the decision to the President. Later, Roosevelt himself was to use exactly the same explanation: ordinary expenses had been reducd in 1933; it was the emergency costs that unbalanced the budget!

Another interesting point is Roosevelt's talk about administrative reorganization. In his Sioux City speech on 29 September he said of the Hoover regime: 'It is an administration that has piled bureau on bureau, commission on commission, and has failed to anticipate the dire needs and the reduced earning power of the people.'[41] Even Samuel Insull at the height of his glory could not spawn holding companies as fast as federal bureaucracy proliferated under the New Deal. Roosevelt was sincere in his desire for more efficient government, but he ignored Hoover's very real accomplishments. Campaigns are waged to win votes.

Early in the campaign President Hoover determined to force the issue on the gold standard. He was convinced that the Democrats planned to tinker with the currency, revive their fearful free silver heresy, resort to fiat money, and destroy the credit of the United States. The President overextended himself on the gold standard and started a senseless argument about how close the country had been to complete financial disaster during the last winter. Hoover believed that he had spared the nation untold miseries by saving the gold standard. Roosevelt's managers let Carter Glass defend Democratic monetary orthodoxy; but just before the election, Roosevelt made one of his famous bloopers by referring to the gold clause in securities as a 'covenant,' a sacred and inviolable pledge.[42]

The Democratic attack on the tariff was designed to appeal to various interests in the country and to appease conflicting views within the party. Where the high tariff was popular, they weaseled; where a low tariff was favored, they attacked the Hawley-Smoot Act and urged substitution of the reciprocal trade agreements program. Hoover repeated the shop-worn arguments in favor of a protective tariff and defended things as they were. His efforts to deny any connection between the tariff and world depression led him into tricky playing with figures. Roosevelt was forced to hedge and then to favor the Hawley-Smoot agricultural rates; and on 31 October at Boston he pronounced in favor of tariffs for industry.[43]

The two candidates clashed directly on farm policy. Hoover defended the Farm Board, the tariff, and other measures to relieve agriculture. Add to these the conversion of submarginal lands to pastures and the farmer would participate in general world economic recovery when it came. In the meantime there must be no 'regimented control of the farmer.'[44] The President's faith was admirably persistent, but of course he knew that the farmer had not been helped much. The Brain Trust's proposals for agriculture were developed by more than a score of men and were contained in Roosevelt's Topeka speech on 14 September. Raymond Moley credits this speech with winning the midwestern farm vote without alarming expected opponents.[45]

The Topeka speech promised much in general and little in detail, and contained so many qualifications and conditions that escape routes were at hand on every side. The Democratic plan would, in essence, be some form of domestic allotment to make the tariff effective. Much of the speech boils down to little except sympathy for the farmer's plight and indignation that Hoover had not solved problems that would have deprived Democrats of a good issue. Roosevelt's crystal ball was cloudy: 'When the futility of maintaining prices of wheat and cotton, through so-called stabilization, became apparent, the President's Farm Board . . . invented the cruel joke of advising farmers to allow twenty per cent of their wheat lands to lie idle, to plow up every third row of cotton and to shoot every tenth dairy cow.'[46] Hoover, relaxed from his strenuous tour of duty, might have indulged in a chuckle when the protesting squeals of doomed pigs were heard in the land as the New Deal slaughter began. But he was too busy lambasting the New Deal to take time out for laughter.

President Hoover saw clearly that the Democratic proposal meant controlled production and subsidies. But he had nothing new to offer.[47] He knew, as well as anyone, the causes of farm problems. He had refused to apply a solution that had a chance of working; he condemned subsidies for agriculture while supporting subsidies for business. The farmers were surfeited with that brand of farm relief.

The long campaign against Prohibition had succeeded in defeating the Eighteenth Amendment and the Volstead Act throughout the country. Hoover recognized this fact and so favored a national referendum with a view to state control. The dry forces, of course, were sadly disappointed when the President in his acceptance speech acknowledged the need for a change and accepted the claim that a majority opposed Prohibition. However, they had no choice but to support Hoover, who might salvage something from the Prohibition wreckage.[48] Prohibition was not a vital issue in the presidential race, but the attitude of wets was reflected in every tavern and brewery that displayed a picture of Roosevelt in 1933.

Public utilities could not avoid being a major point of dissension in the 1932 campaign. The crash of Insull's bloated utilities empire in April was merely the climax in more than a decade of furious controversy. Hoover had made his stand perfectly clear. He favored regulation but opposed everything that smacked of government competition with private enterprise.[49] Roosevelt advocated genuine protection for both consumer and investor. He was opposed to public ownership or operation of all utilities, but upheld the right of communities to do so as a means of holding rapacious utilities in check. Government should develop publicly owned power sites, sell the power to private enterprise, but distribute it itself if necessary to restrain private enterprise. There should be federal development of the St. Lawrence, the Muscle Shoals area, the Boulder Canyon, and the Columbia River as 'a national yardstick to prevent extortion against the public and to encourage the wider use of . . . electric power.'[50] Private enterprise in public utilities would be horrified by this speech; the people would like it.

Neither candidate devoted an entire speech to one of the major issues of 1932: Should there be economic planning by the federal government? Hoover believed that planned economy meant collectivism, a mixture of European socialism and fascism to be insinuated into the American scene.[51] Hoover was not opposed to planning by government within what he defined as its proper spheres of activity. He did not believe in a government-dominated economy with a bureaucracy to plan production and distribution by any industry. Actually, Roosevelt and Hoover were not far apart on basic principles regarding planning. Roosevelt asserted that advanced planning could have prevented tremendous economic wastes, overexpansion of plant capacity, and the piling of surplus on surplus. In several speeches he referred to the need for planning, and sometimes he used words which proved him a poor prophet indeed. Nowhere is this more strikingly demonstrated than in his address to the Commonwealth Club at San Francisco on 23 September.

Roosevelt received a tumultuous welcome to San Francisco. Crowds 'lined Market Street as he drove to his hotel. . . . Old-timers say they had never seen a political visitor received so vociferously.'[52] His speech provided a review of historical lessons in broad and not always accurate strokes. It contained a warning against government catering to interests of special groups while ignoring others. The old equality of opportunity had disappeared in the face of gigantic combinations of capital. 'Our industrial plant is built; the problem just now is whether under existing conditions it is not overbuilt.' Business opportunity has narrowed, being confined largely to small enterprise. No more would the great promoter dominate the scene. Now was the time for consolidation of the economic plant, to re-establish our foreign markets, to adjust production to consumption, to obtain a more equitable distribution of wealth. What we must have was an 'economic constitutional order' in which private economic power must be regarded as a public trust and all property rights must yield to protection of savings. The day of unbridled individualism was over.[53]

President Hoover, in commenting on this Commonwealth Club speech, emphasized Roosevelt's observation that we may have reached the limit to industrial expansion but neglected to call attention to the qualifying 'under existing conditions' phrase. Looking back, it is interesting to observe that only a few years later, when the nations were engaged in World War II, the American industrial plant was expanding rapidly and still unable to meet the demands placed upon it. If we must not condemn a man for not being able to read a book not yet written, we must also remember that one of the measures of statesmanship is the ability to guess with some accuracy what that book will contain. What pained the President above all else were proposals for planned agriculture, government production of power, managed currency, and implications of efforts to curb the Supreme Court. These were threats to verities held sacred. The mild progressivism expressed in the Commonwealth speech was not too far from Hoover's own beliefs.

Even big business had its own idea of a planned economy. Gerard Swope, president of General Electric Company, proposed a system of gigantic monopolies in September 1931. The creation of such trade associations as Swope proposed, and which the United States Chamber of Commerce endorsed, would have resulted, Hoover believed, either in fascism or socialism 'as the result of public exasperation.'[54] During the campaign, Henry Harriman, president of the Chamber, told Hoover that many influential businessmen would support Roosevelt if he did not get behind the Swope scheme. Hoover refused, the monopolists supported Roosevelt, and Roosevelt paid off with the monopolistic National Recovery Administration. This, at least, was Hoover's interpretation.

At Madison Square Garden the President solemnly warned the country that the proposed New Deal would alter fundamentally that American system which had raised the country to such great heights. He was not opposed to change; he was opposed to any renunciation of ordered liberty, freedom and equal opportunity, individual initiative, and the classless society. The American system can remain master in its own house and can meet all the problems that may arise. Measures taken to combat the depression had saved the country 'from a quarter of a century of chaos and degeneration. . . .' To turn from the true path would be to 'embark upon this inchoate new deal which has been propounded . . . would be to undermine and destroy our American system.'[55] A vast bureaucracy would result, with an inevitable transfer of responsibilities to the federal government. The drive for ever greater power would destroy free industry and free commerce, without which other freedoms could not survive.

Hoover's fears, fortunately, were not realized. The New Deal came and cherished liberties remained, although attacks on those liberties were to occur during the Truman Administration, which denounced and fought men who would undermine basic freedoms.

5. 'As We Expected'

President Hoover appeared to have a defeatist attitude when he began the campaign. He concludes his account of the debate with the confession: 'As we expected, we were defeated in the election.'[56] His speeches, lacking the sparkle of confidence, also suffered from a delivery appropriate to the conference room but not capable of arousing enthusiasm. In the days when radio had just come into its own, Roosevelt's splendid delivery gave significance to commonplaces, or people thought it did. Hoover's vocal pedestrianism, his at times mumbling delivery, failed to do justice to many well-written passages. Had the roles been reversed, the outcome might well have been the same but the vote undoubtedly would have been much closer. As the campaign neared its end, the President gained in self-confidence. Perhaps the repetition of his message inspired him to greater efforts, climaxed by the magnificent arraignment of the proposed New Deal which he delivered at Madison Square Garden on 31 October.

There were a few cool-headed observers of the campaign who wished that candidates would stop hiding behind vague generalities, absurd promises, and irresponsible charges. One of these was 'The Drifter,' who satirized the 'point surplus' of both candidates:

It is only a new wrapper for the old baloney. A program which doesn't mean anything can sometimes be made quite impressive if stated in twelve points, and . . . it is easy to slip in a joker somewhere among them without attracting too much attention. Thus it is possible for Herbert Roosevelt to promise the farmers higher prices for their produce in nine points, and in the tenth to conclude casually that of course none of the methods proposed is to be carried out in such a way as to raise the price of food to the consumer. So, too, Franklin Hoover can mesmerize his audience with twelve points for controlling the public utilities, with the off-hand proviso somewhere that no action is to be taken which will disturb the sacred American principle of private initiative and ownership.[57]

When the voters went to the polls on 8 November, there was little doubt about the outcome. Roosevelt received 22,809,638 popular votes and 472 electoral votes. Hoover garnered 15,758,901 popular votes and 59 electoral votes. Norman Thomas led the minor parties with 872,840 votes, a total which probably failed to reflect his real strength. Many potential socialist votes went to Roosevelt to assure Hoover's defeat. William Z. Foster, candidate of the Communist party, had about 103,000 votes. Hoover carried only six states, two less than Smith had won in 1928.[58] It was time for a change, time for a New Deal.

Democrats came as close to making a clean sweep through the nation as any party ever has in a contested election. After the ball was over, Republican hearts were breaking everywhere except in Vermont. In New Hampshire, voters elected a Democrat to replace George H. Moses; Connecticut replaced Hiram Bingham with Augustine Lonergan; Pennsylvania elected eleven Democratic representatives. Northern and Western Democrats for the first time would outnumber Southern Democrats in the House. Only nine states elected Republican governors. Traditionally Republican Michigan, co-hospital at the birth of the Republican party, joined with North Dakota, Oregon and Nebraska to share whatever honor there was in having two Republican senators each.

So ended one phase of the crusade for recovery. For all of his vagueness and nimble dodging in the campaign, Roosevelt had outlined the shape of his New Deal. Hoover was not one of those who believed that the Democrats took over without knowing what they were going to do. Their plans were so definite and to him so alarming that he devoted his last months in office to vain efforts to strengthen conservative defenses.

CHAPTER XVIII

INTERREGNUM

1. *Futile Overtures*

The period between the election of Franklin D. Roosevelt and his inauguration was one of extreme difficulty. President Hoover had been turned out of office on a tidal wave thrown up by voters who did not agree that a nation could not legislate its way out of a depression. For approximately four months, Herbert Hoover was President in name only; the President-elect had no authority, nor did he have a well co-ordinated program to put into effect when he came into power.

In these four months President Hoover endeavored to co-operate with Roosevelt, but it was a co-operation that would have to be on Hoover's terms. What Hoover sought, by his own admission, was a commitment from Roosevelt to continue Republican policies, not to do any of the radical things he had hinted at during the campaign. Hoover was thoroughly convinced that Roosevelt's proposals would wreck the country. There were several matters that demanded co-operation to complete a smooth transmission of authority. Many developments in foreign affairs required decisions: the Japanese war in Manchuria, war debts, the World Economic Conference, and the Geneva Disarmament Conference. In the domestic field, Hoover judged, Roosevelt would want to continue relief, reduce expenditures, balance the budget, reform banking, modify the bankruptcy laws, and maintain sound money.[1]

Roosevelt's reactions to Hoover's proposals show that he was not going to be talked into any kind of effective co-operation. His advisers were wary of traps, and Hoover was not without guile. The President wanted to pull the New Deal's teeth before the country felt the bite, but he was to be denied that solace. Defenders of Hoover charge that the New Dealers adopted policies before the end of the year that renewed the economic slump, destroyed confidence, and caused the national banking panic of February and March.[2]

These charges, often repeated by Hoover and his apologists, are desperate efforts to shift responsibility for the debacle that preceded inauguration. It is notable that the dying Administration, which made such a parade of its efforts to co-operate with the victors, defined co-operation as acceptance and endorsement of the Hoover policies. President Hoover did not ask Mr. Roosevelt how the Republicans could get the New Deal started for him. Yet that, too, would have been co-operation! Democrats were guilty of enough sins of their own without having to do penance for Republican peccadillos.

The post-election panic was the natural result of accumulating events. The National Credit Corporation had failed dismally to thaw out frozen assets, for the freeze was very deep and solvent bankers were not sufficiently interested in rescuing their brethren. Important as it was, the Reconstruction Finance Corporation came upon the scene too late to prevent the depression's climax. Foreign selling of securities and depreciation of foreign currencies drained off gold reserves, depressed the security markets, and contributed to panic long before the election of 1932. Confidence generated by activities of the R.F.C. might have been offset by publicity of its loans, but the Kreuger and Insull failures had delivered their shattering blows before that publicity could have affected the situation. There was an upturn in business after July 1932; but this little flurry of activity has been greatly exaggerated. The country simply hit the bottom and bounced a little. A normally cautious writer believed that the President's program had 'relieved the strain on credits and averted a far-reaching collapse of our financial institutions and business corporations.' Nevertheless, the few encouraging signs of better business conditions did not mean a permanent recovery from economic imbalance.[3]

Given the awkward interval between election and inauguration, it is unrealistic to blame the Democratic party or its leader for the economic chaos of early 1933. There is also great injustice in the comment that the banking crisis was 'the result of three years of drift and blunder' by Hoover's administration.[4] It is equally unjustifiable to blame the Republican party and President Hoover for the catastrophic collapse of the banking structure. A system, a set of institutions, a complex of inherited attitudes and circumstances caused the crisis.

The President's first overture was caused by his concern over war debts and the scheduled World Economic Conference. As early as 10 November, European debtors were demanding readjustment. Hoover was in favor of some reduction, provided he could obtain an integrated settlement that would include lowering of trade barriers, stabilized currencies, and reduced armaments expeditures. Anything that Hoover began, obviously, would be wasted effort unless Roosevelt agreed to it. At Yuma, Arizona, on 12 November, while he was returning from voting in California, Hoover telegraphed Roosevelt to seek a conference on war debts and other problems.[5] The Brain Trust finally decided that the encounter would not be fatal, so the meeting took place ten days later.

Some of the Brain Trust fully expected this move by Hoover. They were convinced that bankers wanted cancellation of the governmental debts in order to make payment of private debts more convenient. They believed that Hoover fully endorsed the bankers' position, so ably represented by Ogden L. Mills; but to get congressional approval of cancellation he needed Roosevelt's support. One of the Brain Trust has stated flatly that in Hoover's opinion the governmental debts 'must be canceled.'[6] If the Brain Trust thus believed that cancellation talk was a bankers' plot, their champion must not be trapped by the wily Hoover and Mills in the conference to follow. There was more than war debts at stake. The Brain Trust feared that the issue might sidetrack their attack on domestic problems, and Raymond Moley, Roosevelt's trusted adviser, believed that the debts should be kept alive as a warning that the United States would not finance another war. Moley refused to accept the thesis of European insolvency and carefully briefed Roosevelt on the subject.

Roosevelt obviously was nervous as Moley and he stepped into the Red Room, where the President stood 'grave, dignified, and somewhat uneasy.' Hoover greeted his guests and then lapsed into silence while Roosevelt exchanged banter with Mills, an old Harvard classmate. The two Democrats smoked cigarettes; the two Republicans preferred cigars; all drank orangeade and water.[7]

The conference lacked cordiality but not lucid exposition. Hoover displayed a complete mastery of the subject as he outlined the problem for his guests. Most of the time he stared at the floor or talked to Moley and merely glanced at Roosevelt to answer a question. He had decided that Moley, not Roosevelt, was the one to educate. The conferees agreed that payments should be demanded on schedule.

Hoover observed that, since the war debts and the proposed economic conference were closely related, a delegation should be appointed to represent the United States in both matters. Roosevelt's attitude was that Hoover should proceed on his own, but the President could see no reason to start something that would be merely a preliminary.[8]

Hoover, alone with Roosevelt for several minutes when the conference broke up, left the room first. Ike Hoover heard him remark about Moley: 'He did not get it at all.'[9] Hoover understood that Roosevelt would confer with Democratic leaders and approve reactivation of the War Debts Commission. At a White House meeting with leaders of Congress, Hoover was astonished to learn that Roosevelt had not conferred with the Democrats. The separate press statements were in basic agreement, but the result was no commitment by Roosevelt. The avenues of negotiation, Roosevelt stated, were open if debtors wanted to use them. This, the President observed, would be futile since 'no foreign power would seriously negotiate with a disappearing administration.'[10]

Hoover continued to press for co-operation in getting the economic conference under way. In a Lincoln Day speech at New York on 13 February 1933 he once more emphasized the need for international recovery, disarmament, maintenance of the gold standard, and co-operation to prevent trade wars. He was convinced that the next major step in remedying the depression must be in the international field 'where the tide of prices can be most surely and quickly turned and the tragic despair of unemployment, agriculture and business transformed to hope and confidence.' To defend themselves, more than forty nations had placed restrictions on exchange and on the flow of goods; an economic war was brewing in which the United States, compelled to take similar defensive measures, would be engulfed in this 'competition of degeneration.' The vicious cycle must be broken, and currency stability was the place to start. Imperfect as the gold standard might be, nothing better had been proposed to stop wild fluctuations. There could be no confidence under systems of managed paper currencies; there must be a restoration of gold standards, and the United States must aid in restoring currencies to a fixed value in terms of gold. Not until then would it be possible to remove the whole galaxy of barriers to world trade. The United States, therefore, had come to the place where three roads forked: one road would lead to stability through international co-operation;

one road would lead to attempted self-sufficiency and controlled production; one road would lead to inflation, abandonment of the gold standard, economic warfare, and final destruction.[11] This speech was an assault upon the New Deal, a reiteration that domestic recovery was dependent upon international events, and an indirect defense of the Hawley-Smoot Tariff. The election was over, but Hoover was still campaigning.

While Hoover had no luck at all in committing Roosevelt to his policies, Henry L. Stimson enjoyed better success. Moley says that Norman Davis made the suggestion that brought the two together at Hyde Park on 9 January 1933; but Stimson reports a telephone call from Felix Frankfurter on 22 December which conveyed Roosevelt's desire to see the Secretary of State. Hoover refused to permit the meeting, until Frankfurter's persistence caused Stimson to believe that something could be accomplished. In a six-hour conference, Stimson won Roosevelt over to the Hoover-Stimson Non-Recognition Doctrine. Evidence was soon forthcoming. Roosevelt on 11 January said he approved Hoover's request for an arms embargo, Stimson reiterated his non-recognition formula on 16 January, and Roosevelt on the next day stated that 'American foreign policy must uphold the sanctity of international treaties.' This sequence of events alarmed the Brain Trust, particularly Raymond Moley, who complained that Roosevelt had not consulted his privy council. This was true. Roosevelt had by-passed Moley by working through Frankfurter. Moley understood the implications of accepting the Hoover-Stimson Doctrine, which meant abandoning traditional concepts of neutrality in favor of collective sanctions, and which would surely lead the United States into a war against Japan, a prospect from which Roosevelt did not shrink.[12]

This criticism does not mean that the Brain Trust was isolationist in the sense used by the one-worlders. It does not mean retreat from foreign contacts, but it does mean maintenance of a genuinely neutral policy. Roosevelt's commitment may not have been serious, nor should it have surprised Moley. During the campaign there was practically no attack on Hoover's foreign policies, nearly all of which Roosevelt could endorse with little qualification. What Moley primarily feared was a series of contradictory commitments: drastic tariff reductions would conflict with the domestic-origin hypothesis of depression and domestic measures to combat it; agreement to reopen the war debts question would lead to commitments binding the United States to European economic measures in an ever-widening circle. Roosevelt's explanation of his approval of the Hoover-Stimson Doctrine was simply a statement that he always had been sympathetic toward the Chinese!

Stimson had also persuaded Roosevelt to discuss war debts and the approaching World Economic Conference. Roosevelt had reached the conclusion that it was not unreasonable to reopen negotiations with the British, since they had paid their 15 December installment. Moley extracted a promise that Roosevelt would insist on his own appointees in any debt discussions, and that they would be kept separate from the World Economic Conference agenda. In the conference on 20 January, Roosevelt, Moley, and Norman Davis met with Hoover, Mills, and Stimson. Moley won the argument when Roosevelt refused to retreat. Stimson, however, tried to rush Roosevelt into agreeing to reverse his position. This final move was checked and Moley, with Rexford Guy Tugwell in tow, conferred again with Stimson, who had Harvey H. Bundy and Herbert Feis in his office. The British, through Sir Ronald Lindsay, were attempting rather delicately to use the debts question in bargaining for making concessions at the World Economic Conference, a policy which Hoover and Stimson approved. Moley, according to Moley, put an end to this scheme.[13]

2. *The Last Lame Duck*

The second session of the Seventy-second Congress, last of the lame-duck sessions, met on 5 December 1932 under a cloud of uncertainties. The November elections had repudiated President Hoover and 158 members of Congress, but the country desperately needed bold and courageous leadership. The presence of several hundred Communist hunger marchers, more or less isolated on New York Avenue, merely added emphasis to swiftly deteriorating economic and social conditions. But the law must be served and 'the exigencies of politics suggested procrastination and obstruction.'[14]

Not upon Hoover alone can the blame for procrastination be placed. The President carried on as though he were to have four more years in the White House. In his recommendations to Congress, in his nominations which Congress ignored, in his steady efforts to pursue policies to fight depression, Hoover displayed a persistent devotion to his own interpretation of the public welfare. As late as 20 February the President urged passage of the bankruptcy bill, ratification of the Great Lakes–St. Lawrence Seaway Treaty, enactment of the Glass banking bill, increased loans by the Reconstruction Finance Corporation to states and municipalities for relief, leasing of marginal lands to reduce farm surplus, repeal of the provision publicizing R.F.C. loans, plans to expand the Home Loan Discount Banks, and authority to embargo the export of arms. This program made no impression on a chaotic, confused, irresponsible Congress.[15]

Since during the campaign Roosevelt had promised a balanced budget and accused Hoover of waste, the President called in Garner and Robinson to suggest that the Congress do the nasty job of balancing the budget before Roosevelt's inauguration. Garner thought it a good idea, particularly in view of the Democratic promise to reduce expenses by one-fourth and to stop the deficits. In his budget message on 7 December Hoover proposed a reduction of $830 million and a manufacturers' sales tax on practically everything except food and cheaper clothing. The budget for 1933–4 would show a deficit of only $300 million instead of $2 billion. Furthermore, Hoover sent to Congress on 9 December his numerous proposals for reorganization that would save money. He did not suggest the very steep income tax increases in higher brackets that could have balanced the budget, but he did recommend a reduction in the number of independent agencies and commissions.[16] He knew, of course, that Congress would not accept the general sales tax.

Leading Democrats and Republicans were in favor of balancing the budget. But on 28 December Roosevelt announced his horror at Democratic acceptance of a sales tax, and that ended budget balancing. There is some justice in the complaint that Roosevelt, who refused to co-operate with Hoover because he had no authority, told Democrats in Congress what to do. What he did was to wield authority while disclaiming responsibility, although Roosevelt denied having attempted to influence Congress on any matter except the proposed sales tax.

There were also rumors that Hoover himself ordered Republicans to block any Democratic program, thus ensuring a special session of Congress that would reveal how planless the Democrats were. Nevertheless, Hoover again on 17 January urged the sales tax as the only practicable way to increase revenues. Roosevelt already had met with Democratic members of Congress to decide on a program for the rest of the lame-duck session, and this meeting decided against the President's tax and reorganization plans.[17]

Faith in budget balancing was very touching. Experts in great number informed the Senate Committee on Finance that a prime need was to balance the budget. Lacking anything better to say, not knowing what to say, representatives of big business repeated the incantation. Myron C. Taylor of United States Steel, Jackson E. Reynolds of New York's First National Bank, and financial wizard Bernard Mannes Baruch spoke to the committee. Some witnesses loftily refused to offer any advice, for which they deserved thanks. Baruch told the committee on 13 February: 'What are we, then, to do? To my mind the road is wide and certain. There is one essential thing—to get people back to work. To do that, we must make money work. To make money work, we must balance the Budget. That should be accomplished first by reducing expenses.' Reduce national expenses to $3 billion and confidence would return, more business activity would result, and more taxes would be collected, thus balancing the budget without further taxation.[18] Mr. Baruch, too, was bewildered.

Champions of federal aid for relief were ready with new bills when the last lame duck assembled. Senator Wagner, who so often had elicited the President's ire, introduced a bill to increase the R.F.C.'s relief and public works program. Again, as they had a year earlier, expert witnesses testified to a need growing greater every week. Edward F. McGrady, representing the A.F. of L., did not exaggerate: 'Living conditions that we have boasted about to the whole world have been utterly destroyed so far as workers are concerned. . . . Children everywhere are suffering from malnutrition, and the damage done to our future generation is going to be permanent.'[19]

Every principle of relief that President Hoover had struggled to maintain was brought under fire by social workers, architects, contractors, engineers, labor leaders, economists, and others who knew whereof they spoke. Their testimony revealed how seriously the vaunted American system had failed to meet the greatest economic emergency in the country's history. One could not ignore indefinitely conditions described by Mrs. Eleanor Patterson, widely known Washington journalist:

So I accompanied some of the workers for emergency relief on their daily rounds. . . . I did actually find children who were cold—and by 'cold' I mean cold to the touch, because there was no heat in the house. . . . I found children who were hungry, because there was no food in the house—no milk, no food whatsoever. . . . I found children who were not hungry, because they were so undernourished that they could not eat.[20]

Senators Costigan and La Follette again joined efforts to introduce a bill calling for a Federal Emergency Relief Board, with an appropriation of $500 million to be raised from a bond issue. Hearings, as Senator Costigan stated, were a continuation of a year's effort. Although Herbert Benjamin, Communist leader of the National Committee of the Unemployed Councils, presented the most gruesome details, far more responsible witnesses told a similar story in more restrained language. Dr. Sumner H. Slichter, Harvard professor of economics, called attention to the great decline in public works, because of local and state economy hysteria; the result was more unemployment.[21] Edith Abbott, dean of the University of Chicago's School of Social Service Administration, warned against social deterioration:

The long delay in the granting of Federal relief has resulted . . . all over the country, in a general lowering of the whole standard of living . . . With larger and ever larger numbers of families coming on the relief list, standards of living have become lower and lower, and that is at a time when the people asking help have been fine, independent, self-respecting people of a type not often seen on the list of relief agencies.[22]

There was appalling evidence of diseases resulting from continued malnutrition among school children in scores of communities.

Officers of the R.F.C. did not appear to speak for the Hoover Administration in this renewed demand for federal relief. Atlee Pomerene, chairman of the R.F.C., revealed that in less than six months one-half of the $300 million made available for relief in July 1932 had been allotted. Whether more was needed he would not say. The R.F.C. president, Charles A. Miller, verified one of Hoover's predictions: 'the public will not put its hand into its pocket and give when the Government is giving . . .' Fred C. Croxton, director of emergency relief for the R.F.C., believed 'that no person has gone hungry, if they made application for help.' But that there was acute suffering he did not deny: 'Wage earners and salaried people who have never before known want are suffering acutely, and have to completely change their standards of living.'[23]

The Seventy-second Congress, if one judges solely by its legislative record, might just as well have passed up its short session after the election. Democratic members would do nothing not approved by Roosevelt. The Congress did pass some 170 public acts and resolutions to build bridges, amend bankruptcy laws, provide for Indians, erect memorials, make appropriations, and close barber shops one day a week in the District of Columbia. Important proposals, except on bankruptcy, failed to win approval. The Collier bill to permit the manufacture of 3.2 per cent beer passed the House on 21 December but died in the Senate; farm relief under the domestic allotment scheme fared no better than Carter Glass's banking reform proposals. The budget remained unbalanced; appropriations had not been reduced to the level of expected revenues; new taxes had not been levied to meet the deficit. The St. Lawrence Seaway Treaty was not approved; the United States still was not in the World Court; some 2,000 presidential nominations had not been approved; the proposed astronomical increases in R.F.C. funds, to be used to relieve unemployment, had not been voted.

During the great argument over relief, little notice was given to Public Resolution No. 45, approved 23 December 1932, which authorized the Secretary of the Navy to sell 'nonregulation and excess clothing' at nominal prices for distribution absolutely free to the needy. Of more consequence was the Philippine Independence Act (Hawes-Cutting Act), which Congress passed over Hoover's veto on 17 January 1933, providing for withdrawal by the United States within ten years of inauguration of a new government. On 8 February 1933 the President approved an act authorizing the Federal Farm Board to give to the Red Cross up to 350,000 bales of cotton held by the Cotton Stabilization Corporation. This cotton could be manufactured, exchanged, or sold in order to acquire clothes, bedding, and other supplies for the needy. These accomplishments do not bulk particularly large in view of problems confronting the country. In spite of its time-consuming debates, the Congress was merely waiting to die— and that suited Hoover. While Huey Long was ranting in the Senate, no 'bad legislation' could be passed.[24]

But the legislative record does not tell the whole story. Important hearings were conducted, and out of these investigations came many ideas which in modified form were to become New Deal measures. Proposals for huge work camps to solve the problem of transient young men were to be reflected in the Civilian Conservation Corps; continued investigation of relief needs further broke down resistance to federal aid; scores of witnesses presented masses of data on the nation's economic problems to the Senate Committee on Finance, precluding the need for a lengthy repetition under Democratic auspices. The Senate Banking and Currency Committee continued its investigations into stock exchange practices and revealed needs for strict regulation. Serious consideration of a compulsory thirty-hour week emphasized a trend later written into law, and Senate hearings on a domestic allotment plan rehashed the farm relief arguments. Wide publicity given to these and other hearings surely helped to pave the way for New Deal measures.

3. *Paralysis*

There is no need to argue the point that many New Dealers and many members of Congress favored inflation by tinkering with money. The silverites hauled out the old arguments. New and old weird proposals received attention in the last lame-duck session the Congress would ever enjoy and the country suffer. It is difficult to see how such efforts were any more unmoral or unsound than causing inflation or deflation by tinkering with credit, a practice frequently indulged in by the Federal Reserve Board. Hoover, too, tinkered with credit by persuading Congress to increase eligibility of paper for discount and to extend credit through new federal agencies. These were inflationary measures, efforts to increase credit, which would increase bank deposits. A runaway inflation through currency tinkering is no more disastrous than a runaway inflation through credit tinkering. Hoover, of course, was opposed to runaway anything; but he believed it was all right to play with credit, wrong to play with money. Several million Americans agreed with him with or without reason. All of this is pertinent to the interregnum because of the accusation that threats of currency tinkering caused increased loss of confidence, uncertainty in business circles, gold movements, currency hoarding, and the banking crisis.

Well-known advocates of inflation were very close to the President-elect. Professors James Harvey Rogers of Yale and George Frederick

Warren of Cornell were seeking inflation by reducing the gold content of the dollar by definition, but they made no wild statements. Among politicians, Senators Burton K. Wheeler, Elmer Thomas, and Tom Connally steadily urged inflationary measures. In the House, John Nance Garner, John E. Rankin, and many of their colleagues tried to put through inflationary measures. Roosevelt himself wanted to experiment with money. In the campaign he straddled the issue, trying to make both inflationists and anti-inflationists happy. When Roosevelt said 'sound money,' he did not commit himself to a gold dollar of any set fineness.[25] Any inkling that currency tinkering was coming, the President believed, might cause a bank panic. Smart people would buy foreign securities and exchange, domestic real estate, and gold bullion, or make other investments that would mean further reduction in bank funds.

There was no more bitter critic of currency tinkering than Herbert Hoover. To him, gold at $20.67 per ounce and 23.22 grains to the dollar was but little short of a sacred formula. Any deviation from the gold standard, from free convertibility, he labeled as collectivism, a general term broad enough to cover anything the President disliked. Managed currency was the forerunner of collectivism; abandon the fixed standard and gone would be the protection of wage standards, control over the public purse, freedom from a currency war with other nations. The fixed standard would prevent governments from confiscating savings by deliberately causing inflation and deflation. The fixed standard was our measuring stick for all obligations. 'In a world of abandoned standards and fluctuating currencies,' he wrote, 'the transactions, the faith, and the confidence of the whole earth was thus able to rest upon the American dollar. What stability there was in international trade resulted from this Gibraltar's clinging to its convertible gold standard.'[26]

There was no general loss of confidence, not even a partial loss, because Roosevelt refused to declare his monetary policies before 4 March. That he would resort to some kind of inflation was generally assumed, but no one can be positive that uncertainty of the New Deal's prospective actions deepened the depression and precipitated the banking crisis. Pro-Hoover versions paint a picture of unrelieved gloom engendered by anticipation of horrible events: the forces of currency tinkering, experimentation, and inflation had been elected; inexperienced braintrusters would guide federal policy; doubts about the soundness of federal credit mounted to alarming degree. As people moved to protect themselves, the Hoover forces said in retrospect, they canceled factory orders and increased unemployment; foreign goods poured over the tariff wall; wise persons sent their capital abroad for safety; runs on banks increased; depositors scrambled to convert their assets to gold, revealing fears 'for the stability of the currency, rather than for the stability of the banks.' Roosevelt refused to co-operate with Hoover to stem the tides of fear. Publicity of loans caused runs on banks aided by the R.F.C., causing at least 1,000 of them to fail. Congress refused to balance the budget, to reform banking, to economize. Promised tariff reduction caused business men to prepare for the event. All this contributed to panic.[27]

The detailed study necessary to prove these charges is all but impossible. Such a study would be a job of such magnitude as to stagger the imagination. Nevertheless, uncertainty about the future could have caused at least some of the difficulties that beset the country during the interregnum.

Before the inauguration, the press reported the fact every time it became known that a money manipulator was near Roosevelt. Carter Glass, so went the reports, refused to become Secretary of the Treasury because Roosevelt would not commit himself to 'sound' money. The rumor was true, but Glass refused because of precarious health. Currency hoarding and gold exports increased sharply in January. Many inflationary bills were introduced in Congress and many, like Adolph J. Sabath's proposal to loan $200 'to every head of a family and to all unemployed ex-service men,' were less than intelligent.[28] With party strength divided as it was, the chance for passage of inflationary measures was practically nonexistent during the interregnum.

The barrage of talk and rumors continued. On 31 January Henry A. Wallace said that the United States should go farther off the gold standard than Great Britain had. Bernard M. Baruch warned against inflation, but Ralph W. Page, a North Carolina banker and son of Walter Hines Page, urged drastic inflation. Professor E. W. Kemmerer, renowned money expert, warned that a national calamity would follow any extensive devaluation of gold. Exports of gold and hoarding increased as by 15 February depositors were withdrawing $15 million a day.[29]

Few people outside of the state were alarmed when Nevada declared a banking holiday of twelve days on 31 October 1932—well before the election of Roosevelt could have caused any loss of confidence. There was, indeed, little confidence to be lost. People were not worried about the soundness of the few dollars they had, but they were worried about the soundness of the banks. What Hoover called 'a wholly unnecessary panic of bank depositors'[30] was unnecessary if depositors would have been willing to see their assets disappear entirely. The fully justified loss of confidence in banks caused the swift paralysis in February 1933. Fear of New Deal monetary policies, while very real, sinks into minor proportions when compared with that also very real loss of confidence that caused a complete disintegration of the banking structure.

President Hoover himself could do little to encourage confidence in banks. He had, of course, been recommending mild reforms since 1929. Now, on 6 December 1932, he informed Congress that 'as a system our banking has failed to meet this great emergency . . . losses and distress have been greatly augmented by its wholly inadequate organization.' Reminding the country that 4,665 banks had failed since 1 January 1930 would hardly increase confidence. The R.F.C. could not solve the problem; it was up to Congress.[31]

Senator Glass once more brought up the measure (S. 4412) he had been working on for two years. By December 1932 many prominent bankers had changed their attitude toward the bill. Charles E. Mitchell, for example, appeared contrite when it was revealed that Percy A. Rockefeller and James A. Stillman, both directors of the National City Bank, had participated in the Anaconda stock pool when the National City Company, the security affiliate, was selling Anaconda stock. Mitchell, with his bank's dirty linen hanging on the public clothes line, was now willing to agree that banks should divest themselves of security affiliates. The continued procession of bank failures also wore down opposition to branch banking. Although much of the banker opposition to the Glass bill had ceased, Senator Huey Long professed to see a tremendous threat in branch banking. The filibuster he organized on 10 January prevented Senate action for more than a week. When the bill came up for a final vote on 25 January it passed by the impressive majority of 54 to 9.[32]

The House, knowing that Roosevelt preferred no banking legislation, buried the bill. As late as 20 February Hoover urged the House to pass the Glass bill. Still there was no action. On 1 March, when Republicans were enjoying needling Democrats because they had made no proposals for tariff reductions, Carroll L. Beedy, a Maine Republican on the Committee on Banking and Currency, unsuccessfully sought a reasonable answer when he asked why the Glass bill was still entombed. Henry B. Steagall, chairman of the committee, replied that the Glass bill, which had been before the Senate for two years, obviously was not emergency legislation. In rebuttal he called attention to his own bill, which had passed the House on 27 May 1932. The Steagall bill, among other significant reforms, proposed a guaranty fund for depositors. Why had not the Senate taken action on this bill, particularly in view of increasingly strong banker support for the guaranty fund?[33]

President Hoover had reason to suppose that Congress would pass legislation to reform the banking system. After the election, Senator Robinson and Speaker Garner had agreed with Ogden Mills and the President that the Glass bill should be pushed through Congress. However, a meeting of congressional leaders with Roosevelt in New York revealed that the President-elect was opposed to such legislation. This opposition was Roosevelt's, and the Democrats', major contribution to the banking crisis; but, in view of the cataclysmic deterioration in the banking structure through 1932, there is little reason to suppose that passage of the Glass bill early in 1933 would have had any significant effect. The panic that came in February 1933 probably would have come in June 1932 had not the R.F.C. rushed to the aid of the Dawes bank. Then was the time for the major financial surgery which Jesse H. Jones and the R.F.C. performed during the New Deal's first year.[34]

Republican apologists have argued insistently that publicity for R.F.C. loans contributed to the banking crisis. One of the last acts of the Seventy-second Congress in its first session was to call for reports from the R.F.C. Democrats feared the R.F.C. loans might find their way back into Republican coffers to finance the 1932 campaign, that banks aided by loans would contribute to the Republican treasury. The matter of publication was nowhere mentioned in that section of the Emergency Relief and Construction Act of 1932 which called for reports:

The Reconstruction Finance Corporation shall submit monthly to the President and to the Senate and the House of Representatives (or the Secretary of the

Senate and the Clerk of the House of Representatives, if those bodies are not in session) a report of its activities and expenditures under this section and under the Reconstruction Finance Corporation Act, together with a statement showing the names of the borrowers to whom loans and advances were made, and the amount and rate of interest involved in each case.[35]

Speaker Garner, before leaving for his home at Uvalde, Texas, ordered the Clerk of the House to turn the R.F.C. reports over to the press. This order may have violated an understanding among Democratic and Republican leaders but it did not violate the law. Publication was legally permissive since it was not expressly prohibited.

When President Hoover signed the Emergency Relief and Construction Act on 21 July 1932, the White House issued a press release stating that Senate leaders had agreed that publicity would not be retroactive and the monthly reports would be confidential unless otherwise ordered by Congress.[36] Publication of names of borrowing banks, it was argued, contributed to loss of confidence, caused runs on the weakened banks, and led to a transfer of deposits. With so many banks in dire straits, the added blow of publicity might weaken them further; on the other hand, it could be argued that depositors would feel more confidence in a bank if they knew that the R.F.C. had come to its assistance.

Speaker Garner, now vice-president-to-be, renewed the drive for publicity when Congress met in December 1932. The House on 6 January 1933 adopted a resolution calling for full publicity on the first activities of the R.F.C. Steagall could see no wrong in this publicity and argued that the people had a right to know where their money was going. Chairman Atlee Pomerene of the R.F.C. protested in vain. Jesse H. Jones doubted if any of the banks aided by the R.F.C. were forced to close because of publicity; many bankers refused to borrow because they feared publicity.[37] Nevertheless, Republicans stoutly maintained that publicity plus fear of Roosevelt's prospective inflation policies caused the general banking crisis.

Here a few facts should be reviewed. For the 1921–32 period, 10,816 banks closed their doors on $4,885,126,000 in deposits. Of this number, 1,614 banks reopened. Those that remained closed had more than $4 billion in deposits. Most of these banks were not members of the Federal Reserve System, although 2,030 of them were. Of the member banks that closed, 203 reopened, leaving $1,688,155,000 tied up in deposits in member banks that stayed closed. During the years 1929–32, a total of 5,761 banks closed; 1,116 were members of the Federal Reserve System. A total of 794 reopened, leaving $2,865,349,000 in deposits in closed banks.[38] Contemplating an average of more than 120 bank closings every month for 48 months in succession, the depositor still uncaught might well prefer socks, mattresses, and buried pots to banks. Publicity given to R.F.C. loans could destroy very little confidence: there was little if any confidence left to be destroyed.

4. *Panic*

Small and large banks all over the country found their troubles increasing steadily in 1933 despite the R.F.C. Neither it nor any other institution could have kept pace with developments. Seven banks closed in St. Louis on 16 January. Four days later, Iowa's legislature authorized the State Superintendent of Banking to operate any state bank for one year without placing it in receivership, which meant that he could keep a bankrupt bank in business. The mayor of Huntington, Indiana, declared a two-day holiday after the town's remaining two banks had declared a moratorium on 24 January. Several companies announced dividend reductions or passed dividends at the end of January, and, perhaps as a result, the stock market broke severely—perhaps, because many alleged causes for market changes were without any foundation whatever. The Mount Carmel, Illinois, America-First National Bank resumed limited operations on 4 February after a nine-day holiday. The mayors of several small cities followed the Huntington example in order to give banks a breather. An increasingly large number of communities without banks in such states as North Carolina, Iowa, Michigan, Tennessee, and Illinois resorted to scrip. By way of contrast, the Corn Exchange Bank Trust Company of New York celebrated its eightieth anniversary by sending stockholders a complete list of its investments. This unprecedented move indicated increasing awareness by banking officials that all banks were suspect.[39]

Banks the country over were growing weaker. In Louisiana, Governor Oscar Kelly Allen proclaimed a holiday for 4 February, ostensibly to honor Woodrow Wilson's diplomatic break with Germany in 1917! But Allen's proclamation, dictated by Huey Long, stopped runs on the Hibernia Bank and Trust Company in New Orleans. In

Detroit, already hard hit by depression in its major industry, the situation was so serious that Governor William A. Comstock declared an eight-day banking holiday for Michigan on 14 February. By that time shortage of money was so severe that 144 organizations in 29 states were issuing token money to carry on business. The Michigan closing came as something of a relief; now the worst would be known. Nevertheless, in spite of increasingly frequent reports of suspensions, embezzlements, arrests, convictions, voluntary liquidations, and the formation of scrip associations, the New York financial center was not prepared for the Michigan holiday.[40]

The Michigan closing precipitated events that caused the banking panic during Hoover's final days as President. Two huge banking groups operated in and around Detroit: the Guardian Detroit Union Group and the Detroit Bankers Company. Each was a holding company controlling member banks, and each indulged in such peculiar banking practices that trouble was inevitable. A R.F.C. loan of $15 million to Union Guardian Trust Company disappeared so fast that its officers soon asked for an additional $13.5 million. But R.F.C. examiners could find no good assets upon which to make the loan. President Hoover entered actively in the negotiations to persuade heavy depositors not to withdraw their funds; if they agreed, the loan could go through. But Senator Couzens threatened to expose the scheme, and Henry Ford decided that the banks might as well close.[41]

Most of these negotiations took place from 9 to 12 February. Banks normally closed on Saturday. Since Lincoln's birthday fell on Sunday, the banks would be closed for the holiday on 13 February. When Ford refused to join the pool and threatened to withdraw his deposits, President Hoover again talked with him and thought he had won him over. But in the meantime the bankers had summoned Governor William A. Comstock to Detroit. On Tuesday morning the Governor issued his proclamation declaring an eight-day banking holiday for the state's 530 banks. The R.F.C. came through with loans of $54 million to the Guardian National Bank of Commerce and promised $20 million to out-of-state banks to prevent their withdrawing deposits from Michigan.[42]

In the midst of this banking crisis, President Hoover delivered his farewell address to 1,500 Republicans gathered for Lincoln Day at the National Republican Club in New York City. The President, in a widely praised valedictory, warned against inflation, urged holding fast to the gold standard, and decried the economic warfare let loose in the world. There must be economic peace 'and we should cooperate to the full. Any other course in the world today endangers civilization itself.'[43] Franklin D. Roosevelt, fishing on Vincent Astor's yacht, the *Nourmahal*, gave no sign that he had heard.

President Hoover had done everything in his power to prevent the impasse that caused the Michigan holiday. Together with Ogden Mills and other federal officials, he had worked desperately but in vain to forestall the crisis. Now the task was to prevent a general panic. News of the Michigan closing spread on 14 February, prices fell on exchanges, depositors withdrew gold for hoarding, and foreign earmarking of gold accelerated. These trends were intensified on 16 February. With time rapidly running out in Michigan, bankers and state officials could not agree on a course of action. Michigan legislators were equally bewildered. Bankers meeting at Grand Rapids voted to keep their banks closed unless legislation were enacted to protect their assets.[44]

Franklin D. Roosevelt was just completing a cruise on the *Nourmahal* when the Michigan crisis came. At Miami on 15 February he escaped assassination by Giuseppe Zangara, one of whose deflected shots mortally wounded Chicago's Mayor Anton J. Cermak. Not even excitement generated by this assault kept the banking crisis from making front-page headlines. After congratulating Roosevelt on his escape, Hoover two days later urged him to make public statements to brush fears away—a great contrast to a Hoover press statement in 1929 that 'words are not of any great importance in time of economic disturbance.' Hoover's letter was a thinly veiled accusation that Roosevelt's election and failure to adopt the Republican program were responsible for the crisis. True, the unbalanced budget, publicity for R.F.C. loans, hoarding, bank closings, increasing unemployment, and lack of reforms all contributed. Now was the time for Roosevelt to reassure the country that there would be no currency tinkering nor inflation, and a balanced budget must be promised.[45]

The budget balancing argument left Roosevelt and Moley untouched. When had Hoover's budgets ever balanced? When Senator David A. Reed of Pennsylvania informed Hoover that Congress would support a proclamation suspending gold payments, the President shied away from what would have been public acknowledgment of defeat for his efforts to maintain what he considered sound money. What he wanted was to commit Roosevelt to ratify 'the whole major program of the Republican Administration; that is, . . . the abandonment of 90 per cent of the so-called new deal.' And if the Democrats refused to do so, theirs would be the blame for the debacle![46] Mr. Hoover was very tired. He really thought that conservative noises from Roosevelt would calm the storm; if Roosevelt refused to execute a sharp right turn, the country would scare itself into a panic.

Saturday and Sunday, 18 and 19 February, were fairly quiet, but only because financial institutions the country over were closed most of the time. On Monday morning, the House of Representatives approved the Senate resolution for repeal of the Eighteenth Amendment, and the Senate spent nearly all of its time in debating the La Follette-Costigan relief bill. If it was worried about banking, there was no indication in the *Record*.[47]

A banking panic of large proportions very clearly was in view as the last week of February entered its second day. The Federal Reserve Board revealed a great increase in money in circulation and a large decrease in Federal Reserve gold holdings. These were ominous signs of hoarding. Some reassurance may have been felt when Lewis H. Douglas, a young veteran of the World War and a conservative member of the House from Arizona, was announced as Roosevelt's Director of the Budget; but also on 23 February there were further revelations by the Senate Banking and Currency Committee, which was having fun with 'Wall Street under oath,' as Charles Edwin Mitchell admitted business sins enough to consign the whole banking fraternity to eternal damnation. The price of United States bonds fell off considerably when many banks sold to increase cash on hand; the Willys-Overland Company went into receivership. Banks in Baltimore spent Friday, 24 February, in paying off depositors as fast as tellers could work. Then Governor Albert C. Ritchie issued a proclamation to close Maryland's banks until 1 March. The Indiana legislature voted to give the State Banking Department broad powers to deal with any emergency. Saturday, 25 February, was a short day in some areas, but there was no respite from growing signs that the crisis was still deepening.[48]

The week that would end with Roosevelt's inauguration began on anything but an encouraging note. Revelations by the Senate Banking and Currency Committee caused Charles E. Mitchell to resign as board chairman of the National City Bank. Many banks in Ohio limited withdrawals. The same restriction was quickly adopted by Kentucky, Indiana, and Pennsylvania. On 28 February the Commerce National Bank in Washington, D.C., suspended; Arkansas restricted withdrawals; Nevada and West Virginia prepared for banking holidays; Maryland extended its holiday; five Kansas banks closed. So many states joined the holiday parade on 1 and 2 March that a general closing obviously was but a few days or hours away.

In those last frantic days of climactic despair, the President never for a moment relaxed his attempts to hold back the forces of disaster. Continuity of effort was difficult in all the bustle attendant upon final packing for moving day, and interruptions were frequent as old friends and faithful aides dropped in to say good-by. Nevertheless, Hoover conferred frequently with Ogden Mills and A. A. Ballantine of the Treasury, with Eugene Meyer, Jr. and Adolph Miller of the Federal Reserve Board, with his California banker friend, Henry M. Robinson, and with members of Congress.

The one purpose of these conferences was to decide on federal action in the banking crisis; but that action was not taken because President Hoover questioned his own power and refused to issue a proclamation to limit banking activities without Roosevelt's concurrence. The old Trading with the Enemy Act might be invoked to limit withdrawals and stop the strain on banks. Mills, Senator Glass, and Attorney General Mitchell doubted that the law was still valid; but Hoover was willing to issue a proclamation if Roosevelt would approve and ask Congress to ratify the step. Mills prepared the order and asked William H. Woodin, who would succeed him as Secretary of the Treasury, to obtain Roosevelt's approval. Roosevelt followed the Brain Trust advice to refuse commitment. The President was positive that a statement from Roosevelt as late as 23 February could have stopped the panic, and that even he could have done so if Roosevelt had supported him.[49]

Hoover turned to the Federal Reserve Board on 22 February to inquire what it proposed to do in the crisis. Governor Meyer responded for the Board three days later: 'While some of the recent developments are disturbing, and many proposals as to ways and means of dealing with them are being made, the Board feels it is essential in times like these that every suggestion be carefully weighed and considered from the point of view of whether it would be likely to bring even greater disturbance and make worse the situation that it is designed to correct.'[50] The Board members, wrangling among themselves, didn't know what to do. Hoover and Mills, disappointed both with Roosevelt and the Federal Reserve Board, then inquired if the Board would recommend some form of federal guarantee of banking deposits and clearing house systems, or allow the situation to drift along. While waiting for a reply, Mills again conferred with Woodin, who had received instructions from the Roosevelt camp to agree to nothing. Meyer's reply for the Federal Reserve Board on 2 March was equally negative.[51]

Later on the same day, while Roosevelt and his entourage were enroute to Washington, Adolph Miller of the Federal Reserve Board urged Hoover to declare a banking holiday to extend through Roosevelt's inauguration. That far the President would not go, but he was willing to use powers in the Trading with the Enemy Act to limit withdrawals and to control exchange. These measures would make a general banking holiday unnecessary. Attorney General Mitchell was called in and advised that Congress should ratify such an action; but Senators Robinson and Glass, also called into conference, reported that Roosevelt would not ask Congress to do anything. The Federal Reserve Board, when it met late on 2 March, rejected Hoover's plan to limit withdrawals and recommended the banking holiday. They asked Woodin to obtain Roosevelt's approval for a holiday proclamation; again Woodin replied in the negative. The hour was then approaching midnight and Hoover, when told of this exchange, insisted that the holiday proclamation was not his plan, and Woodin should be asked if Roosevelt would approve the proclamation to limit withdrawals. And again Woodin replied in the negative. Hoover went to bed at about 2 A.M. on 3 March.[52]

The game was resumed a few hours later on a blustery winter day, when official flags were flying at half-staff in memory of Senator Thomas J. Walsh, who had died the day before. Walsh, returning to Washington with his Cuban bride, was to have been the new Attorney General. But there was one ray of sunshine when Mills reported that major banks had taken measures that would make a general closing unnecessary. When Washington correspondents called on the President for a final press conference, Hoover appeared to be very tired and unhappy: 'Always diffident and almost shy in his public appearances, he was even more so today. That he leaves his office reluctantly and with a feeling of not having had a fair opportunity is obvious,' one reporter commented.[53]

Custom decreed that the President-elect should dine at the White House on 3 March, but Roosevelt considerately sent word that he preferred a simple tea. Apparently Hoover delayed in sending this invitation until the chief usher insisted that the President-elect must be permitted to pay his respects. The Roosevelts, accompanied by their son James and his wife, appeared at 4 P.M. Ike Hoover warned Roosevelt that the President was going to have Mills and Eugene Meyer there to talk about banking. Hurriedly Roosevelt sent a summons for Moley, who showed up when Hoover produced his two advisers. At this conference, which broke up well after five, Meyer urged a closing proclamation, Hoover wanted merely to limit withdrawals and exchange, and Roosevelt said he would talk it over with his advisers.[54]

Principals in both the old and the new administrations had little rest on the night of 3 March. Mills, Mitchell, and Henry M. Robinson conferred with Hoover until midnight, and then Mills, Ballantine, Woodin, Moley, and the Federal Reserve Board kept a vigil at the Treasury. The banking situation was chaotic. Depositors had withdrawn $500 million on 2 and 3 March; Chicago and New York banks could stand little more. When Hoover called Roosevelt at 11:30 P.M., he understood the President-elect to say that he wanted no proclamation issued. The anxious men in the Treasury did obtain approval from Hoover and Roosevelt to persuade Governors Henry Horner of Illinois and Herbert Lehman of New York to issue bank holiday proclamations. Thomas W. Lamont and other New York bankers argued against the plan but finally agreed. Lehman and Horner then issued their proclamations after 4 A.M. on 4 March.[55]

This entire crisis, Hoover maintains, was completely unnecessary. He had been warned by James Rand, a leading industrialist, on 25 February that New Dealers were fully aware of the banking debacle, expected collapse within a few days, and Hoover would get the blame. Then Roosevelt would come to the rescue in a series of dramatic moves. Rexford Guy Tugwell, according to Rand, was his informant. Moley later said that either Roosevelt didn't understand 'how serious the situation was,' or that he wanted things to get worse and then gain credit for himself in solving the problem.[56] If these were the facts, something less than the highest patriotism motivated some of the New Dealers before 4 March. But one must remember that Hoover, by his own admission, had attempted to use the crisis to destroy the New Deal program before it could begin. Who was the pot, and who the kettle?

A few hours more and the banking problem was to be Roosevelt's. Then, after a short rest, Hoover could begin his twenty-five year campaign for vindication. He would, at last, be accepted as an Elder Statesman. The thinning ranks of his own generation imperceptibly merged with new lines brought forward by relentless time. But so long as he might live, through frantic New Deal years, through World War II and Fair Deal years, and into the Atomic Age of sinister missiles and satellites, there would be millions of his fellow Americans who remembered the despair and the gnawing, haunting fear that lay on their hearts even as the heavy gray clouds smothered Washington.

CHAPTER XIX

GREATEST REPUBLICAN OF HIS GENERATION

A raw and cloudy morning greeted more than a quarter of a million visitors who crowded into Washington for the inauguration. President Hoover, rising after four or five hours' rest, ate hurriedly and was in his office at about eight o'clock. There was no time for the usual medicine ball exercise. Between telephone and personal calls, the President vetoed the independent offices appropriation bill because it greatly exceeded his recommendations. Routine matters of no great significance crowded the morning.[1]

Slowly realizing that the hour of release was approaching rapidly, Hoover became genial, and intimate friends 'marveled at his transformation.' He was still in this mood when the car carrying Franklin Delano Roosevelt stopped at the White House portico. The President walked out, greeted Mrs. Roosevelt, then smiled as he shook hands with his successor. During the ride to the Capitol, Hoover replied in monosyllables to Roosevelt's forced efforts to keep a conversation going. Believing that the restrained applause from sidewalk crowds was not for him, Hoover kept his head covered while Roosevelt smiled and doffed his hat.

A few minutes before noon, Hoover took a fresh grip on his unlighted cigar as he signed bills in the President's room. In the Senate chamber such Old Guard stalwarts as Reed Smoot, James E. Watson, and George H. Moses were saying their last farewells. The President appeared to watch Charles Curtis administer the oath of office to John Nance Garner and waited while new senators were sworn in. Diplomats in full regalia formed a double row and greeted Hoover as he walked toward the rotunda. He stood for a moment in the doorway to look over the crowd before taking his place on the platform. The Marine Band played 'Hail to the Chief!' as Franklin D. Roosevelt approached; and Chief Justice Charles Evans Hughes, magisterial in black skullcap and judicial robe, administered the oath of office. While the new President grimly delivered his stirring inaugural to a visible audience of 100,000 and an invisible one of millions, Mr. Hoover listened intently. Occasionally he frowned slightly, his only reaction to a scathing, searing denunciation by implication. When the President closed with his short prayer for divine guidance, Hoover pressed forward to offer congratulations.[2]

The Hoovers drove at once to the station, where a large, cheering crowd greeted them and lingered until the train departed. Mrs. Hoover, Allan, and the Wilburs left the train at Philadelphia to go on to Palo Alto. Accompanied by Herbert, Jr. and Lawrence Richey, Hoover continued to New York and to his rooms at the Waldorf-Astoria. So ended a fateful day in a fabulous career.

There was comparatively little interest in what the former President did or in what he said as the country's attention was drawn to Washington. Herbert Hoover was left with plenty of time to ask himself, 'Why has this happened to me?' He had chosen to be a Republican; he had dared to become a leader of the party. The Republican party was the party of big business, and big business had committed so many economic sins and had created and fostered so much social injustice! For these sins and injustice the leader must do penance for his party, for a party whose principal advocates never acknowledged his leadership. That was the tragedy of Herbert Hoover.

Expecting to preside over a nation that moved forward to ever higher plateaus of prosperity, Hoover came to the presidency with plans and ideas adequate for a future that had already passed. He planned his administration to be one of mild and progressive reform after the farm problem had been met. When disaster struck and crisis followed crisis with unrelenting persistence and increasing intensity, the President fitted emergency measures into his program. And it was a program, with various aspects nicely calculated to create a broad pattern of action. To this dual plan of action, with its integrated progressive and emergency measures, the President applied the principles of his economic and political faith. Anything that could not be justified by those principles he cast aside.

Hoover approached Congress with this integrated program. Industry and labor must co-operate voluntarily to maintain employment; relief, where emergencies dictated, might be on a national scale, but the principal responsibility for relief must remain with state and local governments co-operating with private agencies. Public works, at all levels of government, could supplement private enterprise and take up some of the slack in employment. Reforms in banking, transportation, utilities, and marketing should be imposed by Congress when such reforms were not undertaken voluntarily. There must be economy in government, reorganization to promote efficiency, and the budget must be balanced. This pattern of action did meet with widespread approval in the country.

No one can say better than Mr. Hoover what he hoped to accomplish:

Our program was one of deliberate purpose to do everything possible to uphold general confidence which lies at the root of maintained initiative and enterprise; to check monetary, security, and commodity panics in our exchanges; to assure an abundance of capital at decreasing rates of interest so as to enable the resumption of business; to accelerate construction work so as to absorb as many employees as possible from industries hit by decreased demand; to hold up the level of wages by voluntary agreement and thus maintain the living standards of the vast majority who remain in employment; to avoid accelerating the depression by the hardship and disarrangement of strikes and lockouts; and by upholding consuming power of the wage earners to in turn support agriculture.[3]

No, it did not work. These measures did not stop the depression. And when the New Deal came in, reforms and experiments were pushed with tremendous vigor. They did not stop the depression, either.

Hoover believed firmly that America needed no drastic change in government. The crisis must not be used to expand the powers of national government, nor to increase the power of monopolies in our economic life. Not until late in 1931, when he recommended creation of the Reconstruction Finance Corporation, did Hoover deviate substantially from these principles.

President Hoover believed he was taking bold steps in making any effort to interfere with economic laws. It was a novel idea that the federal government should take measures to stop a depression. No President had ever done so; every chief executive had ridden out the storm. Some, Martin Van Buren especially, had been jettisoned at the end of the cruise. Andrew Mellon headed a cabinet group of liquidationists who would let deflation run its course and in the process concentrate wealth in the hands of still fewer people. Several others, in and out of the Administration, including Mills, Eugene Meyer, and Henry M. Robinson, backed Hoover in the decision to use federal intervention in the economic system.[4] A major fault with the program was its failure to strike hard enough at the basic causes of depressions, the same failure that attended later New Deal efforts.

There is little evidence that Hoover found time for profound philosophical contemplation. He was an organizer, a problem solver, to whom it was almost incomprehensible that people would refuse to take the action so clearly indicated by logical analysis. People would refuse, and they did so because they did not accept the same verities that guided Hoover's thought. This fact Hoover came to accept finally; but it was extremely difficult to admit the validity of principles he had not embraced. Every man, of course, has moments of doubt, periods of pessimism when a sense of futility threatens to engulf the finest idealism. Hoover was by nature optimistic; but he did not permit faith in the eventual triumph of goodness to obscure realities of the moment.

On numerous occasions the President did seem far more optimistic than the facts warranted. He was afraid to let people know his true estimate of the problems they faced. Although there would have been a great psychological advantage in this course had conditions improved, the President's lack of candor in public speeches before 1932 undoubtedly caused a loss of that very confidence he was attempting to preserve. All too frequently the President assured people that things were not too bad, only to be confounded by events far worse than the prediction warranted.[5]

Constantly the President urged the need for confidence. It was unfair of Walter Lippmann to argue that instead of attacking the major governmental or political aspects of the depression, Hoover attempted to exercise a control over economic conditions by admonition and exhortation.[6] Hoover was entirely correct when he told the Indiana Republican Editorial Association on 15 June 1931 that 'Fear and apprehension, whether their origins are domestic or foreign, are very real, tangible, economic forces.' Fear caused people to curtail purchases which in turn affected employment, and fear caused 'a mania for liquidation' disastrous to production and credit. 'We are,' he said, 'suffering today more from frozen confidence than we are from frozen securities.'[7] Several months later, Lippmann himself was writing: 'We are in the midst of a crisis of confidence . . .' And William Trufant Foster, a maverick in economics, declared that American business troubles were 'mainly mental.'[8]

However great the scorn heaped on President Hoover for his insistence on the need for confidence, that need certainly existed. Necessity and confidence cause people to spend and to invest. Without confidence in the future, when fear paralyzes fingers that should be writing checks, people with money restrict their spending and cease investing. If confidence failed to exist to the degree necessary to keep savings flowing into investment, the government had to step in as employer of people who could not get jobs because investment had dwindled to a trickle. This was where the President balked. He saw the danger that new vested interests would be created to resist a return to private enterprise, that the government's watchdog function would be confused with the entrepreneurial function.

The appointment of committees and the conferences Hoover called were of major significance, not for what they did but for what they were. Hoover placed but little reliance upon Congress; when he wanted advice he turned to leaders of finance and industry and very reluctantly to a few labor leaders. At no time, it must be repeated, did the Republican party have a safe majority in both houses of Congress, and in the Seventy-second Congress factions were so well balanced as to produce a stalemate. Under such conditions the very highest political skill might well have been frustrated.

In defending his record, Hoover and his friends have advanced certain hypotheses which may or may not be valid. According to their argument, the major causes of depression lay outside of the United States, in weak spots the world over. The first phase of the depression ended in the spring of 1931, by which time it was apparent that the liquidation process had about run its course. During this first phase, Hoover's measures had cushioned the shock and the continued causes of depression lay outside the United States. Then the central European countries collapsed early in the summer of 1931, thus inaugurating the second phase. In this period Hoover fought the battle to preserve the gold standard, proposed the moratorium, and held chaos in check. Then came the third phase, a more intense battle to preserve financial integrity, which began when England abandoned the gold standard. This was the period of increased trade barriers, general defaults, curtailed production, cataclysmic declines in values, and threatened collapse of banks, railroads, insurance companies, and security markets. The bottom in this process was reached in 1932; the United States was on its way out of the depression when Franklin D. Roosevelt was elected. Fear of the Democrats caused the banking debacle of early 1933; New Deal policies reversed the sound policies begun by Republicans. These are the arguments, the hypotheses, still defended by Mr. Hoover.

There is no question that President Hoover believed he had led the country through the economic swamp when suddenly arose the ogre labeled FDR which frightened us back into the morass: 'The rest of the world turned to recovery in July, 1932, and only the United States marched in the opposite direction with the election of 1932. If the New Dealers had carried on our policies instead of deliberately wrecking them and then trying to make America over into a collectivist system we should have made complete recovery in eighteen months after 1932 . . .'[9] The literary knights of Hoover's Round Table have nailed this sentiment to every lance they flourish in defense of their leader. They protest altogether too much.

The 'President' created by campaign biographers has always been 'an ideal citizen of the republic,' one who embodies all of the ideals and fireside virtues cherished or admired by the people. As a candidate he is presented as an uncommon man; but he must also be identified as Everyman. He must, or should, have a devoted wife; there should be children and dogs; he must be a practicing Christian.[10] Hoover was no exception. His biographers followed the stereotyped pattern and millions believed them. But a President must perpetuate the myth that he is Everyman. Here was Hoover's fatal mistake. He wasn't Everyman—he was something very exceptional, and altogether too busy to work at being anything else.

Like every other President, Hoover suffered because it is impossible for any man to be The President. In its idealized, abstract meaning, the President is the head of the State, leader of the People, oracle of Society. His must be the wisdom no one ever has, the gift of prophecy never vouchsafed to mortals, the omniscience reserved to the Omnipotent. Withal he must be human, with little foibles and quirks to induce smiles or chuckles or affectionate reprimands. The State, the People, the Society, the Government are all ideas; they are simply what individuals together do or are. Together individuals, no matter what the process may be, select one of their number and say to him: 'You are The President,' in much the same way that Aztecs named a god for one year. So, like the Aztecs, we contemplate The President, all the while knowing that he is really John Smith. And in the end we destroy him.

The Herbert Hoover whom the people elected in 1928 never did exist in flesh. That Hoover was the embodiment of an idea, a legendary ideal, a portrait of intentions and not a picture of realities. That Hoover was the Great Humanitarian, the Great Engineer, the Great

Secretary. The trinity was a creation of adulation, publicity, and vicarious materialization.[11] For a while Hoover looked at himself in the public mirror, but the image was drowned in the rush of events.

A good case can be made for the assertion that Hoover had a grasp of social problems unexcelled by any of his predecessors in the White House; but his political and social philosophy required that people must solve their own problems. Government intervention was a denial of a basic tenet of the traditional democratic faith, a lack of confidence in the self-reliant individual. His observations on law enforcement, child welfare, urbanism, juvenile delinquency, housing, child labor, conservation, and many other matters reveal a depth of interest and knowledge expected only from experts. His instructions to commissions and conferences are irrefutable evidence that support this conclusion. Hoover proposed solutions to economic problems that were in accord with a liberalized American tradition; he believed in using the power and influence of the national government to start things, to start discussion, to spread ideas, and to create demands for action.

When his term as President was coming to an end, Hoover made it clear that he was not walking blindly through life. 'The true purpose of living,' he said in a radio address a month before the 1932 election, 'is . . . to place ourselves in tune with the purpose of an Almighty Providence.' All of the mundane activities of man should be directed to enlarging knowledge, 'to give a more generous response to the promptings of the spirit.' He continued to view government as the agency to preserve equality of opportunity among citizens who would be rewarded according to their service and effort. 'Our economic life should be viewed in this philosophy as a means to a high and worthy end.' [12]

Conservative Republicans had no basis for questioning Hoover's orthodoxy. He favored high protective tariffs, opposed government competition with private enterprise, favored self-regulation of business, opposed attempts to attack monopolies or big business except in the public interest, favored economy in government in order to lower taxes, and strongly supported the dribble-from-the-top program for recovery. His advocacy of mild increases in inheritance taxes was more than offset by his support of the manufacturer's sales tax, which was certain to hit hardest the mass of consumers.

Professional politicians complained that Hoover was not one of them, that he was abysmally ignorant of elementary politics. If he was such a neophyte, how was he able to sweep the convention in 1928? That victory was the result of political strength, of a carefully directed campaign and of calculated use of carefully nurtured popularity. As Secretary of Commerce, Hoover had avoided antagonizing party machines by a frank condemnation of the corruption rampant in the 'twenties. He had, for the most part, championed measures subject to little controversy. So long as the temper of the country was dry, Hoover was dry; when wet propaganda scored heavy victories, Hoover was willing to compromise. This record hardly justifies Senator Watson's remark that he knew 'less than a child about politics.' [13]

No man with instincts of a recluse could have achieved success in two decades of public service. There is no evidence that Hoover was generally or habitually aloof, cold, or indifferent toward people; at times he was all of these. Like any normal person, he needed occasionally to escape to his own thoughts, to live in his own imaginings 'and find relief from the pneumatic hammer of constant personal contacts, and refreshment of mind in the babble of rippling brooks.' [14] Hoover did not shirk his responsibility for making decisions, nor did he shrink from their consequences. He did not enjoy making momentous decisions when the evidence pro and con appeared evenly balanced; his conscience told him he had to be right because the course of events, in the growth of institutions and the development of individual lives, depended on the choice he made. Only a fool or a complete egotist can make such decisions without regretting the compulsion of circumstances.

Hoover felt and even resented the burdens of office, particularly the cruel criticism directed against him. He spoke wryly of 'the great variety of persons and organizations who cheerfully and voluntarily insist on acting as hair shirts for the President.' He varied the theme on another occasion and paid his respects to 'certain individuals, newspapers, associations and institutions [who] officiate as haberdashers in this regard, with a high generosity which guarantees both humility and urbanity.' [15] No one could have been more conscientious or more faithful in attending to the duties of his office.

The Republican party has been hard on its three Presidents who displayed leadership of the kind common in the Democratic party. Their immediate lineal predecessors, the Whigs, possessed the same trait. True, the Whigs were very unfortunate in that their two successful candidates died in office. Republicans in 1856, their first campaign for the presidency, sought glitter and gleam in John Charles Frémont. Their next candidate, Abraham Lincoln, proved to be one of only two truly great Republican leaders elected by the party before 1928. The next six Republican presidents after Lincoln were poor stuff for the office. The seventh, Theodore Roosevelt, was an accident deeply regretted by Republican bosses. Taft threatened for a while to be a Progressive, but he fell into line early, and the Grand Old Party got back into its accustomed groove of mediocrity with Harding and Coolidge.

A great many of the Old Guard still active in the 'twenties were veterans of that extremely bitter political civil war that reached a climax in 1912. Their mortal enemies, such Progressives as Norris and Johnson, were still in the Senate. The Old Guard-Progressive feud had been submerged by Wilson's New Freedom, the World War, and the futile efforts to return to normalcy in business buccaneering. Just as Taft was threatened and destroyed by a coalition of Progressive Republicans and Democrats, so, too, was Hoover. The submerged feud broke out in renewed fury during Hoover's presidency, and again a great Democratic liberal was hailed as the country's savior. When Hoover was elected in 1928, the Old Guard feared that he would try to lead and would refuse to be the usual puppet President demanded by party politics. Scorning both Old Guard and Progressives, Hoover would join neither and invited support for his policies through appeals to 'fundamental principles.' With a booming prosperity in force he would have succeeded.

President Hoover probably failed to appreciate the seriousness of the depression until the summer of 1931; consequently, he failed to formulate a program that would enlist popular support. He could have won that support, even without a firm control over Congress, by championing agricultural subsidies, gigantic federal relief activities, and a broad social security program. There is reason to doubt that the country would have accepted the New Deal experimentation before 1932 even had President Hoover been willing to direct the laboratory.

While some sort of a program was being distilled out of the terrific clamor for reform, Herbert Hoover remained true to the philosophy that was the source of his strength. Soon Raymond Moley, who did so much to defeat him in 1932, would write the accurate judgment: 'Hoover, in the abundant resources of his own conscience, can know that he will live as the greatest Republican of his generation.' [16]

NOTES

Although footnotes frequently are combined where feasible for an entire paragraph, they are so arranged that specific citations usually are apparent. In other cases, a series of references in the same note indicates the sources to which the author is primarily indebted.

The following titles occur so frequently that they are abbreviated throughout:

Hoover, Herbert, *The Memoirs of Herbert Hoover,* 3 vols., New York, 1952, abbreviated as Hoover, *Memoirs.* The three volumes in this set are subtitled: *Years of Adventure, 1874–1920; The Cabinet and the Presidency, 1920–1933;* and *The Great Depression, 1929–1941.*

Hoover, Herbert, *The State Papers and Other Public Writings of Herbert Hoover,* ed. by William Starr Myers, 2 vols., New York, 1934, abbreviated as Hoover, *State Papers.*

Roosevelt, Franklin D., *The Public Papers and Addresses of Franklin D. Roosevelt with a Special Introduction and Explanatory Notes by President Roosevelt,* ed. by Samuel I. Rosenman, 5 vols., New York, 1938; 4 vols., New York, 1941, abbreviated as Roosevelt, *Public Papers.*

CHAPTER 1

1. *Literary Digest,* 23 April 1927.

2. Hoover, Herbert, *The New Day, Campaign Speeches of Herbert Hoover 1928,* Stanford, 1928, p. 12. Pertinent for this section are Mazur, Paul M., *American Prosperity, Its Causes and Consequences,* New York, 1928; Nearing, Scott, *Must We Starve?* New York, 1932, Ch. 1; and Corey, Lewis, *The Decline of American Capitalism,* New York, 1934, Ch. 1. Both Nearing and Corey are considerably to the left of center.

3. Altman, Oscar L., *Saving, Investment, and National Income,* U.S. Temporary National Economic Committee Monograph No. 37, Washington, 1940, p. 18.

4. Crowther, Samuel, *The Presidency vs. Hoover,* New York, 1928, p. 25.

5. There were 375,366 persons whose reported incomes exceeded $10,000 in 1928 and 3,675,603 whose reported incomes were less than $10,000. *Congressional Record,* 72 Cong. 1 Sess., 75:213. See also Hallgren, Mauritz A., *Seeds of Revolt, A Study of American Life and Temper of the American People During the Depression,* New York, 1933, Ch. 2; Mazur, Paul M., *New Roads to Prosperity, the Crisis and Some Ways Out,* New York, 1931, p. 167.

6. Berle, Adolf A. Jr. and Means, Gardiner C., *The Modern Corporation and Private Property,* New York, 1932, pp. 18–46; Fainsod, Merle and Gordon, Lincoln, *Government and the American Economy,* New York, 1941, pp. 9–11. Combined assets of the 200 in 1927 exceeded $67 billion; gross assets of the other 302,493 corporations were about $152.5 billion.

7. *Nation,* 3 August 1932, p. 94; Means, Gardiner C., 'The Growth in the Relative Importance of the Large Corporation in American Economic Life,' *American Economic Review,* XXI (March 1931), pp. 10–37; Pecora, Ferdinand, *Wall Street Under Oath: The Story of Our Modern Money Changers,* New York, 1939, p. 37.

8. See Pinchot, Gifford, 'The Case for Federal Relief,' *Survey,* 1 January 1932, p. 347.

9. Goldman, Eric F., *Rendezvous with Destiny: A History of Modern American Reform,* New York, 1953, pp. 309–10.

10. Hamilton, Walton, 'When the Banks Closed,' *America in Crisis,* ed. by Daniel Aaron, New York, 1952, p. 276.

11. Ayres, C. E., *The Divine Right of Capital,* Boston, 1946, p. 15.

12. U.S. Bureau of the Census, *Historical Statistics of the United States 1789–1945,* Washington, 1949, pp. 262, 273, 274, hereafter cited as *Historical Statistics;* Foster, Horace W., 'Our Bank is Now Confidant and Guide,' *New York Times Magazine,* 10 January 1926.

13. Senate Committee on Manufactures, *Establishment of National Economic Council,* Hearings on S. 6215, Washington, 1932, p. 23; Griffis, Stanton, *Lying in State,* New York, 1952, pp. 48–9; [Allen, Robert S. and Pearson, Drew] *Washington Merry-Go-Round,* New York, 1931, pp. 181–3.

14. Hayes, H. Gordon, *Spending, Saving, & Employment,* New York, 1945, p. 52.

15. Madden, John T. *et al., America's Experience as a Creditor Nation,* New York, 1937, pp. 39, 53; *Historical Statistics,* p. 242.

16. Hodson, H. V., *Slump and Recovery, 1929–1937: A Survey of World Economic Affairs,* London, 1938, pp. 5f.

17. *Historical Statistics,* p. 244; Lary, Hal B., *The United States in the World Economy; the International Transactions of the United States during the Interwar Period,* U.S. Department of Commerce, Bureau of Foreign and Domestic Commerce, Economic Series No. 23, Washington, 1943, p. 3.

18. Madden, op. cit. p. 69; Lary, op. cit. p. 4.

19. *Historical Statistics,* p. 233; Benedict, Murray R., *Farm Policies of the United States 1790–1850, A Study of their Origin and Development,* New York, 1953, pp. 167–72; Gee, Wilson, *American Farm Policy,* New York, 1934, pp. 21–2; Bean, L. H., 'Recent Trends in Real Farm Income,' *Annals* of the American Academy of Political and Social Science, CXLII (March 1929), pp. 1–6; McFall, R. J., 'The Farm Income Problem,' ibid. p. 13; Genung, A. B., 'The Recent Trend in the Purchasing Power of Farm Products,' ibid. p. 16; Black, John D., 'Progress of Farm Relief,' *American Economic Review,* XVIII (June 1928), pp. 252–71; Quick, Herbert, *The Real Trouble with the Farmers,* Indianapolis, 1929, pp. 5–6.

20. Baker, O. E., 'Changes in Production and Consumption of Our Farm Products and the Trend of Population,' *Annals,* CXLII (March 1929), pp. 97–146.

21. Blaisdell, Donald C., *Government and Agriculture, the Growth of Federal Farm Aid,* New York, 1940, p. 10.

22. Benedict, op. cit. p. 170; Quick, op. cit. pp. 98–114; Crowther, op. cit. pp. 71–5.

23. Dulles, Foster Rhea, *Labor in America, A History,* New York, 1949, pp. 233–5; Perlman, Selig and Taft, Philip, *Labor Movements,* New York, 1935, pp. 461–8, 521–3; Yellen, Samuel, *American Labor Struggles,* New York, 1936, pp. 251–91.

24. Goldman, op. cit. p. 296.

25. Dulles, op. cit. pp. 228–9.

26. Perlman and Taft, op. cit. pp. 291–514.

27. Quoted by Dulles, op. cit. p. 347.

28. See Douglas, Paul H., *Real Wages in the United States 1890–1926,* New York, 1930, for a thorough study.

29. *The American Labor Year Book 1929,* New York, 1930, p. 80; *The American Year Book—A Record of Events and Progress Year 1928,* New York, 1929, p. 528.

30. Morris, Lloyd, *Postscript to Yesterday; America: The Last Fifty Years,* New York, 1947, p. 65.

31. Johnson, Gerald W., *Incredible Tale: The Odyssey of the Average American in the Last Half Century,* New York, 1950, p. 134. By permission of Harper & Brothers, publishers.

1. *Time,* 3 September 1928.

2. Emerson, Edwin, *Hoover and His Times,* New York, 1932, pp. 583–95; Lane, Rose Wilder, *The Making of Herbert Hoover,* New York, 1920, pp. 3–15; Dexter, Walter Friar, *Herbert Hoover and American Individualism,* New York, 1932, pp. 8–14; Republican National Committee, *Chronological Sketch of Herbert Hoover,* Washington, 1928, *passim;* Irwin, Will, *Herbert Hoover, A Reminiscent Biography,* New York, 1928, pp. 3–8.

3. Irwin, Will, *The Making of a Reporter,* New York, 1942, p. 5; Irwin, *Herbert Hoover,* pp. 8–35; Hinshaw, David, *Herbert Hoover, American Quaker,* New York, 1950, pp. 5–7.

4. Hoover, *Memoirs,* II, Chs. 1–4; Irwin, *Herbert Hoover,* pp. 36–75, 80; Corey, Herbert, *The Truth about Hoover,* Boston, 1932, pp. 124, 157.

5. Moreing was not, as Irwin states, 'a chance visitor to China.' He went there specifically to look over the mining properties.

6. Hoover, *Memoirs,* I, Ch. 6; Irwin, *Herbert Hoover,* pp. 84–98; Hinshaw, op. cit. p. 65; Train, Arthur, 'The Strange Attacks on Mr. Hoover,' *Collier's,* 20 February 1932, pp. 52–4.

7. Hoover, *Memoirs,* I, 55.

8. Liggett, Walter W., *The Rise of Herbert Hoover,* New York, 1932, pp. 98–124, presents a completely unreliable smear used so often by Hoover's enemies as the source of their misinformation.

9. Hoover, *Memoirs,* I, p. 65.

10. Train, 'The Strange Attacks on Mr. Hoover,' loc. cit. pp. 7–9, 51–4; Emerson, op. cit. pp. 116–8.

11. [Allen, Robert Sharon and Pearson, Drew] *Washington Merry-Go-Round,* New York, 1931, p. 52.

12. Peel, Roy V. and Donnelly, Thomas C., *The 1932 Campaign, An Analysis,* New York, 1935, pp. 237-40; West, George P., 'The Success Boys at Stanford,' *The American Mercury,* August 1930, p. 390; Hoover, *Memoirs,* I, Chs. 7–8; Lyons, Eugene, *Our Unknown Ex-President: A Portrait of Herbert Hoover,* New York, 1950, Ch. x.

13. Lyons, op. cit. Ch. xi; Hoover, *Memoirs,* I, Chs. 13–20; Kellogg, Vernon Lyman, *Herbert Hoover, the Man and His Work,* New York, 1920, Chs. viii–ix; Hinshaw, op. cit. pp. 72–87; Hofstadter, Richard, *The American Political Tradition and the Men Who Made It,* New York, 1955, p. 285; *Time,* 26 November 1928, p. 9.

14. Mullendore, William S., *History of the United States Food Administration,* 1917–1919, Stanford, 1941; Lyons, op. cit. Ch. xiii; Hoover, *Memoirs,* II. Chs. 26–9; Kellogg, op. cit. Ch. xi; Hinshaw, op. cit. pp. 88–96; Fite, Gilbert C., *George N. Peek and the Fight for Farm Parity,* Norman, 1954,

pp. 126–7; Paxson, Frederic L., *America at War*, 1917–1918, Boston, 1939, pp. 82–3.

15. Surface, Frank M. and Bland, Raymond L., *American Food in the World War and Reconstruction Period*, Stanford, 1931; Villard, Oswald Garrison, *Fighting Years: Memoirs of a Liberal Editor*, New York, 1939, pp. 445–7; Lyons, op. cit. Ch XIII; Hoover, *Memoirs*, I. Chs. 32–48; Kellogg, op. cit. Ch. XII; Hinshaw, op. cit. pp. 106–12; Gitlow, Benjamin, *The Whole of Their Lives: Communism in America, A Personal History and Intimate Portrayal of Its Leaders*, New York, 1948, p. 221; Browder, Robert Paul, *The Origins of Soviet-American Diplomacy*, Princeton, 1953, pp. 20–21.

16. Liggett, op. cit. pp. 253–4; *The Memoirs of Marshal Mannerheim*, tr. by Eric Lewenhaupt, New York, 1954, pp. 218, 374.

17. Hoover, *Memoirs*, II, p. 21.

18. Ibid. II, 18–26; Wolfe, Harold, *Herbert Hoover, Public Servant and Leader of the Loyal Opposition*, New York, 1956, pp. 82–4; Lyons, op. cit. pp. 175–93.

19. Mencken, Henry L., *Making a President, A Footnote to the Saga of Democracy*, New York, 1932, p. 23; Baker, Ray Stannard, *An American Chronicle*, New York, 1945, p. 477; Cox, James M., *Journey Through My Years*, New York, 1946, p. 341; *New York Times*, 25 August 1919; Field, Carter, *Bernard Baruch, Park Bench Statesman*, New York, 1944, p. 219; Irwin, *Herbert Hoover*, p. 255; Wehle, Louis B., *Hidden Threads of History, Wilson through Roosevelt*, New York, 1953, pp. 81–6; Hoover, *Memoirs*, II, pp. 33–4; Ulm, A. H., 'Hoover Emerges As A Cabinet,' *New York Times Magazine*, 19 September 1926, p. 1.

20. [Gilbert, Clinton W.] *Mirrors of Washington*, New York, 1921, pp. 114–17; id., *The Mirrors of 1932*, New York, 1931, pp. 8–12; Tebbel, John, *George Horace Lorimer and The Saturday Evening Post*, New York, 1948, pp. 186–7; *New York Times*, 16 June 1928; Sullivan, Mark, *Our Times: the United States 1900–1925*, 6 vols., New York, 1926–1935, VI, pp. 540–41; White, William Allen, *A Puritan in Babylon, the Story of Calvin Coolidge*, New York, 1938, p. 201; White, *The Autobiography of William Allen White*, New York, 1946, pp. 586–7; Hoover, *Memoirs*, II, p. 34.

21. Cox, op. cit. p. 341; Oulahan, Richard V., 'Hoover, the Handy, Plays Many Parts,' *New York Times Magazine*, 22 November 1925, p. 16.

22. Lyons, op. cit. p. 201. Hoover in his *Memoirs*, II, p. 186, merely says, 'He made one of the largest offers of remuneration ever paid an engineer.'

23. Hoover, *Memoirs*, II, p. 36; Lyons, op. cit. pp. 221–2.

24. Hoover, *Memoirs*, II, pp. 186–7.

25. Ibid. II, pp. 41–3.

26. Ibid. II, p. 46.

27. Ibid. II, pp. 61f.; Irwin, op. cit. pp. 281–9.

28. Hoover, *Memoirs*, II, p. 77.

29. Ibid. II, pp. 79–91; Irwin, op. cit. pp. 264–71.

30. Hoover, *Memoirs*, II, pp. 101–8; Wilbur, Ray Lyman and Hyde, Arthur Mastick, *The Hoover Policies*, New York, 1937, pp. 125–6.

31. Hoover, *Memoirs*, II, pp. 139–45.

32. Ibid. II, pp. 167–8; Herring, E. Pendleton, 'Politics, Personalities, and the Federal Trade Commission,' *American Political Science Review*, XXIX (February 1935), pp. 21–35; Schlesinger, Arthur M. Jr., *The Crisis of the Old Order* 1919–1933 (vol. 1 in *The Age of Roosevelt*), Boston, 1957, p. 65.

33. *Sixteenth Annual Report of the Secretary of Commerce* 1928, Washington, 1928, p. viii.

34. Owens, John W., 'The Irony of the Harding Cabinet,' *New Republic*, 12 March 1924, p. 65.

35. *Literary Digest*, 30 April, 7 May, 21 May, and 28 May 1927; Speers, L. C., 'The Sort of Man Herbert Hoover Is,' *New York Times Magazine*, 29 January 1928, p. 3; Hoover, *Memoirs*, II, pp. 125–6.

36. [Gilbert] *Mirrors of Washington*, p. 123; *Time*, 27 August 1928, p. 9.

37. Hoover, Irwin Hood, *Forty-two Years in the White House*, New York, 1934, pp. 167–75; statement by Col. James F. Coupal, *New York Times*, 1 August 1931; White, William Allen, *Masks in a Pageant*, New York, 1929, pp. 454–7.

38. White, *A Puritan in Babylon*, p. 363.

39. *Time*, 20 February 1928, p. 8; *Congressional Record*, 70 Cong. 1 Sess., 69:2825–42; Peel, Roy V. and Donnelly, Thomas C., *The 1928 Campaign, An Analysis*, New York, 1931, pp, 5–7.

40. A Washington Correspondent, 'The Secretariat,' *American Mercury*, December 1929, p. 390; [Allen, Robert S. and Pearson, Drew] *More Merry-Go-Round*, Philadelphia, 1932, pp. 287–8; *Time*, 11 March 1929, p. 12.

41. *New York Times*, 25 January 1928.

42. *Time*, 9 January 1928, p. 7, 30 January 1928, p. 7, 13 February 1928, p. 7, and 24 September 1928, pp. 8–9; Myers, William Starr, *The Republican Party, A History*, rev. ed. New York, 1931, p. 483.

43. Irwin, *The Making of a Reporter*, pp. 208–9; id., 'Herbert Hoover,' *American Magazine*, May 1930, p. 128; *Time*, 20 February 1928, p. 7, cites the letter by Col. Thad H. Brown of Columbus, Ohio; *New York Times*, 7 November 1928.

44. Crowther, Samuel, *The Presidency vs. Hoover*, New York, 1928, pp. 137–8.

45. Leopold, Richard W., *Elihu Root and the Conservative Tradition*, Boston, 1954, p. 170; White, *A Puritan in Babylon*, pp. 374–6.

46. Oulahan, 'Hoover, the Handy, Plays Many Parts,' loc. cit. pp. 3, 16.

47. Duffus, R. L., 'College Bred Indeed is Herbert Hoover,' *New York Times Magazine*, 1 July 1928, p. 4.

48. *New Republic*, 21 February 1923, p. 352.

49. Hoover, Herbert, *The New Day: Campaign Speeches of Herbert Hoover 1928*, Stanford, 1928, pp. 41, 179–81, 164; id., *Memoirs*, II, p. 196; id., *American Individualism*, New York, 1923, pp. 9, 12.

50. Wilbur and Hyde, op. cit. p. 6.

51. Hoover, *American Individualism*, p. 48.

52. Address to American Bankers Association, Cleveland O., 2 October 1930, *Congressional Record*, 71 Cong. 3 Sess., 74:203; cf. Hoover, *The New Day*, pp. 154, 182.

53. Speers, 'The Sort of Man Herbert Hoover Is,' loc. cit. p. 231; Hoover, *Memoirs*, III, p. 460.

54. Hoover, Herbert, 'The Paramount Business of Every American Today,' *System*, July 1920, p. 23; id., *Memoirs*, II, pp. 110, 140; id., *The New Day*, pp. 63, 102.

55. Hoover, *The New Day*, pp. 106–7.

56. Ibid. p. 162. Copyright 1928 by the Board of Trustees of Leland Stanford Junior University. By permission of the Stanford University Press, publishers.

57. Campaign address at New York, 22 October 1928, *The New Day*, p. 176. By permission of the Stanford University Press, publishers.

58. *Time*, 12 November 1928, p. 10; Lovett, Robert Morss, 'The Degradation of American Politics,' *Behold America!* ed. by Samuel Schmalhausen, New York 1931, pp. 47–50; Millis, Walter, 'Presidential Candidates,' *Yale Review*, XXII (September 1932), 6; Villard, Oswald Garrison, *Prophets True and False*, New York, 1928, pp. 19–36.

59. *Time*, 26 March 1928, p. 9. Copyright 1928 by Time, Inc. By permission of the publisher.

60. Quoted by Peel and Donnelly, *The 1928 Campaign*, pp. 144–5.

61. Quoted by Myers, op. cit. p. 484.

62. Mencken, op. cit. p. 7.

63. Hoover, I. H., *Forty-two Years at the White House* pp. 176–7; White, *A Puritan in Babylon*, pp. 398–408.

64. Peel and Donnelly, *The 1928 Campaign*, pp. 21–30; *New York Times*, 16 June 1928.

65. Mencken, Henry L., *Making a President: A Footnote to the Saga of Democracy*, New York, 1932, p. 24. By permission of Alfred A. Knopf, Inc., publishers.

66. Quoted by *Time*, 25 June 1928, p. 14.

CHAPTER 3

1. Pringle, Henry F., *Alfred E. Smith, A Critical Study*, New York, 1927, pp. 80–99; Smith, Alfred E., *Up to Now, An Autobiography*, New York, 1929, pp. 3, 8–9; Stone, Irving, *They Also Ran: the Story of the Men Who Were Defeated for the Presidency*, New York, 1943, pp. 285–305; Graham, Frank, *Al Smith, American—An Informal Biography*, New York, 1945, pp. 3–21.

2. Pringle, op. cit. pp. 115, 129–62; Smith, op. cit. pp. 55–88.

3. Pringle, op. cit. p. 237; Smith, op. cit. pp. 204–6.

4. Smith, Alfred E., *Campaign Addresses of Governor Alfred E. Smith, Democratic Candidate for President 1928*, Washington, 1929, pp. 44–7, hereafter cited as Smith, *Campaign Addresses*. Also see Smith, *Up to Now*, pp. 170–371; Pringle, op. cit. pp. 282–7.

5. *Atlantic Monthly*, April 1927, pp. 540–49 and May 1927, p. 721; Moore, Edmund A., *A Catholic Runs for President: The Campaign of 1928*, New York, 1956, pp. 57–79.

6. Dabney, Virginius, *Dry Messiah: The Life of Bishop Cannon*, New York, 1949, p. 177; Cannon, James Jr., *Bishop Cannon's Own Story*, ed. by Richard L. Watson, Jr., Durham, 1955, pp. 413–14.

7. Peel, Roy V. and Donnelly, Thomas C., *The 1928 Campaign—An Analysis*, New York, 1931, pp. 152–69.

8. Ibid. pp. 30–5; *New York Times*, 26–30 June 1928.

9. [Gilbert, Clinton Wallace] *The Mirrors of 1932*, New York, 1931, pp. 41–8; Irwin, Will, *The Making of a Reporter*, New York, 1942, p. 415.

10. *Time*, 24 September 1928, pp. 8–9; *New York Times*, 22 June 1928; Peel and Donnelly, op. cit. pp. 36–46.

11. *New York Times*, 17 June and 25 October 1928; *Time*, 12 November 1928, p. 8; Lief, Alfred, *Democracy's Norris, the Biography of a Lonely Crusade*, New York, 1939, pp. 320–23; Hinshaw, David, *Herbert Hoover, American Quaker*, New York, 1950, p. 143.

12. Smith, *Up to Now*, pp. 385–97.

13. Pringle, Henry F., *Alfred E. Smith, A Critical Study*, New York, 1927, p. 100. By permission of the Vanguard Press, publishers.

14. Peel and Donnelly, op. cit. p. 59. For an excellent collection of campaign cartoons, see *Time*, 15 October 1928, pp. 25–32.

15. Hoover, Herbert, *The New Day: Campaign Speeches of Herbert Hoover 1928*, Stanford, 1928, pp. 12–13. Copyright 1928 by the Board of Trustees of Leland Stanford Junior University. By permission of the Stanford University Press, publishers.

16. Crowther, Samuel, *The Presidency vs. Hoover*, New York, 1928, p. 12.

17. Hoover, *The New Day*, pp. 64, 66, 67.

18. Ibid. p. 171, speech at New York, 22 October 1928. By permission of the Stanford University Press, publishers.

19. Smith, *Campaign Addresses,* pp. 4, 15–16, 153–6.

20. Hoover, *The New Day,* p. 29; id., *Memoirs,* II, pp. 200–201.

21. Hoover, *The New Day,* p. 104, speech at Elizabethton, Tenn., 6 October 1928; Johnson, Claudius O., *Borah of Idaho,* New York, 1936, p. 423.

22. Smith, *Campaign Addresses,* pp. 14–15, speech at Albany, 22 August 1928, and pp. 105–19, speech at Milwaukee, 29 September 1928; Peel and Donnelly, op. cit. pp. 58–9.

23. Willebrandt, Mabel Walker, *The Inside of Prohibition,* Indianapolis, 1929, pp. 303–17; Scott, William Rufus, *Revolt on Mount Sinai: The Puritan Retreat from Prohibition,* Pasadena, 1944, pp. 26–32.

24. Hoover, *The New Day,* pp. 27–9; Peel and Donnelly, op. cit. pp. 64–6; Smith, *Campaign Addresses,* pp. 20–22, 61–76; Lief, op. cit. p. 319.

25. Hoover, *The New Day,* p. 23. By permission of the Stanford University Press, publishers.

26. Ibid. p. 38. Cf. the St. Paul speech, 27 September 1928, ibid. pp. 89–97.

27. Quoted by Fraser, Herbert F., 'Popular Tariff Fallacies,' *Annals* of the American Academy of Political and Social Science, CXLI (January 1929), p. 59.

28. Hoover, *The New Day,* pp. 126–7, 131, 136, speech at Boston, 15 October 1928.

29. Ibid. pp. 157–67; Homan, Paul T., 'The Deepening Tariff Darkness,' *Atlantic Monthly,* May 1929, pp. 680–87.

30. Smith, *Campaign Addresses,* p. 51; *New York Times,* 21 September 1928; Moore, op. cit. pp. 179–89; Myers, Gustavus, *History of Bigotry in the United States,* New York, 1943, pp. 314–27.

31. Dabney, op. cit. p. 181.

32. Ibid. pp. 182–8; Cannon, op. cit. Ch. XVII; interview with Richard Mason Cannon, 17 July 1957; Freidel, Frank, *Franklin D. Roosevelt: The Triumph,* Boston, 1956, pp. 13–14.

33. Johnson, op. cit. pp. 428–9; Timmons, Bascom N., *Jesse H. Jones, the Man and the Statesman,* New York, 1956, p. 148.

34. Myers, William Starr, *The Republican Party, A History,* New York, 1931, p. 498; *New York Times,* 7 November 1928; Cox, James M., *Journey Through My Years,* New York, 1946, pp. 333–4; Stone, op. cit. p. 301; Smith, *Up to Now,* pp. 416–18.

35. *Commercial & Financial Chronicle,* 17 November 1928, p. 2742. By permission of Herbert D. Seibert, editor and publisher.

36. Davis, Elmer, 'Hoover the Medicine Man,' *Forum*, October 1930, p. 198.

37. Hoover, *Memoirs*, II, p. 208.

38. Davis, Elmer, 'If Hoover Fails,' *Harper's Monthly Magazine*, March 1929, pp. 409–18.

39. *Congressional Record*, 71 Cong. 2 Sess., 72:10553.

CHAPTER 4

1. White, William Allen, *A Puritan in Babylon, the Story of Calvin Coolidge*, New York, 1938, p. 418; *Time*, 11 March 1929, pp. 9–10; *Literary Digest*, 16 March 1929, pp. 5–7; *New York Times*, 5 March 1929.

2. *Congressional Record*, 71 Cong. Special Session of the Senate, 4–5 March 1929, 71:4–6. The inaugural address is also in Hoover, *State Papers*, I, pp. 3–12.

3. *Congressional Record*, 71:6; Hoover, *State Papers*, I, pp. 11–12.

4. *Congressional Record*, 71:6–7.

5. Hoover, *Memoirs*, II, p. 217.

6. Johnson, Claudius, *Borah of Idaho*, New York, 1936, pp. 432–3.

7. Page, Arthur W., 'Henry L. Stimson—A Character Sketch,' *Current History*, April 1929, pp. 7–11; *Time*, 11 March 1929, pp. 11–12 and *Literary Digest*, 16 March 1929, pp. 8–10 have good sketches of the cabinet members.

8. Gilbert, Clinton W., 'Andrew W. Mellon, Secretary of the Treasury,' *Current History*, July 1931, pp. 521–6.

9. *Time*, 11 March 1929, p. 12; *Literary Digest*, 16 March 1929, pp. 8–10; Ickes, Harold L., *The Secret Diary of Harold L. Ickes: The Lowering Clouds*, 1939–1941, 3 vols., New York, 1954, III, pp. 88–9.

10. Hoover, *Memoirs*, II, pp. 219–20; Childs, Marquis W., 'The Career of a States-man,' *American Mercury*, May 1930, has a survey of Hyde's career at pp. 29–36.

11. Allen, Robert S., 'One of Mr. Hoover's Friends,' *American Mercury*, January 1932, pp. 53–62; Collier, John, 'The Indian Bureau's Record,' *Nation*, 5 October 1932, pp. 303–5; 'Cabinets and Cabinets,' *Nation*, 12 October 1932, p. 322; [Allen, Robert S. and Pearson, Drew] *More Merry-Go-Round*, New York, 1932, pp. 279–82; Milburn, George, 'Mr. Hoover's Stalking Horse,' *American Mercury*, July 1932, pp. 257–66.

12. *Time*, 15 July 1929, p. 9; Myers, William Starr and Newton, Walter H., *The Hoover Administration, A Documented Narrative*, New York, 1936, pp. 530–42.

13. A Washington Correspondent, 'The Secretariat,' *American Mercury*, December 1929, pp. 385–95; *Time*, 8 April 1929, p. 9.

14. Schriftgiesser, Karl, *This Was Normalcy: An Account of Party Politics during Twelve Republican Years* 1920–1932, Boston, 1948, pp. 281–2; Pollard, James E., *The Presidents and the Press*, New York, 1947, pp. 737–8; Tucker, Ray T., 'Mr. Hoover Lays A Ghost,' *North American Review*, January 1929, pp. 661–9.

15. Peel, Roy V. and Donnelly, Thomas C., *The 1932 Campaign, an Analysis*, New York, 1935, pp. 180–81; address to the Gridiron Club, Washington, 12 December 1931, Hoover, *State Papers*, II, pp. 86–7.

16. For a good analysis, see Pollard, op. cit. pp. 737–72 and Rosten, Leo C., *The Washington Correspondents*, New York, 1937, pp. 39–46; *Time*, 17 June 1929, p. 11.

17. Hoover, *State Papers*, I, pp. 27, 555–6.

18. [Allen, Robert S. and Pearson, Drew] *Washington Merry-Go-Round*, New York, 1931, pp. 324–6; Pollard, op. cit. p. 742; Hoover, Irwin Hood, *Forty-two Years in the White House*, New York, 1934, pp. 209–10; *Time*, 3 December 1928, p. 7. An early article praising Hoover is Oulahan, Richard V., 'Hoover, the Handy, Plays Many Parts,' *New York Times Magazine*, 22 November 1925.

19. *New York Times*, 31 December 1931 and 3 January 1932.

20. [Allen and Pearson] *Washington Merry-Go-Round*, pp. 356f.

21. Macmahon, Arthur W., 'First Session of the Seventy-first Congress,' *American Political Science Review*, XXIV (1930), p. 41; Oulahan, 'Hoover, the Handy, Plays Many Parts,' loc. cit. *passim*.

22. Tucker, Ray T., 'Those Sons of Wild Jackasses,' *North American Review*, February 1930, pp. 225–33; McKee, Oliver Jr., 'Lobbyists Extraordinary,' *North American Review*, January 1930, pp. 82–8; Krock, Arthur, 'Cabinets of Jefferson, Hoover, and Roosevelt,' *New York Times*, 5 March 1933.

23. Senate Committee on Banking and Currency, *Nomination of Eugene Meyer to be a Member of the Federal Reserve Board*, Hearings, Washington, 1931, pp. 4–18.

CHAPTER 5

1. Crowther, Samuel, *The Presidency vs. Hoover*, New York, 1928, pp. 76–80.

2. Hoover, *State Papers*, I, pp. 70–71.

3. Hoover, *Memoirs*, II, pp. 227–8.

4. Homan, Paul T., 'Economic Aspects of the Boulder Dam Project,' *Quarterly Journal of Economics*, XLV (February 1931), p. 215.

5. Address at Eden Park, Cincinnati, 22 October 1929. Hoover, *State Papers*, I, pp. 114–6; *Commercial & Financial Chronicle*, 2 November 1929, pp. 2741–2.

6. Hoover, *Memoirs*, II, pp. 229–35; id., *State Papers*, II, pp. 237–8; Hinshaw, David, *Herbert Hoover, American Quaker*, New York, 1950, pp. 197–9.

7. This policy was forecast in a statement of 15 March 1929. See Hoover, *State Papers*, I, pp. 16–17.

8. Hoover, *Memoirs*, II, pp. 237–9; Hinshaw, op. cit. pp. 199–200.

9. Hoover to Joseph M. Dixon, 21 August 1929, Hoover, *State Papers*, I, pp. 91–6.

10. Hoover, *Memoirs*, II, pp. 239–42.

11. Ibid. II, p. 252; id., *State Papers*, I, pp. 69, 90–91.

12. Hoover, *Memoirs*, III, p. 144.

13. *Literary Digest*, 8 December 1928, pp. 5–7; *Wall Street Journal*, 27 November 1928.

14. Hoover, *Memoirs*, III, pp. 144–5; Pearson, Drew, 'Public Works Face the Ax,' *Nation*, 28 December 1932, pp. 640–41.

15. Hoover, *Memoirs*, III, pp. 143, 147–9; Myers, William Starr and Newton, Walter H., *The Hoover Administration, A Documented Narrative*, New York, 1936, pp. 212–13.

16. Hoover, *Memoirs*, II, pp. 256–66; Wilbur, Ray Lyman and Hyde, Arthur Mastick, *The Hoover Policies*, New York, 1937, pp. 60–87; *Congressional Digest*, XI, pp. 59, 187.

17. Hoover, *Memoirs*, II, pp. 312–19.

18. *Congressional Digest*, XI, p. 170; Hoover, *State Papers*, I, pp. 361–2 and II, pp. 126–7, 134–6; Remington, Harold, 'American Bankruptcy Laws and their Administration,' *Current History*, June 1929, pp. 404–9; Senate Document 65, 72 Cong. 1 Sess., Washington, 1932, *passim*.

19. *Congressional Digest*, XI, 175; Hoover, *Memoirs*, II, p. 273; Hinshaw, op. cit. pp. 196–7.

20. Hoover, *Memoirs*, II, p. 275; Wilbur and Hyde, op. cit. pp. 89–90; Hoover, *State Papers*, I, p. 89.

21. *Congressional Record*, 72 Cong. 1 Sess., 9 December 1931, 72:211. 47 U.S. Statutes 1625.

22. Hoover, *Memoirs*, II, pp. 279–84; id., *State Papers*, I, pp. 162–3, 356–7; Lowry, Edward G., 'A Preface to Hoover,' *Century Magazine*, Autumn 1929, pp. 130–37.

23. 46 U.S. Statutes 259–60; *Congressional Record*, 71 Cong. 3 Sess., 4 December 1930, 74:205–6; Wilbur and Hyde, op. cit. p. 221; Myers and Newton, op. cit. pp. 430–31.

24. Hoover, *Memoirs*, II, pp. 246–8; *Nation*, 21 December 1932, pp. 603–4.

CHAPTER 6

1. *Congressional Record*, 71 Cong. Special Session of the Senate, 4–5 March 1929, 71:6.

2. Raushenbush, Stephen, *The Power Fight*, New York, 1932, pp. 47–124; Pinchot, Gifford, 'The Gigantic Strides of Power Monopoly in the United States,' *Current History*, April 1929, pp. 38–42.

3. Anderson, Paul Y., 'Mr. Hoover's Last Mile,' *Nation*, 9 November 1932, p. 447; *New York Times*, 20 February 1930.

4. 41 U.S. Statutes 1063–77.

5. Hoover, *State Papers*, I, p. 485.

6. 46 U.S. Statutes 797ff.

7. Hoover, *Memoirs*, II, pp. 302–3; id., *State Papers*, I, pp. 155–6; Hinshaw, David, *Herbert Hoover, American Quaker*, New York, 1950, pp. 194–5.

8. Senate Committee on Interstate Commerce, *Confirmation of Marcel Garsaud on Renomination to the Federal Power Commission*, Hearings, Washington, 1932, pp. 1–10.

9. *New York Times*, 24 December 1930.

10. Message to the Senate, 10 January 1931, *State Papers*, I, pp. 478ff and *Congressional Record*, 72 Cong. 1 Sess., 18 June 1932, 75:13329–33.

11. Press Statement, 10 January 1931, Hoover, *State Papers*, I, pp. 485–8; *Time*, 19 January 1931, pp. 11–12; Raushenbush, op. cit. pp. 166–7; Gruening, Ernest, *The Public Pays, A Study of Power Propaganda*, New York, 1931 and Levin, Jack, *Power Ethics*, New York, 1931, cover the power fight.

12. Levin, op. cit. pp. 15–16; Parmelee, Maurice, *Farewell to Poverty*, New York, 1935, p. 142.

13. Gruening, op. cit. traces revelations of propaganda before 1929. The story unfolds in the 73 volumes published by the Federal Trade Commission in 1934.

14. Hormell, Owen C., 'State Legislation and Public Utilities in 1931,' *American Political Science Review*, XXVI (1932), pp. 84–96.

15. Raushenbush, op. cit. pp. 1–46; Lief, Alfred, *Democracy's Norris, the Biography of a Lonely Crusade*, New York, 1939, p. 339; Gruening, op. cit. *passim*.

16. Cooke, Morris Llewellyn, 'Planning for Power,' *A Practical Program for America*, ed. by Henry Hazlitt, New York, 1932, p. 98.

17. Ibid. pp. 99–100.

18. Hoover, *Memoirs*, II, pp. 112–9.

19. Neuberger, Richard L. and Kahn, Stephen B., *Integrity, the Life of George*

W. *Norris*, New York, 1937, pp. 202–21; Lief, op. cit. pp. 244–60; House Report No. 2747, 71 Cong. 3 Sess., 19 February 1931.

20. *Congressional Record*, 72 Cong. 1 Sess., 75:9589–90; Hoover, *State Papers*, I, pp. 521–9.

21. Spargo, John, 'Hoover—The New Phase,' *North American Review*, April 1931, pp. 293–9.

22. Senate Document No. 21, 72 Cong. 1 Sess.

23. Senate Committee on Agriculture and Forestry, *To Create Muscle Shoals Corporation of the United States*, Hearings on S. J. Res. 15, Washington, 1932, p. 45.

24. Senate Report No. 423, 72 Cong. 1 Sess.

25. *Congressional Record*, 72 Cong. 1 Sess., 75:9573–82.

26. *Time*, 18 April 1932, pp. 47–8 and 27 February 1933, pp. 37–8; Childs, Marquis W., 'Samuel Insull,' *New Republic*, 21 September 1932, pp. 142–4.

27. Thompson, Carl D., *Confessions of the Power Trust*, New York, 1932, pp. 232–41; Pecora, Ferdinand, *Wall Street Under Oath, the Story of Our Modern Money Changers*, New York, 1932, pp. 226ff.

28. Childs, Marquis W., 'Samuel Insull,' *New Republic*, 28 September 1932, pp. 170–73 and 5 October 1932, pp. 201–3.

29. 'The Crime Hunt in Insull's Shattered Empire,' *Literary Digest*, 15 October 1932; Flynn, John T., 'What Happened to Insull,' *New Republic*, 4 May 1932, p. 316.

30. *Time*, 17 September 1928, p. 48; Hansl, Proctor W., *Years of Plunder, A Financial Chronicle of Our Times*, New York, 1934, pp. 155f.

31. *Business Week*, 20 April 1932, pp. 18–9; *Nation*, 28 December 1932, p. 627; Danielian, N. R., 'From Insull to Injury,' *Atlantic Monthly*, April 1933, pp. 497f; 'The Loss of Owen D. Young,' *Nation*, 4 January 1933, p. 4.

32. Danielian, 'From Insull to Injury,' loc. cit. pp. 497–8; *New York Times*, 16 April 1932.

33. Richberg, Donald, 'Gold-Plated Anarchy, An Interpretation of the Fall of the Giants,' *Nation*, 5 April 1933, pp. 368–9.

34. *Christian Century*, 28 September 1932, p. 1156.

CHAPTER 7

1. Hoover, *Memoirs*, II, p. 293.

2. 42 U.S. Statutes 941–2.

3. Taussig, F. W., 'The Tariff, 1929–30,' *Quarterly Journal of Economics*, XLIV (February 1930), pp. 175–204, at p. 177.

4. Smith, James Gerald, *Economic Planning and the Tariff, An Essay on Social Philosophy*, Princeton, 1934, p. 139.

5. Collings, Harry T., 'The Basis of International Trade,' *Annals* of the American Academy of Political and Social Science, CXLI (January 1929), pp. 1–10.

6. Filene, Edward A., 'Mass Production and the Tariff,' ibid. pp. 43–8; Wallace, Benjamin Bruce, 'The Case for a Flexible Tariff,' ibid. pp. 61–7; Crampton, George, 'Can the Tariff be Made Scientific?' ibid. pp. 115–9.

7. Staples, P. C., 'Prosperity and the Tariff,' ibid. pp. 51–2.

8. 'Farm Relief and the Tariff,' ibid. p. 122.

9. For a more complete discussion, see Black, John D., 'The Home Market for American Agriculture,' ibid. pp. 124–36 and Gersting, J. Marshall, 'Is the Agricultural Tariff Protective?' ibid. pp. 137–48. Similar conclusions are found in Quick, Herbert, *The Real Trouble with the Farmers*, Indianapolis, 1924, pp. 26–40. See also Seligman, E. R. A., *The Economics of Farm Relief, A Survey of the Agricultural Problem*, New York, 1929, pp. 208–10; Taussig, F. W., 'The Tariff Act of 1930,' *Quarterly Journal of Economics*, XLV (November 1930), pp. 1–21; Zapoleon, L. B., 'Farm Relief, Agricultural Prices, and Tariffs,' *Journal of Political Economy*, February 1932, pp. 73–100. Reed Smoot had his say in 'Why a Protective Tariff?' *Saturday Evening Post*, 10 September 1932. W. C. Hawley gave his views in 'The New Tariff: A Defense,' *Review of Reviews*, July 1930.

10. See Boyle, James E., 'Tariff Handicaps,' *Annals*, CXLII (March 1929), pp. 89–96.

11. *Capitalism and Its Culture*, New York, 1935, p. 468.

12. *Congressional Record*, 71 Cong. 1 Sess., 15 April 1929, 71:25.

13. Lief, Alfred, *Democracy's Norris, the Biography of a Lonely Crusade*, New York, 1939, p. 329.

14. *Congressional Record*, 71 Cong. 1 Sess., 16 April 1929, 71:48.

15. Ibid. 71:52.

16. Ibid. 17 April 1929, 71:64; Hull, Cordell, *The Memoirs of Cordell Hull*, 2 vols., London, 1948, I, p. 133; Johnson, Claudius O., *Borah of Idaho*, New York, 1936, p. 435.

17. 30 November 1929, p. 3378.

18. 25 January 1930, p. 516.

19. Hull, op. cit. I, p. 132.

20. Joslin, Theodore G., *Hoover Off the Record*, New York, 1934, pp. 30–31.

21. Scroggs, William O., 'Revolt Against the Tariff,' *North American Review*, July 1930, pp. 18–24.

22. *Congressional Record*, 71 Cong. 2 Sess., 12 June 1930, 72:10546.

23. Ibid. pp. 10547–52.

24. Ibid. p. 10572.

25. Ibid. 13 June 1930, 72:10616; *Time*, 18 February 1929, p. 13 and 8 April 1929, pp. 11–12.

26. *Congressional Record*, 71 Cong. 2 Sess., 13 June 1930, 72:10625–35.

27. Hoover, *Memoirs*, II, p. 297; id., *State Papers*, I, pp. 314–8; Faulkner, Harold Underwood, *From Versailles to the New Deal, A Chronicle of the Harding-Coolidge-Hoover Era*, New Haven, 1950, pp. 340–43; Roper, Daniel C., *Fifty Years of Public Life*, Durham, 1941, p. 236; Myers, William Starr and Newton, Walter H., *The Hoover Administration, A Documented Narrative*, New York, 1936, p. 439; Soule, George Henry, *Economic Forces in American History*, New York, 1952, p. 322.

28. Berglund, Abraham, 'The Tariff Act of 1930,' *American Economic Review*, XX (September 1930), pp. 467–79 at p. 473.

29. Hoover, *Memoirs*, II, p. 299; Myers, William Starr, *The Republican Party, A History*, New York, 1931, pp. 502–3.

30. *New York Times*, 23 February 1930; *New York World*, 18 June 1930.

31. Soule, George Henry, *Prosperity Decade, From War to Depression 1917–1929*, New York, 1947, p. 266.

32. Hayes, H. Gordon, *Spending, Saving, & Employment*, New York, 1945, p. 9.

33. U.S. Department of Commerce, *The United States in the World Economy*, Washington, 1943, Table 2.

34. Fleming, Denna Frank, *The United States in World Organization, 1920–1933*, New York, 1938, pp. 325–6; Mann, Lawrence B., 'Foreign Reaction to the American Tariff Act,' *Foreign Policy Association Reports*, VI (1930–1931), pp. 261–78; Taussig, F. W., 'The Tariff Bill and Our Friends Abroad,' *Foreign Affairs*, VIII (October 1929), pp. 1–12; Siegfried, André, 'European Reactions to American Tariff Proposals,' ibid. pp. 13–29; Bidwell, Percy Wells, 'The New American Tariff: Europe's Answer,' ibid. IX (October 1930), pp. 13–26; Feis, Herbert, 'After Tariffs, Embargoes,' ibid. IX (April 1931), pp. 398–408; Pell, Herbert C., 'Inefficient, Incompetent or Dishonest,' *North American Review*, January 1932, pp. 16–24; Schivedersky, Herve, 'The Tariff on Sugar, A Case Study,' *Nation*, 2 November 1932, pp. 426–7

35. Salter, [James] Arthur, *Recovery, the Second Effort*, New York, 1932, p. 198.

36. Jones, Joseph M. Jr., *Tariff Retaliation, Repercussions of the Hawley-Smoot Bill*, Philadelphia, 1934, pp. 34–103.

37. *Congressional Record*, 71 Cong. 2 Sess., 13 June 1930, 72:10634–5; Slichter Sumner H., 'Is the Tariff a Cause of Depression?' *Current History*, January 1932, pp. 519–24; 'Presenting the "Tariff Tinkers of '29,"' *Literary Digest*, 9 March 1929, pp. 5–7.

38. *The Recovery Problem in the United States,* The Institute of Economics of the Brookings Institution, Washington, 1936, p. 94.

39. Klein, Julius, 'The Tariff and the Depression,' *Current History,* July 1931, pp. 497–9; Smoot, Reed, 'Our Tariff and the Depression,' ibid. November 1931, pp. 173–81.

40. *The Recovery Problem in the United States,* p. 47.

41. Ibid. quoting League of Nations, *World Economic Survey,* 1932–1933, pp. 16–17.

42. U. S. Bureau of the Census, *Historical Statistics of the United States,* 1789– 1945, Washington, 1949, pp. 243–4.

43. Hayes, op. cit. pp. 5–6.

44. Smith, *Economic Planning and the Tariff, passim.*

45. Donham, Wallace Brett, *Business Adrift,* New York, 1931, pp. 75–81.

46. *The Magazine of Wall Street,* 8 February 1930, p. 603.

CHAPTER 8

1. Hoover, Herbert, *The New Day: Campaign Speeches of Herbert Hoover* 1928, Stanford, 1929, pp. 13–16 for speech of 11 August, pp. 65–7 for speech of 17 September, pp. 139–40 for speech of 15 October, and pp. 150, 171–2 for speech of 22 October.

2. Robbins, Lionel, *The Great Depression,* New York, 1934, p. 53; *Commercial & Financial Chronicle,* 26 October 1929, p. 2578; Miller, A. C., 'Responsibility for Federal Reserve Policies,' *American Economic Review,* xxv (September 1935), pp. 442–58; Willis, H. Parker, 'Who Caused the Panic of 1929?' *North American Review,* February 1930, pp. 174–83; Daiger, J. M., 'Did the Federal Reserve Play Politics?' *Current History,* October 1932, pp. 25–32; Senate Banking and Currency Committee, *Nomination of Eugene Meyer to be a Member of the Federal Reserve Board,* Hearings, Washington, 1931, p. 21.

3. Field, Carter, *Bernard Baruch, Park Bench Statesman,* New York, 1944, pp. 220–21.

4. Myers, William Starr and Newton, Walter H., *The Hoover Administration, A Documented Narrative,* New York, 1936, pp. 10–11; Lippmann, Walter, *Interpretations,* 1931–1932, New York, 1932; pp. 10–11; Edie, Lionel, *The Banks and Prosperity,* New York, 1931, pp. 151–2; *Time,* 23 July 1928, pp. 24–5; Senate Committee on Manufactures, *Establishment of National Economic Council,* Hearings on S. 6215, Washington, 1932, pp. 719–22.

5. Hunt, Edward Eyre, 'America's Increasing Economic Stability,' *Current History,* August 1929, pp. 811–16; Hoover, *Memoirs,* III, pp. 16–17; Myers and Newton, op. cit. pp. 14–16.

6. Galbraith, John Kenneth, *The Great Crash, 1929*, New York, 1955, p. 36; Smith, Rixey and Beasley, Norman, *Carter Glass, A Biography*, New York, 1939, pp. 289–90; Bopp, Karl R., 'Two Notes on the Federal Reserve System,' *Journal of Political Economy*, XL (June 1932), p. 387; Morgenstern, Oskar, 'Developments in the Federal Reserve System,' *Harvard Business Review*, IX (October 1930), pp. 1–7; Miller, A. C., 'Responsibility for Federal Reserve Policies,' loc. cit. pp. 454–5.

7. Lippmann, Walter, 'The Peculiar Weakness of Mr. Hoover,' *Harper's Monthly Magazine*, June 1930, p. 3; *Congressional Record*, 71 Cong. 1 Sess., 71:64; *Stock Exchange Practices*, Senate Report No. 1455, 73 Cong. 2 Sess., Washington, 1934, p. 13.

8. *Stock Exchange Practices*, pp. 15–16; Fisher, Irving, *The Stock Market Crash—And After*, New York, 1930, pp. 1, 20; Nearing, Scott, *Must We Starve?* New York, 1932, pp. 22–9; *New York Times*, 10 November 1931.

9. The occasion was the Sixteenth National Business Conference at Wellesley. *Commercial & Financial Chronicle*, 21 September 1929, p. 1800.

10. Ibid. By permission of Herbert D. Seibert, editor and publisher.

11. James, F. Cyril, *The Growth of Chicago Banks*, 2 vols., New York, 1938, II, pp. 986–7.

12. Schlesinger, Arthur M. Jr., *The Crisis of the Old Order, 1919–1923*, Boston, 1957, p. 158.

13. *Commercial & Financial Chronicle*, 26 October 1929, p. 2579. By permission of Herbert D. Seibert, editor and publisher.

14. *Time*, 4 November 1929, passim; Galbraith, op. cit. pp. 113–23; Hansl, Proctor W., *Years of Plunder, A Financial Chronicle of Our Times*, New York, 1934, pp. 238–45; Fisher, op. cit. p. 9; Lefèvre, Edwin, 'The Little Fellow in Wall Street,' *Saturday Evening Post*, 4 January 1930, pp. 6–7 *et seq.*

15. *Commercial & Financial Chronicle*, 2 November 1929, pp. 2725–6; *Stock Exchange Practices*, p. 71; New York Stock Exchange, *Report of the President, 1929–1930*, New York, 1930, p. 37; Leonard, Jonathan, *Three Years Down*, New York, 1939, has a racy, interesting account at pp. 59–75. More sober treatments are in Fisher, op. cit. pp. 1–20 and his *Booms and Depressions, Some First Principles*, New York, 1932, pp. 90–91. See also Galbraith, op. cit. pp. 93–112; Dulles, Eleanor Lansing, *Depressions and Reconstruction, A Study of Causes and Controls*, Philadelphia, 1936, pp. 160–79; *The American Labor Year Book*, 1930, pp. 22–4.

16. *Commercial & Financial Chronicle*, 17 August 1929, p. 1025.

17. *Stock Exchange Practices*, p. 6.

18. James, op. cit. II, p. 977.

19. *Commercial & Financial Chronicle*, 26 October 1929, p. 2577. By permission of Herbert D. Seibert, editor and publisher.

20. Merz, Charles, 'Bull Market,' *Harper's Monthly Magazine*, April, 1929, p. 642. By permission of Harper & Brothers, publishers.

21. Mazur, Paul M., *America Looks Abroad*, New York, 1930, p. 14.

22. Chase, Stuart, *A New Deal*, New York, 1932, p. 11.

23. Leonard, op. cit. p. 40; Sokolski, A. M., 'American Speculative Manias, Past and Present,' *Current History*, August 1929, pp. 861–8.

24. Galbraith, op. cit. pp. 54–5.

25. *Stock Exchange Practices*, p. 9.

26. *Time*, 7 October 1929.

27. Ibid. 14 October 1929.

28. Ibid. 21 October 1929.

29. Ibid. 28 October 1929.

30. Ibid.

31. Garfield, W. H., 'Guesses for Sale,' *Nation*, 24 August 1932, pp. 162-4. The author concealed his real identity.

32. *Time*, 11 November 1929.

33. Ibid. 18 November 1929.

34. *New York Times*, 31 October 1929.

35. Angly, Edward, 'Prophets Not Without Honor,' *Forum*, May 1931, pp. 272–7; *America Faces the Future*, ed. by Charles A. Beard, New York, 1932, pp. 57–69.

36. December 1929, p. 11.

37. Senate Committee on Banking and Currency, *Nomination of Eugene Meyer to be a Member of the Federal Reserve Board*, Hearings, Washington, 1931, p. 114. Young, when he made this statement, was governor of the Federal Reserve Bank of Boston.

38. 7 December 1929, p. 3511.

39. Pecora, Ferdinand, *Wall Street Under Oath, the Story of Our Modern Money Changers*, New York, 1939, p. 283. By permission of Simon and Schuster, Inc., publishers.

40. Ibid. pp. 70–83; *Stock Exchange Practices*, pp. 156-9.

41. Davis, Jerome, *Capitalism and its Culture*, New York, 1935, pp. 43–246, has a spirited discussion of banking, finance, stock manipulation, and concentration of economic control.

CHAPTER 9

1. Schriftgiesser, Karl, *This Was Normalcy, An Account of Party Politics during Twelve Republican Years,* 1920–1932, Boston, 1948, p. 264.

2. Hoover, *State Papers,* I, p. 191; id., *Memoirs,* II, p. 75.

3. Fisher, Irving, *The Stock Market Crash—And After,* New York, 1930, p. 239.

4. Myers, William Starr and Newton, Walter, H., *The Hoover Administration, A Documented Narrative,* New York, 1936, p. 24.

5. Leonard, Jonathan, *Three Years Down,* New York, 1939, p. 91.

6. Hoover, *State Papers,* I, pp. 134–7; Wilbur, Ray Lyman and Hyde, Arthur Mastick, *The Hoover Policies,* New York, 1937, pp. 129–31; Myers and Newton, op. cit. p. 26; Soule, George, *The Coming American Revolution,* New York, 1934, pp. 161–4; Lamont, Robert P., 'The White House Conferences,' *Journal of Business,* July 1930, pp. 269–71; Cover, John H., 'Our Synthetic Prosperity,' ibid. pp. 317–33; Flynn, John T., 'The Evil Influence of Wall Street,' *Behold America!* ed. by Samuel D. Schmalhausen, New York, 1931, pp. 200–201.

7. Quoted by Crowther, Samuel, *The Presidency vs. Hoover,* New York, 1928, p. 66.

8. Sullivan, Mark, 'The Case for the Administration,' *Fortune,* July 1932, p. 35; Foster, William Z., *From Bryan to Stalin,* New York [?], 1937, p. 222.

9. Myers and Newton, op. cit. pp. 26–8; Hoover, *Memoirs,* III, pp. 42–6; id., *State Papers,* I, pp. 137, 201; *Commercial & Financial Chronicle,* 23 November 1929, pp. 3262–4, has a good summary of these conferences. See also Knappen, Theodore M., 'Business Rallies to the Standard of Prosperity,' *Magazine of Wall Street,* 14 December 1929, pp. 263ff.

10. Myers and Newton, op. cit. pp. 28–31; Fisher, op. cit. pp. 21–4.

11. *Time,* 27 February 1933, p. 9.

12. Galbraith, John Kenneth, *The Great Crash* 1929, Cambridge, 1955, pp. 144–6. For an opposite view, see Brown, Ashmore, 'The Real Hoover,' *Forum,* November 1930, pp. 289–93.

13. *Commercial & Financial Chronicle,* 23 November 1929, p. 3208.

14. 'Cycles of Human Experience,' *Magazine of Wall Street,* 30 November 1929, p. 181.

15. *Commercial & Financial Chronicle,* 30 November 1929, p. 3361. By permission of Herbert D. Seibert, editor and publisher.

16. Fisher, op. cit. pp. 14–18.

17. *Magazine of Wall Street,* 14 December 1929, p. 261.

18. *Commercial & Financial Chronicle,* 23 November 1929, p. 3257, quoting *New York Evening World,* 19 November 1929.

19. *Commercial & Financial Chronicle,* 7 December 1929, p. 3511.

20. *Congressional Record,* 71 Cong. 2 Sess., 72:24–8; Hoover, *State Papers,* I, pp. 146, 214–5; Myers and Newton, op. cit. pp. 34–5.

21. *New York Times,* 8 March 1930; Fisher, op. cit. p. 238. There actually was a Treasury surplus of $184 million on 30 June 1930.

22. Myers and Newton, op. cit. pp. 35–42. For a summary of notable miscalculations, see Angly, Edward, 'Prophets Not Without Honor,' *Forum,* May 1931, pp. 272–7.

23. *Congressional Record,* 71 Cong. 2 Sess., 28 April 1930, 72:7796.

24. Senate Committee on Commerce, *Unemployment in the United States,* Hearings on S. 3059 etc., Washington, 1930, pp. 23, 37–72, 104–7. S. 3061, to provide for better statistical reporting, was signed on 7 July 1930.

25. Hoover, *State Papers,* I, p. 268; *Congressional Digest,* IX, p. 244.

26. *Congressional Record,* 71 Cong. 2 Sess., 8 May 1930, 72:8640–41.

27. Ibid. 72:8639–40; Mazur, Paul M., *New Roads to Prosperity,* New York, 1931, pp. 8–11.

28. *Congressional Record,* 71 Cong. 2 Sess., 8 May 1930, 72:8640–41.

29. Hoover, *State Papers,* I, pp. 375–84.

30. Seldes, Gilbert, *The Years of the Locust, America 1929–1932,* Boston, 1933, p. 74. By permission of the author. For early history of the game, see Davis, Elmer, 'Miniature Golf to the Rescue,' *Harper's Monthly Magazine,* December 1930, pp. 4–14.

31. See *Time,* 12 November 1928, p. 8.

32. McManus, Robert, 'Raskob,' *North American Review,* January 1931, pp. 10–17.

33. Kent, Frank R., 'Charley Michelson,' *Scribner's Magazine,* September 1930, p. 291; Michelson, Charles, *The Ghost Talks,* New York, 1944, p. 15; Hoover, *Memoirs,* III, pp. 219–20.

34. Lyons, Eugene, *Our Unknown Ex-President, A Portrait of Herbert Hoover,* New York, 1950, p. 250; Michelson, op. cit. p. 34; Joslin, Theodore G., *Hoover Off the Record,* New York, 1934, p. 35; Allen, Robert S., *Why Hoover Faces Defeat,* New York, 1932, p. 4; Barclay, Thomas S., 'The Publicity Division of the Democratic Party, 1929–30,' *American Political Science Review,* XXV (1931), pp. 68–72; McKee, Oliver Jr., 'Publicity Chiefs,' *North American Review,* October 1930, pp. 411–18.

35. Moley, Raymond, *27 Masters of Politics in a Personal Perspective,* New York, 1949, pp. 143ff; Michelson, op. cit. pp. 27–34.

36. Kent, Frank R., 'Charley Michelson,' loc. cit. p. 291; Hoover, *Memoirs,* III,

p. 220; *Time*, 8 September 1930, p. 14; [Allen, Robert S. and Pearson, Drew] *Washington Merry-Go-Round*, New York, 1931, pp. 53–5.

37. Allen, *Why Hoover Faces Defeat*, pp. 69–70; *Congressional Digest*, IX, p. 242.

38. Leonard, op. cit. pp. 139–40; Hoover, *Memoirs*, III, p. 195.

39. Lief, Alfred, *Democracy's Norris, the Biography of a Lonely Crusade*, New York, 1939, pp. 343–7; Pollard, Joseph Percival, 'Our Supreme Court Goes Liberal,' *Forum*, October 1931, pp. 193–9.

40. *Time*, 29 September 1930, p. 20 and 20 October 1930, p. 19.

41. Ibid. 13 October 1930, p. 14.

42. Freidel, Frank, *Franklin D. Roosevelt; The Triumph*, Boston, 1956, pp. 162–3.

43. Krock, Arthur, 'The Stakes of '32,' *American Mercury*, February 1931, p. 226.

44. Wolf, D. E., 'A Month's World History—The United States,' *Current History*, December 1930, pp. 432–4.

45. Hoover, *State Papers*, I, p. 468.

46. Ibid. I, p. 469; Krock, 'The Stakes of '32,' loc. cit. p. 230.

47. *Congressional Record*, 71 Cong. 3 Sess., 74:33; Hoover, *State Papers*, I, pp. 428–9. See also Senate Committee on Manufactures, *Establishment of National Economic Council*, Hearings on S. 6215, Washington, 1932, p. 8.

48. Leonard, op. cit. p. 150.

49. Wolman, Leo, 'Unemployment,' *Yale Review*, XX (December 1930), pp. 234–48; Wolf, D. E., 'A Month's World History—The United States,' *Current History*, February 1931, pp. 748–62.

50. *Congressional Record*, 71 Cong. 3 Sess., 16 December 1930, 74:872–8.

51. *New York Times*, 16 January, 4 and 5 February 1932.

52. Myers and Newton, op. cit. pp. 54–69; *Congressional Record*, 71 Cong. 3 Sess., 74:6099; Hoover, *State Papers*, I, pp. 512–7.

53. Krock, Arthur, 'President Hoover's Two Years,' *Current History*, July 1931, p. 494. By permission of the publisher.

54. Freidel, op. cit. p. 165 n. 44.

55. This view was supported by Paul M. Mazur, among others. Senate Committee on Manufactures, *Establishment of National Economic Council*, Hearings on S. 6215, Washington, 1932, p. 687.

CHAPTER 10

1. Wolf, D. E., 'A Month's World History—The United States,' *Current History*, May 1931, pp. 269–77.

2. Hoover, *State Papers*, I, pp. 558, 576, 577.

3. New York Stock Exchange, *Report of the President*, 1931–1932, New York, 1932, p. 2; Hansen, Alvin Harvey, *Economic Stabilization in an Unbalanced World*, New York, 1932, pp. 5–13; Nearing, Scott, *Must we Starve?* New York, 1932, pp. 35–42; Salter, Arthur, *Recovery, the Second Effort*, New York, 1932, pp. 49–63.

4. Myers, William Starr and Newton, Walter H., *The Hoover Administration, A Documented Narrative*, New York, 1936, p. 81; Hodson, H. V., *Slump and Recovery*, 1929–1937, London, 1938, pp. 64–6; Moulton, Harold G. and Pasvolsky, Leo, *War Debts and World Prosperity*, New York, 1932, pp. 301–20; Ostrolenk, Bernhard, 'World Finance, A Month's Survey,' *Current History*, July 1931, pp. xv–xvi.

5. Fay, Sidney B., 'Causes of the German Financial Crisis,' *Current History*, September 1931, pp. 801–5.

6. Wolf, D. E., 'The American-European Economic Conflict,' ibid. June 1931, pp. 428–31.

7. Hoover, Irwin Hood, *Forty-two Years in the White House*, New York, 1934, pp. 192–7; *Time*, 6 April 1931, p. 16, 13 April 1931, p. 12, 1 May 1931, p. 13.

8. Myers and Newton, op. cit. p. 82; Hoover, *Memoirs*, III, pp. 61ff; Stimson, Henry L. and Bundy, McGeorge, *On Active Service in Peace and War*, New York, 1947, pp. 204–5; Lippmann, Walter and Scroggs, W. O., *The United States in World Affairs*, 1931, New York, 1932, pp. 123–31.

9. Myers and Newton, op. cit. pp. 90–93; Hoover, *State Papers*, I, pp. 591–3; Gould, James Thayer, 'The Hoover Debt Settlement,' *Current History*, August 1931, pp. 641–5; Hoover, *Memoirs*, III, pp. 65–72; Stimson and Bundy, op. cit. p. 206; Tugwell, Rexford Guy, *Mr. Hoover's Economic Policy*, New York, 1932, p. 15; *Manufacturers Record*, 9 July 1931, pp. 22–3 and 16 July 1931, p. 15; Hansen, op. cit. pp. 27–43; Seldes, George, *Freedom of the Press*, Indianapolis, 1935, p. 151; Fay, Sidney B., 'Germany's Respite under Hoover Plan,' *Current History*, August 1931, pp. 901–5.

10. Hoover, *Memoirs*, III, pp. 72–8; Gerould, James Thayer, 'Seven-Power Financial Conference,' *Current History*, September 1931, pp. 901–5; Myers and Newton, op. cit. pp. 104–5; Hodson, op. cit. pp. 138–9.

11. Lombard, Helen, *Washington Waltz, Diplomatic People and Politics*, New York, 1941, p. 209; Johnson, Claudius O., *Borah of Idaho*, New York, 1936, pp. 445–6.

12. Hoover, *State Papers*, I, pp. 81–2.

13. Joslin, T. G., *Hoover Off the Record*, New York, 1934, pp. 146–7; Moulton and Pasvolsky, op. cit. pp. 345–8.

14. Hodson, op. cit. p. 139; Hoover, *State Papers*, II, p. 20. There was much less interest in the visit of Dino Grandi, Italy's foreign minister, from 16–19 November. *New York Times*, 17 and 19 November 1931.

15. *Congressional Record,* 72 Cong. 1 Sess., 9 December 1931, 75:213–14.

16. Ibid. 14 December 1931, 75:483–4, 18 December 1931, 75:794.

17. 'Basle Report on German Finances,' *Current History,* February 1932, pp. 701–8; *New York Times,* 25 December 1931.

18. Hodson, op. cit. p. 140.

19. Stimson and Bundy, op. cit. p. 219. For support of Hoover's position, see Auld, George P., 'Reparations,' *Atlantic Monthly,* May 1929, pp. 665–79. An excellent review is Williams, Benjamin H., 'Eleven Years of Reparations,' *Current History,* June 1932, pp. 291–7. Also see Gerould, James Thayer, 'The End of Reparations,' ibid. August 1932, pp. 573–9.

20. *Time,* 19 December 1932, p. 14 and 26 December 1932, p. 5; *New York Times,* 16 December 1932.

21. Madden, John T., Nadler, Marcus, and Sauvain, Harry C., *America's Experience as a Creditor Nation,* New York, 1937, pp. 105-19, 123, 133; Hodson, op. cit. pp. 110–11.

22. Hoover, *Memoirs,* III, pp. 81–3; House Committee on Banking and Currency, *Reconstruction Finance Corporation,* Hearings, Washington, 1932, p. 18.

23. Ibid. pp. 84–8; Hoover, *State Papers,* I, p. 275 and II, pp. 4–7; Myers and Newton, op. cit. pp. 118, 126–9; James, F. Cyril, *The Growth of the Chicago Banks,* 2 vols., New York, 1938, II, p. 1026; Joslin, op. cit. pp. 133–4; Sullivan, Mark, 'Storm Over Washington,' *Saturday Evening Post,* 1 April 1933.

24. Morse, Robert W., 'President Hoover's Plan to Check the Depression,' *Current History,* November 1932, pp. 263-4; Brown, E. Francis, 'American Problems before Congress,' ibid. December 1931, pp. 427–34; *Time,* 8 February 1932, p. 10; *New York Times,* 9–18 October 1931, adequately covers formation of National Credit Corporation units. For banker attitudes, see *Proceedings* of the Twentieth Annual Convention of the Investment Bankers Association of America, Chicago, 1931, pp. 194–203.

25. *Time,* 9 November 1931, p. 57.

26. Ibid. p. 17.

27. Wehle, Louis B., *Hidden Threads of History, Wilson through Roosevelt,* New York, 1952, pp. 71–7; Hoover, I. H. *Forty-two Years in the White House,* p. 214; James, op. cit. II, p. 1026; Hoover, *State Papers,* II, p. 6. House Committee on Banking and Currency, *Reconstruction Finance Corporation,* Hearings, Washington, 1932, pp. 13–18.

28. Ibid. p. 68. This call for a great federal agency pleased Adolph J. Sabath, Illinois Democrat, who had been trying to revive a modified War Finance Corporation for more than a year against the opposition of Hoover, Meyer, and Mills.

29. Jones, Jesse H., with Angly, Edward, *Fifty Billion Dollars, My Thirteen Years with the RFC 1932–1945,* New York, 1951, p. ix; Hoover, *Memoirs,*

III, p. 108; Kies, William S., 'Insuring Against Bank Failures,' *Review of Reviews*, February 1932, pp. 28–9; Knappen, Theodore M., 'The Irony of Big Business Seeking Government Management,' *The Magazine of Wall Street*, 23 January 1932, pp. 386ff; Timmons, Bascom N., *Jesse H. Jones, the Man and the Statesman*, New York, 1956, p. 163.

30. 47 U.S. Statutes 5–12; Jones and Angly, op. cit. p. 4.

31. *New York Times*, 19 October 1952.

32. *Congressional Record*, 72 Cong. 2 Sess., 22 December 1932, 76:871.

33. *Report of the Reconstruction Finance Corporation*, May 9, 1933, Washington, 1933, p. 22.

34. Timmons, op. cit. pp. 168–72; Hoover, *Memoirs*, III, p. 170 n. 2; James, op. cit. II, p. 1030. Hoover defended the Dawes loan in an excellent speech at St. Louis on 4 November 1932. Hoover, *State Papers*, II, pp. 442–6.

35. *Report of the Reconstruction Finance Corporation*, July 7, 1932, Washington, 1932, pp. 1–3.

36. *Congressional Record*, 72 Cong. 1 Sess., 11 July 1932, 75:15041; Hoover, *Memoirs*, II, p. 110.

37. *Report of the Reconstruction Finance Corporation*, May 9, 1933, pp. 1–21,

38. Ebersole, J. Franklin, 'One Year of the Reconstruction Finance Corporation,' *Quarterly Journal of Economics*, XLVII (May 1933), pp. 464–87.

CHAPTER 11

1. *New York Times*, 9, 11, 13 November 1931.

2. Ibid. 2 December 1931.

3. Committee on Agriculture and Forestry, *Agricultural Conference and Farm Board Inquiry*, Hearings on the Agricultural Situation, Washington, 1931, p. 2.

4. Ibid. p. 373; *New York Times*, 25 November 1931.

5. *New York Times*, 3 December 1931.

6. Senate Committee on Manufactures, *Establishment of National Economic Council*, Hearings on S. 6215 (71st Congress), Washington, 1932, pp. 695–6.

7. Ibid. p. 364.

8. *New York Times*, 6 November 1931.

9. Ibid. 8, 9, 17, 20 November 1931.

10. Ibid. 1, 2 December 1931; *Congressional Record*, 72 Cong. 1 Sess., 76:570–74.

11. Brown, E. Francis, 'Mr. Hoover Faces Nation's Problems,' *Current History*,

January 1932, p. 581; *Congressional Record*, 72 Cong. 1 Sess., 75:8; *New York Times*, 13, 23, 26 November 1931.

12. Hoover, *Memoirs*, III, p. 101.

13. *Congressional Record*, 72 Cong. 1 Sess., 75:67, 226–7; *Congressional Digest*, X, p. 290 and XI, p. 53.

14. Hoover, *Memoirs*, III, pp. 101–3; *Congressional Digest*, X, pp. 289–90.

15. *New York Times*, 29 November, 3, 5, December 1931; Senate Committee on Manufactures, *Unemployment in the United States*, Hearings, Washington, 1932, p. 187.

16. *New York Times*, 6, 7, 8, 17 January 1932.

17. Brown, E. Francis, 'Mr. Hoover Faces Nation's Problems,' loc. cit. pp. 525–31; Senate Committee on Manufactures, *Establishment of National Economic Council*, Washington, 1932, p. 114.

18. *Congressional Record*, 72 Cong. 1 Sess., 75:22–3; Hoover, *State Papers*, II, pp. 41–5.

19. *Congressional Record*, 72 Cong. 1 Sess., 75:24–6; Hoover, *Memoirs*, III, 97-100; id., *State Papers*, II, p. 47.

20. 'The Crisis Reaches Washington,' *Nation*, 20 January 1932, pp. 66–7. By permission of *The Nation*, publishers.

21. 'Flaws in the Hoover Economic Plan,' *Current History*, January 1932, pp. 525–31; *Business Week*, 16 March 1932, p. 36.

22. *Congressional Record*, 72 Cong. 1 Sess., 75:244–5.

23. Ibid. 75:673–4; *New York Times*, 18 December 1931.

24. Hoover, *Memoirs*, III, pp. 103–4.

25. Joslin, Theodore G., *Hoover Off the Record*, New York, 1934, p. 143; Hoover, *State Papers*, II, pp. 82-4; *Congressional Digest*, XI, p. 52; Myers, William Starr and Newton, Walter H., *The Hoover Administration, A Documented Narrative*, New York, 1936, pp. 160–61.

26. *New York Times*, 23, 25 December 1931.

27. Ibid. 13 January 1932.

28. Hoover, *State Papers*, II, pp. 102–4; *Congressional Record*, 72 Cong. 1 Sess., 75:1157–8.

29. [Allen, Robert S. and Pearson, Drew] *More Merry-Go-Round*, Washington, 1932, pp. 138–40; Lippmann, Walter, *Interpretations 1931–1932*, New York, 1932, pp. 74–8.

30. Quoted by Herring, E. Pendleton, 'First Session of the Seventy-second Congress, December 7, 1931, to July 16, 1932,' *American Political Science Review*, XXVI (1932), p. 859.

31. Lippmann, op. cit. pp. 105–6, 281.

32. *Congressional Record*, 72 Cong. 1 Sess., 75:24, 221–2.

33. Speech at Hotel Astor, 14 December 1931, ibid. 75:546.

34. Hoover, *Memoirs*, III, pp. 133, 136n; id., *State Papers*, II, p. 105.

35. *Congressional Record*, 72 Cong. 1 Sess., 5 January 1932, 75:1338 and 23 February 1932, 75:4515–16.

36. Brown, E. Francis, 'American Business Perplexities,' *Current History*, August 1931, pp. 748–54.

37. Senate Committee on Education and Labor, *Establishment of Administration of Public Works*, Hearings on S. 2419, Washington, 1932, p. 60.

38. 'The Soak-the-Rich Drive in Washington,' *Literary Digest*, 2 April 1932, pp. 8–9; Brown, E. Francis, 'Congress Wrestles with the Budget,' *Current History*, May 1932, pp. 205–13; *New York Times*, 17 November 1931.

39. *New York Times*, 26 January 1932.

40. Hoover, *State Papers*, II, pp. 165–6.

41. *New York Times*, 4 May 1932.

42. Hoover, *State Papers*, II, pp. 175–81; *Congressional Record*, 72 Cong. 1 Sess., 5 May 1932, 75:9640–41.

43. Among the 142 members of the National Economy Committee were Elihu Root, Jr., John W. Davis, and Alexander Sachs; the National Action Committee boasted such names as Richard Washburn Child, Herbert N. Straus, John Spargo, and Frank J. Loesch. *New York Times*, 5, 6, 7 May 1932. For congressional reactions, see *Congressional Record*, 72 Cong. 1 Sess., 6 May 1932, 75:9721ff.

44. Studenski, Paul and Krooss, Herman E., *Financial History of the United States*, New York, 1952, p. 364.

45. Hoover, *Memoirs*, III, p. 144; [Allen and Pearson] op. cit. pp. 141–2.

46. *Congressional Record*, 72 Cong. 1 Sess., 8 December 1931, 75:25; Hoover, *Memoirs*, III, pp. 121ff; Hazlitt, Henry, ed., *A Practical Program for America*, New York, 1932, pp. 77–92; Westerfield, Ray B., 'Defects in American Banking,' *Current History*, April 1931, pp. 17–23; Willis, H. Parker *et al.*, *Contemporary Banking*, New York, 1934, pp. 632, 636; Flynn, John T., 'Who But Hoover,' *New Republic*, 4 December 1935, p. 93.

47. *Congressional Record*, 72 Cong. 1 Sess., 9 December 1931, 75:233–6.

48. *Nineteenth Annual Report of the Federal Reserve Board Covering Operations for the Year 1932*, Washington, 1933, p. 18.

49. Ibid. p. 9; Hoover, *State Papers*, II, pp. 110–11, 137; Joslin, op. cit. p. 249; *New York Times*, 4, 7, 19 February 1932; Knappen, Theodore, 'Monsieur Laval Presents the Compliments of France,' *The Magazine of Wall Street*, 31 October 1931, p. 48. Rogers had just returned from Geneva and probably had serious matters to discuss with Hoover.

50. Edie, Lionel D., *The Banks and Prosperity*, New York, 1931, pp. 157–65; Sullivan, Lawrence, *Prelude to Panic, the Story of the Bank Holiday*, Washington, 1936, p. 3; Hoover, *Memoirs*, III, pp. 115–17; Hart, Albert Gailord, *Debts and Recovery*, New York, 1938, pp. 51–2.

51. 47 U.S. Statutes 56–57.

52. *Congressional Record*, 72 Cong. 1 Sess., 8 December 1931, 75:24; 47 U.S. Statutes 12–14; Hoover, *Memoirs*, III, p. 111.

53. 47 U.S. Statutes 60; Foulke, Roy A., *The Sinews of American Commerce*, New York, 1941, p. 251.

54. Hoover, *Memoirs*, III, p. 111. By permission of The Macmillan Company, publishers.

55. Ibid. III, pp. 88–94.

56. *Time*, 23 November 1931, pp. 14–15; Mazur, Paul M., *New Roads to Prosperity*, New York, 1931, pp. 115–28; Hoover, *State Papers*, II, pp. 31–4.

57. 47 U.S. Statutes 725.

58. 'Congress Plays its Part,' *Current History*, July 1932, p. 465.

CHAPTER 12

1. Tugwell, Rexford G., 'Farm Relief and a Permanent Agriculture,' *Annals* of the American Academy of Political and Social Science, CXLII (March 1929), p. 281; Saloutos, Theodore and Hicks, John D., *Agricultural Discontent in the Middle West 1900–1939*, Madison, 1951, pp. 290–91. For farm relief proposals, see Kile, Orville Merton, *The Farm Bureau through Three Decades*, Baltimore, 1948; Benedict, Murray R., *Farm Policies of the United States, 1790–1950*, New York, 1953; Gee, Wilson, *American Farm Policy*, New York, 1934; Baird, Freida and Benner, Claude L., *Ten Years of Federal Intermediate Credits*, Washington, 1933; Black, John D., 'The McNary-Haugen Movement,' *American Economic Review*, XVIII (September 1928), pp. 405–27; Fite, Gilbert C., *George N. Peek and the Fight for Farm Parity*, Norman, 1954; and Schmidt, Carl T., *American Farmers in the World Crisis*, New York, 1941. A convenient calendar of farm relief efforts 1918 to 1928 is in Black, John D., 'Progress of Farm Relief,' *American Economic Review*, XVIII (June 1928), pp. 262–5.

2. Shideler, James H., 'Herbert Hoover and the Federal Farm Board Project, 1921–1925,' *Mississippi Valley Historical Review*, XLII (March 1956), pp. 710–29.

3. *Congressional Record*, 71 Cong. 1 Sess., 16 April 1929, 71:42–3; Hoover, *State Papers*, I, pp. 31–5.

4. Hoover, Herbert, *The New Day, Campaign Speeches of Herbert Hoover*,

Stanford, 1928, p. 20; Spillman, W. J., 'Recent Trends Balancing Agriculture in the United States,' *Annals,* CXLII (March 1929), p. 215.

5. *Congressional Record,* 71 Cong. 1 Sess., 16 April 1929, 71:42–3; Hoover, *State Papers,* I, pp. 33–7; *Report of Business Men's Commission on Agriculture,* Washington, 1927.

6. For characteristic pronouncements, see Wilbur, Ray Lyman and Hyde, Arthur Mastick, *The Hoover Policies,* New York, 1937, pp. 43–7.

7. Seligman, Edwin R. A., *The Economics of Farm Relief, A Survey of the Agricultural Problem,* New York, 1929, p. 171; Wieting, C. Maurice, *The Progress of Cooperatives,* New York, 1952, Table 1, p. 11.

8. Hoover, *Memoirs,* II, p. 254; Myers, William Starr, *The Republican Party, A History,* New York, 1931, p. 502; Lief, Alfred, *Democracy's Norris, the Biography of a Lonely Crusade,* New York, 1939, pp. 328–9; Allen, Robert S., *Why Hoover Faces Defeat,* New York, 1932, p. 62.

9. Hoover to Charles L. McNary, 20 April 1929, Hoover, *State Papers,* I, pp. 39–42; Johnson, Claudius, *Borah of Idaho,* New York, 1936, pp. 434–6.

10. 46 U.S. Statutes 11–19; *First Annual Report of the Federal Farm Board,* Washington, 1930, p. 1.

11. Hoover, *Memoirs,* II, p. 255.

12. Hoover, *State Papers,* I, p. 75. Legge resigned on 6 March 1931 and James C. Stone succeeded him as chairman. *New York Times,* 7 March 1931.

13. *First Annual Report of the Federal Farm Board,* pp. 3–30; *Second Annual Report of the Federal Farm Board,* Washington, 1931, pp. 2–35; *Third Annual Report of the Federal Farm Board,* Washington, 1932, pp. 12–46; *Time,* 4 August 1930, pp. 16–17.

14. *Congressional Record,* 71 Cong. 1 Sess., 16 April 1929, 71:51; Pope, Jesse E., 'A Challenge to the Federal Farm Board,' *Atlantic Monthly,* March 1930, pp. 299–308; Cresswell, John C., 'Is Washington Helping or Hindering Business?' *The Magazine of Wall Street,* 22 March 1930, p. 842; Kile, op. cit. pp. 165–6.

15. Saloutos and Hicks, op. cit. pp. 302–3.

16. *New York Times,* 18 July and 2 August 1931.

17. *Third Annual Report of the Federal Farm Board,* pp. 62–73; *First Annual Report of the Farm Credit Administration,* 1933, Washington, 1934, pp. 56–7; Ostrolenk, Bernhard, 'Farmers Quitting Cut-Throat Competition,' *Current History,* August 1931, pp. 727–8.

18. *New York Times,* 5 August 1931.

19. Ibid. 13, 14 August 1931.

20. *Third Annual Report of the Federal Farm Board,* pp. 73–5; *First Annual Report of the Farm Credit Administration,* 1933, p. 57.

21. Hallgren, Mauritz A., *Seeds of Revolt: A Study of American Life and the Temper of the American People During the Depression,* New York, 1933, p. 143. By permission of Alfred A. Knopf, Inc., publishers.

22. Fite, op. cit. pp. 221–42; Schmidt, op. cit. pp. 116–19; *First Annual Report of the Farm Credit Administration,* 1933, Table 42, p. 130.

23. Senate Committee on Agriculture and Forestry, *Farm Relief,* Hearings on S. 123 etc., Washington, 1932, pp. 2–22.

24. Senate Committee on Agriculture and Forestry, *To Establish an Efficient Agricultural Credit System,* Hearings on S. 1197, Washington, 1932, p. 50.

25. Mills to McNary, 8 March 1932, Senate Committee on Agriculture and Forestry, *Farm Relief,* Hearings on S. 123 etc., p. 25.

26. Ibid. pp. 55–62.

27. Senate Committee on Agriculture and Forestry, *To Abolish the Federal Farm Board and Secure to the Farmer Cost of Production,* Hearings on S. 3133, Washington, 1932, p. 52.

28. 'A Dirt Farmer Speaks His Mind,' *Atlantic Monthly,* March 1930, p. 310. By permission of The Atlantic Monthly, publishers.

29. U.S. Department of Agriculture, *Yearbook of Agriculture,* 1931, Washington, 1931, p. 1.

30. Sears, Paul B., 'The Black Blizzards,' *America in Crisis: Fourteen Crucial Episodes in American History,* ed. by Daniel Aaron, New York, 1952, pp. 287–302.

31. *Yearbook of Agriculture,* 1931, pp. 7–9; *Yearbook of Agriculture,* 1932, Washington, 1932, pp. 11, 25.

32. Congressional Record, 71 Cong. 3 Sess., 31 January 1931, 74:3696–9.

33. Ibid. 1 December 1930, 74:7–13; *Yearbook of Agriculture,* 1931, pp. 5–6; Benedict, op. cit. p. 252; Hoover, *Memoirs,* III, pp. 51–2; id., *State Papers,* I, pp. 367–70; Sullivan, Mark, 'The Case for the Administration,' *Fortune,* July 1932, p. 37.

34. A Dirt Farmer's Wife, 'Drought Relief—A Worm's-Eye View,' *New Republic,* 1 October 1930, pp. 175–6.

35. *Congressional Record,* 71 Cong. 3 Sess., 1 December 1930, 74:7; Kellogg, Paul U., 'Drought and the Red Cross,' *Survey,* 15 February 1931, pp. 535–6.

36. *Congressional Record,* 71 Cong. 3 Sess., 9 December 1930, 74:407; *Congressional Digest,* x, p. 4; 46 U.S. Statutes 1032; Krock, Arthur, 'President Hoover's Two Years,' *Current History,* July 1931, p. 491.

37. Hoover to Payne, 10 January 1931, Hoover, *State Papers,* I, pp. 488–9.

38. Ibid. I, 489–94; Seldes, Gilbert, *The Years of the Locust,* Boston, 1933, pp. 95–9; Leonard, J. N., *Three Years Down,* New York, 1939, pp. 159–67; Schafer, A. L., 'When Hunger Followed Drought,' *Survey,* 1 March 1931, pp. 581ff.

39. *Yearbook of Agriculture,* 1932, pp. 26–9 and Table 1.

40. Ibid. p. 11; *Yearbook of Agriculture,* 1933, Washington, 1933, p. 4.

41.   U.S. Bureau of the Census, *Historical Statistics of the United States* 1789–1945, Washington, 1949, p. 233; Martin, Robert F., *Income in Agriculture,* 1929–1935, National Industrial Conference Board Studies No. 232, New York, 1936, pp. 20–21; Douglas, Paul H., *Controlling Depressions,* New York, 1935, p. 89.

42. Kansas State Board of Agriculture, *Twenty-Eighth Annual Report* . . . Topeka, 1933, table following p. 236.

43. Howland, Charles P., 'The Failure of Farm Board Stabilization,' *Yale Review,* xxi (March 1932), p. 503.

44. 'The Great Dirt Conspiracy,' *Forum,* August 1931, pp. 118–23.

45. Wilbur and Hyde, op. cit. p. 159.

46. Ibid. pp. 160-61. By permission of Charles Scribner's Sons, publishers.

47. See Nourse, E. G., 'Can the American Farm be Saved?' *A Practical Program for America,* ed. by Henry Hazlitt, New York, 1932, pp. 59–62; Nourse, E. G., 'What Can the Farm Board do Toward Production Control?' *Journal of Business,* October 1930, pp. 391–401; Ostrolenk, Bernhard, 'The Surplus Farmer,' *Atlantic Monthly,* April 1929, pp. 539–45; Davis, Joseph S., 'The Program of the Federal Farm Board,' *American Economic Review,* xxi (Supplement March 1931), pp. 104–13.

48. For arguments against irrigation expansion, see Peck, Millard, 'Reclamation Projects and their Relation to Agricultural Depression,' *Annals,* cxlii (March 1929), pp. 177–85; Willits, Frank P., 'The Futility of Further Development of Irrigation Projects,' ibid. pp. 186–95; Nourse, E. G., 'Can the American Farm be Saved?' loc. cit. pp. 64–5.

CHAPTER 13

1. Hoover, *Memoirs,* iii, p. 49. For a discussion of the labor force, see Soule, George Henry, *Economic Forces in American History,* New York, 1952, p. 349.

2. Senate Committee on Commerce, *Unemployment in the United States,* Hearings on S. 3059 etc., Washington, 1930, pp. 76, 80.

3. *Time,* 27 October 1930, pp. 17–18; Leonard, Jonathan, *Three Years Down,* New York, 1939, p. 143; *Nation,* 29 October 1930, p. 457.

4. *Time,* 3 November 1930, p. 19 and 17 November 1930, p. 15.

5. Hayes, E. P., *Activities of the President's Emergency Committee for Employment, October* 17, 1930—*August* 19, 1931, Concord, N. H., 1936, pp. 3, 27–8.

6. Ibid. pp. 29, 43, 140–41.

7. Wilbur, Ray Lyman and Hyde, Arthur Mastick, *The Hoover Policies*, New York, 1937, pp. 117, 120–21.

8. Hoover, *Memoirs*, ii, pp. 101, 102–4, 107.

9. Senate Committee on Commerce, *Unemployment in the United States*, Hearings on S. 3059 etc., *passim*; id., *National and State Employment Service*, Hearings, Washington, 1932, *passim*; *Congressional Record*, 71 Cong. 3 Sess., 17 February 1931, 74:5240 and 22 February 1931, 74:9400; House Report No. 2033, 71 Cong. 2 Sess., 26 June 1930; Gard, Wayne, 'The Problem of Employment Agencies,' *Current History*, May 1931, pp. 234–7; Krock, Arthur H., 'President Hoover's Two Years,' ibid. July 1931, p. 490.

10. Lief, Alfred, *Democracy's Norris, the Biography of a Lonely Crusade*, New York, 1939, pp. 335–6; 47 U.S. Statutes 70–73.

11. *Congressional Record*, 72 Cong. 1 Sess., 8 March 1932, 75:5465.

12. Ibid. 75:5471–9. See also Fainsod, Merle and Gordon, Lincoln, *Government and the American Economy*, New York, 1941, pp. 159–63; Lief, op. cit. pp. 385–7; Bussenden, P. F., 'The Campaign Against the Labor Injunction,' *American Economic Review*, xxiii (March 1933), pp. 42–54; 'Labor's Anti-Injunction Victory,' *Literary Digest*, 26 March 1932, p. 13; Gard, Wayne, 'The Injunctive Process in Labor Disputes,' *Current History*, March 1931, pp. 829–33.

13. Epstein, Abraham, 'Faith Cures for Unemployment,' *American Mercury*, January 1931, pp. 94–103.

14. *Congressional Record*, 71 Cong. 3 Sess., 74:33; Hoover, *State Papers*, i, 496–9.

15. Wilson, Edmund, *The American Jitters, A Year of the Slump*, New York, 1932. By permission of the author.

16. Leonard, op. cit. p. 155.

17. *Congressional Record*, 71 Cong. 3 Sess., 9 December 1930, 74:407; Hoover, *State Papers*, i, pp. 459–60. Professor Benjamin M. Squire, Chicago labor expert, testified that neither he nor any one else could say 'what the unemployment situation is in any State.' Senate Committee on Commerce, *Unemployment in the United States*, Hearings on S. 3059 etc., p. 15.

18. *Congressional Record*, 71 Cong. 3 Sess., 9 December 1930, 74:407–8.

19. Hopkins, Harry, *Spending to Save*, New York, 1936, pp. 38, 42; Hoover, *Memoirs*, iii, p. 53; Hayes, op. cit. p. 33.

20. Hoover, Herbert, *The Challenge to Liberty*, New York, 1934, p. 33; id., *State Papers*, i, pp. 500–505; id., *Memoirs*, iii, p. 60.

21. *New York Times*, 7, 12, 13 August 1931; Senate Committee on Manufactures, *Unemployment Relief*, Hearings, Washington, 1932, p. 327.

22. Hoover, *State Papers*, i, pp. 609–10; Hallgren, Mauritz A., *Seeds of Revolt*, New York, 1933, pp. 38–9.

23. Senate Committee on Manufactures, *Unemployment Relief*, Hearings, p. 312.

24. Hopkins, op. cit. pp. 43–6; Hoover, *Memoirs*, III, pp. 150–51; Myers, William Starr and Newton, Walter H., *The Hoover Administration, A Documented Narrative*, New York, 1936, pp. 112–13; Bookman, C. M., 'The Social Consequences and Treatment of Unemployment,' *Proceedings of the National Conference of Social Work* 1932, Chicago, 1933, p. 11.

25. Pinchot, Gifford, 'The Case for Federal Relief,' *Survey*, 1 January 1932, pp. 347ff; Senate Committee on Manufactures, *Unemployment Relief*, Hearings, pp. 211–24.

26. *New York Times*, 16 August 1931; Rogers, Will, 'Bacon, Beans and Limousines,' *Survey*, 15 November 1931, pp. 185ff.

27. *Congressional Record*, 72 Cong. 1 Sess., 75:22–3.

28. Hoover, *State Papers*, II, p. 101; *New York Times*, 4, 5 January 1932; Lyons, Eugene, *Our Unknown Ex-President, A Portrait of Herbert Hoover*, New York, 1950, p. 281; Myers and Newton, op. cit. p. 113; Hallgren, op. cit. pp. 3–12; Davis, Maxine, *They Shall Not Want*, New York, 1937, pp. 16–26; Brown, E. Francis, 'The Unemployment Crisis,' *Current History*, July 1932, pp. 411–16; Senate Committee on Manufactures, *Unemployment Relief*, Hearings, pp. 36–7.

29. Calkins, Clinch, *Some Folks Wont Work*, New York, 1930, pp. 7–22; Howard, Donald S., *The WPA and Federal Relief Policy*, New York, 1943, pp. 44–7; *Fortune*, October 1937, p. 106.

30. [Carter, John Franklin] *American Messiahs*, New York, 1935, pp. 135–9; Raine, William MacLeod, 'Costigan of Colorado,' *Nation*, 29 October 1930, pp. 465–6.

31. Silver, Abba Hillel, 'The Crisis in Social Work,' *Proceedings of the National Conference of Social Work* 1932, pp. 53–64; Bookman, op. cit. p. 6.

32. Senate Committee on Manufactures, *Unemployment Relief*, Hearings, p. 13.

33. Ibid. pp. 28–33.

34. Ibid. p. 49.

35. Ibid. pp. 54–5.

36. Ibid. p. 65.

37. Ibid. p. 313.

38. Ibid. p. 340.

39. House Committee on Labor, *Unemployment in the United States*, Hearings on H.R. 206 etc., Washington, 1932, p. 41.

40. Ibid. pp. 49–50.

41. Ibid. p. 103.

42. Ibid. p. 114.

43. Ibid. p. 131.

44. Ibid. p. 150.

45. Ibid. p. 175.

46. Ibid. p. 122.

47. *Congressional Record*, 72 Cong. 1 Sess., 16 February 1932, 75:4044, 4052.

48. Thomas, Norman, *As I see It*, New York, p. 11.

49. Burns, Arthur E. and Williams, Edward A., *Federal Work, Security, and Relief Programs*, Federal Works Agency, Work Projects Administration, Research Monograph xxiv, Washington, 1941, p. 18; 'Relief Enters the Third Stage and Moves Toward A Crisis,' *Business Week*, 29 April 1932, pp. 14–16; *Christian Century*, 6 July 1932, p. 853.

50. House Committee on Ways and Means, *National Emergency Relief*, Hearings on H. R. 12353, Washington, 1932, p. 34.

51. *Congressional Record*, 72 Cong. 1 Sess., 31 May 1932, 75:11982; *New York Times*, 13 May 1932.

52. House Committee on Ways and Means, *National Emergency Relief*, Hearings, pp. 152ff.

53. Ibid. pp. 262–3; Hoover, *Memoirs*, iii, p. 108.

54. Senate Committee on Banking and Currency, *Unemployment Relief*, Hearings on S. 4632 etc., p. 15; *Congressional Record*, 72 Cong. 1 Sess., 9 July 1932, 75:14957.

55. 47 U.S. Statutes 709–24. Other provisions included R.F.C. loans to finance the marketing of surplus agricultural commodities abroad, Farm Board cotton excepted; loans to start Regional Agricultural Credit Corporations; and loans to aid agricultural marketing co-operatives.

56. *New York Times*, 1 August 1932; Brown, E. Francis, 'The Presidential Campaign,' *Current History*, November 1932, p. 204.

57. Brown, Josephine C., *Public Relief*, 1929–1939, New York, 1940, p. 429.

CHAPTER 14

1. Dabney, Virginius, *Dry Messiah, the Life of Bishop Cannon*, New York, 1949, pp. 133–4; Merz, Charles, *The Dry Decade*, New York, 1931, pp. 5–10; Odegard, Peter, *Pressure Politics*, New York, 1928, tells the League story in Chapter 1.

2. Tucker, Ray T., 'Prophets of Prohibition,' *North American Review*, August 1930, pp. 129–36.

3. [Allen, Robert S. and Pearson, Drew] *Washington Merry-Go-Round*, New York, 1931, pp. 24, 34.

4. Lusk, Rufus S., 'The Drinking Habit,' *Annals* of the American Academy of Political and Social Science, September 1932, p. 46; Sanford, E. P., 'The Unholy Union of Prohibition and Politics,' *Current History*, October, 1929, pp. 58–63; Anderson, Walter, 'The Speakeasy as a National Institution,' ibid. July 1932, pp. 417–22.

5. *Congressional Record*, 71 Cong. 1 Sess., 8 October 1929, 71:4366; Warburton, Clark, 'Prohibition and Economic Welfare,' *Annals*, September 1932, pp. 89, 93, 95–7; Kirkpatrick, E. L. and Tough, Evelyn G., 'Prohibition and Agriculture,' ibid. pp. 113–9; *Commercial & Financial Chronicle*, 2 April 1932, p. 2388.

6. *Time*, 10 February 1930, p. 15.

7. *Congressional Record*, 71 Cong. 1 Sess., 4 March 1929, 71:5; Hoover, *State Papers*, I, pp. 5–6.

8. See speech by Carter Glass, *Congressional Record*, 71 Cong. 1 Sess., 19 June 1929, 71:3097.

9. Hoover, *State Papers*, II, pp. 261–3.

10. *Nation*, 4 May 1932, p. 502.

11. *Bishop Cannon's Own Story*, ed. by Richard J. Watson, Jr., New York, 1954, pp. 383–90.

12. *Congressional Record*, 71 Cong. 1 Sess., 19 June 1929, 71:3100–101; Hoover, *State Papers*, I, p. 63.

13. Pusey, Merlo J., *Charles Evans Hughes*, 2 vols. New York, 1951, II, p. 649; Dabney, op. cit. p. 191.

14. Scott, William Rufus, *Revolt on Mount Sinai, the Puritan Retreat from Prohibition*, Pasadena, 1944, p. 49; Hoover, *State Papers*, I, pp. 67–8, 164; *Congressional Record*, 71 Cong. 2 Sess., 72:2407.

15. The debate ran off and on from 6–10 January 1930. See particularly *Congressional Record*, 71 Cong. 2 Sess., 72:1136, 1190–91, 1275–6, 1377–8, 1383. Facts are summarized in the *Annual Report of the Attorney General of the United States* for each of the fiscal years 1930 to 1933, and in United States Treasury Department, *Statistics Concerning Intoxicating Liquor*, Washington, December 1933, Table 89, pp. 95–6.

16. *Congressional Record*, 71 Cong. 2 Sess., 72:1668.

17. Ibid. 6 February 1930, 72:3129–32.

18. Ibid. 1 April 1930, 72:6269–90.

19. For an enthralling survey of Prohibition gangsterism in Illinois, see *Enforcement of the Prohibition Laws*, Official Records of the National Commission on Law Observance and Enforcement, 5 vols. Washington, 1931, IV, pp. 205–419. See also Johnson, Gardner, 'Wickersham and His Commission,' *Nation*, 21 January 1931, pp. 63–4; Davis, Elmer, 'Founding Fathers and Straddling Sons,' *Harper's Monthly Magazine*, September 1930, pp. 385–8;

McBain, Howard Lee, 'Hurdles for the Hoover Commission,' *American Mercury,* February 1930, pp. 181–8.

20. National Commission on Law Observance and Enforcement, *Report on the Enforcement of the Prohibition Laws of the United States,* Washington, 1931, pp. iii–iv. Hereafter cited as *Wickersham Report.*

21. Ibid. pp. 83, 115–62; Gebhart, John C., 'Movement Against Prohibition,' *Annals,* September 1932, p. 175; Scott, op. cit. pp. 70–73; *Time,* 26 January 1931, p. 11; *Nation,* 4 February 1931, p. 116; Franklin, Fabian, 'The Onward March of Repeal,' *Forum,* May 1931, pp. 307–10; Wolf, D. E., 'A Month's World History—the United States,' *Current History,* March 1931, pp. 911–15.

22. *Congressional Record,* 71 Cong. 3 Sess., 22 January 1931, 74:2889–91, 2976.

23. Ibid. 31 January 1931, 74:3693–6.

24. Ibid. 23 January 1931, 74:2966–71 and 26 January 1931, 74:3158–60.

25. Ibid. 74:4107 *et seq.*

26. Scott, op. cit. pp. 66–7; *Time,* 27 April 1931, p. 18; [Allen, Robert S. and Pearson, Drew] *More Merry-Go-Round,* New York, 1932, pp. 299–319.

27. *Congressional Record,* 72 Cong. 1 Sess., 18 December 1931, 75:772–6; *New York Times,* 5 February 1932.

28. *Congressional Record,* 18 March 1932, 75:6456–8; Hoover's address at Washington, D.C., 19 January 1932, ibid. 75:4780–81.

29. See speech by Senator Robert F. Wagner at Buffalo, 20 May 1932, *Congressional Record,* 72 Cong. 1 Sess., 8 June 1932, 75:12288; ibid. 16 July 1932, 75:15655.

30. *Congressional Record,* 72 Cong. 1 Sess., 15 January 1932, 75:2095, 14 March 1932, 75:6004, 8 June 1932, 75:12282.

31. *Nation,* 4 May 1932, p. 502.

32. *Congressional Record,* 72 Cong. 1 Sess., 28 June 1932, 75:14119.

33. Ibid. 18 June 1932, 75:13333–4.

34. Ibid. 29 June 1932, 75:14325.

35. Ibid. 14 July 1932, 75:15350.

36. Ibid. 13 July 1932, 75:15184 and 16 July 1932, 75:15652.

37. Senate Report 1022, 72 Cong. 2 Sess., 6 January 1933, *passim;* Congressional Record, 72 Cong. 2 Sess., 76:1621–2.

38. Ibid. 14 February 1933, 76:4004–5, 15 February 1933, 76:4141–81, and 20 February 1933, 76:4508–16.

1. *Nation,* 9 December 1931, p. 626; *Time,* 7 December 1931, p. 9 and 14 December 1931, p. 15; 'The Progress of the World,' *Review of Reviews,* January 1932, p. 17; *New York Times,* 6–8 January 1932; Seldes, Gilbert, *The Years of the Locust,* Boston, 1933, pp. 176–7; [Allen, Robert S. and Pearson, Drew] *More Merry-Go-Round,* New York, 1932, pp. 15–16; White, William Allen, 'Herbert Hoover—the Last of the Old Presidents or the First of the New?' *Saturday Evening Post,* 4 March 1933, p. 54.

2. Mayo, Katherine, *Soldiers, What Next!* Boston, 1934, pp. 42–50, 72–83; Burlingame, Roger, *Peace Veterans, the Story of a Racket and a Plea for Economy,* New York, 1932, pp. 12–15, 18–24, 32–8; McManus, Robert Cruise, 'Billions for Veterans,' *Current History,* August 1932, pp. 557–62; House Report 1252, 72 Cong. 1 Sess., 7 May 1932, p. 1.

3. *Congressional Record,* 71 Cong. 3 Sess., 3 December 1930, 74:157–9; Seldes, op cit. p. 173.

4. *Congressional Record,* 71 Cong. 3 Sess., 26 February 1931, 74:6168–70; Hoover, *State Papers,* I, pp. 512–14; Sullivan, Lawrence, 'The Veteran Racket,' *Atlantic Monthly,* April 1933, pp. 393–402. As of 30 June 1932 there were 3,544,251 certificates in force with a face value of $3,514,284,141. National Industrial Conference Board, *The World War Veterans and the Federal Treasury,* Washington, 1932, p. 35.

5. Mayo, op. cit. pp. 156–8; Brogan, Denis W., *The Era of Franklin D. Roosevelt,* New Haven, 1950, p. 18; House Report 1252, p. 2.

6. Hoover, *State Papers,* I, pp. 618–20; id., *Memoirs,* II, pp. 285–90; Burlingame, op. cit. p. 39; Joslin, Theodore G., *Hoover Off the Record,* New York, 1934, p. 123.

7. *New York Times,* 9 April 1932.

8. See House Reports 1242 through 1261, 72 Cong. 1 Sess., 7 May 1932; *Literary Digest,* 23 April 1932, pp. 5–6; *Congressional Record,* 72 Cong. 1 Sess., 18 December 1931, 75:844–5 and 10 May 1932, 75:9967; Brown, E. Francis, 'Congress Wrestles with the Budget,' *Current History,* May 1932, p. 208.

9. *New York Times,* 20 May 1932.

10. Waters, Walter W. with White, William C., *B. E. F., the Whole Story of the Bonus Army,* New York, 1933, pp. 1–13.

11. Ibid. p. 20.

12. Leonard, Jonathan, *Three Years Down,* New York, 1939, pp. 243–4; Waters, op. cit. pp. 39–64; Springer, Fleta Campbell, 'Glassford and the Siege of Washington,' *Harper's Monthly Magazine,* November 1932, pp. 643–4; Report of the Attorney General, 9 September 1932, Hoover, *State Papers,* II, p. 275; *New York Times,* 23 and 30 May 1932.

13. Gitlow, Benjamin, *The Whole of Their Lives*, New York, 1948, p. 228; Browder, Earl, *Communism in the United States*, New York, 1935, p. 43; Magil, A. B. and Stevens, Henry, *The Peril of Fascism, the Crisis of American Democracy*, New York, 1938, pp. 248–9.

14. Spolansky, Jacob, *The Communist Trail in America*, New York, 1951, p. 51; Seldes, op. cit. p. 183; *Congressional Record*, 81 Cong. 1 Sess., 31 August 1949, 95:12529–31; Gitlow, op. cit. p. 228; Joslin, op. cit. p. 264; *Time*, 18 July 1932, p. 11; Springer, 'Glassford and the Siege of Washington,' loc. cit. p. 647; Hinshaw, David, *Herbert Hoover, American Quaker*, New York, 1950, p. 214; *Literary Digest*, 11 June 1932, pp. 8–9 and 25 June 1932, p. 28.

15. Waters, op. cit. p. 127; *Congressional Record*, 72 Cong. 1 Sess., 13 June 1932, 75:12854; *New York Times*, 31 May 1932.

16. For the debate, see *Congressional Record*, 72 Cong. 1 Sess., 14 June 1932, 75:12914ff.

17. Ibid. 17 June 1932, 75:13274.

18. Waters, op. cit. pp. 145–53; *New York Times*, 17–18 June 1932; Seldes, op. cit. p. 186; Hallgren, Mauritz A., 'The Bonus Army Scares Mr. Hoover,' *Nation*, 27 July 1932, p. 71; *Congressional Record*, 72 Cong. 1 Sess., 17 June 1932, 75:13275–7.

19. 47 U.S. Statutes 654, 701.

20. Hoover, *Memoirs*, III, p. 226; Springer, 'Glassford and the Siege of Washington,' loc. cit. p. 648; *Time*, 11 July 1932, p. 21; Waters, op. cit. p. 162; *Annual Report of the Administrator of Veterans' Affairs . . . 1932*, Washington, 1932, pp. 7–8.

21. Waters, op. cit. pp. 164–79; Springer, 'Glassford and the Siege of Washington,' loc. cit. p. 651n.

22. Joslin, op. cit. pp. 267–9; Hoover, *State Papers*, II, pp. 242–3; Waters, op. cit. pp. 181–206.

23. *Time*, 8 August 1932, p. 5; Waters, op. cit. pp. 211–13.

24. Anderson, Paul Y., 'Tear-Gas, Bayonets, and Votes,' *Nation*, 17 August 1932, p. 139. By permission of *The Nation*, publishers.

25. *Time*, 8 August 1932, p. 6; *New York Times*, 29–30 July 1932 has a full coverage.

26. Gitlow, op. cit. pp. 228–9; Hoover, *Memoirs*, III, p. 231; Joslin, op. cit. p. 266.

27. Waters, op. cit. pp. 214–38; Seldes, op cit. pp. 190–91; MacArthur's report in Joslin, op. cit. p. 273; Brown, E. Francis, 'The Bonus Army Marches to Defeat,' *Current History*, September 1932, pp. 684–8.

28. *Congressional Record*, 81 Cong. 1 Sess., 31 August 1949, 95:12531; Gitlow, op. cit. p. 230; Spolansky, op. cit. p. 51.

29. Waters, op. cit. pp. 239–55; *Time*, 15 August 1932, pp. 9–10; *New Statesman and Nation*, 15 October 1932, p. 438. For reports from Johnstown's Camp McClosky, see Senate Committee on Manufactures, *Relief for Unemployment, Hearings*, 72 Cong. 2 Sess., Washington, 1933, pp. 91–104.

30. Allen, Frederick Lewis, *Since Yesterday*, New York, 1940, pp. 83–6; Allen, Robert S., 'The Man Roosevelt,' *American Mercury*, January 1933, p. 19; *Time*, 15 August 1932, p. 10; *Nation*, 14 September 1932, p. 231.

31. Hallgren, 'The Bonus Army Scares Mr. Hoover,' loc. cit. pp. 71–2.

32. 'Tear-Gas, Bayonets, and Votes,' loc. cit. p. 138. See also Mencken, Henry L., 'Commentary,' *American Mercury*, November 1932, p. 382.

CHAPTER 16

1. *Congressional Record*, 72 Cong. 1 Sess., 6 December 1932, 76:51–2.

2. *Stock Exchange Practices*, Senate Report 1455, 73 Cong. 2 Sess., Washington, 1934, p. 7; Brown, E. Francis, 'Reviving American Confidence,' *Current History*, October 1932, pp. 78–85.

3. *National Income, 1929–32*, Senate Document 124, 72 Cong. 2 Sess., Washington, 1934, pp. 10–14; *Nineteenth Annual Report of the Federal Reserve Board . . . 1932*, Washington, 1933, pp. 2–5; *Commercial & Financial Chronicle*, 21 January 1933, pp. 381–99; Slichter, Sumner H., 'Employment Conditions,' *American Year Book . . . 1932*, New York, 1933, pp. 572–3; *Nation*, 17 August 1932, p. 133, 21 September 1932, p. 245, 26 October 1932, p. 385; Douglas, Paul H., *Controlling Depressions*, New York, 1935, p. 31.

4. Deck, J. F., 'The Match Stick Colossus,' *Foreign Affairs*, IX (October 1930), pp. 149–56; Hansl, Proctor W., *Years of Plunder*, New York, 1934, 258–70; *Time*, 21 March 1932, pp. 15, 45–9; *Commercial & Financial Chronicle*, 28 January 1932, pp. 586–8; 'The Passing of Ivar Kreuger,' *Literary Digest*, 26 March 1932, pp. 56–7; Wuorinen, John H., 'Ivar Kreuger's Tragic End,' *Current History*, April 1932, pp. 120–23; id., 'Kreuger's Vanished Millions,' ibid. May 1932, pp. 241–2; Thompson, Ralph, 'The Unfolding of the Kreuger Scandal,' ibid. June 1932, pp. 361–2; *New York Times*, 28 January 1932.

5. Anderson, Sherwood, 'Listen, Mr. President——,' *Nation*, 31 August 1932, pp. 191–3.

6. *Nation*, 6 January 1932, p. 2.

7. Ibid. 14 December 1932, p. 579 and 21 September 1932, p. 243.

8. Hutchinson, Paul, 'Hunger on the March,' *Christian Century*, 9 November 1932, pp. 1377–8.

9. *Nation*, 9 November 1932, p. 441, 3 August 1932, p. 96, 23 November 1932, p. 488, and 30 November 1932, pp. 521–2.

10. *New York Times*, 5–6 December 1932; Cowley, Malcolm, 'Red Day in Washington,' *New Republic*, 21 December 1932, pp. 153–5.

11. *Commercial & Financial Chronicle,* 7 January 1933, pp. 17–18. By permission of Herbert D. Seibert, Editor and Publisher.

12. Ibid. 21 January 1933, pp. 376–8.

13. Hyde, Arthur M., 'Conditions in Agriculture,' *American Year Book . . .1932,* pp. 398–400; McIntyre, E. R., 'Skimmed Milk and Watered Stocks,' *Nation,* 28 September 1932, pp. 281ff.

14. Nourse, Edwin G., Davis, Joseph S., and Black, John D., *Three Years of the Agricultural Adjustment Administration,* Washington, 1937, pp. 21–2.

15. [Carter, John Franklin] *American Messiahs,* New York, 1935, pp. 149–50; Allen, Frederick Lewis, *Since Yesterday,* New York, 1940, p. 86.

16. *Time,* 29 August 1932, p. 13.

17. Gard, Wayne, 'The Farmers' Rebellion,' *Nation,* 7 September 1932, pp. 207–8; White, William Allen, 'The Farmer Takes A Holiday,' *Saturday Evening Post,* 26 November 1932, pp. 6ff; Hallgren, Mauritz A., *Seeds of Revolt,* New York, 1933, pp. 150–54; *Time,* 28 August 1932, p. 13.

18. Bureau of Agricultural Statistics, *The Farm Debt Problem,* Washington, 1932, p. 2; *New York Times,* 21 January 1933.

19. Ostrolenk, Bernhard, 'Prosperity Waits Upon the Farmer,' *Current History,* November 1932, p. 129–34; Saloutos, Theodore and Hicks, John D., *Agricultural Discontent in the Middle West* 1900–1939, Madison, 1951, Ch. xv; Benedict, Murray R., *Farm Policies of the United States,* 1790–1950, New York, 1953, p. 247.

20. White, 'The Farmer Takes A Holiday,' loc. cit. p. 70.

21. *Christian Century,* 7 September 1932, p. 1069. By permission of *The Christian Century.*

22. Hard, William, 'Ingots and Doles,' *Survey,* 1 February 1932, pp. 453ff; *Monthly Labor Review,* January 1932, pp. 27–8 and February 1931, p. 72.

23. 'Industrial Relations and Hard Times,' *Current History,* August 1931, p. 722; Brown, J. Douglas, 'The Manufacturers and the Unemployed,' ibid. July 1931, pp. 517–20; *Monthly Labor Review,* October 1932, pp. 790–91.

24. *Monthly Labor Review,* May 1933, pp. 1015–21.

25. 'Cooperative Self-Help Activities Among the Unemployed,' ibid. March 1933, pp. 451–60.

26. Ibid. pp. 461–70.

27. Ibid. pp. 473–93.

28. 'Gardens for Unemployed Workers,' ibid. September 1932, pp. 495–7, 500–502. The entire self-help movement is surveyed in 'Cooperative Self-Help Activities Among the Unemployed—General Summary,' ibid. June 1933, pp. 1229–40. See also 'Thrift Gardens Relieve Relief,' *Business Week,* 18 May 1932, pp. 13–14.

29. *Twentieth Annual Report of the Chief of the Children's Bureau* . . . 1932, Washington, 1932, p. 7.

30. Senate Committee on Manufactures, *Relief for Unemployed Transients,* Hearings on S. 5121, Washington, 1933, pp. 111–12.

31. 'Survey of Transient Boys in the United States,' *Monthly Labor Review,* January 1933, pp. 91–3; Lovejoy, Owen R., 'America's Wandering Boys,' *Current History,* February 1933, pp. 565–70.

32. Senate Committee on Manufactures, *Relief for Unemployed Transients,* Hearings on S. 5121, pp. 129–33.

CHAPTER 17

1. Gosnell, Harold F., *Champion Campaigner, Franklin D. Roosevelt,* New York, 1952, pp. 1–5. Good books on Roosevelt's career increase steadily. Outstanding among the one-volume studies are Burns, James M., *Roosevelt, the Lion and the Fox,* New York, 1956; Rosenman, Samuel I., *Working with Roosevelt,* New York, 1952; Gunther, John, *Roosevelt in Retrospect,* New York, 1950; Bellush, Bernard, *Franklin D. Roosevelt as Governor of New York,* New York, 1955. The first volume of Frank Freidel's splendid biography is unsurpassed for *Franklin D. Roosevelt; The Apprenticeship,* Boston, 1952. Arthur M. Schlesinger, Jr. has an interesting summary in *The Crisis of the Old Order,* 1919–1933, Boston, 1957, pp. 317–40.

2. Joslin, Theodore G., *Hoover Off the Record,* New York, 1934, pp. 167–8.

3. *New York Times,* 9, 10 January 1932.

4. Ibid. 12 January 1932.

5. Ibid. 26 April 1932 and 15 May 1932.

6. Ickes, Harold L., *The Autobiography of a Curmudgeon,* New York, 1943, p. 253.

7. Benedict, Charles, 'It's the Man—Not the Party,' *The Magazine of Wall Street,* 9 January 1932, p. 329.

8. 'A Reckoning—Twelve Years of Republican Rule,' *Yale Review,* xxx (June 1932), pp. 649–60; Holcombe, Arthur N., 'Trench Warfare,' *American Political Science Review,* xxv (1931), pp. 914–25.

9. Nevins, Allan, 'President Hoover's Record,' *Current History,* July 1932, pp. 385–94.

10. Anderson, Paul Y., 'Wanted: A Mussolini,' *Nation,* 6 July 1932, p. 9; Lippmann, Walter, *Interpretations,* 1931–1932, New York, 1932, pp. 287, 290–91; Catledge, Turner, 'The National Conventions of 1932,' *Current History,* August 1932, pp. 521–6.

11. Mencken, H. L., *Making A President,* New York, 1932, p. 45; *New Statesman*

and Nation, 9 July 1932, p. 31; *Congressional Record,* 71 Cong. 1 Sess., 28 June 1932, 75:14114.

12. *New York Times,* 16 June 1932; 'The Republican Case,' *Saturday Evening Post,* 10 September 1932, p. 3; Mencken, op. cit. p. 52.

13. Scott, William Rufus, *Revolt on Mount Sinai,* Pasadena, 1944, pp. 170–76; Stout, Richard Lee, 'Mr. Wickersham's Platform,' *North American Review,* September 1932, pp. 196–204.

14. *Time,* 27 June 1932; Peel, Roy V. and Donnelly, Thomas C., *The 1932 Campaign, An Analysis,* New York, 1935, pp. 82–90; Joslin, op. cit. pp. 244–6; Catledge, Turner, 'The National Conventions of 1932,' loc. cit. pp. 521–6.

15. Ickes, op. cit. pp. 261–5; Lief, Alfred, *Democracy's Norris, the Biography of a Lonely Crusade,* New York, 1939, pp. 393–404.

16. Peel and Donnelly, op. cit. pp. 92–3; Mencken, op. cit. pp. 113–14, 165, 171–2; Gosnell, op. cit. p. 118; Flynn, Edward J., *You're the Boss,* New York, 1947, p. 90; *Nation,* 6 July 1932, p. 1; *New York Times,* 28 June 1932; *Time,* 4 July 1932, p. 11. The best recent accounts of the convention are Freidel, Frank, *Franklin D. Roosevelt: The Triumph,* Boston, 1956, pp. 291–311; Burns, op. cit. pp. 123–38; and Schlesinger, op. cit. pp. 413–39.

17 .Hull, Cordell, *The Memoirs of Cordell Hull,* 2 vols., New York, 1948, 1, 141; *Time,* 11 July 1932, p. 8; Mencken, op. cit. pp. 161–2; Flynn, op. cit. pp. 104–5; Gunther, op. cit. pp. 270–71; Roper, Daniel C. and Lovette, Frank H., *Fifty Years of Public Life,* Durham, 1941, pp. 258–60.

18. Roosevelt, *Public Papers,* 1, p. 659. By permission of Random House, Inc., publishers.

19. Rosenman, op. cit. pp. 31–2; Freidel, *Franklin D. Roosevelt: The Triumph,* Chs. 2–15, covers Roosevelt's Albany career.

20. Gosnell, op. cit. p. 13.

21. Lindley, Ernest K., *The Roosevelt Revolution, First Phase,* New York, 1933, p. 7.

22. Joslin, op. cit. pp. 15–16, 300–301; Nye, Russel B., *Midwestern Progressive Politics, A Historical Study of Its Origins and Development, 1870–1950,* East Lansing, 1951, pp. 354–6; Brown, E. Francis, 'Roosevelt's Victorious Campaign,' *Current History,* December 1932, pp. 257–65.

23. White, William Allen, 'Herbert Hoover—the Last of the Old Presidents or the First of the New?' *Saturday Evening Post,* 4 March 1933, p. 55. By permission of The Curtis Publishing Company, publishers.

24. Hoover, *Memoirs,* III, p. 233; Stimson, Henry L. and Bundy, McGeorge, *On Active Service in Peace and War,* New York, 1947, pp. 283–5; Villard, Oswald Garrison, 'The Pot and the Kettle,' *Nation,* 7 September 1932, p. 206; Freidel, *Franklin D. Roosevelt: The Triumph,* pp. 364–6.

25. Peel and Donnelly, op. cit. pp. 113–8; *Congressional Digest,* XI, p. 195.

26. MacNeil, Neil, *Without Fear or Favor,* New York, 1940, p. 154.

27. Millis, Walter, 'Presidential Candidates,' *Yale Review,* xxii (September 1932), pp. 1–18.

28. Hoover, *Memoirs,* iii, p. 234.

29. Roosevelt, Eleanor, *This I Remember,* New York, 1949, pp. 72–3; Moley, Raymond, *After Seven Years,* New York, 1939, pp. 41–51; Perkins, Frances, *The Roosevelt I Knew,* New York, 1946, p. 113; Freidel, *Franklin D. Roosevelt: The Triumph,* pp. 356–7. Charles W. Taussig was a nephew of the well-known tariff expert and Harvard economist.

30. Brown, E. Francis, 'The Presidential Campaign,' *Current History,* November 1932, pp. 197–8; Moley, op. cit. p. 52.

31. Munro, William B., 'The Presidential Campaign Opens,' *Current History,* June 1932, pp. 257–64; 'Why This Political Apathy?' ibid. pp. 265–9.

32. Roosevelt, *Public Papers,* i, pp. 669–84. By far the best account of the campaign is Freidel, *Franklin D. Roosevelt: The Triumph,* pp. 312–71.

33. See speech at Cleveland, 15 October 1932, Hoover, *State Papers,* ii, pp. 337–58.

34. Roosevelt, *Public Papers,* i, p. 834.

35. Ibid. i, 651, 672, 750; Hoover, *Memoirs,* iii, p. 252; Hoover, Herbert and Coolidge, Calvin, *Campaign Speeches of 1932,* New York, 1933, pp. 188–9; Allen, Robert S., *Why Hoover Faces Defeat,* New York, 1932, pp. 3–4.

36. Hoover, *Memoirs,* iii, pp. 258–60; id., *State Papers,* ii, pp. 296–7; Hoover and Coolidge, op. cit. p. 14; Myers, William Starr and Newton, Walter H., *The Hoover Administration, A Documented Narrative,* New York, 1936, pp. 251–3.

37. Hoover, *Memoirs,* iii, pp. 311, 316.

38. Hoover, *State Papers,* ii, pp. 378–9.

39. Roosevelt, *Public Papers,* i, pp. 661–2, 760–61, 795–803.

40. Hoover and Coolidge, op. cit. p. 122; Hoover, *Memoirs,* iii, pp. 274–5.

41. Roosevelt, *Public Papers,* i, p. 761.

42. Hoover, *Memoirs,* iii, pp. 280–83; 'The Republicans Try Panic,' *Nation,* 26 October 1932, p. 386; Smith, Rixey and Beasley, Norman, *Carter Glass, A Biography,* New York, 1939, p. 485.

43. Roosevelt, *Public Papers,* i, pp. 763–9, 785, 835–6, 853; Hoover, *State Papers,* ii, p. 343; id., *Memoirs,* iii, p. 293; Hoover and Coolidge, op. cit. pp. 50–52; Myers and Newton, op. cit. pp. 255–6.

44. Hoover, *Memoirs,* iii, p. 302.

45. Moley, op. cit. pp. 44–5.

46. Roosevelt, *Public Papers*, I, p. 709. By permission of Random House, Inc., publishers.

47. Hoover and Coolidge, op. cit. pp. 29–63; Myers and Newton, op. cit. pp. 255–60.

48. Hoover, *Memoirs*, III, pp. 318–22.

49. Hoover, *State Papers*, II, p. 420.

50. Roosevelt, *Public Papers*, I, pp. 729–42; Gruening, Ernest, 'Power as a Campaign Issue,' *Current History*, October 1932, pp. 44–50.

51. Hoover, *Memoirs*, III, p. 329.

52. Wade, Robert E. Jr., 'Can Roosevelt Carry California?' *Nation*, 19 October 1932, p. 350.

53. Roosevelt, *Public Papers*, I, pp. 742–56, 785–6.

54. Hoover, *Memoirs*, III, p. 335.

55. Ibid. III, pp. 338–9; Hoover, *State Papers*, II, p. 408–28.

56. Hoover, *Memoirs*, III, p. 343.

57. *Nation*, 9 November 1932, p. 456. By permission of *The Nation*, publishers.

58. Robinson, Edgar Eugene, *They Voted for Roosevelt, the Presidential Vote, 1932–1944*, Stanford, 1947, p. 183; Peel and Donnelly, op. cit. pp. 230–31.

CHAPTER 18

1. Hoover, *Memoirs*, III, p. 177.

2. Myers, William Starr and Newton, Walter, H., *The Hoover Administration, A Documented Narrative*, New York, 1936, p. 276; Wilbur, Ray Lyman and Hyde, Arthur Mastick, *The Hoover Policies*, New York, 1937, p. 30.

3. Hoover, *Memoirs*, III, pp. 84–96; Sullivan, Lawrence, *Prelude to Panic, the Story of the Bank Holiday*, Washington, 1936, pp. 6–12; Hinshaw, David, *Herbert Hoover, American Quaker*, New York, 1950, pp. 25–6; Donham, Wallace B., 'The Attack on Depressions,' *Harvard Business Review*, October 1932, pp. 45–56; Brown, E. Francis, 'How Real is American Recovery?' *Current History*, December 1932, pp. 335–9.

4. Peel, Roy V. and Donnelly, Thomas C., *The 1932 Campaign, An Analysis*, New York, 1935, p. 45.

5. Tolischus, Otto David, 'Debts and the Hoover Programme,' *North American Review*, May 1932, pp. 389–98; Hoover, *State Papers*, II, pp. 483–6; Hoover, *Memoirs*, III, pp. 178–9; Myers and Newton, op. cit. pp. 279–82; Sullivan, op. cit. pp. 27–30; Raymond Moley, *After Seven Years*, New York, 1939, p. 68.

6. Tugwell, Rexford Guy, *The Democratic Roosevelt, A Biography of Franklin D. Roosevelt,* New York, 1957, p. 256.

7. Hoover, Irwin Hood, *Forty-two Years in the White House,* New York, 1934, pp. 221–3.

8. Michelson, Charles, *The Ghost Talks,* New York, 1944, p. 51; Moley, op. cit. pp. 73–8; Hoover, *State Papers,* II, pp. 487–93; Roosevelt, *Public Papers,* I, p. 867; Hoover, *Memoirs,* III, pp. 176–86; Schlesinger, Arthur Meier Jr., *The Crisis of the Old Order,* 1919–1933, Boston, 1957, pp. 442–5.

9. Hoover, Irwin H., op. cit. p. 223.

10. Hoover, *Memoirs,* III, pp. 179–81.

11. Ibid. III, pp. 188–91; id., *State Papers,* II, pp. 585–95; *Literary Digest,* 25 February 1933, p. 9.

12. Stimson, Henry L. and Bundy, McGeorge, *On Active Service in Peace and War,* New York, 1947, p. 289; Moley, op. cit. p. 94.

13. Moley, op. cit. pp. 99–105.

14. Herring, E. Pendleton, 'Second Session of the Seventy-second Congress, December 5, 1932, to March 4, 1933,' *American Political Science Review,* XXVII (1933), p. 404.

15. Hoover, *State Papers,* II, pp. 597–9; Ayres, Leonard P., *The Economics of Recovery,* New York, 1934, pp. 67–8.

16. *Congressional Record,* 72 Cong. 2 Sess., 76:51–4; Hoover, *Memoirs,* III, pp. 192–3; id., *State Papers,* II, pp. 505–21, 533.

17. Roosevelt, *Public Papers,* I, p. 871; Anderson, Paul Y., 'The Lame Ducks Meet,' *Nation,* 21 December 1932, pp. 610–11; Brown, E. Francis, 'The State of the American Nation,' *Current History,* January 1933, p. 458; Watson, James E., *As I Knew Them,* Indianapolis, 1936, p. 305; Hoover *State Papers,* II, pp. 766ff; Brown, E. Francis, 'The Lame-Duck Congress at Work,' *Current History,* February 1933, pp. 589–95.

18. *Time,* 27 February 1933, pp. 9–10; *Commercial & Financial Chronicle,* 18 February 1933, p. 1139; Senate Committee on Finance, *Investigation of Economic Problems,* Hearings on S. Res. 315, Washington, 1933, p. 14.

19. Senate Committee on Banking and Currency, *Further Unemployment Relief Through the Reconstruction Finance Corporation,* Hearings on S. 5336, Washington, 1933, pp. 117–18.

20. Ibid. p. 20.

21. Senate Committee on Manufactures, *Federal Aid for Unemployment Relief,* Hearings on S. 5125, Washington, 1933, p. 131.

22. Ibid. p. 258.

23. Ibid. pp. 303–13, 330, 331.

24. 47 U.S. Statutes 751, 797–8, 1625; Buell, Raymond Leslie, 'Philippine Independence,' *Foreign Policy Association Reports*, VI (1930–1931), pp. 37–78; Joslin, Theodore G., *Hoover Off the Record*, New York, 1934, p. 340; *Congressional Digest*, XII, p. 89.

25. Lindley, Ernest K., *The Roosevelt Revolution First Phase*, New York, 1934, pp. 64–5; Flynn, John T., 'Who But Hoover?' *New Republic*, 4 December 1935, pp. 94–5.

26. Hoover, *Memoirs*, III, pp. 391–2. By permission of The Macmillan Company, publishers.

27. Sullivan, op. cit. pp. 42–3; Joslin, op. cit. pp. 350–3; Hart, Albert Gailord *et al.*, *Debts and Recovery, A Study of Changes in the Internal Debt Structure from 1929 to 1937 and a Program for the Future*, New York, 1938, pp. 56–8.

28. *Congressional Record*, 72 Cong. 2 Sess., 5 January 1933, 76:1343.

29. Page, Ralph W., 'Bankruptcy or Inflation,' *Current History*, March 1933, pp. 680–4; *Commercial & Financial Chronicle*, 18 February 1933, p. 1139; Myers and Newton, op. cit. pp. 335–6; Moley, op. cit. p. 138.

30. *New York Times*, 19 October 1952.

31. *Congressional Record*, 72 Cong. 2 Sess., 6 December 1932, 76:53.

32. Daiger, J. M., 'Toward Safer and Stronger Banks,' *Current History*, February 1933, pp. 558–64; Brown, E. Francis, 'The President-Elect at Work,' ibid. March 1933, pp. 719–24; *Congressional Record*, 72 Cong. 2 Sess., 25 January 1933, 76:2517.

33. *Congressional Record*, 72 Cong. 2 Sess., 20 February 1933, 76:4553, 5360–63.

34. Timmons, Bascom N., *Jesse H. Jones, the Man and the Statesman*, New York, 1956, pp. 171, 177–8.

35. 47 U.S. Statutes 712.

36. Quoted by Sullivan, op. cit. p. 48.

37. *Congressional Record*, 72 Cong. 2 Sess., 6 January 1933, 76:1361–2; Myers and Newton, op. cit. pp. 325–7; Sullivan, op. cit. p. 49; Jones, Jesse H. and Angly, Edward, *Fifty Billion Dollars, My Thirteen Years with the RFC 1932–1945*, New York, 1951, pp. 82–3.

38. *Nineteenth Annual Report of the Federal Reserve Board . . . 1932*, Washington, 1933, Table 93, p. 151; Mitchell, Broadus, *Depression Decade from New Era through New Deal 1929–1941*, New York, 1947, p. 128; *Congressional Record*, 72 Cong. 2 Sess., 6 December 1932, 76:53.

39. *Commercial & Financial Chronicle*, 4 February 1933, p. 703, 11 February 1933, pp. 933–8; and 18 February 1933, p. 1063.

40. *Time*, 13 February 1933, p. 41; *Congressional Record*, 72 Cong. 2 Sess., 14 February 1933, 76:4090–91; Leonard, Jonathan, *Three Years Down*, New York, 1939, pp. 288–90.

41. Varying accounts are given in Jones and Angly, op. cit. pp. 59–65; Sullivan, op. cit. pp. 83–6; Pecora, Ferdinand, *Wall Street Under Oath, the Story of Our Modern Money Changers*, New York, 1939, pp. 251–6; and *Time*, 27 February 1933, p. 12.

42. *Time*, 20 February 1933, p. 13 and 6 March 1933, pp. 17–18; Jones and Angly, op. cit. pp. 65–6.

43. *Time*, 20 February 1933, p. 9; *Literary Digest*, 25 February 1933, p. 9.

44. Colt, Charles C. and Keith, N. S., *28 Days, A History of the Banking Crisis*, New York, 1933, pp. 10–18.

45. For an eyewitness account of the Zangara shooting, see Moley, op. cit. pp. 138–40, and for a 'Bang! . . . Bang! . . . Bang! . . . Bang! . . . Bang! . . .' story, see *Time*, 27 February 1933, pp. 7–8; Myers and Newton, op. cit. pp. 338–40; Hoover, *State Papers*, I, p. 133.

46. Hoover to Reed, 20 February 1933, Myers and Newton, op. cit. p. 341.

47. *Congressional Record*, 72 Cong. 2 Sess., 20 February 1933, 76:4460; Colt and Keith, op. cit. p. 18.

48. Colt and Keith, op. cit. pp. 24–32.

49. Hoover, *Memoirs*, III, pp. 205–6; Myers and Newton, op. cit. pp. 347–70.

50. Meyer to Hoover, 25 February 1933, Myers and Newton, op. cit. p. 357.

51. Ibid. pp. 361–2.

52. Hoover, *Memoirs*, III, pp. 212–13; *New York Times*, 7 March 1933; Myers and Newton, op. cit. pp. 363–5.

53. *New York Times*, 4 March 1933.

54. Ibid. 5 March 1933; Hoover, Irwin H., op. cit. p. 227; Moley, op. cit. pp. 144–5; Myers and Newton, op. cit. pp. 365–6.

55. *New York Times*, 4, 7 March 1933; *Time*, 13 March 1933, pp. 9–10; Wecter, Dixon, *The Age of the Great Depression, 1929–1941*, New York, 1948, pp. 62–3; Myers and Newton, op. cit. pp. 365–6; Roosevelt, *Public Papers*, I, 870–71; Moley, op. cit. pp. 146–7.

56. Hoover, *Memoirs*, III, pp. 214–15; Myers and Newton, op. cit. p. 356. Myers and Newton left Rand's name out of the letter but Hoover included it.

CHAPTER 19

1. Myers, William Starr and Newton, Walter H., *The Hoover Administration, A Documented Narrative*, New York, 1936, pp. 365–6; Hoover, *State Papers*, II, p. 602; *New York Times*, 5 March 1933.

2. *Literary Digest*, 11 March 1933, pp. 5–7; *Time*, 13 March 1933, pp. 11–12; *New York Times*, 5 March 1933; Roosevelt, Eleanor, *This I Remember*, New York, 1949, pp. 77–8.

3. Address before the United States Chamber of Commerce, Washington, 1 May 1930, *Congressional Record*, 71 Cong. 2 Sess., 8 May 1930, 72:8641; Hoover, *State Papers*, I, p. 291.

4. Hoover, *Memoirs*, III, p. 30; Lyons, Eugene, *Our Unknown Ex-President, A Portrait of Herbert Hoover*, New York, 1950, p. 256.

5. Joslin, Theodore G., *Hoover Off the Record*, New York, 1934, pp. 2–3; Myers and Newton, op. cit. p. 80; Lippmann, Walter, *Interpretations, 1931–1932*, New York, 1932, p. 7.

6. Lippmann, op. cit. pp. 67–8.

7. Hoover, *State Papers*, I, p. 575.

8. *New York Times*, 10 January 1932; *New York Herald Tribune*, 5 January 1932.

9. Hoover, *Memoirs*, III, p. 40. By permission of The Macmillan Company, publishers.

10. I am indebted to Professor W. Burlie Brown of Tulane University, who developed these ideas in 'The Presidential Candidate and the Fireside Virtues,' read at the Houston, Texas, meeting of the Southern Historical Association on 9 November 1957.

11. Lippmann, Walter, 'The Peculiar Weakness of Mr. Hoover,' *Harper's Monthly Magazine*, June 1930, pp. 1–7.

12. Radio address 7 October 1932, Hoover, *State Papers*, II, p. 328.

13. [Gilbert, Clinton Wallace] *The Mirrors of 1932*, New York, 1931, p. 8.

14. Address at Madison Courthouse, Virginia, 17 August 1929, Hoover, *State Papers*, I, p. 88.

15. Address to the Gridiron Club, Washington, D.C., 14 December 1929, ibid. I, p. 187; Hoover to W. O. Thompson, 30 December 1929, ibid. I, p. 197.

16. Moley, Raymond, *27 Masters of Politics in a Personal Perspective*, New York, 1949, p. 28. By permission of the author.

INDEX

AMERICAN HISTORY TITLES IN THE NORTON LIBRARY

DATE DUE

OCT 2 5 2008			